Praise for Thurston ...

SONIC LIFE

A *Vanity Fair* Favorite Book of the Year

A *Rolling Stone* Best Music Book of the Year

"A memorial to the lost petri dish of a downtown scene that made Sonic Youth possible." —*The Washington Post*

"The tale of a record collector geek made good, a seeker after new sounds who in turn became a key architect of experimental rock in the two decades that followed. . . . An engaging memory piece through a golden era of busted toilets and secondhand smoke that now seems as distant as Montparnasse in the 1920s." —*Los Angeles Times*

"Both a herculean work of research and a love letter—to Moore's youth, to underground rock, and to a band that formed in downtown Manhattan in 1981 and went on to change music forever. . . . *Sonic Life* is a big book and it feels like a whole life is poured into it." —*Vogue*

"An edgy valentine to '80s punk." —*San Francisco Chronicle*

"Vivid. . . . [An] excellent memoir." —*The New York Times Book Review*

"A microscopic look at how [Moore's] interests in punk, art, and guitar experimentalism fueled his contributions to one of alt-rock's most daring bands. . . . Moore's memories . . . rock with vivid detail." —*Rolling Stone*

"Downtown scientists, rejoice! For Thurston Moore has unearthed the missing links, the sacred texts, the forgotten stories, and the secret maps of the lost golden age. This is history—scuffed, slightly bent, plenty noisy, and indispensable." —Colson Whitehead, Pulitzer Prize–winning author of *The Underground Railroad* and *Harlem Shuffle*

"Filled with wonderful insights about the New York–based cultural landscape that made him, Moore's *Sonic Life* is essential reading—a moving meditation by a creative force."   —Hilton Als,
Pulitzer Prize–winning author of *White Girls*

"*Sonic Life* works the way Sonic Youth did, with raging appetite for experience, with velocity and nerve, with a total devotion to making art from the resolute stance of starry-eyed fan and unabashed permanent novice. His recall is as amazing as his generosity."
—Jonathan Lethem, National Book Critics Circle
Award–winning author of *Motherless Brooklyn*

"A raw, rollicking document."
—Nell Zink, author of *Avalon* and *Doxology*

"A sensitive and authentic testimony to Moore's commitment to life lived through art and music. Beats with the heart of a true artist and mutineer."
—Viv Albertine, author of *Clothes, Clothes, Clothes.*
Music, Music, Music. Boys, Boys, Boys.

"Vastly entertaining. . . . A more mythic artistic adolescence-slash-storybook New York success story couldn't be imagined. . . . A punk, hardcore, no- and new wave Library of Alexandria."   —*Spin*

Thurston Moore

SONIC LIFE

Thurston Moore is a founding member of Sonic Youth, a band born in New York in 1981 that spent thirty years at the vanguard of alternative rock, influencing and inspiring such acts as Nirvana, Pavement, the Yeah Yeah Yeahs, My Bloody Valentine, and Beck. The band's album *Daydream Nation* was chosen by the Library of Congress for historical preservation in the National Recording Registry in 2005. Moore is involved in publishing and poetry and teaches at the Summer Writing Workshop at Naropa University in Boulder, Colorado.

SONIC LIFE

SONIC
LIFE

A MEMOIR

Thurston Moore

Vintage Books

A Division of Penguin Random House LLC

New York

FIRST VINTAGE BOOKS EDITION 2024

Copyright © 2023 by Thurston Moore

The Library of Congress has cataloged the Doubleday edition as follows:
Names: Moore, Thurston, author.
Title: Sonic life : a memoir / Thurston Moore.
Description: First edition. | New York : Doubleday, 2023.
Identifiers: LCCN 2023005398 (print) | LCCN 2023005399 (ebook)
Subjects: LCSH: Moore, Thurston. | Guitarists—United States—Biography. |
Rock musicians—United States—Biography. | Sonic Youth (Musical group) |
LCGFT: Autobiographies. Classification: LCC ML419.M666 A3 2023 (print) |
LCC ML419.M666 (ebook) | DDC 782.42166092 B—dc23/eng/20230203
LC record available at https://lccn.loc.gov/2023005398
LC ebook record available at https://lccn.loc.gov/2023005399

Vintage Books Trade Paperback ISBN: 978-0-593-46792-3
eBook ISBN: 978-0-385-54866-3

Book design by Betty Lew

vintagebooks.com

Printed in the United States of America
10 9 8 7 6 5 4 3 2 1

For

the Daydream Nation

Contents

BOOK ONE

BOOK TWO

CONTENTS

BOOK FIVE

BOOK SIX

Immersive listening of Lou Reed's double album noise masterwork, *Metal Machine Music*, on heavy rotation in my rural Connecticut bedroom, 1976

BOOK ONE

BOOK ONE

1

EPIPHANY

Gene bounded into our small South Miami, Florida, house, the summer of 1963, a look on his face as if he had located a gift of gold dropped from a psychedelic UFO. In his hand he clutched an article of sonic subterfuge: a seven-inch black vinyl single deliriously titled "Louie Louie," by a group called the Kingsmen. Their name suggested royal knaves, subjects of a British Invasion–informed notion of aristocracy, and not the four hip, sneering roustabouts from the Pacific Northwest that they were.

From that moment onward, my brother's universe and mine would become all flash lightning, "Louie Louie" ringing out repeatedly, a seductive noise machine from on high, the singer wailing, out of control and completely cool, steering us toward an undeniable future—

Okay, let's give it to 'em, right now!

I was five years old to Gene's ten, my response to the record driven as much by the sound as by my older brother's excitement. He reverently spun the single, an artifact from preteen heaven that he had somehow stumbled onto. The only other music heard in our house had been our father's classical records and, more profoundly, the sounds emanating from his hours-long performances at the piano—an instrument that commanded most of the real estate in our modest living room. He worked deliberately through a repertoire of Beethoven, Bach, Brahms, Mendelssohn, and other heavies. Classical music ruled our airwaves.

At least until "Louie Louie" came breaking and entering in.

With that disc in constant revolution, the energy of our existence would change, a new current of electricity introduced. It was as though it had taken the soundworld of our day—our kitchen appliances, our television—and recast it into song, using only guitars, organ, and drums.

The lead singer's voice had the air of a boy smoking a cigarette with one hand while banging a tambourine in the other, an insolent distance to his delivery, a vision of being at once boss and bored.

The flip side of the record was "Haunted Castle," an instrumental with a simplistic chord figure and a suitably mysterious vibe. The fun danger of "Louie Louie" was offset by the cool otherness of "Haunted Castle." Everything about these subversive vibrations suggested to me a new world; they were changing not only my here and now but my vision of what the future might hold for me.

I decided to someday, somehow, be in a band like the Kingsmen.

The first order of business would be my hair. From flipping through the pages of *16* magazine, the bible of 1960s pop-rock teen-idol worship, I could see how the cool cats in bands like the Kingsmen all had bangs grazing their eyebrows, the back of their hair hanging slightly below their collars.

To grown-ups, my little-boy crew cut was *cute*, but after my blinding introduction to rock 'n' roll by way of "Louie Louie," I knew it would no longer do. Forget cute.

After a bit of pleading, I was given permission by my parents to let my hair grow out. Each day I would check its progress, wetting the minuscule strands of my potential fringe so that it might fall onto my forehead, yearning to flick it casually to the side. A few of my classmates at the Epiphany Catholic School took me to task for my preening and faux flicking—

"You don't have long hair, stop pretending."

But I needed the practice.

My father's piano had always been our family's great and sacred object. It cost as much as a car, and we were living on a schoolteacher's wages. But it was a necessary extravagance—not just an outlet for my father but a collective beacon of high art, a reflection, I thought, of our commitment to sound and composition.

But it wasn't for me. What I really wanted was a guitar.

Preferably electric.

Or at least a transistor radio.

Anything that could bring more "Louie Louie" into the world.

2

REFRIGERATOR HEAVEN

In 1947 my father, George Moore, age twenty-two, met Eleanor Nann, two years younger, in music class at the University of Miami, the two falling forever in love. Just a few years prior, each of their lives had been subsumed by war—my mother working as a soldiers' aide at the Biltmore Hotel, then outfitted as a hospital, in nearby Coral Gables; my father enlisted as a military band leader, though with the good fortune not to be stationed overseas. He had learned music theory and piano from his mother, a society pianist.

Both my parents' families had been living in Coral Gables, a charmed and enchanted enclave tucked just below the city of Miami, a paradise of huge banyan trees presiding over narrow streets, their trunks and branches knotty and adorned with thick hanging vines. Green grass lawns were nurtured by tropical rains, which would rage for an hour, then break for high, humid sunshine. Iguanas, lizards, grass snakes, parrots, and peacocks freely roamed. The tolling bells of the Church of the Little Flower—where my parents would marry after three years of dreamtime romance—filled the air, resounding off the walls of homes, some made of old Spanish stucco, others built from coral rock.

My brother, Gene, arrived in 1953, followed two years later by my sister, Susan. I was conceived in the autumn of 1957 in Mount Dora, Florida, in a tiny house outside of the grade school where my father had found a teaching job. For my birth, my mother traveled back to Coral Gables; a family physician delivered me on Friday, July 25, 1958, at 7:37 in the evening. I was named after Thurston "Doc" Adams, my father's stepfather, a larger-than-life character who had become the vivacious patriarch of our extended family. Doc himself claimed to have been named out of his parents' admiration for Thurston the Great Magician and his self-proclaimed

"Wonder Show of the Universe," which had traveled the Southeast early in the century.

At the end of the 1950s, our family of five would relocate, first to Mc-Kenzie, Tennessee, where my father had found a new job teaching at a local college; then back down to Florida a few years later, setting up house in South Miami; before packing up all our belongings once again and heading north, in 1967, to Bethel, Connecticut. My father had found a more desirable academic position, at Western Connecticut State College, in nearby Danbury. He was to teach art appreciation, philosophy, humanities, and phenomenology.

I was ten years old. Leaving behind the perennial sunshine of southern Florida, I would for the first time experience true seasons: dying leaves, snow, and ice.

Before heading north I had been gifted an inexpensive acoustic guitar. The idea was that if I could figure out how to play the thing, I might possibly advance to an electric. The acoustic had nylon strings—not very rock, but they could still make a kind of thrum.

I went to the town hall in Bethel to take lessons with a bunch of other aspiring preteen guitarists. I had stuck an STP decal on the guitar in hopes of imbuing it with a bit of cool—STP being the iconic race car motor oil brand, denoting *speed,* or so it seemed to me. The serious guitarists in the class looked down their noses at my STP machine, particularly as I'd brought it in without a case, naked and battered.

The teacher attempted to show us how to play "Kumbaya." I quickly realized that I would not be returning.

As the seventies got under way, Gene acquired an electric Fender Stratocaster, which he played obsessively. He was eighteen to my thirteen. I managed to glean a bit of fretboard familiarity from simply observing him, watching him play day and night—chordings, fingerings, strumming techniques.

Gene and his hippie friends often sat around our house, endlessly riffing on their axes, spinning records, smoking cigs, laughing, talking about bands and concerts. They each had one group that was all their own, taking it upon themselves to collect every record, becoming the designated aficionado. One guy would be all into the Moody Blues; another would pledge allegiance to Emerson, Lake & Palmer, or Santana, or the

Mothers of Invention. Gene's choice was Jefferson Airplane: San Francisco acid rock with wah-wah guitar leads, far-out lyrics, psychedelic album jackets—all things pretty alien to our rural Connecticut world.

Initiated by the Kingsmen, the expansive music of Jefferson Airplane zapping out of Gene's stereo opened my eyes yet again to rock 'n' roll, a mysterious world far beyond my bedroom window, cast loose from a musical culture that was barely more than a decade old.

When Gene went off to work at one of his various jobs—bagging groceries, mowing lawns—I would sneak into his room and remove his beloved Stratocaster from its felt-lined hard-leather case, playing it until, invariably, I broke a string. Either Gene didn't have any extra strings or I hadn't figured out how to put one on. At any rate, I would guiltily stow the guitar away. He would return home later and race up to his room, only to find that the guitar he'd left in pristine condition now had a broken string. He knew the culprit. Rightfully pissed off, he would warn me to never touch it again.

After a few such instances, he found a solution: the case had a simple lock-and-key clasp. He decided to lock the guitar up, taking the tiny key with him to work. But I quickly figured out how to jimmy open the lock with a screwdriver. And sure enough, as I practiced my rudimentary strumming technique, a string would once again snap, only for the minor drama to repeat itself.

Gene stepped up his security, wrapping an industrial-sized chain around the case, fastened with a formidable padlock. This was daunting at first, but I realized that given a solid pair of pliers and twenty methodical minutes, I could pry apart one of the metal chain links and get inside again. The guitar liberated anew, I would, without fail, break another string, before returning the guitar to its case and spending another twenty minutes rejoining the heavy-duty chain link. Gene, returning home, would head to his room, unlock the case . . . and realize there was no use.

What could he do? His kid brother was as enchanted with the guitar as he was. Eventually he presented me with a crazy-beautiful sunburst Fender Stratocaster to call my own. He had been able to acquire it for next to nothing, its provenance mysterious—likely it had "fallen off a truck."

I wasn't too bothered with its origins, though. I was overwhelmed with excitement and gratitude. I had just turned sixteen years old and now had my first real noise machine.

∽

My days of illicit guitar playing now behind me, I plugged my hot new Strat into Gene's amplifier and large speaker cabinet setup, which he kept in his bedroom. With no one else in the house to disturb—my dad off working at the college, Gene and Sue out with their pals, my mom off somewhere shopping—I blasted away at the instrument, creating squalling, squealing, screeching electric noise. One afternoon in mid-wail, cranking out high-volume crunge, I could just barely make out a pounding on our front door. I ran downstairs only to be met by a shaking, petrified woman who lived across the street, tears welling in her eyes.

"Please . . . can you . . . lower . . . the music?"

—she stammered. *"I'm . . . having . . . a nervous . . . breakdown."*

Gene enlisted in the air force, where he would service fighter jets. To my misfortune, he took his amp with him to his base in New Jersey. I was temporarily bereft, but I soon figured out a solution. I could wire one end of a guitar cable into the back of my dad's cheap stereo receiver, which sat atop the refrigerator in our somewhat cramped kitchen. My wiring was precarious, but it created just enough of a connection for me to send my guitar's signal through the receiver's tiny, crummy speakers. It sounded amazing—crazy and savage, with weirdo distortion, sort of like the first Stooges album, which I had found in a record store discount bin a couple of years earlier, curious about the four stoned-immaculate boys peering out at me from the cover.

I had become a frequenter of the cheap bins by then. Wanting to buy albums, but not having the money to purchase them at full price—usually around three dollars—I would settle on picking up discs with corners clipped off, denoting their unpopular "cutout" status. While many of them proved unrewarding listens, there were some, such as Can's *Ege Bamyasi* and Captain Beefheart's *The Spotlight Kid*, that captured my imagination, that showed rock 'n' roll could be soulful and poetic or else brash and abrasive.

That first self-titled Stooges LP, released in 1969, was a sinister masterpiece of minimalist fuzz. It would become my best friend. When I tried to share it with others, it would be met only with shaken heads. Its submental drone, its delirious, decadent drawl—I had to keep it to myself. It was that first Stooges album, a successor in my heart to "Louie Louie," that I was thinking of as my electric guitar shredded the speakers on my dad's stereo rig, scorching hot atop the humming fridge.

If the first Stooges LP represented a bit of record store serendipity, it had been in discovering the Stooges' second LP, *Fun House,* from 1970, that I'd had my first taste of bin-digging elation: of sifting through the dross and finding a nugget of sonic gold. The Stooges were a long way from what was most popular in music in the early 1970s—"progressive" rock with its emphasis on sophisticated technique, from bands such as Emerson, Lake & Palmer and Yes. The band rarely strayed from their simple, fuzz-box drone, Ron Asheton occasionally punctuating it with his singular brand of wicked lead-guitar psycho-rip. Iggy Pop's vocals sat within the chaos as he poured his inebriated soul into your ear. His performances were notoriously kinetic-bordering-on-manic events (not that I had ever seen them—I'd had to settle for reading about them in the far corners of rock mags). His laments about getting old, at age twenty-two, were to me a thrilling alternative to the foppish, starry-eyed prog rockers crooning about mountains coming out of the sky and standing there.

There was no frill, no jamming, only direct-to-the-heart intensity. It was a hypodermic needle of noise, and to freaks like me listening alone in their bedrooms, it delivered a high like nothing else.

With *Fun House,* the Stooges had taken their sound to an even more blown-out realm. It was hotter and fatter. Music that had once been simply sinister was now downright raving. Each track on the record burst with scalding energy, fairly oozing off my turntable. When the session concluded with the free jazz of "L.A. Blues," it was as if a lid that had attempted to contain all the band's clamor was released at once, the sonic snakes of heavy metal hell creepy-crawling every which way, ravaging my very reality.

With *Raw Power,* released in 1973, the Stooges seemed to be maturing (albeit fitfully), extrapolating out from the four-chord minimalism of their first two masterpiece slabs. They were Iggy & the Stooges now, the music redefined by new guitarist James Williamson's razor-edged leads—sizzling, dark, and hair-raising. Ron brought some excellent bass action to the mix, and Iggy was completely and utterly unleashed, his lyrics like ripped, shiny black leather, a greasy glitter tongue to the stardust rebellion of David Bowie, a newfound champion and cheerleader.

I wanted not just to sound like *Raw Power,* but I wanted to look the part of the animal on the cover—Iggy with his inimitable, cool stare, a spirit aflame with narcotic transcendence, lusting for beauty and bad behavior. There was no other—I wanted to be *that.*

Again, the first thing I needed to do was to get my haircut sorted.

So, sixteen years old in 1974, flush with my motor vehicle learner's permit, I drove to Iron Butterfly, the local hairstyling joint where the older, cool kids went. It was a step up from the old-timey barbers I had previously frequented, my new haircut costing an exorbitant six dollars. But if I could look like Iggy, it would be worth it. I took the *Raw Power* album along and displayed its cover for the twenty-something hairstylist—

"This is what I want to look like."

She didn't understand—

"That's just a normal parted-down-the-middle nothing haircut."

"Yes, well . . . that's what I want."

An hour later I walked out of Iron Butterfly with an embarrassing feathered shag, like the kind John Travolta would wear in *Saturday Night Fever* a few years later. Six bucks down the drain.

The Stooges weren't the only band that consumed me. Two months after *Raw Power*'s 1973 release, the first New York Dolls LP would appear, its cover a revelation: five hetero New York City street rockers dressed in *almost* drag. Their image was a celebration of smart and sexy camp, inextricably bound with the music shredding from the grooves. Producer Todd Rundgren had gently restrained the band's erratic tendencies and, in the process, helped create one of the most focused, fun, and carousing rock 'n' roll albums ever recorded.

As records were prominently displayed in department stores in the 1960s and 1970s, it must have been confusing for many an American music browser to catch sight of a Stooges or New York Dolls album, or, for that matter, David Bowie's *Aladdin Sane,* with its iconic image of Bowie with a lightning bolt painted across his face. These were albums that celebrated the artists' otherness, if not their otherworldliness.

The group Sparks had as much of an impact on me as anything else coming from the makeshift stereo system I had assembled in my bedroom that year. Their 1974 album, *Kimono My House,* was a surprise package of ingenuity and experimental rock song genius, brothers Ron and Russell Mael showing me how rock music could comprise wildly literate, hyper-enunciated epics, songs I found hilarious and straight-up rocking, even as they evinced more prance than swagger.

These bands—along with Alice Cooper, Mott the Hoople, Slade, T. Rex, Roxy Music, and Sweet—all held me captive.

And yet, for all my growing obsession, I hadn't found the wherewithal to actually go *see* any of them in concert. Bethel, Connecticut, was an hour and a half away by train from Manhattan, the city a tour stop for surely every one of them, but my teenage brain wasn't equipped yet to make the connection.

It would eventually, and it would change me. Radically. But until that time came, I contented myself by creating my own gallery of rock 'n' roll, tacking up photos of all my teenage heroes. There were images of Bryan Ferry and Brian Eno of Roxy Music, Iggy, Bowie, the Dolls, Sparks—even "Jim Dandy" Mangrum from Black Oak Arkansas. Each had been ripped from the pages of rock 'n' roll music magazines and mounted onto my bedroom wall, a personal shrine to the glitter gods.

This didn't go unnoticed by my father. He became concerned as to why his son had so many images of these prettified men—their pouty lips, shirts off—emblazoned about his tiny bedroom walls. I wasn't quite sure what to tell him. I never thought about what my fascination with glam rock might say about my sexual proclivities. He must have worried, like many an American parent of the 1970s, that his son was demonstrating some incipient signs of homosexuality.

I basically always knew I was a hetero kid. His suspicion never stressed me out.

I would soon, in 1975, find myself best friends with Harold Paris, a boy who was in fact gay. The two of us would forge a greater bond than any other friendship I had had by that point. More so, we would share a life-defining experience: we discovered punk rock together.

Harold had come into my sights at Bethel High School around 1973. I was fifteen at the time; he, a year younger. Unlike any other boy I knew, he was flamboyant and strikingly effeminate—which, at a small-town American high school in the 1970s, was not only polarizing but dangerous. He would sweep through the halls in striped flares and frilled, half-buttoned shirts, silk ascots tied around his neck, reeking of cologne; his hair was a silver frost with burnt-mercury hints—all of this with a laughing husky voice and gleaming devil eyes. He could be found arm in arm with the most alluring, more experienced older girls, the wildest ones, the ones who had no time for any of the vanilla dudes in the skunk zone of our high school.

I would overhear Harold talking to these girls about the cultural flash points of the time: digging Jane Fonda's stoned nudity in *Barbarella* or hitting New York City to check out Bowie's Diamond Dogs tour. I thought I was the only one following this stuff, or at least the only one in Bethel,

Connecticut. My peers tended to favor the prog rock of Yes, the soft metal of Boston, the denim-shirt balladry of America, and the southern-fried rock of the Allman Brothers Band.

My own interests hadn't escaped the notice of my classmates. They could tell I was into rock music. They probably saw me carrying around copies of magazines such as *Circus, Creem, Hit Parader,* and *Rock Scene.* In the school parking lot, a loudmouthed jock once grabbed a copy of *Creem* I had tucked beneath my arm.

"What is this shit?"

—he sputtered.

He opened the mag to a page featuring a rainbow-haired Todd Rundgren, depicted as a sort of nude, trans Venus de Milo.

"Oh my gawd, this magazine is full of fags!"

He threw it to the ground and bolted off, shaking his head.

A few times, before we became close, I watched as Harold had been thrown to the ground with similar derision by some high school bozo. Being already quite tall, maybe even imposing, I never felt threatened by these know-nothings. If they thought of me at all, they might have seen me as a bit of a class clown: sardonic, smart, nice enough despite my obviously oddball musical interests. Harold enjoyed no such anonymity.

I began learning of and sending out for independently produced fanzines. These were distinct from the rock magazines already in my orbit. They were photocopied and stapled by hand, with titles such as *Denim Delinquent, Teenage Wasteland Gazette,* and *Gulcher.*

Zines were edited and published throughout the early and mid-1970s by rock 'n' roll zealots eager to spread the good word. As a new underground proto-punk culture emerged, they offered reportage from the heart of the rock 'n' roll action. It was through them that I learned of Kim Fowley, the Dictators, Kiss, Blue Öyster Cult, and the Flamin' Groovies.

I began a postal friendship with one of the editors at *Gulcher,* Eddie Flowers, which would continue for a few years. (I couldn't have known, when we started exchanging letters, that his fall 1976 issue would include a scene report I wrote, along with a photo booth pic I sent him of me trying to look tough, a cigarette hanging from my mouth.) Eddie wrote to me of driving back and forth from Alabama, where he had been living, to Bloomington, Indiana, the city from which *Gulcher* had sprung. He was starting a band with a few of the other writers, calling themselves the Gizmos. I asked Eddie about the possibility of me heading out there and joining up with them; I had some tunes I had been working on in my bedroom that I was psyched to share.

"Whoa there, not so fast"

—he wrote back.

"We have too many weirdos as it is."

3

FLAMING TELEPATHS

A long-haired poseur who sang in a local group held court in the Bethel High School cafeteria, acting every part the leading light on all things contemporary rock. He asked me what bands I liked. Everyone in his clique had agreed to worship Yes, the British prog-rock messiahs.

My feelings about Yes were decidedly mixed. I had bought the three-disc live album *Yessongs,* and I recognized the mastery of songcraft evinced by these musos in capes. But too much of the playing was end-less guitar-scale noodle-core for my tastes.

"They're all right, I suppose . . ."

—I said, my true feelings evident in my voice.

I had attended my very first proper concert in early 1974 at New Haven Coliseum, where I witnessed Yes's keyboard maestro, Rick Wakeman, perform his recent album *Journey to the Centre of the Earth.* I had been excited to hear him play, but I found the concert interminably dull.

I didn't relate this to my classmates.

"I'm more into theater rock"

—I said. The Yes lovers looked perplexed.

"You know . . . people like Alice Cooper, David Bowie . . . and Kiss."

Silence.

Followed by a palpable distaste.

The Rick Wakeman show hadn't put me off arena concerts. Soon after, I went to see Peter Frampton, supported by the J. Geils Band, whose singer Peter Wolf bounded onstage proclaiming—

"We're gonna play 'em *allllll* tonight!"

This was excellent news. I had a few J. Geils Band records and had convinced myself that they were pretty damn hot. But the group played only thirty-five minutes—hardly *allllll* their tunes.

Kiss, on the other hand, delivered the rock 'n' roll goods. Their self-titled debut album had showcased bucketloads of high-energy hooks, all the more evident when slotted next to whatever else was being played on the radio in the mid-1970s: the pablum of Seals & Crofts, Anne Murray, Lobo. Kiss constructed short, sharp, hard-rocking tune-grenades primarily focused on booze and sex. They looked amazing too, throwing comic-book kicks and sporting trash heaps of New York City grit and glitter.

Harold and I scored a couple of spare tickets to see Kiss an hour and a half north in Springfield, Massachusetts, hitching a ride from some high school heads we knew. White Crosses were proffered—basically prescription-grade Dexedrine—and we gobbled them down in preparation for some ripping rock 'n' roll rambunction.

Blessed by the parking gods, we scored a space directly in front of the venue. We sat in the car smoking joints, eyeballing an increasingly lengthy queue of teenage animals awaiting entry into the arena. Suddenly, a few feet from where our car was parked, a row of side doors to the arena opened up, and all the teens who had been queuing up on the hill realized they were in the wrong place. They began to run, leaping and whooping down the lawn to the just-opened doors.

We didn't hesitate. Dousing our doobies, we sprang from the car, running at full steam and beating the crazed horde. We became the first ticket holders to enter the building. Once inside and patted down by security, we raced at full sprint toward the massive stage, then stopped, astounded: front row center.

As Kiss was preparing to fry our brains, Harold and I got crushed ever harder up against the guardrails by the army of rabid, heaving youth behind us. It became so intense that we expected to either suffer cracked ribs, lose consciousness, or simply die. Harold looked at me in terror; he was going under, sure to be trampled or suffocated. I reached out and locked my arms under his, trying to ward off the barrage of teenage meat and bone.

Kiss finally arrived onstage, and from the outset they scorched our minds to smithereens. Bassist Gene Simmons was surrounded by flash pots that shot volcanic bursts of fire to the rafters. Close as we were, the heat singed us. It must have been even worse for Simmons, as he pummeled his monster bass. I couldn't figure out how he endured it, his body clad in leather, streams of sweat dripping from his brow onto his Kabuki-painted cheeks. I soon deduced that it wasn't actually *sweat* dripping. He seemed to have some mechanism in his ratted man bun that squirted cooling water down his face, relieving the scorch.

That—along with the huge metal wheels latched to the rafters, grinding unending reams of glitter onto our heads—made for a spectacular impression. Kiss gave everything they had, delivering a supersonic rock 'n' roll circus to us eighteen-year-old school haters. We hung around after the show, dazed and high, as the concert hall emptied and the stage crew began to broom away the mountains of shredded glitter. A teenage girl yelled up to one of the stagehands that she had tossed a bracelet up there and that she really wanted to make sure it got to the right place—which obviously meant one of the boys in the band.

"Sure thing, sweetheart"

—he said, clearly humoring her.

Soon we were told to clear out of the venue. On the ride home I imagined the stagehand locating the girl's bracelet in the debris and personally delivering it to Gene, Paul, Ace, or Peter. The next time they came to play Springfield, Massachusetts, that band member would yell out—

"Hey, which one of you lovely ladies threw this bracelet onstage last time we were here?"

And the teen babe, climbing onto her soon-to-be-former boyfriend's shoulders, would scream—

"Me! It was me!"

—then get pulled up onto the stage, asked to wait by the monitor board while the band continued to shred. Afterward she would race off with them, running and laughing, hopping into their stretch limousine, which would take them to their private Kiss jet, where tall cans of ice-cold Coors flowed like holy water, and away they would fly, instantly married forever in hot rock 'n' roll Kiss-tasy.

Going to see Blue Öyster Cult in Rockland County, New York, later that year would prove not to be so transformative. The band soldiered through their set, pulling all their classic moves—guitars held high, necks crossed in a heavy metal X. But the show was held in an open-pit venue, where teenage douchebags spat Boone's Farm wine on each other and threw lit M-80 fireworks randomly into the air. Stoned and drunken fistfights broke out, the slobbering ding-dongs approaching Harold and me—

"The fuck you fags looking at?"

We eventually got the hell out of there, shell-shocked and dismayed.

～

On Friday, March 19, 1976, three months before I was to graduate high school, Harold zoomed over to me in the school parking lot as the day's classes came to an end. He was already laughing, knowing I was the only other person in town who could understand his enthusiasm—

"Patti Smith is playing in Westport tonight!"

Now was the time.

Since her first poetry reading in 1971 at the Poetry Project in New York City, opening for Gerard Malanga (Velvet Underground whip dancer, Andy Warhol silk-screener, photographer, and poet), Patti Smith had become the gateway drug into everything punk rock promised: an alternative state of creative consciousness. Her performances, accompanied by rock writer and guitarist Lenny Kaye, on bills with the New York Dolls at Max's Kansas City and the Mercer Arts Center, and her downtown theater appearances with radical playwright Sam Shepard, had her name on everyone's lips.

Patti had organically made manifest the persona of whatever punk was going to be. Her appearance was androgynous, and she stripped rock 'n' roll down to its essence, a movement of pure poetry and passion, taking risks, defying expectations, resisting stereotypes, exalting spirituality— and asking no one's permission to do so.

Her journalism in music magazines, her books of small press poetry, her black-and-white countenance among the peacocks of glam rock—all spoke to a new heart for an intellectually charged subculture. Patti Smith exemplified punk rock as art, both beautiful and ugly, a timeless expression of convulsive energy.

There was no way I was going to miss this concert.

I was able to corral a few other teens looking for something— anything—to do. We crammed into one of their cars and proceeded to careen at high speed for forty-five white-knuckle minutes through winding single-lane Connecticut roads to reach the Westport Country Playhouse.

Patti strolled out in a black leather jacket, which she tore off and tossed onto the drum riser. The group leaped into the Velvet Underground's "We're Gonna Have a Real Good Time Together," in homage to the coolest underground rock 'n' roll band of all time. Pumping her skinny porcelain-white fists into the air, she exclaimed her version of Lou Reed's ode to rock 'n' roll love—

We're gonna jump and shout and sing together!

Between songs she spoke to us. No hoary stage spew here. No "How y'all feelin' tonight?" She made us laugh. She compared Republicans and Democrats to AM/FM radio. Smart and commanding, she read poems onstage, got lost in the swirl of electric noise, spat white gardenias out of her mouth.

This was what I had been waiting for: rock 'n' roll transcendence, an experience of mystic deliverance. There was no turning back.

After I graduated high school, the summer of 1976 melted into autumn, New York City's CBGB and Max's Kansas City nightclubs luring me like a siren's song. I wanted to run off and see the bands that I'd by then been reading about and staring at in *Rock Scene* magazine for months. Television, the Heartbreakers, the Ramones, Blondie, Talking Heads, certainly Patti Smith—these were the musicians who had been blossoming together on the radical margins of underground rock, loudly and proudly celebrating the mantle of their forbears: the Velvet Underground, Captain Beefheart, the Stooges, MC5, the Modern Lovers, the New York Dolls. These newer groups didn't aspire to anything so vacuous as playing arenas (or so I romantically told myself). They were artists, alive in the present moment, the new vanguard of punk rock destruction and creation. I wanted in.

4

TODAY YOUR LOVE,
TOMORROW THE WORLD

That October my family's world would be turned upside down. My father was scheduled to have surgery for what had been diagnosed as a benign brain tumor. It was decided that he would be treated in a New Haven, Connecticut, hospital. Relatives appeared from various parts of the country to keep vigil with us. I went with my mother a few times to visit the hospital as my father was tested and, ultimately, prepared for surgery. He seemed as bright and mirthful as ever, even draped incongruously in a hospital gown.

My high school years having recently ended, the question of going to university had been bandied about. I was pretty sure I didn't need any further schooling. My only wish was to go to New York City, to write and play music. But those prospects were decidedly vague. I knew my father, an educator, considered university the best option for an eighteen-year-old. Seeing him in this confusing and compromised position, I decided to do what he thought was best for me. I told him I was going to enroll in the state college where he had been a professor, with the idea of pursuing journalism.

This struck an obvious chord of favor with him. He smiled, saying that a college education was always a worthwhile experience. If I still felt like I wanted to move to New York City, then at least I had given it a try.

It would be the last time we spoke, the last time I saw him alive or heard his voice. In my memory, his hospital room takes on a blue-and-light-gold tone, a sense of amorphous peace pervading it—the solemn joy my father had always manifested.

The day of his surgery, initial reports were that the procedure had been a success. We celebrated that evening, a relieved and happy family. We had been told that even with a successful operation, he might suffer impairments of speech, memory, or movement, but according to a phone call from the hospital, we were in the clear.

On the way home from our visit to the hospital the day before, my mother and I had stopped at a department store. In the record section, I spotted the debut Ramones album that had been released in April. It stopped me in my tracks. Patti Smith and Television had already released independent singles, and they captured the allure of New York City's monochromatic underground music world (or at least as I imagined it, through the prism of *Rock Scene,* a magazine replete with photographic evidence of the milieu). But this eponymous *Ramones* album—this was something incendiary and new, something that demanded my close attention.

The record sleeve itself was strange and seductive in its black-and-white austerity. The four Ramones had been photographed by Roberta Bayley, a young woman with the fantastic credential of being the door person at CBGB. She had caught Joey, Johnny, Dee, and Tommy in her lens as they stood before a graffitied wall in Manhattan, a beautiful and broken playground, their postures conveying tough-kid comic-book energy.

The music turned out to be as radical as what I had heard from the Patti Smith and Television singles, but far more amped and raging. Somehow the band always stayed in the pocket, never succumbing to splatter or loose improvisation, their directness accentuated by the record's stereo setting: Johnny Ramone's guitar in one channel, Dee Dee Ramone's bass in the other.

I didn't have any money, but my mother, sensing my excitement, bought the album for me.

We laughed it up at home the next night, thrilled with the news that all had gone okay with my dad's surgery. Inspired, I slapped the record on, but immediately I had second thoughts. Was this music too weird to play for my aunts, uncles, and grandma?

Apparently not. From the first rocking notes of "Blitzkrieg Bop," everyone in the room sprang up and began to dance. They had no clue who the Ramones were, but they weren't put off by the music's strangeness, especially compared with the radio hits or disco boogie they knew. They simply responded to infectious tunes, moving to the music in celebration of good news.

Late that night, while all were asleep, I heard the telephone ring.

My mother answered. A slow realization crept into my guts: something wasn't right. It turned out that following his operation, my father had experienced internal bleeding. The tumor, when removed, was much larger than the X-rays had shown.

He had fallen into a coma.

We all awoke and waited through the night.

In the early morning my mother, Gene, and I drove the one hour to New Haven to talk to the physicians. The look on the head surgeon's face spoke of failure. Gene and I went in to see my father, my mother opting to stay in the waiting room, unable to deal with whatever awaited.

We found my dad, his eyes shut, air tube in his mouth, IV lines stuck in his arms, nodes attached to his chest. The pumps jerked his body with a hideous whooshing sound, force-feeding him emergency blasts of life. I stood quiet and stunned. I looked at Gene, who first studied the array of gauges, his young engineer's brain whirring, before turning to the sight of our dad, comatose in the hospital bed, then to me. His look attested to the horror of it all: disbelief, dismay, a wave of resignation over the senseless moment we were inhabiting. He broke into tears, something I hadn't seen since we were little boys.

My father remained on life support for a few days, until the call came from the hospital: he would most likely never fully recover from his coma. If he did, it was probable that he would be left with no memory, no motor skills. My mother made the brave decision to let him pass.

After hanging up the phone, she drove by herself to our local Catholic church to pray while I waited for my sister to return home from work. When I told her the news, she threw her keys and handbag down and announced, angry and forlorn, that she was going to take a walk, then headed out to a small dug-out pond that sat between our home and the woods.

We had lost our dad.

I would always wonder what my father would have thought of the life I'd go on to lead. He had filled our house with music, art, and philosophy, but also laughter. He had kept our bookshelves lined with Plato, Aristotle, and Kant, our walls adorned with prints of Renoir, Picasso, and Pollock.

He had introduced me, as a seventeen-year-old professing an interest in writing, to the works of James Joyce and Saint Thomas Aquinas. His influence would lead me, later in life, to the spiritual texts of Saint Teresa of Ávila and Saint John of the Cross, where prose danced with devotion, stood in praise of the ineffable mystery of the divine. If I thought the human condition could be improved by way of an artist's creative vision, that view was informed by the soundworld that he had made of our home.

My mother, sister, brother, and I are quite different people, in our ambitions and in our desires, but we will always hold the essence of my father's truth: that we live and die as nature, in all its complexity and simplicity, blessed with one another as family.

We settled into the reality of our newly detonated universe. Gene would eventually return to his duties at the air force base. Sue would stay close to our home, attending to my mother as a daughter and best friend.

As for me, I would begin to move in three incompatible directions: one in which I enrolled at Western Connecticut State College, as promised to my father; another in which Harold and I became explorers of the New York City punk rock scene; and a third in which I involved myself with local juvenile delinquents—very nearly putting an end to the other two paths.

5

CARBURETOR DUNG

WDRC-FM transmitted out of Hartford, Connecticut, and was where you could hear, usually late at night, music by such lights as Lou Reed, Joni Mitchell, and Roxy Music. I would intentionally leave the station on through the night, thinking that by doing so the songs would seep into my subconscious as I slept.

There was one DJ at WDRC infuriated with all the "unlistenable" records taking up space at the station. He presented a show wherein he would play a track from the offending discs, then smash them to bits on air. This was fantastic, as I finally got to hear music from bands I had only seen pictures of in the farthest margins of rock magazines: Bonzo Dog Doo-Dah Band, Simply Saucer, "Wild Man" Fischer. I found myself more and more intrigued by the psychos and the crazies driving this squaresville DJ to destruction.

WXCI-FM, broadcasting from Western Connecticut State College in Danbury, where my father had taught, was like most college radio stations in those days, free-form and challenging. Late at night, student DJs would go deep, sometimes spinning Nico and John Cale discs. They struck every chord of sonic desire in my body. I would usually hear the tracks I wanted only after picking up the phone and calling in a request—a gamble, and one that didn't always pay off.

"Hey, can you guys play a song from the *Chunky, Novi & Ernie* album?"

"Umm . . . *what*?"

"It came out in '74. Produced by John Cale?"

"Mmm, hold on a second . . . No, we don't have that one, sorry."

Sometimes I would strike gold, though.

"Hi, do you have the new Nico record, *The End . . .* ?"

"Oh, we do, actually—someone just brought that in. How do you know about that?"

"I was reading about it."

"Okay, yeah . . . Well, what do you wanna hear?"

"Can you play the title track?"

I would lie there in my rural Connecticut bed at two in the morning, listening to Nico's incredible nine-and-a-half-minute rendition of the Doors' centerpiece song of internal desolation and societal collapse, sung with unresolved romance and guilt.

When I enrolled at Western Connecticut State in the fall of 1976, my only ambition was to DJ at the radio station. I eventually got to tell the program director that I had been the person calling in and requesting all that outsider rock the last couple of years. He laughed, regarding me first with amusement, then concern.

As I'd told my father, I decided to major in journalism, and I began to write for the *Echo,* the college newspaper. My first assignment was to report on a gig by the musician Nick Seeger, one of the singing relatives of the heralded Pete Seeger family. It was held in the campus coffee shop, and I showed up in my black leather jacket, ripped jeans, and sneakers and watched this young gent singing traditional folk tunes, as well as some of his originals.

After his set I did a quick interview, acting every part the journalist, clutching my notepad and pen. But all I could think about was the fact that he was wearing a pair of wooden Dutch shoes. As he talked about how he had no interest in playing music for money, only for sharing traditional songcraft with listeners, I pondered how he got around in such blocky footwear. How did he drive his car?

Nothing about his music interested me much, nor did his idealism. It went in one ear and out the other. I wrote a snide and snotty piece that, while giving him props for his sincerity and prowess with a banjo, referred to his songwriting as "dire"—a terrible word to use for anyone's efforts. The *Echo* editors made hay out of my screed, ham-fistedly editing the content to fit into the paper's allotted margins, though I can readily admit my review was hastily written, disjointed, and utterly juvenile.

Further editions would print my reviews of albums by Patti Smith, John Cale, and the Ramones. These were written with only a bit more passion and insight (though the editors would ridiculously misspell Ramones as "Remones" and John Cale as "John Cage"). I began to earn a reputation on campus—this new, weird kid writing gonzo stuff in the otherwise boring paper.

After the Nick Seeger piece was published, though, a letter was run from Seeger himself. He was irked that the newspaper had sent such an unprofessional journalist to cover his gig. I was immediately mortified. I hadn't intended to hurt anyone's feelings. I had never even bothered to consider that my copy would be read by the musician himself, a serious, sensitive artist.

Between insulting Nick Seeger and my frustration with the paper over its slapdash copyediting, I was becoming something of a nuisance at the *Echo*. The editors asked that I take a break from music writing. Perhaps I could cover college sports instead?

I walked out. Not just out of the *Echo* office, but off campus.

I left school forever.

The only thing I had really wanted to accomplish was to smoke a cigarette in class, permitted back then. The first class I attended, I waited until another student lit up, then I went for it, puffing away and pretending to listen to the teacher—*whah whah whah whah.*

Smoking cigs in the classroom was excellent, but it wasn't enough to keep me enrolled.

Linguistics had always come naturally to me, and whether or not I was studying journalism, the written word continued to obsess me. Books, magazines, newspapers, liner notes. Typewriters, pens, pencils. Poetry, prose, lyrics, skywriting.

By the early 1970s, due largely to the mainstreaming of underground music writing in *Rolling Stone,* there emerged a community of writers who had a direct affinity with the music they were covering—personas as strange and revelatory as anyone they profiled. These particular rock scribes, their bylines appearing in the magazines *Creem, Circus, Hit Parader,* and *Rock Scene,* contributed as much to my budding notions of creativity as any musical artists.

Lester Bangs, channeling the bebop energy of Jack Kerouac, spilled his blood onto the page. He extolled the chain-saw intensity of Iggy Pop, for him the most potent genius of rock 'n' roll. High on music, weed, booze, and cough syrup, he would hammer away at his typewriter, articulating his love for the jazz saint John Coltrane or, more infamously, his catfights with Lou Reed. By 1976, he was in starry-eyed thrall to the pop experimentalism recorded by Roxy Music and Brian Eno.

To the like-minded, he turned our receptors on to full blast.

Creem, of all the rock magazines in the 1970s, expressed the desire to be both in the scrum with the stoned, hungry audience and at the podium, debating the cultural implications of rock 'n' roll in the aftermath of the idyllic, idealized 1960s. While serving as its editor in the mid-1970s, Lester and his contemporaries subverted the idea of what was "hip." It wasn't running off to the country in a VW hippie bus but hanging tough under the hard lights of the city.

I sent a few record reviews of my own to *Creem*, but I invariably received only rejection slips in return, told my writing was too unhinged, too laden with expletives. I got the message. Still, it was cool they wrote back.

Patti Smith wrote for *Creem* too.

I had seen her byline—styled in all lowercase—in other music mags, but it was *Creem* where her energies seemed to burn the hottest. The first piece of her writing I recall having been struck by was her account of seeing the Rolling Stones' initial appearance on *The Ed Sullivan Show* in 1964. Published in January 1973, Patti wrote that she was "trapped in a field of hot dots" and that "in six minutes five lusty images gave me my first glob of gooie in my virgin panties."

It didn't feel gratuitous or prurient of her; it was a truthful telling of a moment of attraction, one that was honest, delicious, and identifiable for anyone who had fallen in love with the raw spirit of rock 'n' roll the way she had.

Creem would also publish a two-page spread of Patti's poetry, her work stark and striking, announcing the arrival of an important new book, *Seventh Heaven*. Along with the poems, *Creem* would print photos of the writer in action, a raven-haired androgyne in a ripped T-shirt and black leather jacket reciting poetry in New York City.

This was something to stare at.

An agent of change.

Alongside *Creem* there was the more New York City–focused *Rock Scene*, primarily a photo digest that sold itself by placing Led Zeppelin, David Bowie, or John and Yoko on its cover, then peppering its insides with shots taken of the bands carousing at Max's Kansas City, CBGB, Club 82, and the Lower Manhattan Ocean Club. It might feature Wayne County vacuuming her apartment; the Ramones taking the subway from Queens to the Bowery in Manhattan; David Johansen of the New York Dolls and actress-model-downtown-superstar Cyrinda Foxe kissing on the street; Talking Heads looking like art-school nerds, unsmiling with blank stares.

Rock Scene offered a vicarious experience of what was happening in the downtown New York City rock 'n' roll underground. It quickly became a bit too much for me to just wonder and fantasize about.

I needed to get there.

6

DON'T GET TOO CLOSE
OR IT'LL BURN YOUR EYES

There were two cars in our family: a typical 1970s Ford station wagon and a white 1968 Volkswagen Beetle, which my father had used to commute to the college. Since his passing, I, by default, inherited the Beetle. In the remaining months of 1976 and into early 1977, this car would allow me to discover life on other planets.

It began cautiously, as Harold and I made excursions to record stores within a reasonable driving distance, particularly Cutler's in New Haven, known to have the largest inventory of imported albums in the state, mostly thanks to its proximity to Yale. Its singles department was situated in the back, the proprietor proud of carrying all the latest releases from the UK, seeming to welcome the new sound and movement that the media had agreed to label punk. He took immediate notice when I purchased Wayne County's "Max's Kansas City" single, released that summer, as well as the first issues of *Punk* and *New York Rocker*.

Other than Television's "Little Johnny Jewel," Patti Smith's "Hey Joe," and the first Ramones, Dictators, and Runaways albums, there weren't many indications readily available to me of the revolution to come. But there was a palpable vibe that *something* was happening.

I had found a job at a warehouse in nearby Sandy Hook, unloading boxes from trucks eight hours a day, but it didn't last very long; I only wanted to hang out with Harold, play records, see movies, and read rock magazines.

Rock Scene's coverage of the downtown New York City music world grew only more amped up—particularly of Max's Kansas City and CBGB. After Max's began holding performances in its upstairs in the early 1970s, initially as a showcase for new record label signings such as

Bruce Springsteen and Bob Marley (on the same night!), it allowed in the platform-shoed New York Dolls and the shamanistic poetry of Patti Smith.

The culture of celebrity surrounding Max's was intimidating to an eighteen-year-old lost in his thoughts in western Connecticut, an hour and a half away. It was where Andy Warhol had held court, Salvador Dalí and Alice Cooper shared cocktails, Taylor Mead pulled his trousers down, Brigid Berlin pulled her top off, and the artist John Chamberlain traded his priceless sculptures for a steak dinner with chickpeas. CBGB looked more inviting.

As 1976 progressed, I began to see and hear a particular set of names with growing frequency: Talking Heads, the Heartbreakers, Lenny Kaye, Blondie, Television. The scene was entering the national subconscious, Patti yelling, "Happy Easter, CBGB!" at the end of her group's *Saturday Night Live* melee earlier in the year—a shout-out to a magic clubhouse somewhere in the dirty streets of Lower Manhattan.

When the Damned's first single, "New Rose," was released in late October 1976 and arrived as an import from the UK, the Cutler's record store buyer attached a sticker on the outer sleeve describing the disc as being from "England's Ramones." This was for sure exciting news, and I snagged a copy instantly, but upon playing it at home I was taken aback to hear . . . lead guitar! The Ramones had no lead guitar—that was seen as done with, yesterday's rock.

Comparisons aside, though, the Damned single was straight-up amazing in its thrashing one-take, throw-the-sticks-down, let's-go-out-and-cause-some-trouble explosiveness. The flip side was the group's version of the Beatles' "Help!," which jumped off the turntable, a rampaging eaten-up-and-spat-out version of the original, turning the song into a hilarious take on the sanctified entity that had been the Fab Four.

In a one-two punch from the UK came the Sex Pistols' single "Anarchy in the U.K." the following month and then the Buzzcocks' *Spiral Scratch* EP two months after that, both bands informed by each other yet utterly distinct. The Buzzcocks record was four songs hammered out in tightwire precision, with radar-signal dot-dash guitars against an uppity, clipped, Mancunian schoolboy vocal. The Sex Pistols had more swaggering rock 'n' roll attack, obviously indebted to the New York Dolls (rather than the Buzzcocks' nod to the Ramones). Every song on these new records was a solid-gold jewel of punk-pop-rock genius. They soundtracked an intensifying year of transition and explosion.

Not content just to listen, I began constructing songs, which I figured I could offer to Iggy or, by late 1976, the Ramones or the Sex Pistols. For the Ramones I wrote a tune called "I Don't Have to Mow the Lawn No More":

> *I don't have to mow the lawn no more*
> *Or pick my socks up from the floor*

Harold and I scored tickets to see Lou Reed at the Waterbury Palace Theater in November 1976, and we went tripping on crummy blotter acid. Lou's backdrop onstage was a phalanx of television sets all tuned to fuzz and distortion. He had just released his album *Rock and Roll Heart*. He would be not only introducing those tunes but playing some songs from *Berlin,* his downer masterpiece from 1973.

Lou strolled out to the runway in front of the stage, and Harold and I left our seats to crowd at his feet. I was buzzing hard, the golden frequencies of music streaming and whirling around my body. To be suddenly so close to Lou—I felt like I could see the tiny blue veins in the whites of his eyes, my senses heightened.

I was still tripped out on the hour drive back to Bethel, taking the Beetle at twenty miles per hour, barely staying in my lane, apparitions of amorphous beasts lunging out of the neighboring woods. Harold asked me—

"Are you okay?"

"Yeah, yeah—I think so."

The following week we drove, sans blotter acid, to Hartford to catch the Patti Smith Group again, this time with John Cale on the bill. We decided to bolt from our seats and push our way up front. We had come to realize that as soon as anyone in the front rows stood to be closer to the stage, we could spring up and join them, safe in their numbers. The people who remained in their seats began chanting at all of us kids up front—

"*Sit down! Sit down!*"

—then began imploring Patti herself—

"Tell them to sit down!"

"You tell them to sit down"

—Patti responded—

"I'm not their mother."

At which point the band raged into "My Generation," with John Cale joining in, bashing the piano, initially with his fists and then his posterior.

I reached up and grabbed hold of Patti's ankle, and the shock of this breach, the impropriety of it, startled me. I immediately unclasped my grip, embarrassed, flushed with the reality of this person—earthbound, as it turned out, flesh and bone.

It was after this concert that we realized our moment had come—it was time for us to enter into the danger zone of New York City and experience punk rock, front and center.

I still felt drawn to CBGB, but Harold had his heart set on Max's Kansas City, with all its flirtatious glamour. One day in late November 1976, as we sat in his basement playing records, smoking pot, and scissoring photos out of rock magazines, Harold said to me in an epiphanic, giddy, conspiratorial half whisper—

"Let's go to Max's."

It was high time.

We drove the Beetle for an hour and a half until we reached Park Avenue South between Seventeenth and Eighteenth Streets, locating a metered parking spot nearby. Entering the club's hallowed doors around six in the evening, we sat at the bar and craned our necks around the dark space, trying to deduce where the legendary back room was that we had read so much about.

We ordered Coca-Colas, the cheapest drink possible, and feasted on bar nuts. After a few hours of looking and listening, as businessmen came and went and a few oddballs skulked about, we began wondering when and where the music would start.

A girl no older than Harold and I sat near us and began engaging a couple of straight-looking men in banter. She was pale-skinned with black hair, black lipstick, and all-black clothes. Offering the men a litany of personal catastrophes—abortion, suicide, drug use—it was as if she were playing a character out of a film, a parody of punk-kid psychosis.

Sometime after she moseyed off, we queried the bartender: When and where did the music take place? He laughed and said the action was all upstairs. *Oh, of course.* We moved to the stairwell, where a queue of people had already begun forming, including the black-lipsticked depresso girl. The sign on the upstairs door read—

SUICIDE CRAMPS FUSE

We hadn't heard of any of these bands. We knew about Patti, Television, Richard Hell, the Ramones, and the Dictators because they had records out and could be seen in our rock mags. I figured that with names like Suicide and Fuse, those two bands must be straight-up hard rock combos. Cramps just sounded wacko.

We had no idea.

Fuse was indeed a straight-ahead rock 'n' roll four-piece with a New York City swagger, their snarling guitarist, Joey Pinter, a ragamuffin in sneakers and jeans, the star of the band. He wailed and slashed at his axe, making our hearts leap.

This was to be only the second appearance in New York City by the Cramps. I realized something unusual was in store for us when I saw that their singer, Lux Interior, sporting an escaped-convict haircut, sang with the microphone only as high as his waist, forcing him to knock his knees together and crouch in order to yelp out his vocals.

It was ridiculous, but not much more so than the rest of the band. There were two guitarists and a drummer, no bass. Both guitarists were at once utterly beautiful and completely deranged. Poison Ivy Rorschach wore a leopard-print halter top, black latex pants, and pointed high heels, which gave her the look of a gun moll ready to kick a hole in a cop's face. Her black-cat-eyeliner-framed eyes stared darkly into the distance as she chewed gum, wearing an impeccable, seen-it-all sneer, her fingers drawing cool notes from a huge Gretsch guitar. She was astounding and a master of her instrument, all slow death and licentiousness.

Bryan Gregory, who we sat no more than three feet away from, looked like he had just washed ashore from an island asylum. He had black silver-streaked hair that swooped over from one side and fell into his face, greased down into a spike over one eye. He looked like a man who ate rats for breakfast and drank the blood of teenage runaways. He played his polka-dot Flying V as if he were being electrocuted, every sound a sonic slice of fuzz. He psyched us out with a lit cigarette that he rolled from one side of his mouth to the other.

Their drummer, Miriam Linna, was a badass in a Sky Saxon–meets–Moe Howard bowl haircut. She took her sticks out of a 1950s juvenile-delinquent handbag and proceeded to play the most minimal, who-cares rhythms on her bass drum, tom-toms, and snare, with enough stripper-cymbal splash to give the rhythm an insolent sleaze.

Together they sounded like a burned-out battery sputtering into an electric fire, threatening to incinerate the room. I was overwhelmed with joy, but I wasn't sure why. I knew only that it was pure and stunning rock 'n' roll, savagely serenading me in a timeless maelstrom named Max's Kansas City, at that moment the only place on Earth.

The Cramps played a few originals, which they had yet to record, and a handful of tunes from regional psycho-rockabilly outfits, bands that may have had a single or two in the 1950s and 1960s. I would later learn that Lux and Ivy collected such discs from thrift stores and lost-in-time record emporiums across the USA. It had been three years since Lenny Kaye had issued his *Nuggets* compilation of 1960s garage rock "classics." The Cramps took this mining to a whole other level of obsession. Lux would introduce songs naming their original artists—"This next ditty is by the Green Fuz"—and a Pandora's box of underground rock 'n' roll magic would be released.

After all that time spent wondering when and how, Harold and I knew we had come to the right place. Finally, we had done it. We were *there*. Harold sat up straight, his legs vibrating as he chain-smoked Newports, smiling, talking between sets about the energy in the room, alive with the history of the Velvets, the Dolls, and Patti. We sat at one of the communal tables in front of Max's small stage, knowing we were being righteously radicalized.

Two cool girls were sitting across from us, and we struck up a conversation with them. We asked if they had seen the Dolls, and one of them said in an awesome Long Island drawl—

"*Ahh yeah,* we seen th' Dolls millions a toimes."

I asked them how to get to CBGB and the same girl laughed.

"Practice."

She leaned over to Harold, not exactly whispering, and said—

"What's with yuh friend there? He looks like Mick Jagguh?"

—then shot me a salacious wink.

I was in love.

This potentially amazing repartee came to a grinding halt when Suicide hit the stage. This would be no hard rock group.

Two men appeared: Martin Rev in the back with huge, bug-eyed shades that had slits where lenses would normally be, playing what seemed to be some rhythm-box monstrosity, and Alan Vega, the singer, who sported an old lady's wig and a scar on his face, and who stood twitching as he held the microphone, as if he had just been unstrapped from a lobotomy table. He had on a leather jacket completely ripped down one side, the sleeve hanging like the remnant of a recent knife fight.

This looked like trouble—and it was.

As soon as Rev began unleashing electronic loops—equal parts horror-movie noise and Beach Boys melodies channeled through nightmares—Alan started intoning his vocal lines. Overly drenched in reverb, they were interspersed with crazed screams and howls. Each time he broke from the vocals, Alan would lock eyes on someone in the audience who had dared to look away for a second. He would then proceed to grab that person by the hair, wrap his microphone cord around their neck, and scream maniacally in their face.

He walked on top of our table, picked up one of the Long Island girls' drinks, and threw it in her face. She sat there with her mouth open, in total shock and disbelief. Alan proceeded to step on the glass, shattering it, and then, picking up a shard, started slowly cutting his chest as he looked wild-eyed around the room.

He continued whooping into the microphone, the music and his vocals emitting feedback that threatened to tear your head apart. At one point he fell to his knees and wept, delivering lyrics of desire and loss to a girl named Cheree. Martin Rev, meanwhile, remained motionless, playing his electronic keyboard, holding a fixed stare from behind his glasses on the terrorized crowd.

Alan walked across to the table next to ours and flattened his body against some bewildered, ponytailed hippie boy. People started to duck under their tables and barricade themselves with chairs, with a few of the tables upended for further protection.

Harold and I looked at each other. We didn't know what to do. Our money was spent, our table was destroyed. We knew no one else in the venue.

Let's get out of here.

As we drove back to Connecticut, we were both silent for a while. Then we began to laugh. What in God's name was *that*? Together we went over every second of it. Not just Suicide's assault, but the trash action of the Cramps.

Whatever it was that we had experienced, one thing was certain.

We needed to return.

7

CALL HELL

At the tip of Manhattan, where the island narrows to a pointed spear, the streets lose their manicured grid and smash into one another, overlapping into madness. Sliced along the middle runs the Bowery, a beleaguered thoroughfare infamous as New York City's skid row. Among the litany of ancient watering holes for destitute drunks over the last two centuries, there once stood at 315 Bowery a wooden-doored saloon—

CBGB OMFUG.

Inside, on a stage built by musicians, the Ramones would chant to us disconnected and alien 1970s kids—

> *What they want, I don't know*
> *They're all revved up and ready to go*

With the fallout of hippie culture and the karmic sickness of war, New York City was subsumed in waste and neglect. Poets, punks, and painters were arriving now wearing black and calling for a revolution from boredom, exhausted identity, and thwarted ideals.

The politics and pleasure of fun were defining facets of this new punk-art society. Interdisciplinary and intertwined, its members could be found hanging out at CBGB and Max's Kansas City, smoking cigarettes, drinking bottles of never-cold-enough beer, watching Talking Heads—a band that was nervous, short-haired, electric, with an art-school lexicon, singing songs with titles such as "Love → Building on Fire."

Across the Atlantic, Steve Jones, the guitarist and founder of the delirious and bloody-minded Sex Pistols, exclaimed to a bemused music journalist, "We're not into music, we're into chaos." He belonged to a new theater of insolence, an answer to the lumbering rock star of old.

Pistols compatriots the Clash, in a year's time, would send over their own sonic telegram, thrashing out a line in the dirt, a succinct expression of punk rock identity—

> *In 1977 I hope I go to heaven . . .*
> *No Elvis, Beatles, or the Rolling Stones in 1977*

It was a new poetry for cities in dereliction and disrepair. It heralded a new cadre of visionaries coming to town, armed with cheap electric guitars and secondhand books of radical verse.

An article had appeared in the October 1974 issue of *Rock Scene* magazine with a black-and-white image of two young men, Richard Hell and Tom Verlaine, holding a TV set in their arms and staring, affectless, at the camera. Hell and Verlaine, along with their bandmates Richard Lloyd and Billy Ficca, had announced themselves as a new New York City group by the name of Television.

This would be no "Misty Mountain Hop" fantasy world.

No escapist, James Taylor–in-a-rowboat haze.

This was urban art music in love with rock 'n' roll.

This was new.

This was the New York Dolls every Tuesday night in the Oscar Wilde Room at Mercer Arts Center.

This was Suicide across the hall, their demented, nihilist noise rattling the walls.

This was Wayne "Man Enough to Be a Woman" County swinging dildos and toilet plungers around the stage.

This was modern jazz outlier Ornette Coleman wearing a worker's hard hat and checking in with the Art Ensemble of Chicago, in town to share their intellect of soul, sound, and energy in a catharsis of praise.

This was Warhol Factory poet Gerard Malanga snapping a photo of Patti Smith standing on a subway platform, preternaturally underground.

It was Patti who had written the *Rock Scene* story on Television, its title lifted from Bob Dylan—"Somewhere Somebody Must Stand Naked." It would be the first mainstream critical writing on the group, and it read like a prose poem ode to these young street lords. Patti described Tom Verlaine's neck as appearing like a screaming swan.

Television all had short hair, as shocking and off-putting as their sound. Short hair in 1974 was unheard of. Glitter punks like the New

York Dolls all had long hair, as did the Ramones—those bands were pioneers of so much of what punk would always be. In contrast, Richard Hell, Television's bass player and cofounder, would talk about closing his eyes and chopping at his head with scissors to attain the look of the young boy protagonist in François Truffaut's 1959 nouvelle vague film *The 400 Blows*.

Upon reading it, this singular piece of journalism by Patti Smith reverberated in my mind, astonishing and significant. The fact that Television had named themselves after a household object of such banality, a consumer product of mass fixation, was strange and cool to me. The name, along with their shorn locks, felt like a deliberately monotone reaction to the previous few years' bombardment of Bowie-inspired rainbow glam.

When Television first began rehearsing, they were every bit the wild boys. Early video footage shot inside the loft of their friend (and de facto manager) Terry Ork shows Tom Verlaine and Richard Lloyd on their backs ripping the strings off their axes, Verlaine yowling and pulling at his hair, bassist Richard Hell sporadically leaping, drummer Billy Ficca flailing. By the time they began to appear at CBGB, though, they had decided to stay for the most part static—a gesture in opposition to the hyperkinetic antics most other bands were employing.

Hell would continue leaping, though. Eventually and unceremoniously, he would find himself pressured out of the group he had helped create.

It was in June 1974, the same year her article on Television appeared, that Patti Smith recorded her seven-inch single of "Hey Joe," the perennial that had been popularized by Jimi Hendrix. The B side was a spoken-word piece entitled "Piss Factory." It became available that November through ads in *Rock Scene, Creem,* and the *Village Voice.* That single would be as catalytic to my heart and soul as "Louie Louie" had been a decade prior.

It first intrigued me because I had recognized Patti as a rock *writer,* in the pantheon of Lester Bangs and Richard Meltzer, as well as a poet. I wanted to hear what such a writer would sound like on her own record. Upon first listen, the sound and immediacy struck me—it was like a cool-beat whisper, as if it had come directly from an apartment building stoop somewhere in the hallowed vicinity of Bleecker and MacDougal Streets.

"Hey Joe" begins with a recitation on Patty Hearst, the newspaper heiress kidnapped in 1974 by the United Federated Forces of the Symbionese Liberation Army, notorious agents of revolution—

Well, sixty days ago she was such a lovely child
Now here she is with a gun in her hand

—which leads into a minimal piano accompaniment, along with Patti's soulful croon. Her then paramour, Television's Tom Verlaine, brings in scattershot electric guitar action, heightening the song until it's a free-speed spaceship hovering and winging around late-night Manhattan.

The B side, "Piss Factory," rollicks like bop poetry, a contemporary howl for androgynous youth feeling the push and pull of social expectation.

I'm gonna go on that train and go to New York City
I'm gonna be somebody

—the Rimbaud-enchanted poet vows, with tears in her throat, an arrow aimed directly at her own ravished heart.

In the late summer of 1975, Terry Ork, friend and compatriot of Patti, Verlaine, and Hell, founded his Ork Records label to release "Little Johnny Jewel," the first recorded statement by Television. The stark and plaintive tone of Patti's single would cut into further fields of urban smoke with "Little Johnny Jewel." The song first states its case with three descending notes that startle. Verlaine's spoken-sung portrait opens—

Little Johnny Jewel
He's so cool

—and ends with—

All that guy ever said
He said, "I want my little wing-head"

The song fades away on the A side, Verlaine scratching out nervy electric lead guitar, only to hear it rise back up on the B side as the tale finds its dream-bop conclusion.

One year later Ork would release the single "(I Belong to the) Blank Generation," by Richard Hell & the Voidoids. A wild light of the downtown scene, poet and publisher Richard Meyers had taken the nom de plume Richard Hell with a nod to French symbolist poet Arthur Rimbaud's *A Season in Hell* (not unlike the way Richard's fellow runaway and former Television bandmate, Tom Miller, had rechristened himself Tom Verlaine in homage to Rimbaud's older lover and at times rival poet, Paul Verlaine).

Even more than my high school graduation diploma from the spring of 1976, the document that most defined my future that year would be a small ad placed in *Rock Scene* announcing this Voidoids single. The ad, with its deer-in-headlights photo of Hell sporting chopped hair and telescope eyes, read—

CALL HELL

—alongside a New York City phone number and post office box address.

I was a bit wary of telephoning this alien character, so I took a chance and jammed three dollars into an envelope instead. Based on his gaunt, staring visage, I couldn't even begin to think what he would sound like as a vocalist.

I was immediately enthralled upon first hearing him yowl his stray dog yelp of—

> *I was saying "let me out of here"*
> *Before I was even born*

—by far the best first line I'd heard expressing the spirit of this radical rock underworld. Hell was staking his claim as a prophet for a new culture and new identity.

He would have a brief, post-Television musical fling in 1975 with Johnny Thunders's post-Dolls outfit, the Heartbreakers, a writing partnership for what I imagined was one excellent day in an East Tenth Street apartment building. With Dee Dee Ramone and Heartbreakers drummer Jerry Nolan, he would compose the tune "Chinese Rocks," ostensibly glorying in scoring dope.

"Chinese Rocks" was like a balled fist of rock reductivism. In its distilled simplicity, it offered an instant antidote to the overblown progressive rock music that had dominated the 1970s. Its two-chord moves epitomized for me the beauty, power, and epiphany that could be achieved in this new form, a majestic mess of minimalism.

As intriguing as his musical activity was, Hell had also published, in 1973, a poetry book entitled *Wanna Go Out?* on his Dot Books imprint, written by Theresa Stern, purportedly a Puerto Rican prostitute from New Jersey. Theresa Stern was soon revealed to be yet another nom de plume, this time for a collaboration between Hell and Verlaine, the cover image of the "author" a superimposed photo of the two men in drag.

I sent a letter to the offices of Dot Books—which happened to be Hell's apartment on East Thirteenth Street—asking him if he would post me a copy of the book if I mailed him a few dollars. I enclosed a self-addressed stamped envelope, which came back to me in Connecticut, my original letter stuffed inside, with the word "yes" scrawled across it.

Patti Smith's most visible book of poetry, *Seventh Heaven*, had already appeared in the spring of 1972. It would be the first poetry book that most people on the underground music scene would become aware of: the first truly seminal text of punk poetics. *Seventh Heaven* was as illuminating as any of the records being released, its visual aesthetic only more pronounced, its vocabulary rich with religious consciousness, rules of verse both adhered to and tossed aside. Her exultation—

female. feel male

—read as both intimate and precocious. The book's cover photo of the young author was dreamily iconic, her eyes closed, wet black hair fallen into snow-white face.

Verlaine and Hell had already published scattered poems in a few small literary magazines, and Tom and Patti had a collaborative piece, *The Night*, published as a pamphlet inserted into a film journal. These primary documents of Patti and Television were tiny yet startling. They had contemporaries from outside the world of rock too: the word-clearing minimalism of Aram Saroyan and Andrew Wylie; the intellectual, alienated humor of Bill Knott; the New York School chatter of Bernadette Mayer and Ted Berrigan; the experimental texts of Dan Graham and Vito Acconci; the poetry aesthetes of $L=A=N=G=U=A=G=E$ magazine.

Patti, Hell, and Verlaine's distinction from their contemporaries was in heralding the transition from a seemingly exhausted array of "posts"— post-conceptual, post-minimalist, post-hippie—to the rising subculture of punk. When Dee Dee Ramone began writing lyrics in 1974 for his new band, he likely wasn't creating work intended to be in dialogue with any minimalist art or poetry. He and they were simply tuned to the same psychic frequencies, distantly but telepathically connected.

Dee Dee Ramone's brand of writing—pure in its emotion, disenchanted with the preening of the overeducated—was of no less value than the headier works that emerged from the poetry and art worlds. It was this crude motivation to eliminate frill that would inspire me to write and create—pen in hand, hair hanging down to my notebook, scratchy guitar ready to cast spells in spontaneity.

In December 1976, I went on a solo excursion to Cutler's in New Haven. By ritual, I headed straight to the new arrival LPs. I spied one of the employees there, a guy in his early twenties with long black hair and glasses. He often took notice when I arrived, as I would buy LPs by the more curious artists the store carried: Halfnelson, Silverhead, Sailor. I asked him that day if he knew when the first Blondie album was due out. His eyes widened at the mention. It felt cool to impress him.

Cruising the aisles, I invariably checked the Stooges and Velvets bins; they were generally empty. But as I approached the "V" section this wintry day, there stood a Buddy Holly–looking cat—tall, bespectacled, short-haired—staring at the empty space in front of the Velvet Underground placard.

"Not much happening in the Velvets section these days"
—I said.

Startled, he turned to me. He asked if I had heard the *Velvet Underground Live* double album, recently released. I had. It was a remarkable record, Lou Reed's stark urban lyrics charged with the band's otherworldliness.

We began talking—about Lou, John Cale, Nico, Patti, CBGB. It turned out he was graduating that year from the Rhode Island School of Design (RISD) in Providence, the same school Talking Heads had recently emerged from. He told me he had been thinking of moving to New York City to become a comics artist, in the footsteps of Jules Feiffer and Robert Crumb. He was thinking too of starting a band with a few of his fellow art-school escapees.

The Velvets enthusiast introduced himself as J. D. King. A connection to my future was made.

That December afternoon, J.D. asked me if I had seen any copies of *Punk* magazine, of which comics played an integral part. Already a completist, I had sent away for all the issues to date. I had even bought a T-shirt the magazine sold featuring the illustration from the cover of its first issue, published in January 1976, of Lou Reed crossed with Frankenstein's monster. *Punk* was a riotous celebration of all that was beginning to blow up on the New York City scene around, primarily, CBGB.

By calling itself *Punk,* it cemented the term into the culture. It was a sobriquet that rubbed a few pre-punk icons the wrong way, such as Wayne County, who felt disparaged by the word for its derogatory associations with child molesters and jailhouse snitches. Lenny Kaye had already bandied the word about in the liner notes to his *Nuggets* survey of regional records by bands displaying all manner of delinquent attitudes. It was a word the rock writers Dave Marsh and Lester Bangs had been using in their reports on Iggy Pop and his ilk.

And then there it was—

Punk.

It stuck.

Already by the end of high school, there had been a doofus or two who, upon learning I was into the stuff, would derisively sneer—

"Punk sucks, man, that's not even music!"

Hey ho, let's go—we never said it was.

8

CITY SLANG

The first weekend of December 1976, Harold and I went to check out Wayne County & the Backstreet Boys at a joint called On the Rocks, located on the corner of Bleecker and Lafayette Streets. Wayne was a force of nature, vamping, camping, and singing raunchy tunes with titles such as "Cream in My Jeans" and "Fucked by the Devil." Onstage the drag legend moaned about New Jersey rocker Bruce Springsteen, who had that year become all the rage. Wayne thought there was nothing unsightlier than a rock star with hair on his chest.

No more than forty people were in the club, but one of them was Joey Ramone. As we were on our way out, I sidled up to him, astounded to be near someone I had invested so much personal fascination in. At six feet six inches, he was as tall as me, the first rock 'n' roll person I could physically relate to—especially since the standard bearer for lead singers had tended toward the golden god of Robert Plant or the cosmic foppery of Marc Bolan.

Joey was beautiful and strange, slight in frame with a weird, sweet smile. A few kids surrounded him firing questions. I butted in—

"Hey, how was London? What were the Sex Pistols like?"

The others stepped aside, recognizing the way I'd upped the ante. Joey began talking about how the Pistols were cool and all, but they basically just sounded like the New York Dolls, only a bit more sped up.

I knew that the Ramones had played their first gigs in London that past July. As the Clash's Joe Strummer would recount, all the London punks thought the Ramones were going to be more of what they knew of New York rock: the slop and swagger of Johnny Thunders and his Dolls. Instead, what the Ramones offered was rapid-fire, breakneck, concise. It changed the game for how to appear onstage and absolutely destroy.

After the Wayne County gig and our encounter with Joey, Harold and I hopped into my Beetle to make our way back to Connecticut, driving east on Bleecker Street. We had yet to visit CBGB, to my frustration, as 1976, that epic punk year of birth, was coming to a close. I knew the club was nearby, but the city was still, to me, a foreign country of busted-out buildings, trash, bums, and serial killers. My sense of geography wasn't entirely in place.

We began to roll down Bleecker, and I noticed Joey walking down the street with some other cat. I cranked down my window and yelled—

"Hey, Joey, which way is CBGB?"

He pointed straight ahead—

"This way!"

"You wanna ride?"

—I yelled back.

He began to come toward us with an "Okay, sure," but he seemed to be slightly inebriated, and his friend grabbed him by the coat sleeve, tugging him back to the safety of the sidewalk. We were just two geeks from Connecticut in a Volkswagen Beetle, but in New York City in 1976, to hop into a stranger's car was courting trouble.

Harold and I drove a couple more blocks until there it stood, the dirty white awning with the hand-rendered "CBGB OMFUG 315." I had no choice but to pull the Beetle over into a parking spot. We jumped out and walked over—no plans and no money.

What first struck me was how dissimilar CBGB was from everything around it. The other buildings were fairly nondescript. There were derelict hotels for winos to crash out in for a few bucks, such as the Palace Hotel, which had its entrance right next to the club, its rooms situated directly overhead. CBGB sat snug underneath. It had a stucco exterior with two swinging wooden doors and dirty nine-paneled windows on either side; its facade was a holdover from its history as a turn-of-the-century saloon.

Outside the club that night were the requisite hepcats, a few skid row vagrants asking for spare coin, and the ubiquitous street freaks selling loose joints for a buck a pop.

Walking through the wooden doors felt like entering some kind of witch's house. After staring at the *Live at CBGB's* compilation album since it had been released that summer, I could only wonder what the interior was actually like. The front-cover photo depicted neon beer signs hanging from the ceiling, leading off into a mysterious distance.

People were crowded near the entrance. Among them I recognized Richard Hell talking with Roberta Bayley, who was busy collecting money at the door. It cost $2.50 to hear bands, money neither of us had after blowing our chump change at On the Rocks.

I approached Hell and asked him if he could get us in. He looked at me first with confusion, then chuckled and began to lick the entry stamp he had on the back of his hand to see if it could possibly stick to mine. That didn't work at all. Just then Joey bounded in, and I went up to him.

"Hi, Joey, you made it. I was the guy in the Volkswagen offering you a ride."

"Oh yeah, hey, thanks"

—he responded. I motioned to Harold to stay close, and together we trailed Joey into the club, pretending to be his pals.

It worked.

We began our maiden journey into CBGB shuffling along the walkway sandwiched between the bar on the right and the raised level to the left, where a pool table and a jukebox stood. Beneath those beer lights, we headed toward the stage at the back of the room, where the Mumps were about to begin their set.

The Mumps were a band fronted by the awesome Lance Loud, who had come to fame a few years prior as the proud and out gay son from the nationally televised series *An American Family*. Considered the very first reality TV show, *An American Family* was a radically new experiment for the medium. It was particularly impactful, especially for gay teenagers like Harold, to witness Lance pronounce his queerness on national television.

Nearing the stage, I felt overwhelmed. We were walking along a corridor through a place I had fantasized about for the last year. It was then that a beer bottle came whizzing across the room, barely missing my skull before crashing into the void behind the bar.

I was startled but tried not to react. I would never again witness another thrown bottle in the billions of times I entered that room. The moment remained a strange and portentous initiation.

The Mumps were frenetic, with Lance, a rather hunky dude, maniacally doing the frug, the Watusi, and the boogaloo, all mixed into one sweat-drenched, frenzied dance. His bandmate Kristian Hoffman—who had infamously illustrated the "bend-over" girl on the inner sleeve of the first New York Dolls album—was playing keyboards. The band played as though they were at the nexus of the rock 'n' roll universe that night.

Harold and I found a couple of chairs, but a waitress came over to remind us that there was a two-drink minimum, so we got up and kept moving around to avoid her, investigating the room with its wonky wooden floors, its huge burlesque photo boards leaning against the stage walls.

After the Mumps, Blondie clambered onto the stage and tore into "Rip Her to Shreds." The band set off immediate sparks, their tunes hyper-infectious and bopping with pop-punk hooks, Debbie Harry one minute still and focused, then off like a bottle rocket across the stage. The boys in the band looked like cute windup toys, kicking skintight-trousered legs into the air, their skinny ties loose around half-unbuttoned shirts.

The energy in the room was palpable, alive. I felt like I had stumbled into another realm. When Harold and I walked out through the swinging doors and back onto the Bowery, the cold city night swirling around our necks as we headed to the Beetle to put-put our return to Bethel, I felt not like we'd left a club so much as we'd exited a portal from a wholly new sonic dimension.

Harold and I rang in 1977 with a New Year's Eve show by the Patti Smith Group headlining the Palladium, a large theater on East Fourteenth Street, with John Cale and Television also on the bill. Harold had scored some mescaline, which he thought would be a perfect addition to the night.

Mescaline seemed like a scary idea. I had tried acid at that point, but it had mostly been speed-laced crapola. It created hallucinations but never enlightenment—mostly just teeth-gnashing, staying up for forty-eight hours, listening to records, smoking millions of cigarettes, drinking thousands of Cokes, talking endlessly, writing poetry in thrall to Iggy, Patti, and Bowie. Not the worst time, but not what I was usually seeking.

As a rule, I agreed to smoke, drink, or snort anything Harold, or any teen accomplice, had to offer, but I had no real appreciation for drugs, even weed and hashish. Plus I saw no reason to spend money on such substances when there were books and records to be bought with whatever little bits of money I had. The same was true for booze. I preferred focus.

When I went to see bands, I wanted to study every move, each gesture. The code they transmitted with their instruments and amplifiers, to the audience and to one another. The slight smile when their work was appreciated, the nervousness that came with being under mass scrutiny. How individual members processed these variables, and how the group functioned as a collective—these things commanded my attention.

Seeing band members laugh and hug onstage was beautiful. Seeing them disparage each other—or the audience—was no less thrilling, the negative vibration causing the music to sometimes become wired and scary. On a punk rock stage in 1977, the dramas of joy and danger could twist together in a delirious dance.

Without much thought, I swallowed the tab of mescaline, but I knew immediately that it was too strong. We dropped it in the men's room at Tad's steak house—a restaurant chain stuck in a 1971 New York City time warp, where men in private-eye fedoras and rain jackets drank cheap whiskey and scarfed back chargrilled T-bones. We treated ourselves to a New Year's dinner, and by the end of the meal I was becoming disconnected from the physical world. What I could see wasn't pretty; it was Tad's steak house of horrors.

We zombied our way down the street to the Palladium and found our seats, and I sat in a state of tenuous control as Television arrived onstage. I figured if I just maintained my cool, the mescaline's threat of wiping out my sanity would begin to subside and all would be okay.

"A song by Dylan"

—were the only words I remember Tom Verlaine saying to the audience as the band began to play a plaintive cover of "Knockin' on Heaven's Door."

By the time John Cale and his group came onstage, I felt as though I were sliding slowly down the side of a porcelain sink, managing only the barest of friction, my reality threatening to fall into a drain hole never to return. I was gripped by the fear of losing myself completely, another entry on the list of acid casualties. I concentrated on specific thoughts, pinpricks of salvation that I'd cling to, slip from, then hold on to again. I feared that if I closed my eyes, I would be forever vanquished.

Harold was tripping too, though he was hardly as screwed up as I was. He looked at me from time to time, muttering his usual—

"You okay?"

This time I couldn't answer.

I prayed intently. *Dear God, please let me come back from this insanely bad trip, I will forever be your servant.*

The storm slowly subsided, and I gradually began to recognize signals of my existence: breathing, blinking, a toe wiggle.

As the Patti Smith Group came charging out, I felt myself mostly returned. By their finale, a rousing take on "My Generation," we had left our seats and made our way into the hordes pushing to the front, every moment a negotiation as we advanced one step closer, closer again, to where the band was whipping up their incantations.

I noticed Fred "Sonic" Smith of MC5 had joined the group for this song, and it became imperative that I get as near to him as possible—not the easiest thing for a boy of my size, but here was this messenger from Michigan, to me the coolest guitarist not only in Detroit but the whole of the universe. Fred had just released "City Slang," a single by his new group, Sonic's Rendezvous Band, with lyrics only he seemingly knew, powered by a guitar hook that injected the high-energy rock of 1968 Detroit directly into the bloodstream of the oncoming 1977 New York City.

Fred and Patti had become an item. Now here was Fred onstage, unassuming and spectral, as Patti howled and whirled. With "My Generation" culminating in obligatory destruction, all players would eventually leave the stage except for the two Smiths. Like Fred, Patti had a Fender Duo-Sonic strapped on, and she leaned her head onto her sweetheart's shoulder as both their guitars emitted a whistling-bird noise of feedback through the amps.

How this translated to everyone around me, I couldn't say. For me it was an emblematic vision of all I would ever desire from rock 'n' roll—

Transcendence, devotion, sonic love.

9

NEW PLEASURE

Harold became a big fan of the bands Orchestra Luna and the Shirts, two mainstays of the CBGB and Max's scene. Both bands could be entertaining: Orchestra Luna with its cabaret vibe; the Shirts a Brooklyn take on progressive rock, their singer, Annie Golden, winging about the stage like an enchanted dervish-ballerina.

Hilly Kristal, the famed proprietor of CBGB, obviously thought both these groups were the real deal—he had them co-billed at his club on many weekends, where they generated a healthy, like-minded audience, Harold and me included.

But they weren't among the bands I wanted in on. I was more drawn to the ones generating disturbed chaos.

Not so much Harold, though. He became friendly with the members of both bands after they saw him dancing in front of their stages at gigs. He would boogie standing in place, his cigarette held aloft, shirt half unbuttoned, skinny tie loose about his neck, swaying and sashaying, pumping his fist.

I never danced. I got a bit bored with the good-times musicality of the Shirts and Orchestra Luna. It was hard not to be impressed by their songwriting and musicianship, but I was jonesing for weirdo action.

The Dead Boys provided that in trash heaps.

The band had initially been named Frankenstein and featured a couple of the members of another avant-rock Cleveland group, Rocket from the Tombs. Feeling underappreciated in Ohio, the Dead Boys came to New York City with a penchant for pandemonium. Their lead singer, Stiv Bators, had allegedly been the kid who handed Iggy Pop a jar of peanut butter at the 1970 Cincinnati Summer Pop Festival, which Iggy proceeded to smear over his shirtless body and flick into the audience as they hoisted his scrawny frame up into the air. This was really the only credential Stiv and the Dead Boys needed to appeal to us Stooges fans, still barely visible at the margins of the contemporary rock scene.

Word around town was that David Bowie had recently gone to Max's to see two other talked-about Cleveland groups, Devo and Pere Ubu. This surely increased both bands' visibility. They were each purposefully strange, entertaining, and excellent. But the Dead Boys were altogether different. They weren't quirky outsiders so much as hell-bent scoundrels.

Having read about the peanut butter incident, I told Harold we needed to catch these freaks.

We went to see them at Max's the first week of 1977. We sat ourselves a bit near the back of the room, thinking we might otherwise get cut or slashed. After the Suicide scene, our guard was up.

The Dead Boys still had long hair, unlike most of their contemporaries now, and they played a few covers in their set, such as Mott the Hoople's "Death May Be Your Santa Claus." But it was a mostly uneventful night—except that Stiv was so drunk that two bouncers had to physically drag his body off the stage, through the audience, and upstairs to the dressing room. This would turn out to be a regular feature of their sets the times I saw them; I suspected there was a bit of theater going on.

Before long, the Dead Boys would fully relocate to New York City, cut their long hair off, and set up shop at CBGB, Hilly Kristal taking on the role of their manager. It led to wild weekends of bills that included the Ramones, Dead Boys, and Dictators, the most raucous punk rock events of the era.

One night at Max's in late 1976, sitting at one of the long tables abutting the small stage and peering about the smoky room—Lux and Ivy from the Cramps together in one of the banquette tables like surrealist royalty, Wayne County DJing the latest scorchers, fashionistas mixing it up with street trash, punker kids peering through strands of exquisitely messed-up hair—Harold had commented to me about how unfortunate it was that we'd missed the "heyday" of punk.

This was hard for me to fathom, as so much was lit up and happening at that moment. But he was referring to the fact that we had entered the scene a solid two years after many of the bands we loved had taken root. The Fast, the Planets, Blondie, Tuff Darts, Wayne County, Television, Patti Smith, the Ramones, the Dictators—all had been together at least since 1975, a few even earlier.

It would be the Heartbreakers, though, who would truly galvanize the underground music scene in New York City, turning it into a genuine street-rock experience. Harold and I would catch as many of their gigs as possible. They represented a downtown 1970s lineage, connecting the glitter trash of the New York Dolls and Kiss to the neo-beatnik vibe of Patti Smith and Television.

This dynamic would form a defining essence of punk rock, where the intellectual passions of literature and art collided with the street smarts of the working class. It was Richard Hell meeting Johnny Thunders, Malcolm McLaren meeting Steve Jones.

Whether or not punk's "heyday" had passed, it was 1977 when the floodgates truly burst open. The audience for the music had been growing exponentially, the early bands on the scene proving formidable performers after having worked the stage for so many nights.

The Ramones, who could be notoriously *un*together in 1975, would by 1977 deliver consistent thrills each time they played—which they did a lot. They had been touring nonstop and were at the apex of their assault. Blondie, Television, Talking Heads, the Dead Boys—all were ripping it up to a remarkable level.

Harold and I remained open to anything that caught our eyes, that targeted our rapacious receptors. We would hunt down a copy of the *Village Voice* midweek to see what was in store, then pick what we hoped to attend. Espying a card-sized ad for *Unmade Beds,* a film by Amos Poe, one of the first downtown punk auteurs, and featuring Blondie's Debbie Harry, I convinced Harold to drive with me the hour and a half into the city to see the ultra-low-budget film—if only because I loved the tagline in the ad, which read simply ". . . depressing."

There were the activities of the avant-garde and free jazz community happening on any given night at Ali's Alley, the Brook, the Ladies' Fort, and Environ. Musicians Anthony Braxton, Sun Ra, Sunny Murray, and Milford Graves played constantly, often in the same neighborhoods as CBGB and Max's. Tom Verlaine would name-check Albert Ayler's record *In Greenwich Village* as a direct inspiration for his music. Seeing that album in record bins, with its swirling psychedelic typeface and an image of Ayler in full force with his soprano saxophone, I would harbor a long-gestating curiosity toward his music (which I would only years later immerse myself in).

An intriguing review of minimalist composer Philip Glass's 1977 LP, *North Star,* was enough for me to persuade Harold to check out a Glass performance in uptown Manhattan on the first of May that year. Glass's ensemble was austere, with three keyboardists, three horn players, and a single sound mixer arranged in a square formation, the musicians facing one another in the room's middle, the audience seated around them. This music was truly unlike any I had yet to encounter, the lengthy repetitions mesmerizing to the point where my body struggled to remain conscious—not due to boredom but to the deep and droning narco-magic of the sound, which brought me to a meditational peak, my mind rendered blank.

Though punk rock had entered the 1970s music stream as an unbridled, gloriously untutored noise, it always gave itself license to draw from the lineages of pop, funk, reggae, and experimental music. The dynamism of the category was such that it could be both elitist and populist at once. Elvis Costello's more traditional songster voice, along with his minor-key guitar moves, was a far cry from the squalling crunch of the Sex Pistols, the Clash, and the Damned; but all of it came from an urge to topple the dinosaurs that preceded it.

The first bands of the British punk explosion to visit New York City offered a curious insight into a world with its own defining tenets, radicalized by its own social reality. Hearing the Clash sing "White Riot"—their call for revolution aimed at England's working- and middle-class white youth, urging them to rage against the racial imbalance dividing the country— was quite different from punk in the U.S., whose defiance tended to take shape in the ragtag cross-dressing of the New York Dolls, the heady experimentalism of the Velvet Underground, the avant-gardism of Sparks and Alice Cooper, and the primal assault of MC5 and the Stooges.

Of course, these same bands were important to the British underground too (particularly Sparks, who would find incredible fame overseas while remaining a perennial cult group in the U.S.). England could rightly claim David Bowie, Marc Bolan, and Roxy Music as its homegrown visionaries—artists who would be accepted by punk worldwide, transcending any of the boundaries presented by cultural differences.

When Brian Eno released his experimental rock recordings *Here Come the Warm Jets* and *Taking Tiger Mountain (By Strategy)* in the mid-1970s, followed by Iggy and Bowie releasing their two collaborative albums, *The Idiot* and *Lust for Life* (inspired by the *motorik* and *kosmische musik* of German groups like Neu! and Kraftwerk), they defied the norms of the commercial music world. It may not have been punk per se, but it was generally seen as informing what was to *become* punk. These experimentalists would rightly sit alongside new music coming from the UK's younger bands: X-Ray Spex, Siouxsie and the Banshees, and the Adverts in London; the Buzzcocks, the Fall, and Joy Division in Manchester.

So a David Bowie appearance at Max's Kansas City to take in Devo was a significant validation by rock royalty. So would Lou Reed sitting at CBGB to check out the Ramones. Bowie and Reed may not have been ground zero punk rockers, but their identities and music were prescient, and they were clearly dialed into punk as it was evolving.

Nothing was or would ever be sacred in this newfound movement.

Crucifixes and swastikas were bashed into each other, if only to see what insane noise they might make together. There was no respect and no shame, only opportunities for upheaval. This gleeful nihilism, intentionally repellent and thrilling at first, would grow stale by the beginning of the 1980s, devolving into provocation for its own sake. Tasteless references to genocide would be a testament not to punk's ability to shock but to its purveyors' weakness of imagination. As exciting and exploratory as the noises of London experimental music collectives Throbbing Gristle and Whitehouse were (music that would prove to have a modest impact on my own, outside of their theatric trappings), their usage of Nazi iconography and serial killer and sexual abuse imagery could be seen only as abhorrent and immature, at the time and only more so in hindsight.

There was little room for subtlety in this burgeoning scene. SEX shop designer Vivienne Westwood and her impresario partner, Malcolm McLaren, dressed up the insolent and antagonistic Sid Vicious with swastikas and the youngster Siouxsie Sioux with a swastika armband. It may have been motivated by fuck-the-world giddiness, but as time progressed, it could be viewed only with mortified regret, at least by Siouxsie.

Not by Sid, though—he would die before he got old.

10

THE WONDERS DON'T CARE

After that first excursion to Max's in 1976, Harold and I initiated our punk rock voyages the same way, repeated countless times. We grabbed a few cans of Coca-Cola and packs of Kool and Newport mentholated cigarettes, then hopped into my Beetle and shot off to the Big Bad Apple. The cigs would be huffed and the Cokes slurped all the way across the Saw Mill River Parkway merging with the Henry Hudson Parkway, which would then drop us right onto the cobblestoned West Side Highway, where we would zigzag into and through Manhattan until we located either Max's or CBGB.

If we departed Bethel early enough, we would spend time bopping into Gotham Book Mart on West Forty-Seventh Street, as that was the place Patti Smith poetry broadsides could be bought. Inside would be stacks of independent poetry books and assorted ephemera, including photographs of Allen Ginsberg, Frank O'Hara, Marianne Moore, Sylvia Plath, and William Burroughs—all at various events, signings, and salons.

My attraction to bookstores was exponentially magnified by this shrine to books, with its wrought-iron sign exclaiming WISE MEN FISH HERE. My father had taken me on bookstore jaunts in the early 1970s, driving to the surrounding towns that had secondhand emporiums, dusty with stacked tomes, a cat or two lounging about. He would ask the proprietor where the philosophy and music sections were, and I would drift through the aisles, the smells of aged paper and cloth board lighting up my senses.

Punk rock was in full bang by 1977. All the energy exchanged among artists had galvanized into a living scene, with new bands and artists coming into New York City as if called by a siren, intoxicated by the radical promise of this new insurgency.

To identify with punk rock was to be utterly of the moment, in the now. The music might borrow from older genres, but it demanded that any aspiring punk rocker excise all pre-1976 musical statements from their mind. All the LPs I had owned as a teenager—the ones I'd alternately enjoyed and maligned, by Led Zeppelin, Pink Floyd, Black Sabbath, Yes, ELP—had been relegated to a few crates in the cellar of my mother's house in Bethel. Now it was only the glittering trash of the Bowery for me, fantasizing I might share a few beers with Cyrinda Foxe, Wayne County, Richard Hell, Debbie Harry, or Lenny Kaye.

There were certain acts Harold and I wouldn't miss: the Dead Boys, the Dictators, Blondie, the Mumps, Helen Wheels, the Heartbreakers, the Voidoids, Television, the Ramones, Talking Heads, and Patti. They would offer us entrée to the bands on their bills from farther afield: the Fans (Atlanta), the Nuns (San Francisco), the Dils (Los Angeles), the Mutants (Detroit), Rubber City Rebels (Akron), Bound & Gagged (Boston), the Poles and the 'B' Girls (Toronto).

The records being released in 1977 spoke to punk's developing style and aesthetic—confrontational, nihilistic, defiant. Each new recording would deliver a direct attack, composed with hot-off-the-griddle hooks, tempered by pop sensibilities, and oiled with rock 'n' roll louche and soulful abandon. Every document was both a fresh building block and a challenge to the next player.

In early January, the Ramones issued their second album, *Leave Home,* a perfect continuation of the first record's template—*1-2-3-4!*—but amped up like a pile driver. Blondie's debut album had also just appeared. Blondie had emerged as the perennial downtown opening band, a bit of novelty next to the more "serious" pronouncements of Television, Patti Smith, and Talking Heads. The group would herald a manifesto of "fun," which ran against the prevailing New York City punk-poet vibe, but the kids in the clubs got it—to them, *fun* was where it was at.

Television's debut album, *Marquee Moon,* would appear around the same time, a masterwork of focused and modern songcraft centered on the interplay of its two visionary guitarists, Tom Verlaine and Richard Lloyd, countered by Verlaine's cryptic lyrics, all UFOs, graveyards, and snakes vibrating out of their skins.

"White Riot," the Clash's first single, was released at the end of March, as was Elvis Costello's debut single, "Less Than Zero." The first Clash LP followed soon after, sounding thin and scrabbly, the singing gruff, Joe Strummer's spittle all but audible in the grooves of the record. Strummer, Mick Jones, and Paul Simonon looked fantastic on the cover, insolent and ready to fight. They wanted only to take rock music by the collar and swing it up against the wall.

The Adverts' "One Chord Wonders," an early, self-reflective critique on punk music, would be released in April. It was followed by the Jam's first single, "In the City," with Paul Weller's educated bullyboy take on the British mod that had been put forth a decade earlier by the Who.

Harold and I would first hear these new records at Max's between bands. The DJs there (usually Wayne County) would be supplied with test pressings, and they would be blasted through the PA. Hearing the Dead Boys' "Sonic Reducer" or the Runaways' "I Love Playin' with Fire" the first time, cranked and glorious, was as awesome as anything else happening in that room on any given night.

When Talking Heads' "Love → Building on Fire" was first spun, it was as though the trio had denied the entire vocabulary of rock, offering a minimal and stunning vision of love as a work of arson. Harold and I would look at each other every time we heard these tracks, acknowledging what we knew to be true: that we were in an exclusive space, experiencing the greatest music being made in the Western world.

The Damned would be the first of the wave of British punk bands to play in the U.S., appearing at CBGB the first weekend of April 1977 on a co-bill with the Dead Boys. The two bands were a perfect marriage, all spit and venom. Harold and I attended all three nights, each of them flat-out scorching, but on Easter Sunday, Hilly Kristal had booked the Patti Smith Group to play too. It was billed as "La Resurrection." Patti had spent the last few months undergoing intensive rehabilitation after plummeting off a stage while on tour, and she was raring to rock again. This show was to be her return. The band disseminated flyers that declared her—

OUT OF TRACTION, BACK IN ACTION

As the Damned/Dead Boys show came to an end, the club tripled in attendance, to the point where bodies could barely move. I attempted to go fetch a couple of bottles of beer and found myself chest to chest with Damned guitarist Brian James, who was not happy about this insane glut of human crowding.

"What is this?"

—he said, scowling—

"Oh, I get it, it's New York. *Wankers!*"

As we squeezed by each other I remarked—
"It's Patti Smith . . ."
The look I received from him was enough for me to keep any further commentary to myself.

The universe of what punk could be—in music, art, fashion, literature, film, and attitude—would expand throughout 1977 in ways that no one could fully predict. Each week became more hectic than the last, with new bands and records constantly spurting forth.

By May, the Ramones, the Heartbreakers, Blondie, Television, Talking Heads, Cherry Vanilla, and Wayne County would all be representing New York City in the UK, while that country's own scene was busy combusting. The weekly music papers in London attempted to make sense of the country's furious outpouring of music, embracing the scene they had agreed to market as "new wave," the sobriquet coined to expand upon punk's promise.

At this point a machine gun of music was let loose. The Heartbreakers' "Chinese Rocks" single was finally released. The first single by Generation X would flip the Who's "My Generation" onto its back—

> *Your generation don't mean a thing to me!*

At the end of May, the Sex Pistols would release their second single, "God Save the Queen," proving the band to be a full step greater than "Anarchy in the U.K." had ever suggested. When Johnny Rotten implored—

> *God save the Queen*
> *We mean it, maaan!*

—it was as much exhaustion at royal family worship by the British working class—1977 being the silver jubilee year for Queen Elizabeth II—as it was a harangue and tease of the hippies and their leftover peace-sign speak. In June the record would hit number one on the British music charts, offending one audience as it thrilled another.

Harold and I found ourselves whipping back and forth between Bethel and Manhattan in these months, the Beetle feeling the strain of the miles as my heavy foot floored its accelerator. With my brother still in the air force and my mother and sister trying to find solid ground in the void left by my father's passing, I was focused only on getting from one day to the next.

I worked jobs at local donut shops, drove a school bus for a short while, and pushed a broom at the local Columbia Magnetics factory, where recording tape was manufactured—huge spools kept in airtight spaces moving through futuristic machines overseen by men in white lab coats with clipboards.

I tuned in, delighted, as David Bowie presented Iggy Pop to all of North America on the afternoon television talk show *Dinah!,* hosted by the 1950s apple-pie-and-soda-pop sweetheart Dinah Shore. After asking Iggy about his practice of pouring hot wax over his body and busting his teeth on microphones, Dinah asked—

"Do you think you have influenced anybody?"

Iggy's response—

"I think I helped wipe out the sixties"

—would throw Bowie into a paroxysm of laughter, nearly causing him to fall off his chair. I could see how these men loved each other and the other's company, both of them beautiful beyond compare.

At nineteen, for all my will and desire, I couldn't quite figure out how to pull up stakes and actually *live* in the big city. My family's house in Bethel was perfectly safe and sound—if still bearing the trauma of loss. There was nothing much to push me out. Plus I really didn't know anyone in New York City.

I had no inkling, in the summer of 1977, where life would take me. I would sit in Harold's basement rec room as he played albums by Sparks, the Ramones, Skyhooks, Blondie, and others. Harold gladly ventured with me all across downtown Manhattan, but he was just as happy to stay put and hang out with me and no one else, sitting at my feet, tying and untying my sneaker laces in an act of benign intimacy, an unspoken distance between us always preserved. I suspected that if I reached out to touch him, he would respond, but I knew it was a place I had no natural desire to explore. I felt guilty for my heterosexuality—that I couldn't reciprocate what I imagined he felt.

Sometimes our closeness as best friends betrayed a sharp edge. If I failed to drop by his place because I was hanging out with someone else, he would become testy and tight-lipped. We would head out in his car for drives through the endless winding, hilly roads of western Connecticut, not saying anything to each other.

Caught in the free-floating haze of those weeks and months with Harold, I became more and more impatient. We continued to hit New York City as much as possible, to see anything and everything Max's and CBGB had to offer. But I began to pray for some radical angel to wink their eye at me, inviting me across the sonic threshold into the only future I cared to dream: a devotional life in service to rock 'n' roll.

11

ANOTHER PLANET

CBGB, in the summer of 1977, continued to place rickety wooden chairs and tables in front of the stage, but as gigs by a few of the more popular bands began to attract significantly larger crowds, these ancient furnishings would become ridiculous obstacles that took up too much real estate.

Driving in to see Patti Smith play there in mid-July, Harold and I knew enough to get to the club by late afternoon and situate ourselves in line outside the club's saloon doors, as the queue would progressively snake down Bowery and around to First Street. Homeless winos, their clothes and beards smeared with city grime, would beg for loose coin or, in states of inebriated lunacy, serenade the people in line with loud, caterwauling Bowery barroom songs, from Gene Kelly (*"Taaaaake me out to the ball game!!"*) to Frank Sinatra (*"Strangers in the niiiight!"*). At times they would be swishing a bottle of rotgut wine in one hand and raising a huge roasted turkey leg in the other.

These culinary quirks, affordable even on a vagrant's budget, could be procured from the deli across the street. We would pop into the place ourselves for cigarettes (and, at times, a turkey leg—they were hearty, all the better drenched in watered-down hot sauce), slipping our cash through a hole at the bottom of a hard plastic divider, yellowed with age, separating the cashier and register from anyone thinking of sticking up the place—something that had surely happened too many times before.

The night of Patti's show, we were able to score a couple of seats near the stage as people plowed in, our bodies and chairs rammed into each other, the waitresses yelling at us through the tumult to order something, given the two-drink minimum. Just when we thought it couldn't get any more crowded, the waitstaff began pushing their way through the throng, shouting—

"Move! Move! Move!"

It was like Moses parting the Red Sea. They picked one of the tables up into the air and slammed it down, right next to where Harold and I sat cowering, then banged a candle in a fat red jar onto the empty table. Then, through the violent wake, came William Burroughs and his assistant, James Grauerholz, special guests of their friend Patti.

Harold and I looked at each other in amazement. We were all but elbow to elbow with Burroughs, the Beat legend, who was dressed in a dapper suit and tie, glancing at us with steely, seen-it-all eyes. Grauerholz reached over to light the bard's cigarette.

Patti later took the stage, all burners on high, wearing black leather trousers and a white T-shirt. Everyone immediately stood up, including us (though not Burroughs and Grauerholz). She sauntered like a panther, ready to rip the place apart, knowing her Beat mentor was in attendance. I bit the bottom of my lip, staring at this feral vision within arm's reach, and she quickly caught my eye, the tallest boy in the room, and bit her lip back at me, then grasped the microphone to split the night wide open.

As the steamy July got under way, the Sex Pistols' third triumph, "Pretty Vacant," was released, easily out-motoring the competition, a killer rampage of a record, the group at the peak of its power. With this single and the Ramones' "Sheena Is a Punk Rocker" becoming the broiling soundtracks for our punk rock ecstasy, we could hardly imagine anything more seismic.

But on the thirteenth of July, in the demolition zone that was New York City, all manner of hell would be unleashed.

The day had begun with intense heat and humidity. Harold and I headed into the city from Bethel to hang out at CBGB, as had become our custom. A record-breaking heat wave had instated itself that morning, and by early evening low-slung lightning bolts began to aggressively zap across the sky.

As we drove south on Broadway from Fourteenth Street, we noticed the lights in some buildings randomly switching off. Turning east onto Bleecker Street, we heard the clacking of streetlights and could see electricity shutting down in patterns on either side of us. By the time we parked and walked over to the club, the entire area was utterly blacked out.

Hilly stood outside CBGB holding a candle. We hung out on the street with him, waiting and wondering if the power would return anytime soon. Within an hour, the feeling that chaos was about to erupt was palpable. Police and firetruck sirens became more and more constant. Distant shouts and screams echoed through the streets, punctuated by sounds of breaking glass. Car and store alarms offered a discordant soundtrack to the pitch-blackness of the city, usually lit up at all hours of the day. Hilly decided to lock up the club; it seemed obvious the power wasn't about to return.

With the streetlights out and the yellow taxis slaloming between speeding cop cars and fire engines more recklessly than usual, it was nearly impossible to navigate the Beetle through the grid of the city. Vagrants had begun to build bonfires in trash cans in the middle of the avenues, taking it upon themselves to direct traffic. Anarchy reigned.

The blackout, caused by lightning strikes upon a power grid already on its knees, broke down the walls of economic privilege. A disenfranchised and demoralized citizenry began raiding stores for food, clothing, televisions, stereo equipment—anything historically denied people by the systemic poverty that pressed upon their daily lives. While there were those who looted for sheer kicks, most were spurred on by destitution, anger, and desperation.

By the time Harold and I made it to the West Side Highway, we could see fires licking buildings where Upper Manhattan merged into Harlem and then the South Bronx. Helicopters buzzed overhead, aiming high-powered light beams into the detonated blocks. We retreated to the safety of Connecticut.

A week after the blackout, with electricity fitfully returning, disco in all its permutations—its music, dancing, and style—would return undimmed. Through the summer of 1977, it would ramp up in intensity, the music industry's new gold mine.

The much-discussed rift between punk and disco was real, and to a horde of puerile punk boys, disco was nothing more than a vapid, escapist rush, a scene that favored double-knit slacks, silk shirts, and layer-cut hairdos—anathema at the venues I frequented. Disco would prove itself in time to be an organic and innovative music, evoking a wholly modern, collaborative joy for Black and white, gay and straight, rich and poor listeners alike, later informing the hip-hop emerging from the South Bronx with its rhythmic sophistication and melodic pleasure.

New York City may have been segmented, generally along neighborhood borders, dividing it along lines of race, ethnicity, class, and more. But New Yorkers had a psychology informed by living in a city dense with humanity, awake at all times of the day and night, everyone in everyone else's face: an unspoken sense that all of us were in the same wild boat. The two movements, punk and disco, not only coexisted but crossed paths. They could no more be kept apart than the passengers of a subway car at rush hour.

The Dead Boys, after building up a rabid fan base at CBGB, celebrated their one-year anniversary by playing a show at the club, barely a week after the blackout. It would prove them to be one of the greatest, most notorious punk rock groups in the world. The boys pulled out all the stops—guitarist Cheetah Chrome shredding hotwired licks, lead singer Stiv Bators going totally off the rails.

Stiv—with a hilarious sneer like that of a rat-faced 1950s juvenile delinquent—chomped on bubblegum while he sang, then stuck a part of the wad to the microphone, stepping backward to see how far he could stretch it. He wore slices of bologna safety-pinned to his T-shirt that he would blow his nose into, then eat off the floor like a dog.

During a fairly long instrumental section of a song, he brought out a vibrator and jammed it down his tight black leather trousers, vibrating himself to an orgasm. Later in the gig, he crawled behind the drum kit, then slithered out through the kick drum, puking all the while. The set came to a finale with him dragging a girl—innocently bopping along with the other punkoids—onto the stage, then pulling her top off before tongue-smearing peanut butter across her body, as she and her friends screamed and yowled in shock and delight at the comic-book craziness of Stiv's theatrical assault.

It was a legendary night of punk rock chaos, providing a belated soundtrack to the madness of the preceding week's blackout.

Both Talking Heads' and the Heartbreakers' first LPs were released a few months later: the former, *Talking Heads: '77*, was a glowing ember, a promise of a visionary future; the latter, *L.A.M.F.*, was dull junkie rock, already stuck in the recent past.

Everything the Heartbreakers promised musically would ultimately be crystallized through *Never Mind the Bollocks, Here's the Sex Pistols* appearing in the fall of 1977. This record would destroy anything and everything in its wake with a relentless, razor-sharp mix of multiple guitars (all played by Steve Jones) in solid time with Paul Cook's spot-on, gunshot drumming. Johnny Rotten, offering his working-class truth with a glorious howl in the face of all that was deemed proper, guided the album to become a quintessential punk rock masterpiece from beginning to end.

It was followed by a further riptide of revolutionary tunes. As 1977 came to its close, the Damned would have their fifth single and second album released; the Ramones, their third album; and Generation X, their second single. Though there were more radical entries in the annals of punk outside of such high-profile acts (such as the ramshackle clatter of the Fall in Manchester, the deliberate noise solipsism of Throbbing Gristle in London, and the brat minimalism of Teenage Jesus & the Jerks in New York City), it was possibly Wire's *Pink Flag* that challenged the genre's course the most.

Dressed in muted builder's wear, neither smiling nor shouting, Wire brought an altogether new energy to the movement, stripping emotion and romance away from the creative act in a way that proved to be as effective as Joe Strummer on his knees overcome by passion. Wire became a template for disaffected youth—for those without the propensity toward flash that flourished in other corners of punk.

I knew something new and different was being put forth when I put on *Pink Flag* at home with Harold. He had always found the dress-up of punk essential to the music's value, and he cast a cold shoulder to the record. Not his cup of tea, this whole mono-dynamic, glam-less stuff. I found it alluring, painstaking, purposeful.

Was it boring?

Or was it earth-shattering?

Who knew?

Who cared?

What could possibly be next?

12

CAN'T STAY AT HOME, CAN'T STAY AT SCHOOL

J. D. King, the tall drink of water I met at Cutler's Record Store in early December 1976, had passed me his address and phone number that day. I proceeded to write him long letters on yellow tablet paper expounding on my experiences—about seeing bands at CBGB and Max's and hoping sometime soon to be on those stages, starting new-wave-punk-rock fires for the world to be scorched by.

By the late summer of 1977, J.D.—along with some of his RISD pals—had relocated to 85 South Street, a loft space at the very tip of Manhattan overlooking the infamous fish markets, where trucks and trolleys full of that day's catch were delivered onto docks lit overhead from midnight until morning. He wrote, inviting me to play bass guitar in a group he was forming. I owned no bass, had never even played one, and only really wanted to play electric six-string guitar—so that was what I brought along for our first get-together.

We sat on his bed, smoking cigarettes, drinking instant coffee, and sharing guitar ideas. J.D. had songs that utilized a few simple chords: D, A, E, and G. I showed him some of my own song ideas, basically down-stroked barre chords. We realized his more Lou Reed–ish strumming aesthetic and my Ramones-inspired thrash might make for a cool mix.

I began driving the Beetle almost daily to J.D.'s South Street loft. His loft mates were fellow RISD grads Bill Komoski and Randy Ludacer, along with Randy's two younger siblings, Ken and Hal, who had arrived fresh from their family home in the Long Island suburbs. The three brothers, super skinny and male-model handsome, quickly formed a group they aptly named Ludacer, the siblings upfront with guitars and vocals, with Bill enlisted as drummer.

I watched Ludacer rehearse, the boys affecting a decidedly un-rock attitude, all furrowed brows and knock-knees. I was still in the sway of performers like Cheetah Chrome, so to see these lads looking so severe, maintaining their deliberately nerdy, anti-rock stance, was novel—almost cute.

The music was good, though. Ludacer had short, engaging, angular songs, and they looked pretty cool onstage at the few gigs they scored around town. But Randy, as Ludacer's big brother leader, would soon become progressively more interested in neo–bossa nova, changing the band's name a few times before the three brothers went their separate ways. Hal Ludacer, notably, would be welcomed among the downtown art and fashion cognoscenti, gorgeous in his androgyny, and would be name-checked in a filmed interview with Jean-Michel Basquiat, the artist recounting how the two poor lads would scour the Mudd Club floor for loose change.

As for J.D., he had begun forming his own band with the artist John Miller, also a RISD grad. John had some music experience, having banged around with the artists Mike Kelley and Tony Oursler in a mysterious project named the Poetics. As our developing group rehearsed, I would crash on the floor in my sleeping bag in J.D.'s section of the loft.

Our drummer, Dan Walworth, came up with a name for us, Room Tone—video art lingo for the sound one doesn't notice in an enclosed space until it's recorded. The name sounded serious and hip, nerdily academic. I thought it was perfect. It was a band name that evoked short hair and penniless pockets in straight-legged trousers of uneven fit. It suited our developing aesthetic to a tee.

We would take long walks together at night, hitting every spot where punk rock and art cohabitated. First and foremost there were the music venues Mudd Club, on White Street, and Tier 3, on West Broadway. In between we would stop into Dave's Luncheonette, on Canal Street and Broadway, as it was the only semidecent place below the West and East Village open all night. With a little coin you could have a coffee or an egg cream and a grilled cheese sandwich with some chicken noodle soup. Harold and I had often stopped there after long nights at CBGB and Max's, so as to gorge on late-night hot dogs, grilled and split on toasted, buttered buns, and lime rickeys concocted with sugar syrup, fresh lime juice, and seltzer, before scurrying back to Bethel in the Beetle. Now that I was beginning to situate myself in the city and hang out with these art-rock boys, it meant a lot of hanging at Dave's Luncheonette: killing time, smoking cigarettes, watching the incredible waitresses with their beehive hairdos chewing gum and asking with their thick New York City accents—

"What's it gonna be, honey?"

The booths would be taken up by locals who still had vapors of the 1940s in their eyes, mixed with punks and artists barely out of their teens—kids soon to be christened Beastie Boys—not to mention the rather notorious roustabouts of the Mudd Club–Tier 3–Club 57 axis: Basquiat, Diego Cortez, Anita Sarko, Cookie Mueller, David Wojnarowicz, Ann Magnuson, Glenn Branca, Lydia Lunch, Haoui Montaug, Sara Driver, Jim Jarmusch. Nobody was famous or anything—except for maybe Cookie Mueller, having already graced the silver screen as a John Waters movie star. But at Dave's we all felt like film stars on a set of our own making.

Hilly Kristal attempted to expand the CBGB empire by opening a new venue on Second Avenue in late December 1977. It would be called, fittingly, CBGB's Second Avenue Theater, in a building that once housed the Anderson Theatre, renowned as the place where the final Yardbirds concert in New York City had been recorded. Harold and I went there on New Year's Eve to see the Patti Smith Group with Richard Hell & the Voidoids—one of the only shows ever at the spot as, by early 1978, the place would go belly-up. Hilly had been facing a lot of pressure from fire marshals, so, in fear that their new enterprise might be closed down, Hilly's wife, Karen, would patrol the aisles yelling at punkers to extinguish their cigarettes and joints.

Hilly and Karen's concerns were well-founded. Many a time, to Hilly's annoyance, men had marched into CBGB in full firefighting suits and with axes, interrupting gigs and turning the lights up while they inspected for faulty sprinkler and alarm systems—really looking to extinguish the scourge of punk. Attendees would continue to just hang out, smoke, drink, and laugh, waiting for the party poopers to do their business and go on their way.

But at CBGB's Second Avenue Theater, the policing just felt silly and embarrassing. Here we all were, imagining we were part of the most cutting-edge-music scene in rock history, only to have to hide our cigarettes from Hilly's wife, who for her part didn't look to be enjoying her role as punk rock hall monitor.

At the end of Patti's set, rousing as ever with the added wow factor of

Bruce Springsteen coming out to play on "Because the Night"—the song he and Patti cowrote, a genuine hit—a slew of New York City rockers, from David Johansen to Richard Hell to Ross "the Boss" Friedman from the Dictators, hit the stage for a sing-along.

Before the count-off, though, Patti began reciting, dramatically, the Pledge of Allegiance. She held her citizenship close and was adamant in praising its principles, even in the face of the nation's greed and racism. As she recited the pledge, my attention was drawn to Hell, who stood there with his bass, rolling his eyes at what he apparently saw as a bit of corn-ball pandering. It dawned on me that the luminaries of the underground scene, whom I had imagined speaking with a collective voice, might not actually see eye to eye.

This was to be another night cut short by fire marshals. They clamored in, citing the place for overcrowding, and that was that.

Walking past the shuttered theater soon after its short existence, the venue hassled to closure by a slew of city ordinances, I would find words graffitied on the wall, a phrase that would have a greater influence on me in the years to come than I could have known—

NO WAVE

A week after the New Year's show, Harold and I returned to the city to see the Ramones headline at the Palladium, with the Runaways and Suicide on the bill. This was a big deal for the Ramones as they steamrolled further into the public consciousness, the Palladium a considerable step up in size from CBGB and their other usual haunts.

Suicide's debut album had been released just the previous week. My first listen was an odd experience. It took the blood and pathos and psychosis I associated with the duo and placed it into a space of isolation. Unlike with their live set, the listener had the safety of a volume knob.

There was still nothing remotely as confrontational as Suicide in the 1970s, but their presence was more subdued when it was projected from the Palladium's large stage, far from the terror and intimacy of upstairs at Max's. The band that had so disturbed Harold and me was received with a disinterested shrug by most of the tristate attendees milling about the room.

The Runaways, from Los Angeles and produced by the mind of sleaze-core impresario Kim Fowley, stood out for the sheer brilliance of the musicians. They mixed the gut pleasure of glitter with skin-shredding guitar licks and scantily clad lyrics. Their first two albums were a steady assault of Sunset Strip dynamite, and when they played the Palladium, they were in flames.

We would see the Runaways again that March at CBGB, and they would destroy the place. They outplayed and out-rocked every band I had heard when it came to killer-rific action. Seeing Lita Ford swing her long Southern California hair around like a whip, hearing her play her high-energy lead guitar—it was mind-melting and exquisite. Joan Jett, with her short black Suzi Quatro cut, leather jacket, and bad-to-the-bone snarl, was beyond beautiful as she delivered her fierce, devil-may-care vocals.

At a lot of CBGB shows in those days, an assortment of cliques could be found at the front of the stage. Some would go on to start bands of their own, putting them that much closer to their idols. The Student Teachers, the Blessed, and Spicy Bits, made up of New York–area kids, could often be found up front, laughing and dancing, sometimes even working as CBGB's door people.

Possibly the weirdest individual of the pack was Bradley Field, a boy from Cleveland, Ohio, whom I would watch with intrigue. He had a pronounced mental-patient haircut and a precocious, snaggletoothed grin. Bradley looked lost and skittish, like a friendly, but wild, dog that had somehow found its way into the center of a CBGB Dead Boys pit.

There were a lot of nutsos from Cleveland running rampant in downtown New York City around 1977: Bradley, but also Adele Bertei, Miriam Linna, and Jim Jarmusch, intersecting with other young and restless crazies like Lydia Lunch, James Chance, Jean-Michel Basquiat, Arto Lindsay, Mary Lemley, Gordon Stevenson, Sumner Crane, and Vincent Gallo, not to mention slightly older freaks like Diego Cortez, Anya Phillips, Eileen Polk, and Debbie Revenge.

I would catch sight of their likes at gigs, always standing a few measures away, sometimes wishing one of them would ask me to come hang out or join their band, or maybe make out behind a torn curtain.

But they never did.

By 1977, I had noticed flyers pasted around record stores and telephone poles indicating that Bradley Field was a member of a group named Teenage Jesus & the Jerks. It was, I thought, the most ridiculous and possibly the *worst* band name ever. When I saw the band mentioned in the *Village Voice*, I thought the listing must be some fluke occurrence, a crazily named band that would vanish from my sight like so many others.

But it didn't. It kept appearing alongside certain other bands, forming a concurrent adjunct to the Patti Smith–Blondie–Television–Talking

Heads axis. Sharing the mantle of that graffito outside of CBGB's Second Avenue Theater, these would be the "no wave" acts. They were darker, stranger, and dirtier than their punk-inflected contemporaries. With names like Mars, the Contortions, the Gynecologists, Theoretical Girls, Arsenal, and DNA, they were the underground to the underground.

These bands never seemed to covet the celebrity or harbor the ambition of the top-tier groups in town. "No wave" was not, as yet, an immediate signifier, nor did it point to an obvious group identity. It was suggested that Lydia Lunch, the infamous queen bee of Teenage Jesus & the Jerks, had coined the genre's tag; also that it had been promulgated by an article on the sub-scene in *New York Rocker*.

Whatever its origins, I couldn't claim to be too intimate with any of the musicians at its core. I could see they were more my age than any Ramones or Blondie member, which was enough to capture my interest. Other than that, though, I didn't exactly fall in love with the music or the artists. In fact, after reading an interview with Lydia in *SoHo News*, where she dismissed Patti Smith as a barefoot hippie, I felt downright conflicted about them.

But that would all change soon enough.

In early March 1978, I went with the South Street gang to a benefit for *X Magazine*. Harold came with us but decided to bail so he could see the new wave singer Rachel Sweet play in the West Village at the Bottom Line. He and I had continued to grow apart when it came to the music we connected to and identified with. I was gravitating toward the more nihilistic, subversive elements, while Harold was drawn to the glamorous and more accessible new wave groups. The buzz we had first shared in 1976—our awakening to the downtown New York City punk explosion—had, by early 1978, begun to fade. I wanted now to move to the city for real, to play in an art-rock band, to delve deeper into the parts of the music and art scene that moved me—which more and more, as the months progressed, became synonymous with no wave, a scene Harold was dismissive of.

The *X Magazine* benefit turned out to be a signal moment. It was ostensibly a fundraiser for an artist-run print journal, started earlier that year by Collaborative Projects Inc. Each page of the new journal was created by a single artist or group, who used a Xerox to reproduce their anticapitalist ire or simply to elicit shock. COLAB, as it was known, coexisted with a number of like-minded corollaries, but it was the so-called New Cinema—featuring the filmmakers Beth B and Scott B, James "Jamie" Nares, Vivienne Dick, and Eric Mitchell, among others—that received most of my attention. Their no-budget Super 8 films were cast with artists who would turn out to be no wave luminaries, a community that became only more alluring to me in their smart and erotic subversion.

Teenage Jesus & the Jerks was the most renowned musical group of that bunch, though they didn't play the *X Magazine* benefit. The Contortions, though, did perform, along with the Erasers, DNA, Theoretical Girls, Policeband, and Terminal.

DNA was a trio of guitarist-vocalist Arto Lindsay, drummer Ikue Mori, and keyboardist Robin Crutchfield. Arto was rail thin, wearing a button-down shirt tucked into straight-legged trousers, his glasses barely staying on his face as he scratched out abstract scrawl from his electric twelve-string guitar and delivered his vocals in hoots and yowls. Ikue, comparatively serene, had not a cymbal at her kit as she established rolling patterns unlike any you'd expect to hear in rock music. Robin stood behind his keyboard with an odd, distant manner, offering short punctuations of dark notes.

Following DNA was Theoretical Girls, who came out with a way more bloodthirsty energy. Glenn Branca, the guitarist, began the first song by playing hypercharged beer-bottle slide on a beat-up electric six-string while the others created a tumbling arrhythmic tumult. It was the first time I'd see Branca play, and far from the last.

The act billed as Policeband would turn out to be just one man, Boris Policeband. He began his set before he even arrived at the venue. Standing more than six feet tall, Boris had been a fixture all over the downtown scene, strapping around his body a phalanx of police scanners that buzzed and whirred with radio noise, which he fed into a headphones-and-microphone headset, allowing him to repeat what he heard from the police radio. Donning an ever-varying assortment of sunglasses, he would accompany his pronouncements by sawing at an electric violin hooked up to a tiny amp attached to his belt.

I would later see Boris hanging out at Barnabus Rex, an artist bar on Duane Street in TriBeCa where the no wave community, particularly those residing more around SoHo, spent time. He was standing by the coatrack in the back near the bathrooms, chittering and chattering, a living noise sculpture.

"What's happening, Boris?"

—I asked while heading to the loo, the response a distorted—

"ZxxckkzXxxzZzhHxxxzzXx . . ."

Boris did nothing at the *X Magazine* benefit but step out in front of the audience—there was no stage—and do exactly what he had been doing all night while in the audience. He was a mysterious figure whose presence always lit up the joint, heightening the mood to where performative subversion begat pleasure.

The Contortions came out next, and for as memorable as their opening acts were, they stole the show. Pat Place, androgynous with short-cropped blond hair, played an insistent slide guitar against the funk minimalism conjured by guitarist Jody Harris, bassist George Scott III, drummer Don Christensen, and keyboardist Adele Bertei, all of them completely ablaze. The band's leader and saxophonist, James Chance, reacted to the art kids sitting on the floor in hip lethargy by leaping onto their bodies, blindly punching and kicking anyone who happened to be in the line of fire.

Chance pissed off a few people, mostly the East Village residents who happened to be in the room, unprepared for these rabid no wavers. A few onlookers went so far as to get up and take a swing at James, who was busy sweating and gyrating. He was undeterred by them, only goading them further.

I didn't know it then, but it was a watershed event—for me and for the downtown scene. This, more than any other, was the night punk rock in New York City was waylaid by a new breed of troublemakers. Having rollicked for two years in the trenches of CBGB and in Max's experimentalism, the no wave artists were knives out now, slashing the canvas for fresh blood.

And there was, indeed, blood in the air. Johnny Blitz, of the Dead Boys, was stabbed five times during a violent street altercation in April 1978, and he would be hospitalized. In early May, CBGB presented a benefit in which bands from all over downtown came in support of the much-adored drummer. It featured the Ramones, the Dictators, the Contortions, the Mumps, Steel Tips, Suicide, and a dozen others.

Overlapping with the Blitz benefit was a multi-night event listed as BANDS AT ARTISTS SPACE. It was a survey of this new so-called no wave scene, held at the eponymous gallery deep in the heart of SoHo. No less than Brian Eno would attend a few of those shows, soon deciding to capture the bands for a curated LP called *No New York*.

No New York could have been a seismic event for these up-and-coming artists. Instead it provoked sniping and infighting, focusing as it did on only the East Village contingent of no wave—the Contortions, DNA, Mars, Teenage Jesus & the Jerks—while ignoring the SoHo contingent—Theoretical Girls, the Gynecologists, Arsenal, Tone Death.

This partitioning would have the unfortunate effect of deflating and fracturing the scene, even as it was just beginning to receive more serious critical attention.

Whatever contingent you declared allegiance to, you couldn't deny the essential role of Lydia Lunch. Lydia's presence on the downtown scene was entirely compulsive. She offered soul-shredding evocations of pain, lust, and boredom, all in a singular and explosive complex of art, literature, and performance. She had arrived as a teenage runaway in 1975, bringing with her a vision of poetry as psychological firefight—a weapon with which to strafe the bombed-out Lower East Side. She saw New York City in the 1970s as a postapocalyptic playground, a view that she transmitted through her total incineration of what she loved: rock 'n' roll. It was at once a gesture of reclamation and renaissance.

The sound of Lydia's electric slide guitar on Teenage Jesus & the Jerks records—accompanied by a voice whose lyrics were both terrorized and terrorizing—was the sound of every alien artist in the city looking to find sense in a reality infused by perversion and absurdity.

For all that intensity, though, she was also just a delightful figure to behold—witty and smart, prepared to eviscerate the first person who dared to challenge her right to express herself.

No wave, even more than the general punk scene it developed within, was remarkably gender inclusive. Though the media liked to highlight the "women of punk"—whether Patti Smith, Debbie Harry, Tina Weymouth of Talking Heads, Exene Cervenka of X, Penelope Houston of the Avengers, Chrissie Hynde of the Pretenders, Nina Hagen, Siouxsie Sioux, Pauline Murray, the Raincoats, the Slits, or Vivienne Westwood—the youth genuinely involved with the movement never seemed to dwell on such gender distinctions. That isn't to say that sexism had no place. There were those punk rock blokes who thought they were somehow more advanced practitioners of the genre. But punk was all about creativity in disregard to such conventional matters as *technique*. Parading the hot licks of previous rock "gods" wasn't going to get you noticed in this world. As it was, the most interesting bands were the ones who didn't bother (or even know how) to play traditional tropes—who dismissed the accepted notions of musicianship, leaving them liberated to experiment, by any means necessary.

If punk was predicated on defiance of musical norms, the Slits, the Raincoats, and Teenage Jesus & the Jerks went even further than the Ramones or the Sex Pistols. They approached their instruments without any apparent regard for even the most basic tenets of what rock music *should* be. The most radical among them were truly creating new forms in the music.

The hoary expectations of rock fully stripped away, it was a time when female-centric groups struck the era's most significant, radical, and fascinating chords.

Certainly one of the most striking female voices in punk was Poly Styrene, lead singer and lyricist of X-Ray Spex. Poly and the band flew to New York City from London in March 1978 and played a few nights at CBGB. Harold and I attended, as did just about everyone in the tristate area with an ear turned toward the new music rampaging out of London. CBGB was rammed as we hustled to the front, able to sit in a shared chair pushed up tight to the stage. Seeing musicians as young as I was being fully in the moment, confident and powerful, every song a moving, rushing, grooving organism of sound and energy, was earth-shattering.

The set ended with X-Ray Spex's first single, "Oh Bondage Up Yours!" As singer Poly Styrene came to the title chorus, she shouted—

Oh bondage!

—then placed the microphone into the face of the closest person to her. As it happened, that night it was me. I had no choice but to just go for it—

Up yours!

It would be my first live performance.

13

PUFF THE MAGIC

Other than my six-second duet with Poly Styrene at CBGB, my debut playing live was our band's first and only gig as Room Tone, in the late spring of 1978, at an artists' loft teeming with young moderns in skinny-lapel jackets, ties, and green-on-the-vine intellectual ambitions. John Miller, the RISD artist and Poetics member, joined us to sing a few of his self-penned tunes.

When we finished, I sat on the wooden floor next to Harold, who told me that I was great, his eyes alight and proud. I had broken through a wall, gone from being a witness to an actual performer. It felt amazing, the reality of it coursing through me—the feeling of standing there with an electric guitar strapped on, being received and perceived by these people I barely knew.

After this first gig, though, John Miller would decide to focus on his art career. Room Tone crystallized into a four-piece: J.D., me, Bob Pullin on bass, and Dan Walworth on drums. The fact that J.D. and I were six feet six inches tall would have been pretty striking in itself, but Bob was nearly seven feet tall. Dan, he of "normal" stature, had recently, and surprisingly, procured a drum set that had belonged to Angus MacLise, a founding member of the Warlocks and the Falling Spikes, the bands that had begat the Velvet Underground.

There was discussion one evening about how the name Room Tone was a bit too similar to Talking Heads. They both came from the language of video art. I thought that relationship made it cool, but for the RISD cats it was too unoriginal. We cast about for names, struggling to reach a consensus but having fun all the while. J.D. came up with the name the Coachmen. It sounded like some generic 1960s band, one of the groups playing the Middle American restaurant circuit, entertaining customers with versions of "Rawhide" and "Cool Water." It was so unhip and outré that we had to choose it.

I still preferred Room Tone.

Harold often rode with me to rehearsals at South Street, as any chance to go to New York City was preferable to being stuck in Bethel. He would take off record shopping, then return, sitting around and waiting for me to finish before we headed back home. He didn't much care one way or the other for the older artist boys I was hanging out with. I suppose he was jealous of the way they drew my attention away from him, and their sardonic art-school knowingness rubbed him the wrong way. One of the Ludacer boys made fun of Harold's newly purchased Patti Smith Group *Easter* album because it had a song entitled "Ghost Dance" on it. The boy chuckled and emitted a sarcastic, smirking Indian war whoop. Patti Smith and Johnny Thunders were both a bit corny for these art rockers. I had been sporting a Johnny Thunders *Dead or Alive* T-shirt around that time, which I thought was super punk rock and cool, but it didn't fly in this crowd.

Other than Harold, I still had a few pals from my high school days, particularly Michael Koproski, who shared my abiding love for pre-punk rock 'n' roll—those bands that spoke to the hormonal adolescent in me, such as Montrose, Bachman-Turner Overdrive, Three Man Army, and Judas Priest, not to mention the big shots: Alice Cooper, Aerosmith, Black Sabbath. Michael and I banged around with a few other high school dudes in the years just before and after graduation, using fake IDs to sneak into local bars at night.

A big favorite of the New England rock bars in 1978, years before they became huge on the MTV metal circuit, was the band Twisted Sister. They were "cutting edge," playing covers of David Bowie and Lou Reed alongside their originals. But when I began to hear people refer to them as *punk,* I became incensed.

"Twisted Sister are *NOT* punk!"

So committed was I to this idea that I told Michael Koproski the next time Twisted Sister came to town, I was going to go see them while wearing my *Punk* magazine T-shirt, walk up to the stage, and flip the bird right in the singer's face.

Well, the day came and a carload of us pimpled dweebs went to the Fore 'n' Aft bar in Danbury, Connecticut, so I could confront Twisted Sister. The place was buzzing as we marched in and settled into a booth, ordering a round of watered-down drinks in plastic cups. I was anxious—I was hardly a confrontational person—but with Koproski and these other guys certain I could never actually do such a thing, I felt obligated to prove them wrong.

Twisted Sister came onstage rocking out of the gate, singer Dee Snider really putting on a show, all wigged-out curls, red lipstick, and leopard-print tights. It wasn't the Ramones or Dead Boys, but it was certainly kicking up a storm. Still, I needed to make a statement, if for no other reason than to draw a line between what I saw as real punk and fake punk—even if I could hardly articulate what exactly that meant.

The dudes at the table were waiting, goading me, so I downed my vodka and 7UP, walked up to the stage, and stood there with a scowl. Dee Snider saw me staring at him, this gawky teen. He pointed at me, then pranced over to sing in my face, perhaps in solidarity—I was wearing my *Punk* T-shirt, after all, with Lou Reed cartooned on it, in this Podunk bar where everyone else was either a biker or a cowboy wannabe.

Then I did it—flipped the bird directly in his face.

Dee's eyes widened. He proceeded to prance backward, pretending to spit on the stage in front of me in mock offense. The guitarist Jay Jay French, in teardrop motorcycle shades, smiled at the action. He was either happy to see Dee being flipped off or just amused by my self-serious teen face.

Freaked out, I spun around only to find the older types in the bar looking at me quizzically, this beanpole of a teenager with his obvious distaste and mystifying gesture. They let me pass. Mike Koproski and the gang were watching, huge grins of amazement and satisfaction on their faces. They made motions of wanting me to leap onstage and actually tussle with Dee, but this bit of insanity was quickly defused and we hightailed it out of there.

I was notorious all the way home that night.

Between high school graduation and my eventual move to New York City, I would find myself roaring around with teenage monsters at loose ends, devoid of responsibility and discipline. Nights were spent driving aimlessly around the spindly Connecticut roads of Bethel, Danbury, New Milford, Redding, and Newtown, 8-track tapes of Bad Company and Boston cranked and blasting, distorted, challenged by the variable speeds of the tape moving across dirty, resin-gooed tape heads.

One bonkers night, I was whipping around the country roads of

Redding with a girl named Robbie who was wild with trouble, seeking out whatever action a teenager might hope for in rural 1970s America. Redding was the home of Mary Travers from the famed Peter, Paul & Mary folk trio. We all loved knowing she lived there, proud to have this musical legend in our midst. That night, as I slalomed my family's Ford station wagon around the bend where Mary's house sat, I suddenly lost control of the wheel. The car slammed into the stone wall outside her home, its huge rocks rolling out onto the street, the front fender of our car sheared off, the window cracked where Robbie's head had bashed into it. Smoke puffed from the crumpled hood, though the engine kept on humming.

I rammed the gear shift into park and asked Robbie if she was okay. She was startled but only laughed—there was no blood, only a bit of a spreading bruise. A woman came running out of the Travers home and approached us wearing a shocked look of concern, asking if we needed help.

"No"

—I said, a bit bummed that this woman was not Mary herself. Probably just the housekeeper.

"Is this the house where Mary Travers lives?"

The woman didn't answer; she just looked at me with incredulous confusion.

"Can you please tell her I'm sorry? I'm a fan."

For all my joyriding and gallivanting, I still needed some kind of employment, if just to afford the gasoline it took to get around. I had a job for a while working the midnight-to-dawn shift at a Mister Donut shop, an all-night Bethel coffee joint, where I filled donuts full of jam and custard and waited on the late-night miscreants who stumbled in. Often it was drunks who sat at the counter, drinking weak coffee throughout the night until dawn came.

Some real delinquents came flopping in, a few I recognized from high school—kids who had yet to figure out how to grow up and who put my own minor delinquency to shame. One of these boys befriended me after I allowed him to hide in the back kitchen when he came scooting in with blood on his hands. He claimed he had busted a window while breaking into a gas station. After robbing the till, he ran over to Mister Donut, the only place open so late at night.

Outside, I could see cop cars whizzing around looking for the guy. I went back into the kitchen to check on him. He was pulling out blood-soaked five- and ten-dollar bills from his dungaree jacket. I gave him free coffee and donuts, and after he settled, he started talking to me about girls, records, movies, our mutual friends. He began coming by Mister Donut on the nights I worked. We eventually began hanging out quite a bit outside of the shop, driving aimlessly around in my Beetle, looking for something to do, mostly finding trouble.

Trouble was attractive—dark, palpable, unsettling to me to the point of nausea and yet still addictive. This kid, a year or two older than I, was well acquainted with trouble. He was born into it, having been severely abused by his father while growing up. Cruising around Fairfield County together, he would instigate car chases with the random teens tooling around Danbury and Bethel, mostly kids with 1970s hotshot cars such as Chevy Novas and Camaros. It was ludicrous to challenge them while driving a Volkswagen Beetle, but we didn't care. We zigzag raced, me always at the wheel, shifting and grinding the manual transmission, my left foot stomping at the clutch while my right foot banged from the accelerator to the brake. We would whip around rural residential streets, sometimes across lawns and parks, families and baseball teams scattering as they heard us roar a bit too close.

One sunny, blue-skied afternoon, we had been racing along, taunting some hot-rodding young dude, when the other guy made the mistake of flipping his middle finger at my copilot. He responded by hurling empty beer bottles, which had been rolling around in the Beetle's back seat, out his window at the guy's car. Freaked out, the other driver decided to wail the wrong way up onto the off-ramp of the highway, zooming headlong into speeding traffic, albeit on the shoulder, in hopes that he might lose us and our beer-bottle attack. Instead we followed right behind him, the oncoming traffic whizzing by us, people's faces gawking out their windows at how dangerous and utterly stupid we were.

The next exit we peeled off down to the main road, my heart pounding out of my chest and my eyes popping from their sockets. Still, we kept chasing at high speed, our prey driving back onto the highway (this time going in the correct direction). With his pedal obviously to the metal and his superior car, he quickly lost us.

We decelerated just as a cop car flew by, siren screaming, cherry tops flashing. We could see that his target was the middle-finger-flipping speedster we had been playing cat and mouse with. The cop pulled the boy's car over, and as we approached, the officer was stepping out his driver's-side door while peering down at a citation booklet, ready to write him a ticket.

Insanely, as I slowly passed the kid's car, my friend tossed one final empty beer bottle out his window, straight into the kid's face. The look of *NOOO!!!* in the boy's eyes seared itself into my brain, the police officer somehow completely oblivious to what was happening. We just drove the hell away, delighted by our purposeless vindication.

On an early winter day, the snowy ground hard and crunching beneath our feet, my friend came to me with the ridiculous idea of robbing the house next door to my family's. Having just been released from the juvenile detention center in nearby Cheshire, Connecticut, he was no stranger to this sort of thing. I registered the absurdity of his suggestion—how could I not? But I was unmoored and raring for action, enough that it didn't take much cajoling to convince me. He showed me how to break a window with a T-shirt wrapped around your fist and how to retreat backward so our footprints could not be so easily traced.

We ransacked the place. While my criminal pal searched for money, I, true to form, took the opportunity to grab a copy of Joni Mitchell's *Court and Spark,* which I had found in one of the bedrooms, leaning against a stereo speaker. (It wasn't my proudest moment, this act of juvenile burglary, but Joni's song "Raised on Robbery" still brings a smile to my heart.)

Someone at a neighboring house saw us as we were climbing out the window and alerted the cops. I didn't return home until later. My sister said the cops had come by looking for me. I called my jailbird accomplice, and he suggested we beat a retreat out of town. I jumped into the Beetle and picked the boy up, and we hit the highway with the notion of driving out to the Michigan suburb that his estranged family had relocated to. The Beetle, mechanically compromised from the constant back-and-forth to Manhattan, broke down in Ohio. We hitchhiked the rest of the way.

En route we dined and dashed from pizza parlors and stole candy from highway rest stops. We slept in freezing derelict buildings or in the crash pads that kids who picked us up invited us to. Reaching his family's house, unwashed and famished, I could tell they were spooked by our being there—especially given the way the boy's father, a violent and abusive drunk, had routinely beaten the hell out of my friend when he was a kid. When the father heard that his wayward ex-con of a son was in town, he arrived at the house, banging on the door and yelling—

"Get those junkies out of my house!"

Which I supposed meant us. Mom and sister thankfully kept the door chained shut from the inside, preventing him from entering. I half expected him to kick the door down or smash through a window, but he, thankfully, retreated to whatever bum bar he had stumbled out from.

I left the next day, hitchhiking my way back to Bethel. It was the early winter of 1977, shortly before Christmas. The highways were a series of trucks and cars whipping by, spraying ice and snow, but I persisted and got enough rides to make it back within forty-eight hours. As I hobbled down Main Street, a cop car cruised by, screeched to a halt, and demanded I get in.

I recognized the cop; he was a dude a few years older whom I had known from Bethel High School. He shook his head at my sorry state as he hauled me into the police station. My mother bailed me out, and I appeared in court in handcuffs and leg manacles—a bit dramatic for breaking and entering. But it was part of the show, and in some way, this was, I thought, the role I had asked for: the boy up against the rules and regulations of a society he wasn't sure he wanted to belong to.

Released, I caught a few connecting buses back to the forgotten town in Ohio where the Beetle patiently awaited me, repaired at a local service station, then drove it back to Bethel for fourteen straight hours.

After paying a misdemeanor fine negotiated by a local defense attorney, I got off having only to see a probation officer every week for a few months. Still, my name and criminal offense appeared in the local paper, and it humiliated my mother. Harold came over and cried. Why would I get so involved with such idiocy? Even I realized that there was an element of acting out in it, still feeling at loose ends after my father's death. We all felt that way in my family, so this wasn't some profound insight, but my response was by far the most destructive.

I decided to take it as a sign. My close call with the law told me that it was time to do something bold—to get out of this small town and move to New York City once and for all. It was where I could write songs, play guitar in a band like no other, write books of poetry, spend my days and nights in deep-soul streets of inspired energy.

A place where I could be protected by rock 'n' roll, where I could fall in love at any given moment.

The Coachmen—(left to right) Bob Pullin, J. D. King, Thurston Moore, and Dan Walworth—strolling the no wave streets of Lower Manhattan, 1979

BOOK TWO

14

FOR WHAT IS A PRAT

Spending more and more of my time at the South Street loft, I scoured the *Village Voice* for a place of my own.

I could live with an old man rent-free if I didn't mind taking care of him: walking him, feeding him, giving him his meds. Economically sensible as it was, it seemed depressing, possibly dangerous. I had never heard of anyone living to tell such a story. I passed.

After looking at some real ratholes, I settled on a third-floor walkup at 512 East Thirteenth Street between Avenues A and B. The rent was $110 per month, a manageable enough sum—if I could land a job.

The building was typical for the East Village in 1978, especially for the stretch that residents called Alphabet City. No buzzer system at the door; tiny black-and-white-tiled floors, all chipped and grimy. The tenant above me was a barely functional ex-con and drug addict who had a couple of high-strung rottweilers, which he would drunkenly whip and yell at throughout the night. Above him lived an alcoholic couple who stumbled up and down the stairs. When I crossed their path, they would urge me to take a sip from their sloshing bottle of booze. The woman once began screaming maniacally in their apartment, then proceeded to climb down the fire escape at the front of our building, yowling—

"Help! Help me!"

She tried to open my window, sobbing and bleeding, begging me to protect her from her husband, who had evidently smashed a bottle over her head. I noticed him trundling down after her, just as drunk and clumsy as she was, trying to grab her by the hair and drag her back into their hell zone. I didn't own a telephone so I couldn't call the cops. I pretended not to know how to open the iron gates that barred the window.

The ex-con upstairs had a strung-out buddy with no teeth who would hang with him once in a while. He would see me, cackle, and call me "Slim." I must have amused him, the skinny, tall, corn-fed boy just out of his teens living in this godforsaken building. One afternoon, I ducked out of the rain into a doorway on Avenue A, only to find no-teeth guy standing there as well seeking refuge. He was delighted to see me—Slim, of all people! He told me that I should think about selling drugs for him and his friend. He said I could make good money. He added that I could fuck him in the ass if I wanted—

"I'll suck your dick too."

I politely turned him down before leaping back into the downpour and heading home.

Each time I approached the corner of Avenue A and Thirteenth Street, I would break into a sprint to my doorway. It ensured, among other things, that I wouldn't get stopped by the local teens, who thought nothing of ganging up on a new guy in the neighborhood, mugging him for money or kicks. I would be on high alert whenever I headed east toward Avenue B too, a crime scene waiting to happen. I took a chance late one night, walking quickly to a bodega on Avenue B and Thirteenth to grab a pack of cigarettes and a can of Pepsi. On the way back, three kids strolled by, all of sixteen years old. One of them eyeballed me and slapped me on the back, saying, "Hey," before continuing toward Avenue B.

I picked up my pace, and sure enough the kids backpedaled, surrounding me. They wanted money—ridiculous, as I had probably three dollars on my person. They threatened me with a knife, and I froze. One boy reached into my back pocket and took my wallet; another snatched my bag with the Pepsi and the cigs. They said if they saw me again, they'd kill me, then ran off laughing and yelling, throwing the soda can past my head and onto the street, where it sputtered. I swooped it up and bolted the half block back to my apartment, shaken and terrified. After gathering my senses, I opened what was left of the Pepsi, slowly sucking on its fizzy sweetness, wishing I could smoke a thousand cigarettes.

For weeks I was gripped with paranoia whenever I left my place, mostly from the possibility of seeing those same street kids again, whether in the neighborhood or on a nearby L train subway platform—but it never happened. I had a slow, sober realization. The demons at play in this teeming metropolis were largely figments of my imagination. The crime and violence were real, but they were more or less arbitrary. Also, I probably shouldn't be walking alone around Alphabet City at three in the morning.

The drug-dealing dude with the rottweilers disappeared one day. It was after I had heard a relentless, low moaning outside my doorway, coupled with an insistent thumping. The sounds from around the neighborhood were always disturbing and alien, so I put up with it for a while, but I eventually opened the door to see what was going on.

I found the toothless guy who had propositioned me lying on his back, his feet crumpled against my door. He must have been bleeding for some time from some unseen wound, because the entire hallway was swamped in blood. I sensed that he was expiring, his leg jerking spasmodically against the door. I leaped over the lake of blood and ran upstairs to bang on the ex-con's door. I told him his friend was in trouble. He hurried down, eyeballed the situation, and told me he would take care of it. I leaped back over the bloody dude and into my apartment, staying there for as long as I thought it was safe.

I could hear him dragging his friend's body—*clunk, clunk, clunk*—up to his room, then the *thunk* of it hitting the floor above my ceiling. Eventually the landlord appeared with the police, and I told them what I saw, nothing more, nothing less. Cleaners arrived, scrubbing and disinfecting the hallway, but there would always remain streaks of dried blood in the cracks of the aged tile. The guy upstairs soon vacated the building, escorted by cops, his dogs mysteriously gone with him.

A single mom soon moved into the building, one of the only other white residents, the building primarily occupied by Latino and Black tenants (much like most of the neighborhood). She had two little kids who never seemed to attend school. She was also a heroin addict. The last I saw her was while she was pushing her baby daughter in a stroller along First Avenue, obviously on a junk nod.

Her little boy would sometimes knock on my door, with all the innocence of a ten-year-old as he came in, and we talked. Within a couple of years, I would see him performing magic tricks in Tompkins Square Park, hoping to cadge a bit of coin. A few years later I would be hanging with a few people on the sidewalk in front of the Saint, a venue the musician John Zorn had founded to present free improvised music. I watched as two kids began hassling a friend of mine, poking at him a bit, then laughing and trotting off. I recognized one of them as that same boy. I wanted to say something to him, now a teenager—to see if he remembered me, that nice guy who had lived in his building, who had let him hang out and talk while his mother was lost upstairs in a haze of heroin—but I just watched him disappear toward Avenue D, deep into the savage streets of Alphabet City, and wondered where kids like him end up, what their stories might sound like, hoping they might somehow be delivered from the tragic dice roll they'd gotten.

The Fender Stratocaster my brother, Gene, had given me was my only possession other than a chair and a mattress. I had no dresser. The clothes I wore were primarily bought from the open bins in front of Canal Jean Co., a remainder store on Canal Street (it would eventually move to a building on Broadway in SoHo). Shirts, trousers, and shoes could be had for a dollar a pop there. They were all "irregulars," mistakenly sewed such that buttons didn't quite match buttonholes, for instance. They weren't considered very hip by any contemporary boutique standard, which at that time favored either hippie-funk flash or colorful-disco glam. The "look" of downtown no wave wasn't retail-supported. If it aspired to anything, it was the uptown aesthetic of Fiorucci or the London-punk influence of Trash & Vaudeville on St. Mark's Place. But those places were prohibitively expensive, especially compared with Canal Jean, and people on the downtown punk streets tended to struggle to make ends meet.

The clientele at CBGB and Max's didn't dress punk in any way that would have been endorsed by London's King's Road—no bondage gear, safety pins, or teddy boy accoutrements. If you walked into a club looking like that, it would be obvious that you were from way out of town or had seen pictures in magazines and thought that was what punk was. Or else it simply meant you had money.

The button-down shirts from the Canal Jean bins had tiny collars, and the trousers were all straight-legged and cuffed, a bit of a neo-bumpkin look about them—particularly when the trousers rode above the ankles, a fate I had more or less accepted for myself, being so tall. I certainly wasn't the only poor art-rock nerd outfitting myself from these rag boxes. The entire no wave scene, all of whom seemed to live in and around my home on Thirteenth Street and Avenue A, was wearing the same duds.

The skinny ties and skinny-lapel suit jackets many of us sported, also cheap and vintage, gave the scene a derelict yet debonair feel. The inexpensive winter coats most commonly available at Canal Jean were made from old-man tweed, the kind a 1950s private detective would wear. When walking into Tier 3 or Mudd Club, it was obvious that we all had shopped, or stolen, from the same bins.

I had devoured Mickey Spillane books growing up—Mike Hammer, Spillane's protagonist, ruminating about how he loved the summer rain, as it washed away the scum of New York's infested streets. Manhattan still had a bit of Mickey Spillane in it during the 1970s, at least in the no wave clubs below Canal Street where I hung out. Bands like the Lounge Lizards, led by John Lurie and his younger sibling, Evan, both of whom looked like they were straight out of a noir flick, wore the style perfectly, accompanied by dangling cigarettes and blue-mood sax and piano.

There was a young Latino couple living on the ground floor of my building. They knocked on my door one day and gave me some pro-socialist literature, asking if I would be interested in organizing a protest against the landlord, who, typically, was lax about protecting the building and raised rents without explanation. They invited me into their apartment for coffee, the place nearly as spartan as mine: all they had was a bed, a hot plate, and a large, ripped poster of Che Guevara on the wall.

 I was noncommittal. I didn't have any point of reference for their activism, as a geeky kid from Connecticut whose only experience with protest was when my father took me to a peace march after Martin Luther King Jr. was assassinated, ten years prior. Sometime after our meeting, I heard a commotion downstairs—the landlord had shown up with some muscle to forcibly evict the insurgent couple.

I needed an amp if I wanted to really play my Stratocaster, and I eventually procured a tiny one at a Connecticut yard sale. I played in my apartment, noise that could most likely be heard by other tenants, but it was no louder than any of the yelling and stomping going on all day and night. At some point, new people moved in across the hall, and one evening I heard a *tap tap* on my door. It was a petite, pretty Latina girl in a bathrobe asking if she and her boyfriend could send an extension cable through their back window, across the airshaft, and into my apartment, so they could feed off my electricity until they got their payments together. They would pay me for what they used, of course. I acquiesced. She kindly queried about my guitar too and about me being a musician.

 After about a week I realized I was being conned. These cats were never going to pay their share of my electric bill. So I unplugged them. My neighbor came over again, wondering what happened. I said I felt like one week was enough and that they should find another solution. The next night when I entered my apartment, I noticed the door was unlocked. Someone had come in and plugged the cable back in. From what I could tell, they had crawled on a plank between the two airshaft windows, reconnected the electric cord, then walked out my door, unable to lock it behind them.

The boyfriend had a rather imposing vibe, so I didn't confront him, I simply unplugged the power again. The next time I returned, the same thing—cord plugged back in, door unlocked—but now the Fender Stratocaster my brother had given me, my small guitar amp, and my cassette player were missing.

I knocked on their door and the girl answered. I explained the scenario. I could see her boyfriend sitting on the couch with another dude watching TV.

"It wasn't us"

—he said, not looking at me.

His friend, also not taking his eyes off the TV, added—

"You shouldn't live in this neighborhood."

I realized that if I disconnected them again, I might be attracting more than theft. So I left the extension cord plugged in and hoped they would eventually recognize how lame this situation was for me, their nice neighbor.

A few days later I heard yelling in the hallway. It was the landlord, once again, accompanied by yet more thugs. He threw my electricity-cadging neighbors out. It seems they hadn't paid him any rent since they'd first moved in. The landlord saw me checking the scene out, then pointed his finger at me and warned—

"And I better not have any more trouble from you!"

I wasn't entirely innocent. I too could be a bit in arrears with my monthly nut.

All I had left to my name were my single bed mattress plopped on the floor, a tottering stack of books I had procured from various secondhand bookshops around town, and two cassettes—the Rolling Stones' *Some Girls* and Bob Marley's *Exodus*—with nothing to play them on. I was heartbroken at having the Stratocaster suddenly gone. It wasn't the last time a guitar of mine would be ripped off, but it was the most jarring, my innocence at once vanquished, an initiation into the big, bad world of the big, bad city.

I didn't have many friends in the neighborhood, even if I recognized some musicians and artists my age prowling around. Over on Twelfth Street between Avenues A and B was an infamous apartment where the no wave rat pack of James Chance, Sumner Crane, Lydia Lunch, and Jim Sclavunos were living together. A block west, in the building Jack Kerouac had lived in two decades prior, was where Allen Ginsberg, Peter Orlovsky, Arthur Russell, and Richard Hell were currently decamped.

The only way I could pay the rent for my own modest dwelling was to borrow it from my mother, but that couldn't go on forever. I scanned the want ads and saw that I could make a few bucks taking part in a drug-testing experiment. I went to the location in the ad, somewhere off Fourteenth Street around Union Square, and, at eight in the morning, got in line with a collection of street crazies, punk psychos, and a few relative innocents like myself. We were to get a hypodermic needle stuck into our arms full of some experimental vaccine, then to sleep the night on prison-style bunks in a large warehouse space. Easy enough money, I thought.

I received the shot and prepared myself to bed down, all the while listening to the jabber of the maniacs around me. I looked forward to receiving my paycheck the next morning—thirty fat dollars. Within a few hours, though, I felt violently ill and began to puke endlessly into a bucket by the bed. Only a few of us were in such a state; most of the others were getting through it, whatever "it" was.

The following morning, after collecting the dough, I decided that I should probably find another source of income.

So I became a foot messenger.

As a foot messenger I walked through every neighborhood in Manhattan, entering countless buildings, peeking into strange apartments, once in a while receiving a tip, which I would generally use for a subway token to lighten the burden the miles put on my legs. The pay was entirely insufficient; as I walked, I would keep my head down, scanning the pavement for the gleam of errant coins. A few dollars gathered were enough to buy me a ticket on either the Metro-North train to Bethel or the less expensive Hudson line to Brewster, New York, a half hour outside Bethel, at which point I could hitchhike to my mother's house for a little decompression.

New York City in the summer of 1978 was at the bottom of its nosedive. With growing economic disparity, street crime was a normalized part of daily life. There was a general attitude of weary resignation. But there was also a shared sense, among my peers, that we were living in this city for the ineffable connection it afforded us—the wild community of artists, poets, and musicians giving voice to an environment rife with trash, chaos, and absurdity.

Spying Joey Ramone, Johnny Thunders, Lydia Lunch, Howie Pyro, Pat Place, Neon Leon, James Chance, or Cheetah Chrome and his amazing girlfriend, Gyda Gash, walking on the streets in sunlight, it was as if I were seeing owls who, through some error, were out and about during the daytime. They would appear to me like characters out of a Fellini film, as they stepped over spilled garbage cans or dodged around uncorked fire hydrants shooting water onto broiling concrete.

In the summer, almost everyone was out on the streets, sitting on building stoops or in cheap folding chairs on the sidewalks. The cost of air-conditioning was a luxury to most anyone living below Fourteenth Street. Along with fire engine and cop car sirens, the sounds of Mister Softee ice-cream trucks, their prerecorded music a worn-out, wobbling tape loop, would serenade us in the late afternoons.

The Sex Pistols had come over to tour the USA in January 1978, but, by manager Malcolm McLaren's decree, they didn't play the major outposts of New York City or Los Angeles. Instead, the punk lords plowed through Georgia, Tennessee, Texas, Louisiana, and Oklahoma, ending it all with a bedraggled performance at the Winterland Ballroom in San Francisco, California, where they would unceremoniously split up.

Punk rock had by then entered an alternate reality, for those of us devoted to its glory. To hear jokes about Johnny Rotten and Sid Vicious on *The Tonight Show Starring Johnny Carson,* the highest-profile television program in the U.S., could only suggest that an end was near. Word went around that the Pistols were going to play New York City after all, despite the news of their apparent breakup, but it was not to be.

McLaren still had plans for his musicians. He whisked guitarist Steve Jones and drummer Paul Cook off to record in Rio de Janeiro, with vocals by Ronnie Biggs—notorious as one of the infamous Great Train Robbers, by then escaped from English prison and living in exile.

As for Sid, he nearly OD'd after the Winterland gig, then again on the way to New York, eventually making it to London, where he would reconnect with his girlfriend, Nancy Spungen of Philadelphia. After recording incredible cover versions of the Frank Sinatra nugget "My Way" and the Eddie Cochran rockers "Somethin' Else" and "C'mon Everybody" and playing a gig at the Electric Ballroom with ex-Pistol bassist Glen Matlock and Damned drummer Rat Scabies, Sid left with Nancy for New York City, where they would live out their final days.

The two immediately hooked up with ex–New York Doll Jerry Nolan, who had just formed his own band, the Idols. Like Sid and Nancy, he was a straight-up junkie, subsisting on heroin substitutes from various methadone clinics around town.

Nolan set up the closest thing to a Sex Pistols gig to grace New York, an act initially called the Music Industry Casualties, to play Max's Kansas City on September 7. When the ad first appeared in the *Village Voice,* it mentioned that Sid would be joined by the Dead Boys' Cheetah Chrome and Jeff Magnum. By the following week, the group was listed simply as "Sid Vicious and his Crew." The Dead Boys were booked to play CBGB that same night, so those maniacs weren't likely to be involved; but Nolan's bandmate in the Idols, guitarist Steve Dior, convinced the Clash's Mick Jones, in town mixing their second album at the Record Plant, to join Sid's group. It would be Jones, Nolan, ex-Doll Arthur "Killer" Kane, and Dior himself. This was the first time any member of the Clash would appear live in New York City (a good five months prior to the Clash's seismic throwdown at the Palladium in February 1979).

Whomever the band's lineup would ultimately comprise, there was no way Harold and I were going to miss it. Sid playing at Max's was the closest thing to compensation we'd get for the Sex Pistols blowing off New York City earlier in the year. The general feeling around town was that, as denizens of the birthplace of punk, we had been ripped off by the band breaking up. The fact that the Pistols had died their crummy death in San Francisco of all places, the city where punk's nemesis, the hippie, had been born, only added insult to injury.

Harold and I arrived at Max's in the late afternoon of the seventh, knowing that the gig would be sold out pretty quickly. There were about twenty people in line along Park Avenue just above Fifteenth Street. We joined them and waited, waited, waited. Finally, after cramming our way into the upstairs room, we grabbed two seats at one of the long tables pointing to the tiny stage. The audience that filed in was a mix of the usual characters with a new French-speaking, leather-pants-wearing punk contingent.

Again we waited, waited, waited.

Finally the opening band, which no one wanted to see or hear, came on. They were called Tracx, and they were so *not* punk it didn't even register as funny. No one had ever heard of this band before (or has heard from them since), and they got killed by the audience. For thirty minutes, it was nothing but jeers and hoots before Tracx slumped off the stage.

Again, we waited interminably for Sid to come on. The place was jammed, drunk, smoked out, shifting discernibly from bored to belligerent.

And then they came.

Pushing through the audience first was Sid, followed by ex–New York Dolls bassist Killer Kane, then Jerry Nolan hand in hand with Nancy Spungen, then drummer Steve Dior and, to everyone's leaping heart, the one and only Mick Jones from the Clash.

They assembled behind the stage's curtain. When Sid stuck his head through it to deliver the almighty Sid wink, we knew we were in for crazy times. The curtain at last scrolled open, and Mick Jones led the band through classic Dolls and Pistols originals, as well as the 1950s Eddie Cochran tunes Sid had recorded in London. Nancy was playing, to some degree, a tambourine.

The audience went ballistic through it all. Chairs and tables were decimated. People spat, threw drinks—pure mania. The leather-trousered French freaks pointed their fingers at the stage howling—

"Seeeed! Seeeed Veeeesshus!"

After the first song a girl yelled—

"I love you!"

—to which Sid responded in his North London street drawl,

"Shut your fucking mouth, you stupid fucking cunt."

I had seen bands get spit on before. The musicians would usually scowl or, worse, complain. Sid spat back. You could see his goobers plonking into the French punks' eyeballs.

This was *waaay* better than any old Sex Pistols gig would have been.

This was the flower and the poison in one glorious crash and burn.

15

NO GOLDEN THROAT

A magazine shop named SoHoZat opened in 1978 on the east side of West Broadway, just north of Canal Street. It was a grungy and desolate strip back then, with a fenced-in vacant lot across the street and a scrapyard next door. There was no other retail to speak of nearby, besides the army surplus stores on Canal.

SoHoZat was a subcultural paradise. It was the only place to find the Los Angeles fanzines *Flipside* and *Slash*, as well as *Search & Destroy* from San Francisco. Seeing images of Los Angeles punk bands from the 1970s (Germs, X, the Dils, the Weirdos, the Screamers, Bags), it was easy, as a newfound New York aesthete, to react with inarticulate derision. Their dyed hair, chain necklaces, leather-studded wristbands, and ripped clothes marked them as London copycats, especially if you couldn't hear the music.

I could tell from the zines, though, that Los Angeles had more people my age performing in bands, especially compared with those at the shows I was seeing at CBGB and Max's. The Ramones, Hell, Patti, Television, the Heartbreakers—they were all heading into their fourth decade. Only the no wave bands were near my age, then twenty. But for as much as their music kept me riveted, I could see that this new generation of musicians were lunatics—living in bombed-out basements, surely having bondage sex and shooting amphetamines into their skulls. San Francisco seemed to have a weirder, more art-school version of punk brewing, with bands like the high-concept Crime, Negative Trend, the Avengers, the Offs, the Mutants, and the designed-to-offend Dead Kennedys.

Mostly I preserved my East Coast snootiness, but I was intrigued by West Coast punk. One Los Angeles fanzine I loved was titled *Trudie.* It consisted of only pictures and stories about a Los Angeleno punk girl named Trudie Arguelles who looked astounding with goth black hair, eyeliner, and lipstick, all adorning a pale white face at odds with the L.A. sunshine. When San Francisco's the Nuns played CBGB that summer, I went out of curiosity, and a few of the punk girls I recognized from *Slash* and *Flipside* happened to be there, visiting I suppose. I spotted L.A. punk legends Alice Bag, Hellin Killer, Kid Congo Powers, and, sure enough, Trudie.

The Nuns were okay. It was cool to see the punk "ice queen" domina-trix Jennifer Miro at her keyboard. But my attention was drawn more to the L.A. underground celebs at the front, pogoing and making sure the band had some audience energy. Everyone else was just sitting at their tables, eating burgers and fries, drinking tepid beers (it's possible they were there to check out Akron, Ohio's great Rubber City Rebels, who were also on the bill). When the Nuns finished their set, Alice Bag screamed for more and began kicking the stage with her deadly black pointed shoes. I sat there alone, watching her intense energy, besotted and enchanted. I wished I wasn't so shy so I could say, *Hey, I love the Bags, you're amazing.* Or, better still, run off on a punk rock honeymoon with Trudie.

As it was, making friends with people my age in the scene mostly eluded me—due to my innate shyness more than anything. I certainly didn't have the confidence to attempt anything intimate. I would catch the eye of other loner kids on the streets around my building, obviously there to connect with the punk life, but we rarely exchanged words.

A rather flamboyant punk ran across Avenue A one day as I was bop-ping around and asked me excitedly if I played drums.

"Uhh, no . . . but I play guitar."

He muttered—

"Damn . . ."

—before running back to his friends, whom I recognized as a band named Tina Peel.

Another time, a rather bodacious punk girl followed me out of the shop Manic Panic onto St. Mark's Place and loudly whispered—

"Pssst, hey you . . ."

I turned around and she gave me a wink, then slipped back inside the shop.

Did I even respond? No.

I walked home to Thirteenth Street, dazed.

For a while I kept seeing this tall-as-myself boy with wispy white hair skulk-ing around the streets accompanied by a very Dee Dee Ramone–looking cat in a black leather jacket. They eventually disappeared; I later realized they were Greg Sage and Dave Koupal, who had started a band in Portland, Oregon, named the Wipers. Before 1978 was over they would release their first single, "Better Off Dead," which had a snarling vocal, a bit of feedback guitar floating around its edges, and hypnotic chiming chords that made the hairs stand up on the back of my neck.

In a year when the most popular music in the world was the disco groove of Donna Summer and, on the big-rock front, the Who's *Who Are You* and the Rolling Stones' *Some Girls,* regional punk music had been spreading through the towns and cities around the globe. Bands like the Wipers proved that punk wasn't a flash in the pan or a passing phase, but that it had inspired a reconsideration, reinvention, and renewal of rock 'n' roll as art. Some of the higher-profile punk bands managed to become somewhat integrated into the culture, though the music on the whole remained fairly marginalized—certainly compared with the arena rock of Bruce Springsteen, Kiss, and Aerosmith.

The downtown New York City fanzines that began appearing in the summer of 1978 were born of the same energy as the bands they featured; at times, they were produced by the same people. *Beat It!* and *NO* were two that émigrés to the East Village no wave scene were involved in, *Beat It!*'s look defined by the photos and layouts of Julia Gorton, along with her editorial partner, Rick Brown, who played in the no wave groups Blinding Headache and Information. Julia had created a specific design by ripping the borders of her photos and placing them on stark backgrounds of either black and white or flat pink. She had an obvious eye for the damaged glamour of the artists she was lensing. I would tear her artwork out from the fanzine and tack the pages to my apartment wall.

The principle of sharp cuts and haphazard—yet focused—placement was exemplified too by the flyers of Glenn Branca (of Theoretical Girls and the Static). Glenn would eschew most nontext imagery, emphasizing words to an almost fetishistic degree.

I read these fanzines alone in my apartment, knowing they were made by people my age living somewhere close by. It seemed like most of the punk and no wave activity in the East Village was spurred on by connections coming out of New York University, where friendships had already been established, as well as on loose collectives moving into the city from outside, with Ohio and Florida seemingly generating some of the most interesting characters.

I shared space with these people—we went to the same clubs, eateries, shops—but always I stood at a social remove. Besides hanging out with the Coachmen and the Ludacer boys, I really didn't have any other close friends in town. At least, not yet.

Some West Coast punk singles caught my eye in the record stores around Manhattan, but I used whatever money was in my pocket—hardly anything at all—on discs coming out of the UK and New York scenes.

Wire had released two singles in 1978: "I Am the Fly" and "Dot Dash"—both astounding in their unity of pop hooks and grey-toned crunch, and a majestic leap from the miniatures heard on their *Pink Flag* album. A band out of Birmingham, England, named Swell Maps would release "Read About Seymour," a single that flared off the turntable like a wild, clattering gem, mixing elements of Krautrock with its homegrown, outside-of-London punk-pop otherness.

The Rough Trade record shop in London would release "Paris Maquis," by a Parisian band named Métal Urbain, the first single on the shop's own imprint. It was as weird and relentless as the Wire and Swell Maps sides, with two whipped-cream, fuzz-frazzled guitars parrying each other against a hyperkinetic drum machine and electronic sputter, backing a vocalist singing about state control, a spiked-wrist-banded fist in the air as he denounced—

"Fasciste!"

The Paris scene had a direct connection with London more than any other city—due not just to geography but also to the relationship between Malcolm McLaren and the French rock 'n' roll freaks Michel Esteban, a graphic artist who had been involved with the early CBGB scene, and Marc Zermati, who had been releasing proto-punk records on his Skydog label since 1973. All three had been part of an early 1970s Paris collective by the name of Les Punks—basically hard-core Lou Reed enthusiasts who tracked the connective tissues from Lou, Iggy, the Dolls, the Ramones, Hell, Patti, and Television to the Pistols, the Clash, the Damned, the Slits, Siouxsie, and onward.

Esteban would start a label he'd christen Rebel, which would release "3 E," a fantastic, stuttering, train-derailing masterpiece, the first recording by the New York no wave band Mars. He would go on to cofound the ZE label with the downtown music and art aficionado Michael Zilkha, which released New York City–centric singles by Lester Bangs, Suicide, the Contortions, Kid Creole, Lydia Lunch, and the first records by Esteban's partner, the poet-singer Lizzy Mercier Descloux.

Lizzy, while hanging around New York City, had been friendly with

Patti and Hell. She could be seen jumping onstage at various no wave gigs. A book of her poetry, *Desiderata,* with an intimate foreword by Patti, had been floating around.

I was hardly hooked into this social world of French punk luminaries (let alone Patti's or Hell's), but I was very intrigued by Lizzy's book. Her solo album, *Press Color,* was a curious invention too: a no wave–disco hybrid, the music modern, sparse, and off-kilter, with fractured grooves and a nouvelle vague urbanity. I became enchanted by Lizzy, her black-and-white visage on *Press Color* androgynous, cool, smart, young. She was like a contemporary Jean Seberg from Godard's *Breathless.*

I convinced Harold to join me in hearing her perform one night. He was hardly impressed, the music too scratchy and atonal. Harold wanted hard-glam kicks.

I wanted only to daydream about this French poet-rocker whom I would never meet.

St. Mark's Church, home to the St. Mark's Poetry Project, of which Patti and Hell were chief proponents, suffered a nearly ruinous fire, and a benefit was held at CBGB in late October 1978. Advertised to perform was a host of New York City poets mixed with local musical acts. Harold and I went on one of the nights, primarily on the off chance of seeing Lou Reed or Patti, and without any real knowledge of who the poets and writers involved were.

I had seen Ted Berrigan, then lauded as the Poetry Project's central voice, on the East Village streets for some time, always in the vicinity of Gem Spa, on the corner of Second Avenue and St. Mark's Place. Gem Spa was a genuine New York City rock 'n' roll landmark, the location for the back cover photograph on the New York Dolls' first LP. Harold and I would always go there to steal the expensive English music papers. I would order a couple of chocolate egg creams (frozen milk, seltzer, U-Bet syrup; no egg, no cream)—Gem Spa made arguably the best in town—and while the gent at the window concocted the delicacy, Harold would stick the music papers under his shirt.

Berrigan was stocky, in his mid-forties, and had a scruffy beard, thick black glasses, and a cigarette constantly in his mouth. On the street, I would invariably see him with a crew of young writers, who followed him as he held court. I would listen to his incessant tenor, wondering if he was some kind of cult leader.

When Berrigan strode through CBGB on the night of the St. Mark's benefit, I realized he was a big deal in this world. He certainly was to Hell. When the Voidoids took the stage, Richard began by reading "10 Things I Do Every Day," a classic of Berrigan's, in which the bliss of the banal is illuminated in verse—

> *read books*
> *see my friends*
> *get pissed-off*
> *have a Pepsi*
> *disappear*

—before Hell and his band blasted off.

Harold and I spied Elvis Costello bustling about the club, startling because he was wearing a black leather jacket and dungarees—unlike the knock-kneed dweeb holding an electric guitar that we'd seen in magazines. On a visit to the basement toilet, I found myself peeing next to the guy. Some excitable kid recognized him and began yammering.

"Hey, Elvis!"

That prompted some other dude, sitting in one of the stalls, his trousers around his knees, to shout—

"Is that Elvis Costello? Oh my god, I love you, stay there, I want to meet you!"

Elvis quickly zipped up his fly and sped back upstairs.

During their set, the Voidoids decided to try their hand at "Shattered," the Rolling Stones' ode to 1970s New York City. They invited Elvis onstage to play guitar and sing along, the energy in the room shooting through the ancient, plastered ceiling.

That same October, a week prior to the St. Mark's benefit, Sid Vicious had been arrested after his girlfriend, Nancy, had been found knifed to death in their Chelsea Hotel room. This news raged like wildfire all across town, with conflicting stories and police reports. Sid was hauled off to Rikers Island prison, where ten days later he attempted suicide.

That same week his ex-Pistols best friend, Johnny Rotten (né Lydon), would premiere his new project, Public Image Ltd (PiL), releasing their first single, "Public Image," a scathing statement of identity theft, driven by bassist Jah Wobble's heavy dub measure against a snaking guitar line from Keith Levene. Their debut album would soon follow, a huge departure from the Pistols, all psychedelic noise guitar; slamming, reverbed drums; and dark dub bass, with Lydon wailing in despair—*I wish I could die*—before breaking into spurts of lunatic laughter. It was a furious and disturbed album that refused to comply with any standards except its own. As the new thing from the former Rotten, it was incredibly significant: a call to wipe out notions of punk as a generic form.

On other fronts, Siouxsie & the Banshee's first album, *The Scream*, would be released, after more than a year of my seeing and hearing news about this group, which had been formulated from the very first participants in the London punk underground. The LP had been preceded by a single, "Hong Kong Garden," offering an enticing depiction of the band's excellence and promise. Siouxsie Sioux sang with commanding and glorious tone, clear and vibratory, wrapping her voice and energy around the room and straight into your bones, her band playing along at full steam with swirling-rock propulsion. The sound of John McKay's guitar seemed unleashed from the place where Bowie collided with the Pistols. *The Scream* was experimental, relentless, serious, and only hinted at the goth-playfulness of their songs to come.

Other than the blistering revelation that was Métal Urbain, one of the first and most revolutionary documents to come from a non-English-speaking country was the Swiss band Kleenex's scintillating 1978 single, "Ain't You" / "Heidi's Head," the band exuding razor-sharp, angular, loudspeaker-ripping punk minimalism, singing in Swiss-inflected English, and presenting one of the first all-female fronts of energy on the scene.

The Slits and the Raincoats, from London—whom we wouldn't be able to hear in the States until their first releases in 1979—were the only other bands that most of us were aware of at the time comprising all women. Gender politics weren't the defining aspect of these bands' lyrics, but the cool aggression of the playing—confident, mysterious, surprising, bold, and funny—would destroy any stereotypical notion or expectation of what young women's rock music was supposed to be.

This was punk, a welcome space to pronounce your sexual identity, politics, love, hate, or indifference, without the judgment or permission of anyone else. Even though a boys' club mentality would often rear its head inside the scene, punk was at its heart defined by freedom. Within its liberated universe, debate, opinion, argument, and activism prevailed. Skinheads, peace punks, anarcho-punks, art punks, queer punks—all could cohabitate and converse within its sentient walls.

Except nazi punks—they could fuck off.

16

MERE ANIMAL IN A PRE-FACT CLAMOUR

Punk would die in 1979, but not before it had invaded, infected, intersected, interrupted, disrupted, deflowered, empowered, enlightened, frightened, heightened, harangued, heralded, chewed up, swallowed, spunked, debunked, spit out, flunked out, stunk up, fucked up, sucked up, pissed off, and tongue-wrestled the entire culture of music, art, and literature the world over.

On the second of February, Sid Vicious was found dead in a West Village apartment from a hot shot of heroin. I was visiting my mother in Bethel when Harold broke the news to me. I yelled at him, stunned and angry—

"What? Are you kidding me!?"

We immediately flicked on the TV and waited for the news. Sure enough, there it was, a body bag being carted out of the apartment building. Sid's mom had been in town to lend some support, but she too had drug issues. Considering the hellish events in Sid's world the last year—which included bottoming out with the Pistols, OD'ing, waking up to find Nancy dead, being tossed into prison, then slashing Patti Smith's brother's face with a broken bottle at a gig right after being released—Sid's death, while a jolt, was hardly unexpected.

It would alter the state of mind of the punk scene. Its king, its clown prince, our salvation from the dreariness of conservative expectations, had left the planet after barely twenty-one years. The frivolity of the movement, the who-couldn't-care-less insouciance of it, was diminished by his loss.

The music, though, would not stop.

A couple of weeks after Sid's demise, the Clash would play their first concert in New York City. It had been two years since their inception, but instead of playing Max's or CBGB, as a new arrival from London usually might, they appeared at the significantly larger Palladium. Harold and I knew better than to miss this gig, and it proved worth the wait, a ballistic game changer, the Clash sprinting out, guitarist Mick Jones grabbing his microphone—

"C'mon, Strummer!"

Joe Strummer came bounding onto the stage and strapped his guitar on. The band kick-started the night by blasting out "I'm So Bored with the USA." The entire audience sprang to their feet, galvanized by the thrash. Strummer stayed rooted at center stage, stomping his feet, raging into the microphone, pulling at his hair, while Jones and bassist Paul Simonon leaped up and off Topper Headon's drum riser, windmilling their axes, intermittently crisscrossing each other as they flew from one end of the stage to the other.

The Ramones had famously schooled the London scene upon their visit in 1976. The Clash returned the favor in 1979. After the shock of Sid's passing, the Clash brought life hurtling back into the despairing punk community.

As the Clash began to command huge venues, a band of their London contemporaries, the anarcho-punk group Crass, was keeping things far more radical. Crass released their 1979 album, *Stations of the Crass,* each track slamming into the next, fed by extreme noise guitar, primal drumming, and the voice of singer Steve Ignorant declaiming the imbalance of power everywhere he looked.

After performing no more than seven gigs in London beginning in late 1977, Crass had come to New York City in June 1978 to play a handful of gigs. Very few people had any real clue as to who they were, only that they'd arrived from London and that their name was curiously close to the Clash.

One of the gigs they played in New York City that summer was on a bill with a few local no wave groups at 33 Grand Street, a performance loft space deep in the dark streets of SoHo, belonging to Jeffrey Lohn, from the band Theoretical Girls. Crass played last, and they were unlike just about anything and everything that was happening that night, let alone downtown—each member dressed in black with armbands tied to their shirts. They proceeded to thrash out a furious, serious howl.

The few of us in the room were mostly Lower Manhattan–dwelling artists. What anger we nurtured was mostly toward the ants that had invaded our communal peanut butter jar that morning. But these guys were crazed, yelling, the guitar player thrumming dissonant downstrokes on his strings—totally open, no fretting, just *whaammm! whaamm! whaaamm!*

We all looked at each other like, *What the hell is this?*

It was completely and—for us slackerly, art-school-ish malcontents—incongruously militant.

New bands started popping up everywhere downtown in 1979, with a fair amount of musical bed-hopping going on. Some musicians and artists appeared in three or four different groups at any given time, collaborating on short-lived projects (some of which would never advance beyond the rehearsal room), everyone trying out different permutations, hardly defined by notions of competition.

Hearing one of the first gigs by the all-female group Ut, I felt as if the entire bottom had fallen out of what I knew to be rock music. Ut was not only beyond punk and no wave; they were almost beyond comprehension. With each piece of music, the members would switch instruments, suggesting an unusual degree of musicianship. Their songs clashed and shuddered with total disregard for any traditional approach, but unlike many of the bands who eschewed standard ideas of rock (even to the point of chainsawing their instruments in half onstage, à la the Plasmatics), Ut seemed as if they were clawing their way up from some primordial ur-language, allowing their shapes and forms to be defined from an intrinsic, organic drive.

The Ut performance made me feel anxious and impatient. It was as if the band had created a society unto itself, in which members could come and go as they pleased, moving from station to station—all within the context of a singular performance. It was a model of sonic democracy that stuck with me and that would prove significant for what lay ahead of me.

The downtown scene bloomed into an array of influences and proclivities, different styles melding into one another. The art-school nerds who had been cued off by Talking Heads moved further into disjointed pop experimentation; no wave bands were becoming far more formidable than their off-the-wall craziness might have first suggested.

The Contortions became tighter and more funk focused, finding a balance between rhythm-section grooves and the spasmodic noise of their guitars and keyboards. DNA was transformed by the inclusion of ex–Pere Ubu bassist Tim Wright, who would further distinguish the band, bringing the added attraction of a heavy, swooping low end, not to mention a player who was truly "out there"—tight trousers, black leather shoes, curly hair falling into his angular face, a glint of mischief in his eyes, cigarette dangling, stepping about the stage like a demented marionette.

The Dead Boys and the Heartbreakers would continue to play rousing rock 'n' roll, offering cheap-booze kicks, flipping the bird at authority, and taking no prisoners. But most of the other bands that drew from the Dolls and Stooges playbook seemed to be holding on to a bit of yester-year's glory.

J. D. King accepted a job that required him to sleep nights inside the Dia Art Foundation's gallery at 393 West Broadway in SoHo. He was tasked with intermittently polishing, and ostensibly protecting, Walter De Maria's sculpture *The Broken Kilometer*.

Dia had been founded in 1974 by the German art dealer Heiner Friedrich with his wife, the Houston oil heiress and art-collecting philanthropist Philippa de Menil. It existed as a rather mysterious entity in the art world. The foundation eschewed publicity while funding long-term spaces and studios for installation artists such as John Chamberlain, Donald Judd, Dan Flavin, La Monte Young, and Marian Zazeela. Dia had installed *The Broken Kilometer* in 1979, to be exhibited at the gallery in perpetuity—until the end of time, supposedly.

The work utilized the entire space. It was constructed of five hundred solid brass rods positioned on the gallery's large wooden floor in five parallel rows of one hundred each. The idea, at the time at least, was that the rods were to be kept immaculate—a nice, relatively undemanding job for J.D.

He would soon be offered some other, more remunerative work and asked if I wanted to take over the sleeping and polishing gig. So I began attending to *The Broken Kilometer*. Initially I polished the rods as the job required, but I soon realized that it made absolutely no difference— there were no security cameras, and the rods didn't look much different after I'd finished. So I just read books and lay awake in my sleeping bag instead.

Walter De Maria was a conceptual artist and composer who, in the very early 1960s, with the composer La Monte Young and choreographer Simone Forti, had staged happenings in San Francisco, before heading east to New York City. Once there he ran an art gallery, as well as became the drummer for the Primitives, a group with Lou Reed and John Cale, before they rechristened themselves the Velvet Underground.

Getting paid minimum wage to sleep with a bunch of brass rods was a pretty good deal. And coupled with our Coachmen drummer, Dan Walworth, playing a kit once owned by Angus MacLise, I felt as though I were part of the Velvet Underground's sprawling lineage—even if my employment at the gallery would last for only about a month.

My waking hours, when not working at such strange jobs, would be spent either in the company of the Coachmen and Ludacer gang, all huddled together in their large South Street loft, or simply prowling the downtown streets—hanging out at the record stores Bleecker Bob's and Free Being, or the Strand, the mighty St. Mark's Bookshop, or the funkier East Village Books.

We rarely had gigs, though we continued to rehearse. Nights would often find us carousing through the streets, looking for kicks. SoHo was fairly abandoned, TriBeCa only more so, and Wall Street, at the southernmost tip of Manhattan, was simply a desolation zone after six p.m. Our two bands would take cans of spray paint and find places to emblazon our names, joining the other tags on the street. No wave bands spray-painted their names fairly judiciously at that time, sharing space with the graffiti abstractions of true street writers and new-energy taggers, like the omnipresent SAMO. Flyers for gigs, dance events, poetry readings, and other random pronouncements were plastered everywhere, all rubbing up against one another in a living exhibit of real estate reclamation.

Besides spray-painting, we delighted in minor vandalism, primarily breaking off hood ornaments and collecting them in sacks or ripping telephone receivers out of phone boxes. A few times we spotted giant spools used by telephone companies to wind up their long cables. Unspooled, they would sit on the street, these massive abandoned wooden wheels laid on their side, until they could be collected. We would upend them, then roll the giant cylinders into the middle of the avenues, the traffic thin after three in the morning, and set them wilding chaotically down the road before smashing into parked cars, hopping curbs, sometimes surprising the hell out of a suddenly oncoming Checker cab or pedestrian.

It was destructive, but in our giddy sense of entitled recklessness, and as people not yet willing to accede to the responsibilities of adulthood, it felt perfectly in tune with the tarnished atmosphere of our city, the yellowed lights of the streetlamps buzzing and flickering over trash-strewn avenues, a place where youngsters like us would hop over scurrying rats the size of armadillos and dodge cockroaches as big as ferrets.

We weren't out looking for trouble, not really.

We were just kittens.

17

BOYS BUILD FORTS

The Coachmen were granted a Monday night "audition" slot at CBGB in early March 1979, a kind of showcase for bands trying to get in with the venue. We were joined by a slew of unremarkable groups from parts unknown. There were no sound checks, and it was a bit of a crapshoot who would play in what order.

The audience was primarily made up of the bands' friends and families. No one interested in coming to CBGB to hear what made the club famous would purposefully choose to visit there on an audition night. The music was hit or miss; some surprises might emerge, but they were rare.

Audition night at CBGB was a rite of passage. If Hilly thought you had "something," he'd *maybe* let you play a midweek gig, either at the bottom of the bill or in the clean-up slot at the end of the night, after the headlining act finished up, usually at around two or three in the morning.

CBGB on a weeknight, when the room wasn't so hectic, felt more like a neighborhood hangout. A few lazy felines would amble up onto the equipment riser behind the stage and take a snooze while the bands churned. Hilly's dog, Jonathan, a lanky, pointy-faced saluki who was already a star in the pages of *Punk,* was comfortable enough to stride out onstage sometimes, curling up next to a microphone stand.

A dilapidated yet functional kitchen was stuck in the back next to the dressing room, neither of which had a door, just small hovels with band graffiti layered on every inch of their walls and ceiling. As the club became more and more populated toward the end of the 1970s, the kitchen was shut down and turned into a second doorless dressing room. The toilets at the bottom of the basement stairwell in the back would only sometimes have doors themselves, but they were eventually disposed of, as they kept falling off their hinges. There was hardly ever a toilet seat to be found. The toilets, the broken mirrors, the air ducts—everything there was marked by graffiti too.

When our Monday night slot came, we performed for the few people who'd come to see us: the artists Mike Glier, Bill Komoski, and Mary Lemley, along with the Ludacer boys. I had never played on an actual stage before, and the fact that I was appearing on the one at CBGB, even though it was only an audition night, felt remarkable. I double strummed my guitar with such velocity that I sliced off a fingernail, cutting through the underlying skin such that blood sprayed on the pickups and pick guard, splattering them in red. After a couple of songs, I tore off some old gaffer tape stuck on the wooden floor and wrapped it around the bleeding finger, which required me to switch my pick from my thumb and index finger to my thumb and middle finger. I figured that if the gaffer tape held and I just stood there with my hair hanging in my eyes, affecting a bored scowl, nobody would pay me or my wound too much mind.

We retreated to the dressing room, and our guests gathered around to say how much they had liked our performance, offering polite congratulations—mostly to the other guys in the Coachmen, their fellow RISD grads. I was just some young, tall, skinny kid from nowhere, not really part of their history.

But I was indeed *there,* enlisted by J. D. King, who was well respected by all of them. I was also bleeding, which was maybe a bit too much for their art-school ideas of propriety. Only Iggy Pop and Alan Vega were permitted to bleed onstage. Art-school bands just didn't do that.

One guest entered the dressing room and, without acknowledging me—though knowing I could very well hear him—said smirkingly to another—

"Did you get any on you?"

The artist Jenny Holzer was in attendance that night too. She turned out to be instrumental in presenting opportunities for the Coachmen to perform outside the forbidding doors of the local club network. She had moved to Manhattan in 1976 after earning her master of fine arts at RISD, where she'd connected with J. D. King. She then joined the Whitney Museum's lauded independent study program.

Jenny was already fully into producing her "truisms"—personal statements of intellectual and radical activism, placed among the patchwork of signs strewn across the city. PRIVATE PROPERTY CREATED CRIME on a lighted billboard in midtown Manhattan or TURN SOFT AND LOVELY ANYTIME YOU HAVE A CHANCE on a theater marquee.

She became involved in organizing, along with Coleen Fitzgibbon of the COLAB artists collective, a show called *MANIFESTO* at 5 Bleecker Street, a storefront a half block west of CBGB. It ran for most of April 1979. *MANIFESTO* called for local artists to submit textual and icono-graphic pieces of communication. J.D. had been asked to submit a piece, and he presented a sheet of paper displaying his lyrics to a Coachmen tune entitled "Girls Are Short." We recorded the song in a tiny record-ing studio in the West Village so it could be played at the Bleecker Street space, among other sound-art pieces.

Jenny invited the Coachmen to play a gig later the same month up in the South Bronx, at a new gallery named Fashion Moda, conceived by the Austrian artist Stefan Eins. Fashion Moda would be among the first spaces to create a formal exchange between the downtown art scene, mostly white and college-educated, and the city's burgeoning culture of graffiti artists, primarily Black and Latino.

Graffiti, hip-hop, and break dancing had begun to gain recognition from the downtown art community by then. They were seen as indig-enous expressions of the city, unlike the work of arrivistes like us. When the Ecuadorian American graffiti artist Lady Pink, a native of Astoria, Queens, connected with Jenny Holzer, it generated a thrilling dialogue—art as a means not only of self-expression but of political exchange.

The Coachmen, with the Ludacers and Mary Lemley, all took the sub-way up to Fashion Moda. Mary, Jenny's loft mate at the time, was nearer to my age than the others. She was fabulous, and unlike most of the crea-tures inhabiting the downtown art lofts, she was friendly and sweet. She began seeing Ken Ludacer, which made my heart droop, but I never really thought I had a chance with her. My shyness around the people I admired would take years to subside, if it ever did.

J.D. had put forward the idea of having Mary share vocals with him on some of the songs he had been writing, as he never cared too much for his own singing voice. I thought his vocals were cool and odd, with their idiosyncratic talk-sing tenor, but nevertheless I was quietly thrilled that Mary was going to be singing with us.

The racial divides within the boroughs of New York City were extreme, and walking from the Jackson Avenue subway station to Fashion Moda at twilight, we must have been a sight to behold. Geeky white no wavers didn't turn up often in the streets of the South Bronx. Families were sit-ting on their stoops enjoying the warm summer evening, obviously enter-tained by the visitors in ill-fitting clothes tripping along with their guitar cases. The women and children—there seemed to be few men around—laughed and howled at us—

"Oh my heavens—you people lost?"

Little kids ran around us, pointing at me with my skinny-legged pants, ripped at the knee, my vintage suit jacket, my short-chopped hair, and Mary with her punk do combed sleek, her pointed black heels.

"Look at that lady!"

—they screamed, delighted. We were freaks from another planet, albeit ones who lived half a dozen miles south.

Come showtime at Fashion Moda, there were no more than a few people in the gallery: Stefan Eins, Jenny Holzer, Mike Glier, Lady Pink, and Joe Lewis, a young poet and artist closely connected to the gallery and to the performance art scene downtown. We played our set, only Joe Lewis taking it upon himself to dance, flailing demonstratively.

It was hard, in those waning months of the 1970s, to imagine that the city's fortunes might ever change. New York's near-bankruptcy had been destroying its infrastructure since at least 1975, with one-fifth of public workers laid off, resulting in an extreme shortage of firefighters and police on the job. Fires in impoverished neighborhoods, whether by accident or by arson, were simply left to burn. A brochure with a hooded skull and the words "WELCOME TO FEAR CITY" would be handed out to tourists arriving at airports, issued by the New York City police, with tips for survival—mainly staying away from the subways and avoiding the streets after six in the evening. Subway cars were ravaged tin cans, broiling hot in the summer, freezing in the winter, consistently malfunctioning. Fights and robberies weren't unusual. Graffiti seemingly covered every exposed inch of vertical surface—subways, buildings, street signs. Some of it was ornate and astounding, the rest a chaos of tags and unintelligible scrawl.

Living on Thirteenth Street between Avenues A and B, I was no stranger to dilapidation, though it was hardly as intense as only a few blocks farther east, toward the East River, where rows of buildings stood gutted, their windows so many black eyes. (And that still had nothing on sections of the South Bronx.)

Lying in bed in the middle of the night that July, my two front windows open, secured by rickety metal grates, a cheap fan clacking as it pushed the humid air into something resembling a breeze, I would listen to the life below: teens yelling at each other from either side of the street, men sitting in their cars honking their horns long and loud for reasons I could never fathom. No one would dare complain—to do so could be to invite a brick through your window.

One particularly steamy night, someone decided to play a cassette of a Richard Pryor comedy album at stadium volume, huge speakers sitting atop their car hood. I awoke at three in the morning shocked by the loudness, wondering if there was an actual live concert happening in the middle of the street. I saw out my window all the families in the neighborhood sitting on stoops, children racing about, leaping off cars. Small fires in trash cans illuminated the spontaneous scene, people happily whooping it up as they listened to Pryor's routine on the insanity of America.

With the opening of the Mudd Club in 1978 and Tier 3 in 1979, both located just below Canal Street in TriBeCa (Mudd Club on White Street, which was shut down and almost barren at night; Tier 3 on the southeast corner of White and Broadway, the air still dense with the aroma of the nearby thread-making factories), the downtown music scene's center of gravity shifted south, away from the well-worn trail between CBGB and Max's Kansas City.

The Mudd Club had been founded by Teenage Jesus & the Jerks "manager" Diego Cortez, downtown provocateur and fashion designer Anya Phillips, and filmmaker Steve Maas. The sound system had purportedly been designed by Brian Eno, who had been hanging around town working with Talking Heads, as well as recording his contentious *No New York* album.

The Mudd Club (which cofounder Anya Phillips had originally named the Molotov Cocktail Lounge) had a minimal interior. An oblong bar sat at the front entrance leading into an open, windowless, industrial-sized space, a few tall loft-style pillars supporting the high ceiling. The stage, snug to the left side in the back of the room, was tiny, with one of the pillars somewhat obstructing its view. Raised about five feet up from the floor, it made for unwieldy real estate. Behind the stage were stairs leading down to another room, where bands could hang out and any overflow from upstairs could spill over.

Tier 3 had been founded by a young woman named Hilary Jaeger, and it was distinct from the Mudd Club, its character looser, funkier, unwashed. Colorful murals by the artists Jean-Michel Basquiat and Kiki Smith adorned the club's walls. Just inside the entrance, a bar was situated to the right and the playing room was a step down to the left, the stage lower and wider than the Mudd Club's and that much easier to perform on.

Many nights, alone and wandering, I would sit on the loading dock outside of Tier 3 and smoke cigarettes, listening to the city thrum as if it were a huge instrument of brick and concrete. The sounds of trucks and taxis resonated through the urban valleys. The dock was a bit of a local hangout zone, and it had an ageless feeling, a variety of nightlifers always coming and going from the club.

I would laugh overhearing Shannon Dawson—whom I recognized from Test Pattern, his group with Al Diaz and Jean-Michel Basquiat—holding court on the sidewalk. Jean-Michel would come bounding out, and they would stroll off into the four a.m. night, lit up by streetlights, off to see what was happening elsewhere.

Their departing energy left a void. I'd watch them saunter off, envious of their camaraderie, then walk myself home, alone, to my tiny apartment on Thirteenth and A.

The Coachmen figured we could get a gig at either the Mudd Club or Tier 3, but the process proved to be even more difficult than that of CBGB or Max's. Tier 3 was swamped with demo cassettes from every band below Fourteenth Street, piles of audio solicitations from acts ranging from DNA to an up-and-coming singer named Madonna Ciccone.

The Mudd Club was simply impenetrable. Our South Street gang had all gone there from the moment it opened. We caught the initial solo outings of ex-Television-guitarist Richard Lloyd as well as the Feelies, in their revved-up, Velvets-inflected majesty, and readings from William Burroughs, sitting behind his grey metal office desk. The DJ one night would be Cookie Mueller, the next night James Chance, the next night Richard Hell.

The DJ booth at Tier 3 wasn't unlike the one at the Mudd Club, though Tier 3 would sometimes host Harry Smith behind the turntables, with his scruffy white beard and heavy-rimmed glasses. Harry was the legendary music archivist responsible for curating the *Anthology of American Folk Music* albums, released in 1952, compilations of regional recordings that captured the disparate, disappearing vernacular of the American musical landscape since the turn of the century.

He seemed to be in the right place.

Traipsing back and forth between Tier 3 and the Mudd Club, sometimes multiple times a night, became a ritual for all of us no wave boys and girls. The route from White Street to West Broadway—with a break at Dave's Luncheonette once in a while—could be as social as the gigs themselves. Club hoppers would compare notes with those heading in the opposite direction, gleaning how dead or alive each spot was. If our bands had an upcoming gig, we would join together in wheatpasting flyers along this pathway, where we invariably met other wheatpasters vying for the same wall space. We were eager to stake a claim but also not to flyer over each other—there were tricky politics involved.

All us Coachmen and Ludacer boys went to see the Raincoats play their first stateside show at Tier 3, a gig I was immensely excited to catch. The band was raw and alive, playing all the songs from their first album, ending with a ramshackle take on the Kinks' "Lola." They sounded great, clattery and loose, leaping about, allowing whatever mistakes they made to be charmed assets. A few bands from London found gigs at Tier 3, all of them young and startling. There was A Certain Ratio, minimal and direct in their greyscale funk, and Madness, who ska-rocked the place to bits.

During the Raincoats gig, J.D. came running into Tier 3 complaining about how some other group kept wheatpasting their flyers over the ones we had wheatpasted ourselves, which announced the CBGB engagement on May 1 that we were psyched to have locked down. He told us he had had a shouting match with the crazed singer of the other band about proper wheatpasting protocol.

I followed him outside; there was still some beef brewing. The other group apparently comprised a pair of twins and an agitated guy with short hair save for one long strand falling over his right eye to his cheek. They were called Circus Mort. The twins, I would later learn, were Josh and Dan Braun. The singer's name was Michael Gira.

It seemed every time one of the Coachmen wheatpasted a flyer on a post box or light pole, the Circus Mort crew would paste one of theirs on top of it—and vice versa. This was no small slight, but I decided to stay out of it. I went back inside Tier 3, still besotted by the Raincoats. J.D. joined me, but he was less than impressed with the band. He yelled into my ear—

"They're terrible. We're much better than they are! All these people here watching a band that can hardly play, and no one comes to see us! They can't even play 'Lola,' for chrissakes!"

Two bands, 8 Eyed Spy and Bush Tetras, proved that there was plenty of room for further experimentation and excitement to be heard from the no wave movement in the spring and summer of 1979, as some players on the scene began to employ more traditional, if not accessible, tropes in the music, a music that originally, and radically, eschewed such moves.

8 Eyed Spy was a particular, magnificent case in point, formed as a

vehicle for Lydia Lunch to perform in a more straight-ahead context than her previous bands of pure abrasion—especially her first band, Teenage Jesus & the Jerks. Joined by Jim Sclavunos, Pat Irwin, Michael Paum-gardhen, and the Contortions bassist George Scott III, 8 Eyed Spy was groove-based swamp rock, with the unexpected thrill of hearing Lydia actually singing instead of just shouting—which made her that much more astonishing.

The Bush Tetras were the new project from Contortions guitarist Pat Place, who had gone from slide guitar to actual fretting; Cynthia Sley, tall and draped over the microphone singing in a drop-dead monotone; Laura Kennedy, scowling and totally badass with her bass; and Dee Pop, the cute and street-savvy boy on drums, playing minimal punk-funk beats on such songs as "Too Many Creeps" and "Snakes Crawl"—classics of the era.

Bush Tetras and 8 Eyed Spy gigs during the summer of 1979 were epiphanies. I would stand agape. They were, I thought, the coolest rock groups I'd ever seen and heard.

At the start of that summer, the Coachmen were invited by Jenny Holzer to play in her loft at 515 Broadway between Spring and Broome Streets. It turned out to be the overflowing downtown art world gala of the season. Standing by the stairwell among the people making their way into the space, I was surprised and delighted to see a lovely, pale, redheaded girl whom I had recently, and fleetingly, encountered, wondering if I'd ever see her again.

We'd met at a Patti Smith show at CBGB earlier that May, a bit of a last-minute announcement advertised as a "Bob Dylan Birthday Bash." When I became aware of it, I immediately hustled over to the club, only to find a queue snaked along the Bowery. I barely made it inside to join the crush and maneuvered only three-quarters of the way in along the bar before a wall of bodies prohibited further progress.

A couple of girls next to me looked uncomfortable, jostled and smushed by the crowd, and we smiled at each other in our shared misery. When Patti hit the stage, it was all but impossible to see anything unless you were up close or, like myself, tall enough to get a lighthouse view. I noticed a few people sitting up on the bar to get a better look, and I asked one of the girls if she wanted to hop up too. After a shy nod, I hoisted her onto the bar, her feet dangling in front of me, long red hair falling across her face.

She was astounding.

The atmosphere only intensified for me as Patti invited Ronnie Spector onstage to sing a duet of "Be My Baby." I was more enchanted by the beaming girl atop the bar than anything going down onstage, but when the crowd later dispersed, she was gone. I skulked home through the wet streets, wistful at the thought that I might never encounter her again.

So when I saw the same girl enter Jenny's loft, my heart leaped. I mustered a—

"Hey . . ."

—and she smiled back at me with recognition.

We escaped to the rooftop together, where other party people were milling about, the clouds in the night sky lit up by the after-hours electricity of Manhattan below, the gleaming moon dusky above.

She told me her name was Pam. She was originally from Sweden but had been living in London the last few years, studying film and connecting with the punk and art scenes there. She seemed to know a few of the artists prowling about the party. We hung out for a while, our interests seemingly mutual.

We talked about anything and everything that night—music, film, books, New York, London, punk—all the while sharing cigarettes. Her eyes were green sapphires, gleaming. We made arrangements to have coffee together at some time, but I still had no telephone, so I wrote down my Thirteenth Street address and asked her to come by if she ever wanted to. I told her all she had to do was simply yell up from the street. Pam recognized my address with a bit of surprise. It was the same building a writer friend of hers lived in.

Soon it was time for the Coachmen to play our set, in between the groups Ludacer and the Static. The Static was a trio comprising Glenn Branca, Barbara Ess, and Christine Hahn. I had seen Glenn's band Theoretical Girls at the *X Magazine* benefit. His new trio produced jarring songs, with shredding guitar squall and loping, thumping rhythms from Barbara's bass and Christine's drumming. They had just released what would be their one and only record on Branca's Theoretical Records label. The A side, "My Relationship," featured Glenn repeating the song title over and over into a state of repetitive psychosis, as the trio's playing slowly unfolded into chaos. The B side, "Don't Let Me Stop You," was just as wild, Glenn's detuned guitar building to a threatening dynamic, then morphing into an almost-punk symphonic beauty. It was an incredible record, and one that would point me in new directions when it came to my own guitar playing and composition, post-Coachmen.

Pam arrived at my place a few days after the Jenny Holzer party, yelling up from the street—

"Hey, Thurston!"

I threw my keys out the window in a sock.

When she knocked, I let her in, her face blushing red and happy. She bustled around the apartment, flustered, neither of us sure of how to talk to the other. Before too long, another knock came. I opened the door to meet, for the first time, the older writer friend of hers whom she had mentioned, who had an apartment on the top floor of my building. I realized the two of them had also made plans to meet. It seemed that maybe I was a bit of a stopover point, a courtesy. They soon split, off to wherever they had planned to go, and I sat back on my bed—the only place to actually sit in my apartment—deflated and bummed out.

I would later become friendly with the writer, Russell Epprecht, who I surmised was in love with Pam (though he had seemingly resolved to allow her her freedom). He and I would get into heady conversations about spirituality, art, and literature. It was through Russell that I would meet Peter Cummings, a long-standing friend of his. A half decade older than me, he lived nearby in his own Lower East Side hovel. Peter was a poet as well as a performance and visual artist whose mystical experiences in Morocco and Big Sur, California, had left him with an openhearted and open-minded sense of wonder.

I would eventually become close to Peter, a daily friend and confidant. He was quirky, charming, and odd, with a dark and sardonic take on the life of an artist, living nomadic in the city. Peter and I would wander the East Village talking about love and music, poetry and poverty. We would step into Kiev Restaurant and find a table with the plates yet to be cleared off, then while perusing the menu we'd snarf the remaining uneaten blintzes and pierogi. When the waiter came by to give us the hairy eyeball, we would excuse ourselves, announcing that something had unexpectedly come up, then quickly hightail it out of there.

Peter's friendship was a welcome change from the solitude I'd become used to, often being alone for days on end. Even though I connected with the South Street gang creatively, I never felt so close to any of them that I could drop by unannounced and simply hang out. Harold and I remained friends, though he would come into town only once in a while, usually when there was a gig he wanted to check out. Likewise, I would hop on the train and see him in Bethel. But the we-only-have-each-other dynamic that had defined our friendship had changed, as I became engaged in these newer relationships in my tiny, but growing, downtown social scene.

Peter began to visit almost daily, intoning my name from the street—not yelling, just speaking it in a speedy monotone—

"Thurston, Thurston, Thurston"

—that would catch my ear, the voice so differentiated from the rest of the noise outside. I'd throw down my key and he'd trundle up. We'd smoke a little weed, which he always seemed to have, then shoot the breeze, feeling ageless, unhurried, with no particular place to go.

Peter had struck up connections with various poetry and performance scenes downtown—the Poetry Project and the Nuyorican Poets Cafe on East Third Street. From time to time he would score gigs reading.

As for Pam and me, after those first fleeting encounters in the summer of 1979, we would soon become romantic. She would hang out with me on South Street while the Coachmen rehearsed and join me on excursions to Connecticut, allowing us to break away from the madness of the city and also for me to have her in my heart without distraction. My mother, brother, and sister met her and were happy for us.

Pam's time in London had coincided with the punk explosion, and she told me of having spent those days hanging around with the various radical musicians, writers, and artists there. We shared a fascination with Wayne County, whom she had seen play in 1976, when he was rocking every venue on the London punk scene. After Wayne transitioned to Jayne, we went to Jayne's unveiling at Max's, an utterly raucous riot, Pam joyful and exultant in celebrating this awesome legend.

There was more to her story than I realized. She revealed to me that she had a young son from a relationship in the UK. The boy was clearly very dear to her, and the separation from him and his father wrenched her. Even though she and I were the same age, this was alien and adult stuff for me—more than my young and naive brain could fully comprehend.

Selfish frustration would overwhelm me. I longed for Pam's presence, yet days skipped by with no communication from her, not helped by the fact that I still didn't have a telephone. All I could do was walk endlessly through the streets of the East Village, SoHo, and TriBeCa, harboring an obscure hope I would come across her. I would sometimes leave the city on a bus to Bethel and, if she wasn't with me, would peer forlornly out the window, succumbing to misery, certain this girl was never going to be mine forever.

Despite those misgivings, the summer progressed and so did our budding relationship. It felt like all might soon be perfect in my universe—until July 3. Pam and I had made plans to see each other that day, but she never arrived for our get-together. Concerned, I called her from the pay phone on the corner of Thirteenth Street and Avenue A. Her phone only rang and rang. I tried again every few minutes.

No answer.

The next morning J.D. came by my apartment unannounced, which was unusual for him. I knew right away that something wasn't right. He sat on my bed, lighting one of my cigarettes. J.D. explained to me that Pam had been the victim of rape the day before.

He related the details as he had heard them. It seemed the assailant had forced his way into the Duane Street apartment Pam had been caretaking. He told me that while she was being assaulted, she could hear the telephone ringing. I realized it could only have been me, calling her again and again. I imagined the torment she must have gone through—trapped, violated, the ringing phone a reminder of her helplessness.

When I at last saw her again, I could only think to hold her, giving what comfort I knew how to offer. Despite the violence she'd suffered, the invasive terror she'd endured, she remained strong and sober. Still, I could sense the shock beneath the surface.

My feelings for her were undiminished, but I could sense her emotions clouding over. She moved apart—not only from me, but seemingly from everything. I opened my heart to her on the street one afternoon. I told her I wanted her to be mine forever. My plea was drowned out by fire engines roaring past. Pam could see I was struggling with my words and my feelings. She gave me a slight smile of understanding as we stood there together, the noise of the city raging around us. She had been hurt, and assuaging my twenty-one-year-old heart was not what she needed to be dealing with just then.

She came over to my place later that day and we just hung around— our words muted, a remote sadness tamping the joyful fire we had once shared. She put on an old overcoat of mine, one that had belonged to my father. She told me she needed to go somewhere and would come back soon, but she was gone.

Rape is a violation beyond the comprehension of many; it was certainly beyond mine, a young man just barely out of adolescence. I had little clue then the stamp such violence could leave on a survivor's being, the way it could permeate their life. I knew only that Pam's infernal experience instilled in me a vigilance toward sexual violence, one that I would never shake.

18

YOU GOT ME

The Coachmen played the Botany Talk House, a club in midtown Manhattan situated in the flower district, in June 1979. The storefronts on either side and across from the club sold wholesale flora, much of which was spread along the sidewalks, lending the area a sweet scent of nature at complete odds with the city's more familiar stench. Botany Talk House would become a hot spot for us, allowing our band to play a few more dates, a decompressed vibe compared with those of some of the other clubs we'd so far played.

The following month we somehow found ourselves playing a coveted Saturday night slot at CBGB. It was a dream, though we were paired with two groups we had never heard of, one of them being a goofy metal act. I could sense J.D.'s displeasure and frustration, having gone to so much trouble—rehearsing, landing a gig, wheatpasting flyers everywhere—only to find ourselves on a bill with such random and utterly incompatible bands.

We found a more like-minded community at A's, the performance art and music loft on Bleecker between the Bowery and Chrystie Street named after artist Arleen Schloss, who lived there with two young gents, R. L. Seltman and Tod Jorgensen. These three curated "Wednesdays at A's," evenings of music, dance, readings, exhibitions, and performance. Tod had been critical to the downtown scene in an unlikely way. He had overseen the color Xerox machine—a rare contraption in 1979—at Jamie Canvas, the rollicking art supply store on Spring Street in SoHo.

I would stop into A's each Wednesday night, usually after ambling about for a while, just walking, walking, walking. I would cruise all through downtown, from Fourteenth to Chambers Street. I would roam through Little Italy, beautiful and glorious, lit by yellow streetlights and the neon glare of Italian restaurants and delis, the smell of red sauces wafting through the air. Elderly women in housedresses and slippers would sit behind folding tables preparing Sicilian arancini, deep-fried risotto balls laced with ragù, mozzarella, and peas. For fifty cents, they could curb my appetite for a few solid hours.

The only affordable alternatives were to be had along East Houston Street, either the Yonah Schimmel bakery on the corner of Forsyth Street, for a knish jammed with yellow mustard and sauerkraut, or Katz's Delicatessen a couple of blocks east, for a split grilled frankfurter with the "works" on a toasted bun, ideally downed with a Dr. Brown's cream soda. If you were feeling flush, a couple more bucks could get you either a hot pastrami or a corned beef sandwich on rye bread, doused with mustard and coupled with a large sour green dill pickle. The pickle was key, as it helped you digest all those cured meats. At times a pickle was *all* that was needed, and the pickle stores on the Lower East Side's Essex Street—huge barrels of briny vinegar pickles set up on the sidewalk, sometimes so acrid your eyes would water—were perfect for an emergency crunch fix.

The A's crew was very welcoming of the Coachmen and just about anybody else active on the downtown new art scene. When we played there, the audience would actually gather around us and *dance*. Our first shows at A's were with other new groups, some more ad hoc than others. On any given night we might play with the no wave trio Ut, the strange psycho-rhythmic group Liquid Idiot (soon to be rechristened Liquid Liquid), Suicide vocalist Alan Vega (the singer whose show had so terrified and entranced Harold and me three years prior), performance artist Eric Bogosian, or Arleen Schloss herself.

A few of our gigs would be shared with whatever incarnation of a band Jean-Michel Basquiat was in, from Test Pattern to the Manmade Jazz Band. The first time I heard him play any kind of music was at A's one evening. A simple Magic Markered flyer was taped to the front door of the building reading: SAMO. I supposed that whatever was happening upstairs, it must be connected to the person who had been spray-painting that cryptic moniker all across SoHo.

Climbing up the stairs, I met Arleen, who greeted me with her gentle smile and her gleaming, beatific eyes, always so loving and smart. Maybe twenty people were hanging around the space, sitting in chairs, smoking, having a coffee or a beer, ready for anything. I was surprised to find that SAMO wasn't some performance artist but three guys my age who frequented the same clubs and outposts that I habitually hit: Club 57, Tier 3, Mudd Club, Gem Spa, the Sounds and Free Being record stores on St. Mark's Place, the Leshko's and Odessa coffee shops on Avenue A, the Binibon restaurant on Second Avenue.

SAMO turned out to be a trio of Jean-Michel, Al Diaz, and Shannon Dawson. I immediately became smitten with their music, its experimental otherness mingled with the rhythms of the street. Shannon, cocky, tall, and thin, would bleat minimal trumpet lines while Al, scruffy and with a preternatural sense of groove, played Latin percussion on congas. Jean-Michel stood in front of a tabletop junk-electronic setup, generating atonal noise while chewing on a plastic straw. It sounded great—fresh, raw, and smart.

When the identities of the infamous SAMO graffiti trio were eventually outed in the *Village Voice,* mostly focusing on Basquiat, it riveted the downtown world. Those tags had been everywhere—oblique, erudite, head-scratching, and oddly elegant.

I had noticed, alongside SAMO's graffiti, another tag: BOY TOY. It caught my attention, as it was not the typically male-centric writing generally found. BOY TOY would turn out to be the work of Madonna Ciccone, who lived a few streets away from my apartment, also banging around the Mudd Club and Club 57 world.

Appearing the same night as SAMO was Mania D, four young women from the Berlin punk-art social scene, which was centered around the venue SO36, run by the artist Martin Kippenberger. Mania D's appearance that night had the stark aesthetic of late 1970s subcultural Berlin: short hair combed at specific, hard angles; dark and tribal eyeshadow; an androgynous energy. It was oddly complemented by the loose thrift store attire of the New Yorkers in the room, myself and the members of SAMO included.

Mania D's music was as minimal and angular as their style, with cool swaths of saxophone from Eva Gossling, who would soon leave the band to live and play with Basquiat for a while, the two of them finding a spot to crash and cohabitate in one of the available studio rooms at A's.

More than any other performance space at the time, A's welcomed the entire downtown artist community to come share new ideas, with some nights featuring more than a dozen acts, from bands to dancers to poets to film presentations.

In 1979, I heard Glenn Branca play there as he began to introduce and develop his compositions for multiple electric guitars. I had seen his groups Theoretical Girls and the Static. Now he had taken to placing flyers around downtown that featured his face, serious and handsome, with LOUD GUITARS printed across them.

I thought I was prepared to deal with whatever he threw down. I was not. It was like hearing the sounds of the amplified rock noise in my head become manifest.

His music at A's that night was as revelatory for me as hearing Patti Smith, Television, or the Ramones had been only a few years before. Each of his compositions was completely instrumental, Glenn just one of six electric guitarists alongside a bassist and drummer. I stood stunned as the pieces unfolded. The guitars, which I had no idea were in nonstandard tuning, sounded like jets burning down a tarmac, only to lift off into a polyphonic stratosphere.

Glenn frenetically nodded, cued, pointed, and shouted at the other musicians to prepare for the next movement, which would shred forward toward faster, dizzying heights, Glenn gnashing and shaking his head, his ratty sports jacket flapping atop a half-unbuttoned shirt, sleeves loose and ragged, the agitated and pulsing air around the room coming utterly undone from energy and noise.

As the band set up for the piece "Dissonance," an oil drum was rolled out. Glenn enlisted a young gent to wallop the bottom end of it with a sledgehammer—*BLAMMM!*

The music was ferocious and amazing. A few of the listeners in the room jammed their fingers in their ears before escaping the din and retreating to the sidewalk downstairs. But I was mesmerized. This was exactly what I imagined a band could sound like but had yet to find. It was what had been gestating in my heart and brain—primal, experimental guitar action, propulsive, manic, negative, and beautiful, loud enough to create unlikely harmonics and dissonant tonal colors that could work their magic into and out of my bones.

When we first connected, Pam had been working a job at a small organic grocer on Prince Street in SoHo. She told me of a kitten there that had strolled in one day and decided to take refuge in the back of the store, by the veggie-juicing zone. The employees had named the feline Sweetface, but the owner of the store said the kitty couldn't stay.

So, hiking down to SoHo, I collected little Sweetface, put her in a cardboard box, and walked her back to my East Village home. She mewed with anxious concern, poking her paws out the folds of the box top.

Sweetface became an excellent roommate.

The streets of SoHo, in the late 1970s, had grown progressively residential, the once-industrial factory floors turned into lofts and occupied by artists and their families at a time when rent was as low as it could be, given the city's fiscal doldrums. There was hardly a restaurant to be found there, other than a few coffee shops and diners. One coffee shop I regularly visited was situated on Lafayette Street just south of Spring Street. I had caught Sid Vicious sauntering in a few times back when he was still alive, most likely because of the methadone clinic nearby.

Many of the art galleries downtown proliferated along SoHo's West Broadway, the local population of artists routinely spotted bounding around the streets, the male practitioners carrying themselves like serious, chain-smoking, paint-splattered, bearded visionaries. Spring Lounge, otherwise known as the Shark Bar—there were a few large plastic and stuffed sharks nailed to the walls—on the corner of Spring and Mulberry Streets was the watering hole of choice for many of these bedraggled SoHo artists.

Basquiat, living in a cheap apartment nearby on Crosby Street just off Prince, would cruise in and out of Shark Bar, as did Glenn Branca and his paramour and sometime bandmate, the artist Barbara Ess, the two living two blocks away at 8 Spring Street. I imagined the musicians and artists in this east-of-Broadway area, where SoHo and Little Italy rammed into each other, were probably paying not so much more in rent than my $110 a month—maybe even less.

After dark, SoHo was more vacant than the East Village, where a heightened street life teemed. In SoHo, it never felt necessary to ping-pong from one side of the street to the other to avoid interacting with someone up to no good. And the farther east you walked on any of the cross streets—Spring, Prince, Broome, or Grand—the deeper you'd find yourself in Little Italy, which held the promise of further safety, as it was looked after by old-school organized crime groups. No one dared to mug, rob, or burglarize on these streets. You might disappear if you tried. There were a few wiseguy clubhouses in the neighborhood, and in the summertime, they kept their doors open, their members sitting around on the sidewalks outside in folding chairs, smoking cigars and reading newspapers.

Ray's Pizza on Prince, between Mott and Elizabeth Streets, had arguably the best pizza in Manhattan. It was the perfect spot to enjoy the rich language of Little Italy while supping on a slice—the perfect balance of mozzarella and tomato sauce, the crust impeccably toasted from a broiling-hot oven. Mott and Mulberry Streets exhibited the old-world character of Little Italy, their delis and bakeries blowing irresistible smells onto the street. The Parisi Bakery, on Elizabeth Street, made beautiful eggplant parmigiana and potato and egg sandwiches, which had the power to lift your entire cellular system from the sidewalk to heaven.

The families living in Little Italy struggled as much as most in the city, though the neighborhood maintained an intense pride of place. St. Patrick's Old Cathedral on Mott Street stood in Roman Catholic auster-ity, though the stretch of Elizabeth Street from Prince to East Houston Street had become so fetid and destroyed that to walk up or down it was like stepping through a portal of abandoned hope.

The Bowery, where men lost to the world lived in a pit of alcoholic despair, was only one block east, and it seemed as if the most severe cases, aimless and demented, often crawled over to Elizabeth Street, only to expire where they fell. Bodies of bums in rags could be found flopped in random spots, oblivious to the vermin scattering around beat-up trash cans. It was safer, although just barely, to cruise along the Bowery—at least there were actual living people walking around.

The poet John Giorno had a place on the Bowery, the "Bunker," where William Burroughs lived as well. It had been a YMCA back at the turn of the century, before becoming live-work spaces for artists such as Fer-nand Léger and Mark Rothko. In 1979, the steps to the building would be home to any number of defeated souls, boozing, crowded around fires lit in steel-mesh trash cans swiped from the street corner. Burroughs would enter and exit in his slow gait, his cane and fedora pushed forward, the men giving way with unspoken respect for this man of letters.

A block east on Chrystie Street was where Sara D. Roosevelt Park divided Little Italy from the Lower East Side and where mostly Jewish families lived, pushing up against Chinatown to the south. The park, run-ning from Canal to East Houston Street and Chrystie to Forsyth Street, was a strip of city-choked trees, brown weeds, and concrete. It housed its own community of debauchery. Inside could be found encampments of prostitutes, homeless transients, drug dealers, and wayward winos.

The prostitutes were hard-core Amazonian women, many over six feet tall with high heels, miniskirts, and ratty fur coats, which they would flash open to cars tooling by. It was not so rare to witness three or four of the women all leaning into the windows of an automobile full of men or boys, negotiating—tough as nails, ready to attack or run if need be. A cop car would cruise by, and they would scatter into the darkness and bare trees of the park, their heels clacking on the pavement. Like the men on the

Bowery, they too would create trash can bonfires in the winter, dozens of them in skimpy clothing, gathered around, yelling to each other and laughing.

Walking along Chrystie Street late at night, I would be invariably and aggressively solicited—

"Hey, honey, want a date?"

"Wanna go out?"

—the sound accompanied by whispering weirdos stumbling in and out of the shadows—

"Loose joints, coke, speed, *whatchoo looking for?*"

19

NATTY ROACH

I was able to find a job that actually paid pretty well: climbing up tall ladders in SoHo galleries and scraping old paint off of vintage tin ceilings so they could be repainted, usually bone white. This was a nine-in-the-morning-until-seven-in-the-evening neck-breaking, arm-shattering, toxic hell of a gig, and a lot of us young locals playing in bands, making art, and banging around the streets took it so we could earn a bit of actual coin. But the work was ultimately too terrible and painful, and after a few intense days I decided I'd rather be penniless.

I had been hipped to a job opening at Printed Matter, a bookstore on Lispenard Street in TriBeCa. They needed someone to do a bit of cataloging of their inventory. Hired immediately, I sauntered through my days performing whatever filing tasks they required of me, bemused by the place I found myself in.

Printed Matter, founded in 1976 by a collective of downtown artists, established itself as a library of periodicals and books created by artists, for artists, of artists. Most intriguingly, it saw the production of the book itself *as* art. I was a babe in the woods here. Still, I saw *any* job as an intrusion on the lifestyle I desired—to be free and fully engaged with rock 'n' roll. It was a feeling I would never completely resolve. The job at Printed Matter lasted only a short while, anyway. After one paycheck, I was let go.

I needed a job that would let me pay the rent and buy peanut butter and cigarettes. Foot messenger work had educated me to every inch, nook, and cranny of Manhattan, but it offered barely enough income to buy a lousy pack of smokes. So I took a tip from Coachmen drummer Dan Walworth to apply at Design/Research, a hip home furnishings store on Fifty-Seventh Street between Madison and Fifth Avenues. He had heard that Chris Frantz, the drummer of Talking Heads, had held a job there as a shipping clerk, and because of his band's touring schedule, especially in 1979, he could no longer commit to the hours.

Design/Research hired me to replace Chris, and I would work there until the business filed for bankruptcy later that year. It was a remarkable place to work, considered the very first "lifestyle" emporium, carrying designer furnishings by Marcel Breuer and acting as the primary U.S. distributor of Marimekko textiles from Finland—gorgeous, simple designs with hand-rendered flower motifs and broad swaths of color.

I worked in the basement with a Jamaican lad who was my age and who would school me on what and what not to do on the job. The sales employees upstairs were mostly young, beautiful people dreaming of being actors and models, many of them flamboyantly gay. They would take their quick lunches in the basement, dishing about their boyfriends. Some of them were involved with each other and smooched openly, much to the displeasure of my Jamaican workmate who, after they would scoot back upstairs, would mutter—

"An abomination."

He would then sit in the corner and read the Holy Bible.

I was becoming immersed in reggae music, mostly through the prism of English punk bands, and I asked my Design/Research friend about Jamaica. He regaled me with stories of his Caribbean island paradise. With only limited opportunities for employment there, his family had immigrated to New York City, but he seemed rankled and frustrated by his displacement.

We spent some hours in that basement discussing the Bible. In the years prior to his death, my father had found, in his study of philosophy, a great interest in Catholicism. He invited priests to our house for liturgical discussions. Like many devout Christians, my Jamaican friend had literalized so much of the allegorical aspects of the Bible, to the point of prejudice, bigotry, and judgment. I tried to convince him that sexual persuasion might not be defined by religious and political tenets, but I would be met with only sour looks.

In the rear of our basement workspace was an area where two locked and rusted metal doors in the ceiling lifted out onto the sidewalk of Fifty-Seventh Street. The area had been jammed full of old empty boxes, packed to the rafters, for quite some time. Every once in a while, a huge New York City cockroach would scuttle out from behind them. I would freak, but my Jamaican friend would just stomp on it with a loud grunt.

I brought in a mixtape of reggae singles I had made with records procured from reggae shops far out in Queens, and we would sing along with Errol Scorcher's "Roach in de Corner"—

> *There's a natty roach in de corner*
> *Bim! Kill 'im!*

There had been a reggae station on the AM dial in New York that advertised these Jamaican-owned record vendors. I would write down their addresses, find a map, and figure out how to get to where they were. It required a lengthy subway ride out from Manhattan, then a walk through streets of primarily Jamaican and African American neighborhoods. The stores were small and cramped, Rasta gents smoking spliffs, seemingly amused, like everyone else on the street, by this tall, gangly punker ambling in and buying reggae singles at ninety-nine cents a pop. I would choose the sides by feel—they were all from independent labels, with a multitude of names alluding to Black majesty, sound, and marijuana.

One day we were asked by our store manager to remove the old boxes from that back space. As I tugged on a particularly large and soggy box, I felt hundreds of little *objects* falling onto my hair and into my shirt. I immediately realized it was a rain of giant cockroaches, skittering and scattering. I began screaming, madly flicking them off my body and tugging them out of my hair. My Jamaican friend only laughed, tears in his eyes, clapping his hands as he jumped up and down singing—

> *There's a natty roach in de corner*
> *Bim! Kill 'im!*

I became friendly with Michael Shamberg, one of the salespeople at Design/Research who discovered I was into punk and no wave and was a regular at the downtown clubs. Michael had been involved with setting up a New York base of operations for the Factory Records label out of Manchester, England. I shared my enthusiasm with Michael for the Factory bands A Certain Ratio and Joy Division, and he asked me if I would be interested in playing guitar with his girlfriend, Stanton Miranda, a keyboard player and songwriter.

I had seen Miranda (as she preferred to be addressed) perform as a member of the no wave band Arsenal, and I was intrigued by the offer to play with her. I soon visited their Sixth Avenue midtown apartment, guitar in tow. Michael introduced me to Miranda, who was petite, friendly, and, like myself, a bit nervous about meeting someone new. We were around the same age, still clinging to that feeling of life being a forever happening. She had a keyboard set up in the apartment with a couple of small amplifiers.

Inspired by the sounds I'd been consuming and that had been gestating inside me, I started thinking that, with my electric guitar, I might dispense with any reliance on traditional notes and chords in favor of the wild and scattershot noises I could create along the instrument's neck. I began to see music not just as something composed but as sounds that could be created spontaneously, if the right sense of openness could be conjured, the mind freed to the possibilities of chance and magic. But I had yet to really play or express myself in this way with anyone.

The songs of the Coachmen were built upon basic chords, albeit through the liberating lens of punk rock, as informed by the Velvet Underground. I was curious what would happen if I simply allowed myself to make musical noise, while the musicians around me created rhythmic stability. This didn't come out of any intense familiarity with the free improvisation or free jazz scenes, which were then quite active. It had more to do with what I was hearing on wild nights at A's, as well as the unfolding attraction and resonance I felt toward the fringier factions of no wave.

I had heard the Human Arts Ensemble, a legendary free jazz group from St. Louis, play at A's one night. I sat on the floor at their feet, lifted off the ground into space, transported by the energy of their collective improvisations. I had no context for the music, only that it fit into the values of experimental rock music that I had always found myself attuned to.

My first time hearing Glenn Branca's guitar instrumental ensemble at A's, with its unforgettable oil-drum smash, had had the same effect—especially during something that happened at the end of that set. Wiped out by the performance, Glenn was approached by a black-haired cat with a beat-up guitar case. I could see Glenn negotiating with this person about what was most likely being proffered—that the two play together. There seemed to be a connection between them. I watched as Glenn agreed to a duo set.

I surmised that this other person was Rudolph Grey, if only because his name had been next to Glenn's on the sign at the door downstairs. The two plugged in, and instead of the rigid constructions of Glenn's ensemble pieces, it turned into free-form electric guitar squall. The room was already ear-exhausted from the Branca ensemble performance; I could tell most people had heard more than they could process, earning this duo a perfunctory reception at best.

But my curiosity was piqued. I was intrigued to see and hear Rudolph, his head down, filterless cigarette smoldering in his mouth, running his fingers across the fretboard in total free play, his amp overdriven and blasting, seeming very much in the moment. It didn't quite shake me up, didn't spark instant epiphanies the way other performances had. But there was something curious and almost touching about it, even as it was radical and revealing.

Both these moments may have been resonating with me still on that first meeting at Miranda's pad. It may be that I simply wanted to score the vibrations and frequencies of my adopted city: the late-night distant, grinding wheeze of mysterious trucks; the symphony of car horns, chaotic in their human-provoked interplay. Whatever it was, I was ready to play and emote in a new way.

Miranda had a few electric piano and drum machine riffs she'd been working on. I asked her to just play them—or *anything*—and I would come up with some ideas, throw out a bit of free-form wilding from my electric six-string.

We played together for about ten minutes, then stopped. She smiled with a bit of curiosity in her eyes. I said—

"That was cool, let's do some more."

Another ten minutes or so, and I ramped up the abstraction, more confident in how I could locate and land, whip around and dance, with the tonal moves from her keyboard.

We took another break. Miranda asked—

"Do you always play like that?"

"I do now."

Miranda was sweet, with a kind voice, and I enjoyed playing with her. But I wasn't sure we had too much of a musical future together. We sat and talked about different bands and the people we knew. She mentioned she had been rehearsing with a trio named CKM.

The "C" for Christine Hahn, who I knew as the drummer in the Static.

The "M" was for her, Miranda.

And the "K" was for a girl named Kim.

20

BREAKING THESE ROCKS

Because of systemic mismanagement, Design/Research would go into liquidation, its doors shut by the end of the summer of 1979. I was all at once out of work, paying the rent suddenly a more desperate concern. I scrutinized the job offerings in the daily papers, circling a potential listing for a shipping clerk position. The address in the ad was for a record mastering studio named Masterdisk uptown on West Sixty-First Street near Lincoln Center.

After a fairly undemanding interview, I was given the job, taking over for a young man named Howie Weinberg, who had moved up the ranks to become an actual mastering engineer. Howie had learned to work with record-cutting lathes from Bob Ludwig, chief engineer there all through the 1970s. My job would be to simply box up lathe-cut reference discs for either shipment or hand delivery to studios around Manhattan.

I was a bit stunned at first to see high-profile musicians such as Bryan Ferry and Judy Collins hanging about the place to hear their forthcoming albums being cut, mostly in Bob Ludwig's studio room. Howie cut the lesser lathes—which, in 1979, were mostly punk, no wave, spoken word, and hip-hop sides. I would hear him mastering Kurtis Blow's "The Breaks," running the track over and over, applying the final equalizer details to the jam before it would be sent off for manufacturing.

Howie invited me to accompany him downtown one evening to Big Apple Studios to be part of a crowd making ambient party noise on a new track of Kurtis's to be titled "Christmas Rappin'." I decided to go home to my lonely apartment instead. I was often shy about entering into new social scenes in New York City, retreating into the safety of solitude. It wasn't yet obvious that hip-hop would be the most significant and radical audio art form of the late twentieth century. I certainly blew it by not taking Howie up on his invite.

Starting in the summer of 1979, my new friend Peter Cummings and I began to drop into Club 57 on St. Mark's Place between First and Second Avenues. Peter wanted to check out some of the poets and the performance action going on there. But an evening at Club 57 would hardly be as dry as a night of poetry readings might suggest. The readers and performers who put on shows and threw parties there were fully aware of how dull these disciplines could be, and they were determined to turn them on their heads, creating a hilarious and crazed atmosphere of theatrical experimentation, satire, and recklessness.

The people who made Club 57 one of the most exciting spaces downtown in the late 1970s were an amazing, beautiful, and vibrant crew. It was a scene of fantastic girls and queer boys—including the fabulous Klaus Nomi and notorious John Sex—having the time of their lives, staging impromptu drag queen revues, forming ad hoc bands, and screening films, the more bizarro and terrible the better. If you weren't laughing and getting loose at Club 57, you were in the wrong place.

The club was in the sublevel of an ancient Polish church, investing the atmosphere with an edge of sacrilegious naughtiness. Like the soft disparity between the SoHo and East Village no wave scenes, there was a Club 57 versus Mudd Club divide, though many would cross it—I did, at least. All I know is that Club 57 was nutso and fun, while the Mudd Club felt more self-serious, more careerist. The allure of wealth would soon come creeping into the entire downtown art scene, but at Club 57, money was always regarded as something that only uptown squares aspired toward—it was boring, embarrassing, easy to laugh at.

I attended a few evenings of the Monster Movie Club, where uproarious grade-Z horror flicks would be shown, only for the whole place to shout at the inane dialogue on the screen or else scream in earsplitting mock terror when a monster cut someone's head off.

There were so many cool girls there that when a bunch of them, including Ann Magnuson and Wendy Wild, came together to form an in-house band they called Pulsallama, it was as if a fun bomb had gone off. Pulsallama's sets were rollicking, fearless, and spirit-soaring, with cheap guitars and keyboards and multiple percussions, all the members dressed in thrift store ball gowns and leopard-print pullovers. There was tons of shouting and whooping, a delirious and debauched scene.

Before 1979 was over, David Bowie would enlist Klaus Nomi and performance artist Joey Arias, two of Club 57's most beloved habitués, as members of his ensemble on *Saturday Night Live*. It was a moment of national visibility that encapsulated and galvanized the downtown underground scene of queer creativity, its shockwaves electrifying and inspiring the culture into the next decade.

On a rainy August afternoon, I went to see the Patti Smith Group in Central Park. Patti had come out onstage riding a broom, and her band battled for the soggy sold-out crowd, but it was difficult to enjoy her set with raindrops splattering your face. I had come alone, and I overheard someone saying that the group was planning to play a secret CBGB show afterward. I jumped on the subway and headed downtown, where, sure enough, a queue had formed out the door. I was just early enough, though, gaining entrance to join the crush.

The group avidly blasted through their set, but as I stood there, still a bit waterlogged, I felt a shift taking place: the initial ecstasy that this band had once unleashed, in me and on the scene, had become overwhelmed by what was coming from more recent and radical voices. They performed a new tune, "Dancing Barefoot," as moving as anything they had written so far. But it seemed to me that Patti was off to a new place, an experience beyond solely working in a rock 'n' roll band.

This would be their last gig at CBGB, and in New York City, before playing a handful of shows in Europe. Patti would then disappear from the scene for years, setting up house in Michigan with ex-MC5 and Sonic's Rendezvous Band guitarist, Fred "Sonic" Smith, raising two children and living a marriage made in sonic heaven.

It felt as though one of the anchors of the New York music world had been pulled. Patti Smith had been a primary catalyst for so much of what punk had become: manic, messy, impassioned, inspired, enraged, enlightened, impetuous, impolite, and intensely direct.

Where the scene would drift off to next was anyone's guess.

Three of the most interesting bands from the UK—the Slits, This Heat, and Cabaret Voltaire—would release their debut albums in September and October, each, to me, a masterpiece in the way they furthered ideas of what a rock band could be. So were the new offerings coming from Public Image Ltd and the Clash, who released their multi-LP opuses *Metal Box* and *London Calling*, respectively.

For their part, the Slits had joined forces with dub reggae maestro

Dennis Bovell to record their first album, stepping out of the chaos of punk noise into a dimension of composition so astounding, artfully orchestrated, and evocative that its significance as a harbinger of new musical forms would be perfectly clear from the first revolution. The LP jacket was at once playful and confrontational, the trio draped in mud, topless and regal in statuesque poses. It was a decimation of gender prejudice, no erotic nudge and wink. The opening song, "Instant Hit," about their pal Sid Vicious, would convey their conflicted affection for the doomed singer. The final song, "Adventures Close to Home," held a poetic truth rarely heard in the bellowing caterwaul of the punk-boy brigades—

> *Don't take it personal, I choose my own fate*
> *I follow love, I follow hate*

The Coachmen, at the beginning of November 1979, played a rousing show at A's, joined by Liquid Idiot, Jean-Michel Basquiat's Manmade Jazz Band, and a Xerox art exposition of pieces by Basquiat, Kenny Scharf, Carolee Schneemann, Ray Johnson, and many others. I interacted with some of the artists, musicians, performers, and filmmakers at the performance space, though most were a generation or so older than me. Soon enough I would be more connected to people my age, but as the 1970s came to an end, I still felt like the youngest person in any room.

In contrast to A's, the gatherings at Jenny Holzer's loft, where I had connected with Pam earlier in the year, were far less funky, with a pronounced art-school vibe about them. I felt closer to the softer, more considered gazes around the room. There was something nearly erotic to me about the studied sophistication, the more subdued tenor of these parties. They intrigued me more than the let-it-all-hang-out-ness of other venues. I was grateful for the times the Coachmen gang would hang around there, drinking the cups of Café Bustelo coffee Jenny would offer us, smoking cigarettes, talking, laughing, and dishing about other artists and musicians.

Our last performance at Jenny's would be in early December with Harry Toledo, a group named for its chief songwriter. It turned out to be one of the last times I consorted with that particular art crowd at all, the new decade holding new and curious transitions for my future.

The drummer from Harry Toledo's group was a young gent named Dave Keay. He expressed genuine enthusiasm for the Coachmen's music. With Dan Walworth deciding to exit the band, we rang up Dave and he quickly joined us. The change was intense and immediate. The simplicity of Dan's playing, direct and unfettered, was now replaced by a more propulsive force, which amped up the volume and energy of our band to a significant degree. I would miss Dan's minimalist approach, but having a more traditional rock drummer allowed new voltage to flow.

We were invited back to play A's that New Year's Eve on a bill with Alan Vega and Liquid Idiot. It was a fantastic way to welcome in the 1980s. It would also be the first time in a few years that I would spend New Year's Eve without Harold, who had decided to stay at home in Connecticut with some of his new friends.

Pam had returned from her journey, after leaving because of the nightmare she had experienced in the city that summer. The two of us spent the Christmas holidays at my mother's house. But this New Year's Eve gig would be the only time we would have together before she headed back to England, our paths not crossing again until decades later.

The evening was a celebration of the oncoming open vista of the 1980s. Liquid Idiot played first, a trio I had seen a few times at A's. They were always an odd affair, their music playing like exercises in sound abstraction, moving from woozy and tripped out to fully discombobulated. It was a formula explored by a growing number of art-rock groups on the scene, with varying results. The trio would soon change their name to Liquid Liquid and focus on hyper-rhythmic groove music, a completely refreshing, startling, and increasingly popular sound on the downtown scene of the early 1980s.

Alan Vega ran tapes through an amplifier, creating beat-machine propulsions reminiscent of what his Suicide partner, Martin Rev, had employed, though more stripped down and raw. With a less demonic demeanor, Alan sang new tunes such as "Jukebox Babe" and "Speedway." He would be the first musician from the ground zero of downtown punk and experimental music to offer me words of encouragement and advice. Running into each other on the street in the months to come, we would stop and talk about the time we had together at A's. His enthusiasm for the Coachmen's music seemed heartfelt. He would tell me adamantly—

"You gotta make a record, man."

He'd continue—

"That's the only way people will take you seriously. And it's the only way to get gigs in these places."

But the Coachmen had no money to make a record. We could hardly afford to record a demo cassette.

21

11,000 VOLTS

The Coachmen barely made it into 1980.

Before our drummer Dan departed the band, we had managed to record five songs in a small jerry-rigged studio in a midtown apartment, mainly to have a tape to encourage clubs to give us a shot. We had a few more tunes in our arsenal, but they would remain ghostly pieces on scattered cassette tapes, filed away in unmarked shoeboxes and junk drawers.

I hoofed our demo around to Max's, CBGB, Mudd Club, and Tier 3 in hopes of scoring further gigs. The cassette fell into the purgatorial void where all demos go. Only Hilly, who was usually around CBGB during the day, physically accepted the tape. We sat together at the entrance on a couple of wobbly barstools, and he talked to me about the logistics of running a club—the expectations and realities of musicians wanting to get a foot in the door. He mentioned that he had seen me in CBGB the last couple of years. He knew the Coachmen had played the dreaded Monday audition the previous spring, followed by a couple of other nights.

By the end of our conversation, he had offered me a Sunday night slot at the end of January, the first month of a new year of a new decade. We'd be billed with a couple of bands he thought the Coachmen might be compatible with.

On the night of the gig, we rolled our little amps in across the floor of rugged broken wood and raced through a perfunctory sound check. We would be joined by A Band, who had been on the scene for a while, the project of artist and songwriter Paul McMahon and ex–Theoretical Girls drummer Wharton Tiers. Also on the bill was a band named the Fluks (later the Flucts). It was something of a toss-up whether the Fluks or the Coachmen were going to play first. As gig time approached, the Fluks' guitarist and singer approached me—

"Do you know if you guys are playing first or second?"

I could sense this person, around my age, had been hoping to play second, the hotter slot. It was a common conflict, to the point where more aggressive groups would commandeer the stage with their gear at just the right moment, before anyone else could claim the primo spot. J.D. had already been adamant in telling us that the Coachmen were *not* going to play first.

So, as instructed, I said—

"Our band is definitely playing second."

The trio of Fluks came on first, and they were interesting—assertive, jittery, and strange, with songs that were straightforward in structure but arch and angular in sound. After the Coachmen set, I was relieved to see that the guy from Fluks, who had been a bit rankled by my earlier demand, was smiling, enthused about how our bands shared similar musical language.

He introduced himself as Lee Ranaldo.

Lee and Fluks drummer David Linton showed up at a Botany Talk House gig the Coachmen played a month later—surprising, as I knew of no people who ever came to see the Coachmen simply because they *liked our music*. If there were any regulars at our gigs, it was the Jenny Holzer contingent.

Three nights later we played Max's Kansas City for our first and only time. I was anxious about the night. Beyond the club's place in punk's history and my own, would we tall guys even fit on the stage? Somehow we did, though the gig was attended by only a dozen or so people. Regardless, we knew we were having our moment in a hallowed space, the same stage from which Iggy Pop had leaped up and cracked his head open, where Lou Reed had worked out his new material, where Patti Smith had read poetry while opening up for the New York Dolls, where Sid Vicious had spat into the void.

A fanzine from Brooklyn, simply named *Ffanzeen,* published the first and only article about the Coachmen, featuring a photo of us with our new drummer, Dave Keay, all four of us looking properly dour and unsmiling. Dave's girlfriend at the time was the French composer Elodie Lauten, daughter of the jazz modernist Errol Parker. She had studied minimalist composition with the legendary La Monte Young. Elodie's work as a composer was searching and otherworldly. She had pitched the *Ffanzeen* editor the idea of having the Coachmen appear. It would basically be a short interview, along with a brief questionnaire. One of the queries the editor asked was "Who is your best friend?" I had written in—

"Harold."

When I showed Harold the fanzine, he was extremely touched. But the truth was that we were becoming increasingly distant from each other, as I found myself becoming more and more entrenched in life away from Bethel, drawn into the seductive and swirling maelstrom of Lower Manhattan.

Harold still trained in from time to time and stayed at my apartment. We would hang out at the record and bookstores as we always had—Bleecker Bob's, Discophile, Sounds, St. Mark's, East Village Books. We would peruse the magazines and newspapers at Gem Spa or poke around the Revenge and Manic Panic punk "boutiques," sometimes catching a gig or a movie. Or we would just sit on one of the stoops of St. Mark's Place, watching the downtown scene flow by.

The energy along St. Mark's Place between Second and Third Avenues held within it an intoxicating and radical history. In the 1960s it had housed the celebrated Dom, where Andy Warhol's *Exploding Plastic Inevitable* took place, the Velvet Underground and Nico performing drone rock masterpieces of distortion and beauty while Gerard Malanga whip-danced with the enchanted Edie Sedgwick and wild girl Mary Woronov. Downtown society was fully represented on St. Mark's Place, with its burned-out hippies, punks in various stages of below Fourteenth Street poverty or uptown wealth, a mix of Latinos, African Americans, gays, straights, street kids, drug dealers, drunks, tourists, and no wave aesthetes prowling up and down the block, everyone checking everyone else out, even as a marketplace of various sundries for sale sat at our feet on rows of blankets and split-open cardboard boxes. During warm-weather days, you might find records, books, jewelry, and household items available from these vendors. It wasn't unusual for a car or an apartment to be broken into only for the ripped-off items to appear soon after on St. Mark's sidewalks, hawked by the perpetrator.

Harold and I would traverse the streets in the frigid winter ice, rain, and snow, making our way to and from CBGB, Max's, or St. Mark's Cinema, figuring out which avenues had the least freezing winds blasting through them. Broadway was notorious in the deep winter as a tunnel of insanely cold air blowing from the tip of Manhattan, where the Hudson meets the East River, straight north to Central Park. Turning a corner onto Broadway, the wind chill could drop to well below zero degrees, turning each nostril into a cavern of frozen skin, every breath into an ice cloud emitted through cracking lips. Homeless people constructed cardboard box housings atop subway grates, wrapped themselves in any shreds of fabric they could procure.

The two of us still hit the gigs by the bands that first lit our fuse: the Heartbreakers, Blondie, the Planets, the Fast. But as time went on, Harold began expressing conflicted feelings about the no wave scene and my attraction to it.

We had seen the band Mars back in the fall of 1977, when they performed on a bill with Richard Hell & the Voidoids at the Village Gate. Mars played discordant, rambling, falling-down-the-stairs music. They looked like they sounded—dark and otherworldly. The guitarist and singer Connie "China" Burg, tall with long dirty-blond hair, dressed without the least bit of glam-punk pretense. I became transfixed by Mars, eager to know more about them and their cacophonous bliss. Harold would only look at me with pure displeasure—this was not the Mumps.

"I kinda like it"

—I'd say.

"It's terrible"

—he'd reply.

Once on a walk with Harold I had picked up the Mars single "3 E" from one of the blanket sellers on Astor Place. Harold saw my reaction as I locked eyes on the record, offered for one measly dollar. With a half smile, he said—

"Oh . . . you should get that."

It was a concession, in its way—an admission that we weren't the unit we once were.

Another day while record-store hopping in late 1979, I picked up the Contortions' *Buy,* the album cover an odd, gender-fucked portrait of Terence Sellers, a writer on the downtown scene who had recently published a provocative book entitled *The Correct Sadist.* The image had a feeling of otherness to it, a whiff of intelligence, of transgender fluidity. Harold was unimpressed.

"It's ugly"

—he said.

When he spent the night at my apartment, Harold tucked into the sleeping bag he had brought with him, laying it on the floor next to my bed, as there was very little space elsewhere. One night after lying fitfully on the hardwood floor, he slid into the bed next to me. I soon felt him touching me. I shunted his hand away, and he made a quiet sound of dismay before dropping back to his sleeping bag.

The next morning he packed up the small vintage suitcase he was proud of, and I watched from my window as he walked west on Thirteenth Street to catch the subway to Grand Central Terminal. He seemed so alone out there, disappointed that I wouldn't respond to him the way he wanted.

I waited a few hours until I was sure he was back in Bethel before I rang him asking if he was okay. He was surprised; he told me he was touched that I called. Still, our lives veered apart and, within time, irrevocably. By the end of 1979, he had come out as gay to his family and friends, soon finding a gentle and devoted partner in Bethel. He spent less and less time in New York, content in the genuine love he'd found.

I was happy for his happiness, but I also felt a pang of loss knowing that my partner in discovering this magnificent city and the all-out glory of punk rock as a portal into worlds of wonder was, for the most part, settling down to a domestic lifestyle.

22

ECSTATIC STIGMATIC

The band I wanted to see more than any other in the universe in 1980 was Public Image Ltd. Their *Metal Box* set was a radical key for what I was feeling at the core of my creative soul—their experimental noise guitar moves interplaying with dub, and John Lydon going deeper into his psyche than the Sex Pistols had ever suggested.

Their debut New York City concert would be at the Palladium on Sunday, April 20—which just happened to be the same night that the Coachmen were booked to play at a club in midtown called S.N.A.F.U. I was despondent about missing PiL—and it would only get worse. While at work at Masterdisk the following Wednesday, I recognized Ed Bahlman, the proprietor of 99 Records. He was there to retrieve some reference discs for the first release on his label, a twelve-inch by Glenn Branca. Ed and his partner, Gina Franklyn, were running 99 Records out of a storefront at 99 MacDougal Street, and they were the two retail people in the city who best had a finger on the pulse of what was new and fresh coming out of London.

Talking to Ed about how cool it was that 99 was starting a label, I asked him if he had seen PiL at the Palladium. Of course he had, but he said the show last night was way better. My stomach hollowed out—

"What show last night?"

"The one at Great Gildersleeves"

—he said.

"It was unannounced. And completely amazing."

I walked around in a daze the entire week, wondering how I had missed this other show. What was I doing on Tuesday night, April 22? I was home alone in my apartment eating a peanut butter sandwich and watching a rerun of *Three's Company* on a tiny black-and-white television set while sitting on my unmade bed—totally unaware that PiL was play-ing a not-so-secret secret gig a few blocks away.

For the longest time I would think about how I had missed the most extraordinary night of post-punk ever. I would bring it up to various peo-ple I'd meet throughout the years and invariably hear the same reply—

"Oh yeah, that show was fantastic—probably the most incredible gig I've ever been to."

As springtime approached in 1980, news came that Manchester sensa-tion Joy Division was coming to tour the USA. I instantly purchased a ticket for their appearance at Hurrah, only to hear, the day before the show, that the singer Ian Curtis had died, apparently by suicide. It struck a confounding note in me. I didn't have any experience with suicide. Ian Curtis, a musician only two years older than I was, singing in a band so new and remarkable and choosing to take his own life—it didn't register with me; it made no sense. His seizure disorder, his pain, and his medica-tions were a foreign country.

A couple of weeks later, on the first night of June, the South Street gang and I headed to the opening of *Times Square Show,* an art happen-ing curated by people from Fashion Moda and COLAB. They had taken over an abandoned massage parlor on the corner of Forty-First Street and Seventh Avenue and invited more than one hundred artists, from SoHo to the East Village to the South Bronx—anyone and everyone who had some connection to punk, new wave, no wave, hip-hop, graffiti, film, poetry, music, and sculpture.

This event would herald a new identity for the New York art scene, energizing and exposing interdisciplinary work that operated below the radar of the established art world. I never considered myself a full-fledged member of this collective; I was really only interested in seeing, hear-ing, writing, and playing music, punctuated with my obsessive prowling through record stores and various musty bookstores dotted along lower Broadway from Fourteenth to Eighth Streets, and writing poetry, my only other creative outlet.

And wishing I had a girlfriend.

The Coachmen would perform in early August at the Plugg Club on West Twenty-Fourth Street in what would amount to our final show as a band. The Plugg Club was both the living space and performance venue of the impresario Giorgio Gomelsky, who had famously run the Craw-daddy Club in early-1960s London, where the Rolling Stones and the Yardbirds—bands Giorgio initially managed—had first played.

On this midsummer night, Miranda brought along her friend and bandmate Kim Gordon, apparently so she and I could meet. I could tell there was a bit of matchmaking going on when we were introduced, but I was okay with that. My heart was still shaken from Pam having left the city, but I was trying to keep an open heart and mind.

I sat down next to Kim on a bench, and we began to talk—about music, being in a band, living in the city. I remember sharing with her my sense that if an artist feels like they are doing good work, then if people take notice, that's cool, and if not, then that's just the way it goes. I told her I couldn't imagine being anxious, competitive, or envious about any of that.

It was an unusual sentiment to express to a stranger, and I'm not sure why I spilled it, but Kim seemed to go along with it. She was a few years older than me. Her face was obscured by a pair of flip-up shades, which she had clipped onto her actual glasses, and she was wearing a small-brimmed cap. Despite the glasses and hat, I could make out her smile and glimpse her eyes, which were sweet and smart, beautiful in their blue-grey hue.

After the Coachmen finished our set, Kim and Miranda said they were heading downtown to grab a bite at Magoo's, an artist bar and restaurant on the corner of Sixth Avenue and Walker Street in TriBeCa. I helped load the Coachmen's amps and drums back into the South Street build-ing, not really registering that the gig we had just played was to be our last, though I had been sensing a general feeling among the other band members that the lack of any real critical attention toward our group had become increasingly deflating, if not wearisome. At the same time J.D. and Bob had "real" careers to focus on as graphic artists.

After the load out, I hustled to Magoo's hoping to reconnect with Miranda and Kim. They were still in the restaurant, though it looked as if they were about to split, as it was past two in the morning. Hanging out with them was Nina Canal from the group Ut. Nina's presence downtown was heavy; she had been appearing and recording with the most interest-ing and radical artists on the scene for years. Miranda and Kim had met up with Nina to see if she'd be interested in joining their trio, expanding it to a quartet.

Nina seemed excited by the prospect of joining forces with the band. CKM had performed only one gig, under an earlier name, Introjection.

They had formed after the artist Dan Graham introduced Kim to Miranda and Christine Hahn (ex-drummer of the Static). His notion had been for Introjection to act as a sort of backing band for an event at which he had been invited to perform, in the spring of 1980, at the Boston Film/Video Foundation, by a young Massachusetts College of Art and Design student named Christian Marclay, who had been instrumental in introducing New York's downtown art and no wave participants to the local Boston scene.

Dan's performance, as such, would involve him standing at the front of the video space, rattling off droning descriptions of the members of the seated audience, as Introjection performed free-form music behind him.

Also with the three young women at Magoo's was George Scott III, the bass player from the Contortions, 8 Eyed Spy, and the Raybeats. Miranda introduced the two of us and suggested that George and I get together sometime to play—yet more matchmaking going on. George gave me his phone number, and we planned on finding a time to play, maybe with Miranda joining us. Or Nina. Or Christine. Or Kim. Or all of us.

George left the restaurant with a friendly wave and his celebrated large smile, and soon after Miranda, Kim, and Nina split, a tentative idea left hanging in the air that we might all connect again sometime.

Through the summer of 1980 I continued to work at Masterdisk, attempting and often failing to be there at nine in the morning. I tended to either stay out all night or lie awake until dawn listening to the noise of the city. Not having a phone at home made it harder for me to call in sick and for the business manager at Masterdisk to reach me. My excuses for missing work or arriving late had been wearing thin. At times I would bail from the city to go off to Bethel for a few days, then return to Grand Central Station, where I would drop a dime into a pay phone and tell a story to the manager at Masterdisk, a very nice woman who kept giving me breaks, about how I had had a family emergency and needed to leave town all of a sudden.

I tried to bat away questions of why I hadn't rung her earlier. I'm sure she saw through my lame excuses. The truth was that working in an office couldn't compete with my obsession: to play in a rock 'n' roll band.

I received a picture postcard from Kim at my Thirteenth Street apartment, which came as a pleasant surprise. Other than the dreaded electricity bill from Con Edison, mail was scarce. She had written from a fishing encampment on the Klamath River up in Northern California, where she had been spending the summer with her family and their friends. The postcard depicted a comedic scene: fishermen in their boats all jammed into one hot spot at the rushing mouth of the river, all of them attempting to hook a few steelhead salmon.

I had run into her a couple of times before she left the city—first at an 8 Eyed Spy gig at Tier 3, where she appeared wearing a blue-and-white vertically striped shirt with matching trousers, her shoulder-length brown hair tied into a short, off-center ponytail, still sporting flip-up shades. We didn't talk much, but I watched her as she nodded her head to Lydia Lunch's new caterwauling group, curious to know more about who this cool-looking artist girl was.

A few nights later, after an Erasers gig at the Ear Inn on the far west side of Spring Street, I noticed Kim cruising toward me while walking an Australian shepherd. I must have told Miranda that I was planning on being at the Ear Inn that night, and she must have relayed that info to Kim, because she didn't seem surprised to find me. I was happy to see her and knelt down to give her friendly dog a few scritches behind the ears. I asked her where she was headed. She replied that she was on her way to the Ear Inn to check out the scene. She added—

"And I knew you'd be there."

It was unusual to see someone with a dog in the city, at least in our scene of young artists and musicians. Having a cat was one thing; they were more or less self-sufficient, requiring only a minimum of attention. Kim's Aussie was named Egan, and he was handsome and alert, his tail shorn off as per breed standard.

Together we walked across downtown to the East Village. We found some late-night food at a diner on Second Avenue, Egan tied up outside, attentively waiting for his master, once in a while issuing a bark to let her know what time it was. Kim told me she had been staying far uptown at the apartment of the SoHo gallerist Annina Nosei. Leaving the diner, I asked how she was going to get up to Annina's with Egan so late at night, as animals weren't permitted on the subway unless they were Seeing Eye dogs. A taxi seemed luxurious. She said she was okay. I was too shy to kiss her, even politely on the cheek, though I wanted to. So I simply said—

"Okay, see ya around"

—and stuck my hand out, feeling immediately foolish. She cocked her head slightly, half smiling, before returning my handshake.

I walked to my apartment smitten and a bit mortified, my desire over-whelmed by my lack of confidence. I was clearly no Lothario. I was twenty-two years old but with a teenage brain, slow to transition to adulthood.

It seemed certain to me that anyone young and living in the big city making art and music had to be living a wild and sexually active life. I was envious of people on the scene, who I imagined were jumping into each other's beds, always loose and uninhibited. I was too reserved to ever be that way, could hardly approach, let alone try to pick up, anyone.

The punk scene had been glorified, at least since 1975, for its embrace of promiscuity. The New York Dolls exemplified a kind of radical heterosexuality—the boys could prance and gesture about the stage in effeminate attire, but we all knew they fell into the beds of the hottest women. By the time the Ramones, Heartbreakers, and Dead Boys entered the limelight, the celebration of raunchiness had extended to an embrace of sex work. A 1978 issue of *Cheri* magazine had the Dead Boys cavorting with soft-porn pinup girl Cherry Bomb, slobbering over her ample nudity, their trousers pulled down. Some of the more extreme and liberated young ladies popping into CBGB early on would seemingly find fun performing public fellatio on such nutjobs as these, though many of the male musicians from this particular faction of punk had replaced their sexual desire with flaccid junkie lust. A heroin high was said to supplant the libido, along with just about everything else.

But what did I know? The truth was that neither hard-core sex nor drug action figured very much into my world. Boys have always wanted to be in rock bands to get laid, or so it's said. But that was just not a defining factor for me. To be in a band was to locate and achieve an emotional pleasure charged by an organic, if not spiritual, creative impulse—a wholly other kind of eros than the one found by those blessed bed-hoppers.

23

ON THE PROMONTORY

Michael Shamberg, my former colleague from Design/Research, contacted me in the autumn of 1980 and asked if I wanted to make a few dollars helping out a crew filming a conversation with the artist Vito Acconci. All I would need to do was carry some film gear from a van, which we would drive from Manhattan to Brooklyn.

Vito's studio was a sprawling floor in a building on a desolate street beneath the Brooklyn Bridge, a stone's throw from the East River. Typically, among this crew of SoHo artists, I was the youngster of the group. There was a palpable reverence for Vito, as his work since the 1960s—as a language poet, radical performance artist, and post-postmodern architect—was a model for the intellectual concerns of young artists rolling into New York City. With such pieces as his 1972 *Seedbed* (which found the artist lying hidden beneath a ramp on the floorboards of a gallery, purportedly masturbating as he described, in his gruff, amplified voice, what he fantasized were the gallery visitors' movements above him), Vito Acconci had become an infamous and mythological presence in the Manhattan art world.

I was immediately taken with a girl moving about Vito's studio, seemingly no older than myself. She was ethereal, very thin, with almost translucent skin and a shock of egg-white hair. Whatever else was happening in the room—the crew setting up lights, once in a while being asked to hold random pieces of equipment—I was interested only in this astounding person.

As I sat by one of the large windows huffing cigarettes with Michael and a few others, she eventually strode over, smiling and full of energy, to join us for a smoke. Michael introduced her to me as Anne DeMarinis; he told her about how I had been playing guitar with his partner, Miranda. By the end of the evening, after some pleasant discussion—during which

I discovered she was Vito's girlfriend and also a pianist—we decided to try our hand at playing music together sometime. We exchanged numbers.

I soon began taking the subway over to Vito and Anne's Brooklyn studio, on a desolate, cobblestoned street with hardly a recognizable business or residence in sight. The area was governed by industrial activity by day, abandonment by night. It made for a creepy and unnerving journey.

The original idea had been for Miranda to join us as well, possibly to play bass, but she decided to bow out. Anne and I began to work on song ideas, which both of us had to some degree. The minimal, mostly minor-key guitar riffs I introduced were immediately complemented by Anne's obviously learned piano playing. We would take breaks, and I would sit with her and Vito, drinking coffee and smoking cigarette after cigarette, listening to records in their open kitchen. Vito was completely besotted with punk rock, its audacity and the way it rubbed up pleasingly against art-school inventiveness. He bought every new record that was released.

Entering Vito's loft one rehearsal day, Anne scurried over to me and whispered—

"Oh my god, do you know Dan Graham?"

"No."

"Well, he's here, sitting in the kitchen talking with Vito—he is such a freak."

I had no idea what she was talking about, though I could see there was indeed another person in the space. He was closer to Vito's age, all of forty years old—which, to a twenty-two-year-old, seemed fairly ancient—and he sat talking with Vito, in serious engagement. Vito introduced me to Dan. I noticed they were playing *Totale's Turns (It's Now or Never)*.

"How's the new Fall record?"

—I asked.

Dan went into a protracted analysis of the band, the recording, and the singer Mark E. Smith, referring to the Fall as a sort of contemporary equivalent to 1960s-era Kinks, a band for the British punk working class. While he talked, he pulled at his scruffy black facial hair with one hand, scratched the back of his head with the other. Vito had a smile on his face; he could see I was a young pup all at once caught up in the intellectual hurricane of Dan Graham. I liked the man immediately. The conversation turned to the Leeds art school band Gang of Four and the news that their next album was to be titled *Solid Gold*. I told Dan I thought the album's title was brilliant, taking the generic language of a pop greatest-hits package and recontextualizing it for their own experimental, politically charged agit-rock.

An American family, Bethel, Connecticut, 1971. Left to right: my father, George; mother, Eleanor; brother, Gene; sister, Sue; and me at thirteen

Harold Paris (seventeen) and me (eighteen) in suburban Connecticut, 1976, hair shorn, no sleep, driving back and forth to CBGB and Max's every night of the week to see Television, Patti Smith, the Ramones, Richard Hell, Blondie, et al., the future in full effect

The Coachmen, 1979. We were the tallest art rock band on the downtown scene. Left to right: Bob Pullin (bass), J. D. King (guitar, vocals), Dan Walworth (drums), and skin-and-bones me (guitar) at twenty-one

Sonic Youth come together between SoHo and the East Village. Left to right: Kim Gordon, me, Richard Edson, and Lee Ranaldo

Sunday matinee show at CBGB in late 1981, appearing with Dark Day (featuring ex-DNA member Robin Crutchfield) and Don King (with ex-Mars members Connie Burg and Mark Cunningham), the no wave torch passed forward

Michael Gira would enlist Lee or me to play bass as he began formulating Swans into the molten monolith of expressionistic din it would become. Here he joins Sonic Youth at a benefit for the White Columns gallery at Danceteria in May 1982.

Carving a crucifix into the stage of CBGB in 1982 during a chaotic noise interval (to the displeasure of the soundman)

Sometime in early-eighties New York City with Rhys Chatham, the heart and soul of downtown experimental music. I would play with Rhys's groups a few times, but mostly we enjoyed posing heavily in backstage hallways. *SoHo News* journalist and champion of the scene Merle Ginsberg is at Rhys's right.

Lydia Lunch's In Limbo project of deadening dirges featured Konk and Sonic Youth drummer Richard Edson, ex-Contortions and Bush Tetras guitarist Pat Place, onetime Sonic Youth drummer Jim Sclavunos playing saxophone, and me on bass. Performing one of our few live shows at Danceteria in early 1983

Backstage at Danceteria in 1983 with our then drummer Jim Sclavunos, who would go on to record the bulk of *Confusion Is Sex* with us before departing for further vistas that included Panther Burns, the Cramps, and Nick Cave & the Bad Seeds

Glenn Branca's ensemble was the only place to be as far as radical guitar exploration went (the keyboards here built as "extended" guitars). It took me on my first journey outside the USA, performing here in Poitiers, France, early summer 1983. Left to right: Amanda Linn, Barbara Ess, Glenn Branca, Margaret De Wys, Greg Letson, Lee Ranaldo, Stephan Wischerth, me, Arleen Schloss, Axel Gros, and Dan Witz

Sonic Youth's first gig in Europe, in Lausanne, Switzerland, the summer of 1983, with Bob Bert back in the drum saddle. The fact that we knew no one in these audiences allowed us to unleash our most intense performances yet.

For a November 1985 gig christened Blood on Brighton Beach, we performed on a jerry-rigged stage stuck precariously in the damp sand, the waves crashing close by, our amps whipping out sound mixed with howling wind and salt air. Later that night we played again in the tiny Zap Club on the boardwalk. Here I sit backstage, young and dazed at twenty-seven.

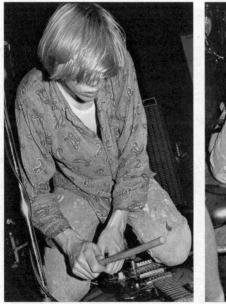

Noise psychedelia live in Los Angeles, 1985, where we would find a second home for our post-punk explorations

All members of Ciccone Youth accounted for in Los Angeles, 1986, including new drummer Steve Shelley. Mike Watt (of the Minutemen and fIREHOSE) collaborated with us on a split-single in tribute to Madonna, us playing "Into the Groove," Watt playing "Burning Up," against popular demand.

In the glorious dressing room of the notorious City Gardens club in Trenton, New Jersey, early summer of 1987, on a bill with Dinosaur Jr. and Das Damen

Dan laughed a high-pitched chortle. I could feel him sizing me up, recognizing in me a genuine "punk" source.

Meeting up with me after her return to New York City, Kim related that she had found a modest railroad apartment on the third floor of 84 Eldridge Street, between Hester and Grand Streets on the Lower East Side. She was excited about moving downtown after having had to relocate around the city from one artist's apartment to another with her modest belongings.

She was employed as an assistant and receptionist for Annina Nosei's new gallery at 100 Prince Street, and she invited me to the first group show to be held there, at the end of September. It would feature the artists James Casebere and Mike Kelley.

I appeared at the gallery at around seven—openings usually ran from six to eight o'clock—and saw people I knew from Jenny Holzer's loft. I was wearing a recently acquired old-man private-eye raincoat, the no wave fashion of the moment, as I sidled up to Kim, who seemed genuinely pleased that I came by.

She introduced me to Annina, a stately, beautiful Italian woman with a sharp and friendly energy. One of the artists in attendance was the same person who had made the snarky comment about my bloody finger at the Coachmen's CBGB debut, a year and a half back. He walked over to me, squinting at my short, choppy hair and my Canal Jean irregulars.

"Nice raincoat."

Kim had to stick it out for dinner and drinks afterward, but I split, heading over to Tier 3 to hear Arto Lindsay tear it up as the new guitarist in the Lounge Lizards.

Not long after the gallery event, Kim and I met for lunch at Ray's Pizza on Prince Street, then walked over to check out her new apartment on Eldridge Street. Up two flights of stairs, we entered a small kitchen area with a bathtub next to the sink. There were two gated back windows looking over a rusted fire escape and, beyond that, a view of a nondescript housing project. Toward the front of the apartment was a small middle room opening onto another equally sized room with two windows looking out over Eldridge Street. A young Chinese Canadian artist, Ken Lum, was busy scraping and painting the walls, preparing the place to be habitable. He had been suggested by Dan Graham, who Kim explained owned the apartment directly above.

"Dan Graham?"

—I said.

"I know him. We just met over at Vito and Anne's place in Brooklyn."

Kim told me that Dan was a close confidant, a connection she'd made through the artists John Knight and Mike Kelley. Kim and Mike had originally made the drive from Los Angeles to New York City, staying in the shared loft of Cindy Sherman and Robert Longo, two artists who had recently moved down from Buffalo, New York. With small-world fittingness, their loft happened to be in the same building on South Street where the Coachmen lived and rehearsed. Mike had returned to the West Coast, but Kim decided to stay in town, enchanted by the New York art scene, particularly the interdisciplinary action happening around no wave.

After settling into her freshly scraped and painted apartment, she invited me over again. I arrived at Eldridge Street and shouted up to her window—

"*Kim!!*"

Her head bobbed out.

"Hey you"

—she said with a smile, before tossing her front door keys down in a sock, which I caught like a charm from the sky.

A wooden plank sat atop the bathtub in the kitchen, functioning as a table of sorts. The only other items in the apartment were a thin foam mattress and a guitar, which I immediately recognized. I had played this very guitar with the Coachmen earlier in the year; it had been lying around our South Street rehearsal loft. The guitar belonged to another RISD guy, David Bowes, a skinny, pale blond cat with a calm and beatific vibe. He had come down to New York City around the same time as J.D. and his pals.

The guitar was a black Korean-made Drifter, a six-string solid-body electric, cheap and rugged. Evidently, after I'd played it, he left it at Jenny Holzer's loft, where unbeknownst to me Kim had crashed for a spell. Jenny's roommate, the artist and sometime Coachmen co-vocalist Mary Lemley, offered the guitar to Kim since she didn't have one of her own.

So there it was, this Drifter guitar I had banged around on the last couple of years, sitting in Kim's first New York City apartment.

She had recently purchased a battery-powered Lectrosonics Moose practice amp, which was about the size of a small end table. I sat on her floor playing the plugged-in Drifter for some time, its presence helping alleviate the nervous intimacy of our being alone together for the first time.

I had it in my head to ask Kim if she wanted to play with Anne and me, so I soon introduced them. We met at Dave's Luncheonette one early evening. I was a bit anxious bringing these two women together, in part because I recalled Anne's queasiness toward Dan Graham, with whom Kim was close. Kim certainly was aware of Anne's partner, Vito Acconci, and the historical relationship Dan had with Vito dating back to the mid-1960s, when Dan had helped Vito attain his first gallery exhibit as a visual artist. I was relieved that Anne and Kim seemed to get on well, recognizing and appreciating each other's connections to the art world, as well as their shared interest in experimental music.

The situation at Masterdisk hadn't improved; I still found myself continually oversleeping and skipping work. I would eventually, after a final warning, be unceremoniously fired.

Without even the pretense of a day job, my days became unmoored. I stayed awake through the nights, falling asleep around nine in the morning, then waking anytime between five and seven in the evening, at which point I would bop from Tier 3 to Mudd Club to CBGB to Club 57 to Max's to Dave's Luncheonette to Kiev—the city open and purring at all times.

This was bad news for my landlord, who was becoming more and more agitated, as I was in constant arrears on my rent. It was a new decade, and I had turned twenty-two in July. I had no money and no job, was on the cusp of eviction. But I was enchanted with an artist from California five years my senior, rendering the rest of it almost irrelevant. All I needed to satisfy my soul was to form a band, to make a dream come true.

Kim came by my pad a few times, amused by the fact that I had no dresser, only a pile of shirts stacked in a corner. The single piece of art on my wall was the cover of an album I had found in a junk shop, entitled *Let's Dance the Ska,* by Lord Gayle and the Seasiders. It was lime green, with a line drawing of a young, joyous Jamaican couple dancing.

Kim and I began to spend every moment together. By her invitation, I soon abandoned Thirteenth Street to move in with her and Egan on Eldridge Street, bringing along my kitty-cat, Sweetface. Those first weeks living together, we spent endless hours walking through the city, connected by the slow, vibrant hum of having found each other. We both seemed to realize pretty quickly that we were in love. Our shared interests had been fostered by our friendships in the downtown social milieu, which kept our own friendship strong.

Kim possessed a sensitivity that could be emotionally raw or coolly distant, depending on the environment. It was obvious that she was genuinely devoted to being an artist, a stance that she embodied naturally and that attracted me profoundly. Her feminism was a radical revelation to me, and it would inform my own self-awareness. I sensed that I had something that thrilled her too, a younger, somewhat-on-the-loose rock 'n' roll boy, expressing my own organic intellect and my penchant for humor.

Whatever the reason, we found ourselves in harmonious enchantment, an existence of timelessness and wonder that, in our youth, felt natural and promised.

24

ATOMIC BONGOS

I invited Coachmen drummer Dave Keay to play with Kim, Anne, and me, and we rehearsed in a soundproof room set up in Vito Acconci's studio loft. With Anne behind her electric piano and Dave at his kit, Kim and I shared the two guitars at our disposal: the black Drifter and a cheap Harmony electric I had found at a yard sale in Connecticut. I threw down a few song ideas. Anne had a couple as well, as did Kim.

Kim's were songs she had been working on with CKM, one called "Cosmopolitan Girl," in which she recited the copy from a *Cosmopolitan* magazine ad. To have those words spoken-sung in a dispassionate monotone by a tomboyish-looking young woman in flip-up shades was most likely not the image *Cosmopolitan* had been suggesting, which made the song's commentary on female desire and identity that much more charged. Another tune she proffered was "Teenage Men," the lyrics sung in a similar way, only this time evoking both adoration and criticism of her subject: young men playing loud guitars.

Kim and I had agreed that one of the most interesting proponents of new music in our scene, hands down, was Glenn Branca. Kim had met Glenn through Dan Graham some time before I had, and, like myself, she was in awe of his music. Glenn, along with his compatriot in high-volume electric guitar minimalism Rhys Chatham, as well as the other male guitarists they employed in their ensembles (such as the artists Robert Longo and Richard Prince), were the most obvious muses for "Teenage Men." Kim's song suggested that these were effectively teenagers in men's bodies, which made them at once alluringly cute and irresponsible—a recrimination I would often feel her applying to me in our years together.

Shortly before Kim and I connected, I had seen a "Musicians Wanted" ad in the back of the *SoHo News*. Glenn was seeking guitarists willing to play in "weird tunings," it said. Considering the ferocious and radical sounds he created, "weird tunings" felt like an understatement. Maybe he wanted to soften the blow for any unsuspecting guitarists.

I rang Glenn immediately and he answered, telling me to come by the next day. I soon found myself sitting in his kitchen, in the home he shared with the artist Barbara Ess. Glenn offered me coffee while lighting one of his countless filterless Pall Mall cigarettes. He handed me one of the guitars lying around in random corners of the apartment. He was eager to see if I had any familiarity with playing harmonics, in which the fingering hand gently mutes and then quickly releases the string on various harmonic-friendly frets, while the plectrum hand performs a quick pluck. He also wanted to know whether I could double strum.

Harmonics I had been loving and working with for some time, and double strumming was my default mode, as opposed to the typical downstroke of punk or the more regular swinging stroke of classic rhythm guitar. I showed him my lightning-speed double strum, offering—

"I'm more into triple strumming, actually."

Glenn eyed me with bemusement and a bit of a *well, that won't be necessary* look. As I left the building I ran into Lee Ranaldo, the Fluks guitarist who had come to a few of our Coachmen gigs. He had his guitar case in hand, also coming to meet Glenn.

The only phone number I could give Glenn was at Masterdisk, but he never called. I mentioned my audition to Kim later on, who mentioned it in turn to Glenn. She told me his reaction: that I was *too wild* and that *he didn't want to be the person to tame me.* I was somewhat flattered, though also taken aback at the "wild" comment. Kim had referred to me as "wild" once, right after we first met. I realized that perhaps that was the way I was being perceived, some wild child on the SoHo art-rock scene.

Whether the description fit, I just *really* wanted to play guitar with Branca.

After I was fired by Masterdisk, Kim and I subsisted off whatever coin we could scrounge together. Cigarettes and coffee were our first priority. Then, when we could afford it, food. Tuna fish, mayonnaise, onions, and potatoes were fairly inexpensive, and Kim was remarkably creative in her preparations, even when we were working from just scraps.

Anne, Kim, Dave, and I continued to get together at Vito's to work out song ideas. No one had been designated as bass player, though Anne had a bass guitar in her studio. She played it on a couple of the numbers we were working on, as did Kim and I, though we mostly stuck to the Drifter and Harmony electrics, all of us except Dave sharing vocals.

I hadn't sung with the Coachmen. To sing into a microphone amplified through a small PA, which Anne owned, was altogether new, strange, frightening, and thrilling. Anne had a nice, pitch-conscious voice. Kim tended to sing in her more distinctive shout-speak. I was, I hoped, coming out of the Tom Verlaine, Richard Hell, Joey Ramone, and Lou Reed school.

I had it in mind to reach out to George Scott III, of the Contortions and Raybeats, to see if he wanted to play bass with us. Regretfully, I never made the call. The news in early August that he had died from a toxic mixture of narcotics was heartbreaking—he had been a beautiful, rambunctious musical light, all of a sudden gone. His death, as well as those of several other well-loved members of the late-1970s downtown community, suggested the end of a moment, as we stared into an unknowable future.

That year saw the selling of the 1950s Hollywood actor–turned–California governor Ronald Reagan as a Republican presidential hopeful. Reagan had at first seemed like a long shot, particularly with the meltdown of the Republican Party following Richard Nixon's resignation in 1974, still in our collective memory. But after four years of Democrat Jimmy Carter's presidency, conservatives crafted new strategies to regain the White House and displace Carter's softhearted diplomacy. Promising a return to some fairy-tale "great" America—in thrall to capitalism, prioritizing the Christian values of the so-called moral majority—Reagan soundly trounced Carter.

Artists and musicians from all movements, particularly the underground ones, disparaged the rebranding of America as "Reagan Country." But it was the voice of the punk rock kids that could be heard the loudest. In affluent communities in Reagan's own Southern California, where money, home, surf, and sand were most explicitly exalted, the idea that youth might embrace the same values as the "Me Generation" was disturbed by the advent of hardcore, a music far more amped and primal than the first generation of punk.

Hardcore would hardly be exclusive to Southern California. Bands and fanzines sprang forth all across North America, powering a politically informed collective that ran in direct opposition to Reagan's America. The hardcore scene, as a whole, was hyperaggressive, testosterone charged, and, even more than the original punk movement it had spawned from, populated by teenagers.

Anti-Reagan messaging became more explicit in the New York City music and art scenes as well. It could be found in the politically conscious groups Mofungo, the Scene Is Now, and V-Effect; the Manhattan-based hardcore group False Prophets; the satirically named Reagan Youth; and hip-hop, which had risen in prevalence from street-conscious party music to acts of resistance against social oppression. With portable boom box cassette/radio players becoming increasingly available and affordable, the streets of 1980 were even louder than those of the previous decade, alive with creative and surprising frequencies.

Our apartment building on Eldridge Street in the Lower East Side stood in what was then a mostly Jewish neighborhood, though that was quickly changing, as other ethnicities migrated in and neighborhoods merged. Next door was a housing complex that was primarily occupied by Chinese, Black, and Latino residents. Chinatown, just to the south, brought in an influx of Chinese Americans, just as many Jewish families were leaving.

Our landlord owned and ran a fabric business on the ground floor of our building. He would invite me into the back of the store, drawing a glass of fresh seltzer from a water cooler by his desk, surrounded by large spools of linen, regaling me with stories of the fantastic old days when Yiddish-speaking families populated the neighborhood. He would bemoan the changing identity of the street.

Living on Eldridge was quite a bit calmer than East Thirteenth Street, though it still had an intensity to it. It was best to keep vigilant, especially after dark—creeps from all corners of the city might cross your path at any time. Having Kim's dog, Egan, bound about with us as we walked from here to there seemed to be a good deterrent to anyone considering any funny business.

Kim asked me to fly to California in the late summer of 1980 to meet her family. Landing in Los Angeles, we were picked up by some friends of hers, who drove us from the airport to her parents' house in the Rancho Park section of west Los Angeles. With the car windows open, I was immediately struck by the air, laced with the scent of bougainvillea flowers, dry and sweet. Coming from East Coast cities, those greyscale metropolises with their towering monoliths, I found it enchanting to see Los Angeles, a sprawl of suburban lawns, palm trees, and sunshine.

We traveled up to Berkeley to visit Kim's closest friend, whom she had shared a house with in Venice Beach in the early 1970s. We then made our way farther north to Klamath, California, where Kim's mother, father, and older brother were staying for their annual summer fishing trip.

I was welcomed with kindness by Kim's parents, her mother, Althea, a seamstress, and her father, Wayne, a UCLA sociology professor, both of them erudite and endearing. Her older brother, Keller, approached me with a hearty hello and immediately offered to show me around the encampment.

Klamath was primarily Native American grounds, with territory divisions for nontribal people to camp and fish for steelhead salmon. That's what the Gordons did, starting at the break of dawn, with a posse of friends and associates—educators, documentary filmmakers, eccentrics, intellectuals, a garrulous mix of Los Angeles characters. By sunrise, Klamath River would be a cavalcade of small boats, fishing fanatics put-putting about in circles, tossing lures into the river in hopes of hooking breeding steelhead. Each evening there would be a communal campfire, with masses of fresh fish grilled by Wayne on an upturned barrel loaded with briquettes and firewood. It was an idyllic, almost mystical world of giant Sequoia trees and rich, verdant glory.

We both found odd jobs after returning to New York City, though hardly anything with much stability. One fortuitous day I was offered an exciting gig at the Squat Theatre, located on West Twenty-Third Street, a legendary space founded by a radical Hungarian theater troupe. The Contortions, the Sun Ra Arkestra, the Lounge Lizards, and Defunkt had all become mainstay attractions there, the room buzzing nightly with downtown funk and punk energy. Eszter Balint, the daughter of one of the main overseers of the theater, had grown up acting in many of the plays being presented there. She was just fourteen years old in 1980, but had already proved herself a considerably talented musician and actress, and was cherished by the downtown community.

Mary Lemley, the artist and occasional Coachmen singer, yelled out to me from the back of a yellow taxi one day. She had been hanging around with Eszter, and they both wanted to hit some party, but Eszter was supposed to DJ at Squat that night. They asked if I would fill in for forty bucks. I gladly agreed.

I had never DJed in my life.

I couldn't think of a better thing to do in the world than to play records for a crowd of people into cool music. I had amassed a few boxes of seven-inch singles from thrift stores and junk shops across the city: surf and garage rock bands, reggae sides I'd purchased in Queens, as well as a slew of punk singles.

Kim and I met Mary and Eszter at Squat, and Eszter gave me a quick tutorial on how to use the two turntables and mixer. It was all pretty basic. Kim and I huddled in the DJ booth together, and I began to spin discs.

Nico, the legendary Warhol figure and Velvet Underground singer, was due to perform that night. Nico played quite a bit at the Squat, as well as acting in some plays there. It had been a while since I had seen her in concert—usually at CBGB, almost always on the same bill as her Velvet Underground compatriot and producer John Cale. She still maintained her utterly distinct presentation, the harrowing and strong voice, heart-struck and exotic, accompanied by the stirring alien drone of her harmonium.

As the evening ended and we began stuffing records back into the shopping bags we had brought them over in, Nico flung open the door to the DJ booth. Her face looked as pale as the winter moon, her eyes bloodshot and wet, mascara dripping to her cheeks. She asked if I had seen a certain someone.

I was caught in her intense glare.

"No one's been back here except us."

She gave me a three-second stare, anger rising within her, then slammed the door shut.

Kim and I looked at each other, acknowledging with nervous amusement what we had just experienced. I collected the forty bucks, and we got the hell out of there.

Kim had written an article entitled "Trash Drugs and Male Bonding," an observation of a performance by Rhys Chatham's group, in a new art journal called *REAL LIFE*. It was about musicians snorting tiny canisters of Locker Room, a cheap amyl nitrite head rush commonly available at street-corner bodegas. I thought the title of the piece would make for a cool band name.

Our bandmates liked it too, though we decided to truncate it to simply Male Bonding. But by the time we had scored our debut gig, at A's, our name had changed again, this time to Red Milk, conjured together around Vito and Anne's kitchen table one afternoon.

With a lineup and a name, the four of us, in the second week of

December 1980, gathered our two amps and drum kit from Anne's studio in Brooklyn and took a taxi to Manhattan. It had been a snowy, cold winter afternoon, and we had to carry the gear a few blocks to where taxicabs might possibly be located—cars, let alone taxis, were a rare sight in this desolate area of Brooklyn (which, in years to come, would be designated DUMBO by real estate developers—Down Under the Manhattan Bridge Overpass).

After what felt like forever, we sloshed our wet amps, drums, and bodies into a Checker cab, then rode, stunned and freezing, to our first gig. The audience was sparse at A's, though both Vito Acconci and Dan Graham attended to lend their support. We needed a third amplifier, so I walked a few blocks to fetch the Moose from our apartment. Once we started playing, though, we realized something was terribly wrong. Dave's drums were pretty much all Anne, Kim, or I could hear. The song structures we had practiced went missing in action, Dave's whamming percussion plowing and pummeling forward, Anne staring at me in confoundment and panic. A lot of our vocalizing was supposed to be shared by the three of us, working off one another. This became impossible and even ridiculous; we couldn't hear one another, much less sing together. And the Moose was woefully underpowered next to the other two amps.

We had only four or five songs. Each one was a chaotic failure.

When this catastrophe ended, we speechlessly broke down our gear, pushing it to the side of the room to make space for the next act.

Anne, Vito, Kim, and I left A's to sit in a Chinese restaurant until the end of the night, before hauling our gear back from whence it came, stunned by how horrendous we had been. Vito tried to cheer us up, reminding us that the night's experience, like everything in life, was simply and essentially absurd.

We were confused and humiliated.

Red Milk, after one gig, was finished.

25

I DREAMED I DREAM

After the disaster at A's, I decided all that was needed to recalibrate our group was a new name. I suggested the Arcadians.

The Arcadians of mythology were peaceniks, a gentle people who communicated through song. They were the antithesis of the warmongering Spartans, the muscle-headed aggressors. The name was a bit at odds with the current crop of monikers on the scene, not that there was any real aesthetic consistency among them, other than a taste for subversion.

It barely snowed at all in New York City in January 1981, but it was one of the most bone-chilling winters in the city's history, temperatures below zero degrees Fahrenheit at mid-month, which was exactly when our next show was as the rechristened Arcadians. The night would begin as a replay of our first gig, pushing amplifiers on rickety casters across the bare and frozen cobblestone streets of Brooklyn, nearly succumbing to hypothermia while waiting on taxis willing to pick us up. Only this time we'd be headed to CBGB.

Midweek nights at CBGB favored neighborhood bands rather than the higher-profile blowouts of the weekends. It was encouraging to see people attending the gig who were curious to hear us: a few musicians around the Glenn Branca–Rhys Chatham axis, artists associated with Vito Acconci and Dan Graham, and people who recognized both Anne's and Kim's credentials on the scene.

For all my time attending shows and a few parties here and there, I was still a mystery to most of these people—the young, tall, skinny boy standing gawkily between Anne and Kim, playing a ratty Harmony electric guitar held together with duct tape.

Our set that cold night was solid, especially compared with the one at A's the previous month, though CBGB's stage monitors didn't altogether help our cause. While there were a couple of monitor wedges on the front of the stage, there were also massive monitor horns hung from the ceiling to the left and right of the stage, which had the potential to feedback with an eardrum-decimating screech or else simply blow your head off with a howling roar.

Invariably around the thirty-minute mark of a group's set, the soundman would announce through the monitors from his post in the middle of the room—

"You got one more song, let's wind it up, guys."

Which meant a new band's moment of glory at the legendary club would soon be over.

Paying rent, not to mention the electricity and telephone bills, became more worrying. So did buying groceries and cigarettes. Kim and I had no choice but to find real jobs. Kim began waitressing at Elephant & Castle, a slightly upscale restaurant in SoHo with a British flair. But after about a month, she was let go for, as she related, "not smiling enough."

I found a job as a dishwasher at FOOD, a cafeteria-style restaurant on the corner of Wooster and Prince Streets in SoHo. In 1971, the post-conceptual "anarchitect" Gordon Matta-Clark, along with his compatriot artist friends Carol Goodden and Tina Girouard, had decided to open the place. The idea was to offer a kind of "intervention" to the lack of nourishing eats around SoHo, then dilapidated, as well as to employ local artists in need of sustenance and coin. By the time I got a job there, the original founders had moved on (Matta-Clark having died tragically in 1978), but not before the eatery had become a hot spot for the downtown art world.

I shared my dishwashing job with a few other young men making minimum wage, all of them either Black or Latino. The chefs and preppers were young, hip aspiring artists, dancers, actors, and musicians. They were paid a bit better than we were.

The best part of working in a restaurant, whether it was Elephant & Castle for Kim or FOOD for me, was that we could bring home (or smuggle out) takeaway platters. FOOD especially was bountiful in this respect; it kept us alive for the few months I worked there.

Whenever there was a lull in the kitchen, I would skip out the side door onto Wooster Street to smoke cigarettes and hand out loaves of day-old bread to any homeless people ambling past. Musicians stopped by at times, wheatpasting their gig flyers—the walls of Wooster Street were prime real estate for that purpose. They might ask me to refill their slop buckets, which I would supply from the dishwashing sink taps.

The artist Keith Haring, whom I knew only casually from hanging out at the same nightspots, would pop around FOOD, knowing he could get his wheatpaste bucket reliably refilled. He had been slapping up xeroxed sheets that he had constructed from front-page headlines of the *New York Post,* cut up and reworded, such as—

REAGAN: READY TO KILL

Wheatpasting flyers around downtown was still an integral part of being in a band or, in Keith's case, sharing your visuals. Refilling your bucket wasn't always easy; not every restaurant was amenable. I found that the all-male St. Mark's Baths worked pretty well. The men cruising about in their bathrobes would look at me wondering if I was going to stick around, but I had my mind set on other things, namely promoting an upcoming gig.

A couple of cheery prep cooks at FOOD realized I was a musician in a band. They too had a group. Together we were able to land a gig, just five days after the Arcadians' first CBGB appearance, at Inroads, a SoHo performance space on Mercer Street, just north of Prince. It was a decent place to hear free jazz and experimental music, as well as see theater and dance shows. Jazz players, from avant-garde violinist Billy Bang to the scabrous improvising trio Massacre to the high-octane industrial trio Borbetomagus, would throw down their boundary-crashing concepts on any given night.

It was these farthest-of-far-out ensembles that I kept crossing paths with as I attempted to book the Arcadians. Vying for the same venues left us competing but also commiserating with each other, listening to and attending each other's gigs. It was exciting, the sense that there were new sounds coming up, post–no wave, post-1970s, and—a sobriquet soon to define a generation of underground experimental music—post-punk.

Anne, Kim, Dave Keay, and I were rehearsing at Vito's studio in early December 1980 when news broke that John Lennon had been assassinated outside the Dakota, the home he shared with Yoko Ono and their son, Sean, on West Seventy-Second Street across from Central Park. It was impossible for us to continue playing or to do anything else other than monitor the TV news for what was happening around the Dakota. Dave became visibly upset, tears welling in his eyes. He excused himself to catch the subway back to his apartment to grieve. For the following week, thousands upon thousands of people gathered outside John and Yoko's home singing, weeping, lighting candles, and laying flowers.

A few months earlier, while working at Masterdisk, I had delivered acetates to the Record Plant at the same time that John and Yoko were recording *Double Fantasy* there. Of course, a few Beatles fanatics were hanging around outside, waiting for a glimpse of the two. After the assailant was apprehended, a photograph circulated in the news of John outside the Dakota signing an autograph for his future assassin. It made my blood run cold.

The same week, the *SoHo News* mentioned another death in the world of rock 'n' roll, a lesser name but one that meant something to those in the underground of American punk. Darby Crash, singer of the infamous Los Angeles band the Germs, had ended his life with a fatal heroin overdose. Darby had been born in 1958, the same year as me. That this twenty-two-year-old had belonged to a local milieu rampant with kids around our age made me realize how different—how much younger—the Los Angeles scene must be from New York City's.

It wasn't just the scene's youth that set it apart. The punk music in Los Angeles seemed to be defined by people who had actually grown up there, attending the various high schools dotted around the region, which made their sound more of an indigenous affair. Much of the downtown New York City art and music world was defined by people who had migrated to the city. The truly indigenous expressions of New York City, in the 1970s and onward, were not so much happening in punk but in salsa and hip-hop—music enacted by youth who had come of age in the actual geography of the city itself.

There were a few roustabouts my age banging about the downtown scene, but it was still mostly inhabited by older folks (which to me meant anyone in their late twenties or beyond).

That would soon change.

In early February 1981, seemingly the entire downtown art world swarmed into Long Island City, in Queens, for the opening of the Diego Cortez–curated group show *New York/New Wave* at the P.S. 1 Contemporary Art Center. The exhibit was a bursting-at-the-seams update to *Times Square Show* a year prior. More than one hundred artists were included in *New York/New Wave,* their work filling the massive, reconstructed turn-of-the-century schoolhouse. Contraptions of art hung everywhere, pieces by established luminaries colliding with work from

COLAB-associated aesthetes, Fashion Moda–spotlighted graffiti artists, and various scenesters from the Mudd Club–Club 57 circuit.

The year would get only more amped for the twenty-year-old Jean-Michel Basquiat, who became the breakout artist from *New York/New Wave*. The poet Rene Ricard soon published a laudatory profile of him in *Artforum*. Basquiat, by 1982, would have his first major solo show at Annina Nosei's gallery, a little more than two years after I had visited Kim there.

Jean-Michel would become the first person from our downtown punk and no wave scene—our community of outsiders, aliens, runaways, and seekers—to become an actual living legend. And deservedly so. Madonna Ciccone, whom the world would soon come to know by her first name alone and who had had an intimate connection with the young artist, would be close behind him, as would Keith Haring. But Basquiat was the first true supernova to explode from our streets, showering the universe with color, magic, energy, light, sound, and vision.

Dave Keay had been invited to play in a new lineup for ex-Television guitarist Richard Lloyd. It was a big deal for him, but it meant our group, the Arcadians, was now drummerless. I decided to reach out to Richard Edson.

I had met Richard a few times at A's when the Coachmen played there. He had been living at the space for a while in a shared room with another artist and had been playing percussion in one of Arleen Schloss's ad hoc groups, as well as in a band named Body (soon to change their name to Live Skull). He let it be known to me that he was available to play together, if the situation ever arose.

Richard invited Kim, Anne, and me to his rehearsal spot, a basement on Second Avenue between Fourth and Fifth Streets. He was auditioning us as much as we were auditioning him. The joint was dark and tiny, with just enough room for Richard's kit, which sat across from a large black furnace, noisily heating the tenements above. Over his drum stool, a small window sealed with soot and mold let in a dull glow from the world outside.

We had carted over a couple of small amps with our guitars and keyboard, and we began setting up. I sensed Richard was a bit wary of us, but he was welcoming, with a wide, expressive smile and happy, slightly mischievous eyes. His nose was fantastic; it pulled down his face, giving him a cool-cat look that matched his bebop voice, somewhere between an alto and soprano, a sweet nature always dancing in his phrasings.

His kit was pretty stripped down, with only a snare and kick drum, a hi-hat, and a crash cymbal, along with a set of attached bongos. As we played the few songs we knew, Richard tapped along, his drums tight and pointillistic. It was less rocked out than we were used to with Dave Keay. Richard established a groove, while Anne, Kim, and I tore about on our instruments.

Anne's keyboard punctuations were the most pronounced. They were a stark contrast to the loose action Kim and I were laying down. I was doing what I did, creating slashing noise and droning double-strummed chaos. I could hear Richard attempting to incorporate bongos into our sound, which was completely at odds with the mania emanating from our amplifiers. I could sense some frustration amid the din, but we continued to wail.

My eyes were shut and I was fully in the zone when I heard Richard yell out—

"Whoa! Whoa! Hold up!"

He was staring at his bongos, which were dotted in red. He looked at me, then at my hand, dripping crimson. Evidently, I had cut my thumb open again, this time on the metal stalk that had once held a volume knob on my cheap guitar. It wasn't the second or even the third time. The truth was that it happened more or less whenever I got carried away, as I certainly had been in that moment.

Richard wasn't sure whether to get angry at me for defacing his instrument, but his good humor prevailed. He said—

"Yo, from now on *you cannot be spraying blood on my drums.*"

While I wrapped tissue and gaffer tape around my thumb, Richard said that he liked what we were doing, but that the music would be far more effective if there was some semblance of an arrangement, guitars locking into a rhythm so changes could be audibly established.

This sounded reasonable enough. We complied, if only with a shrug. I picked up the bass to play a song idea we had been working toward, finding myself immediately syncing with Richard's playing. He responded with a gleam in his eye: *That's the ticket!* What he really wanted more than anything was a groove to bite into, and recognizing this, I jammed out some bass guitar hooks, further locking into his hungry rhythmic energy.

We rehearsed a few more times with Richard, but our band—such as it was—was entering a dislocated space. Anne had begun expressing interest in the music happening among the more reserved, studied art-school bands on the scene, particularly a new ensemble called Off Beach. When one of the musicians from that outfit suggested that what our band was doing was less impressive or effective than some of the more progressive streams emerging in downtown music, I could see Anne taking the message to heart. She obviously respected this musician's perspective.

"He knows these things"

—she said with a sigh.

It was pulling us away from the kind of energy I had been focusing on: Branca's brutalist ministrations, as well as my growing fascination with bands operating well outside the art world—an encroaching slew of hardcore groups, mostly from the suburbs and outer boroughs.

Feeling Anne's interest wane, I decided to take a more controlling hand. There was magic unfolding and developing within us and our music—I could sense it—and I had no desire to let it slip away. This group was going to move forward; I would instill it with my vision of what it should be: the experimental group I had been dreaming of forever.

I had been holding a band name close to my heart for quite some time, waiting for the perfect moment to share it. I hid it greedily, as if it were a diamond fallen from the heavens, a secret rendezvous with an endless future. It was a group name for every dream I dreamed about rock 'n' roll:

Sonic Youth.

Sonic Youth at home in the crosstown traffic of New York City, 1982. Left to right:
Bob Bert, Kim Gordon, Lee Ranaldo, Thurston Moore

BOOK THREE

BOOK THREE

26

FREUNDSCHAFT

I had first been struck by the word "sonic" in the nom de guerre of Fred "Sonic" Smith, the guitarist of MC5. It was also the name of the 1960s Pacific Northwest garage rock group the Sonics, whose first album featured the raw fuzz splatter of songs like "Psycho" and "Strychnine," which I had found in a used bin for ninety-nine cents in my early teens. "Sonic" was the coolest-sounding word in existence. Attaching "youth" to it was inspired by my intoxication with reggae and dub music, the word consistently appearing in lyrics, Jamaican youth fighting off oppression and disenfranchisement.

Kim, Anne, and Richard seemed okay with the name change. I sensed they could see and hear how it had the power to galvanize us, to create a new vision for who we could become.

We were due to play at Club 57 in the early spring of 1981. I created a flyer, the first with our new name, using an image Kim had drawn of my head bent in repose while lolling about in our Eldridge Street apartment. As an artist, she had been creating work in various disciplines for as long as I'd known her, but I hadn't seen her take pencil to paper and draw a representational image in this way before. The realization that she possessed such skill made me see that I had so much more to know about and learn from her.

Even as she disregarded this tossed-off drawing as nothing special, I was charmed and delighted by it. I made a few flyers, modifying our name in some instances to Fucking-Youth, for no real reason other than to draw attention to the band through play and confusion. I also wanted to establish a bit of edge and mystery to us, inspired by the raw energy of the hardcore flyers I had begun spotting around town. I wheatpasted both versions on every lamppost, mailbox, and wall below Fourteenth Street, paying attention not to paste over any upcoming gigs by other groups or Keith Haring's increasingly ubiquitous crawling-baby graffiti. Keith's baby was something seen one day in the subway, then on a wall, then another wall, a telephone booth, another telephone booth.

While walking with Richard Edson along Houston Street one afternoon, he pointed at one of Keith's babies on the bottom of a lamppost. We smiled in recognition of this sweet, rascally image and the young artist who created it. It was enchanting and evocative, resonating as much, if not more so, than the typically bold street art gestures of the day.

Despite my efforts at marketing, the Club 57 gig attracted only a handful of people. Still, I felt newly empowered by our band name, untethered from how I had acted onstage previously. I stepped up the guitar noise, at one point playing slide guitar using a shaken-up beer bottle, which gushed over my left fist and onto the strings. A fellow musician approached me after our set, asking, with a hushed curiosity, if I had been trying to channel masturbation.

I hadn't actually considered it. All I'd really wanted was to make a bit of wet noise.

Richard had been using the last name Smith—as opposed to Edson—at this point, possibly to separate what he was doing with Sonic Youth from his other projects, such as the new funk-centric collective he had been involved with named Konk. The musicians in that band (including trumpeter Shannon Dawson, whom I remembered from Test Pattern and SAMO) were steeped in a lineage of rhythmic Lower East Side street music coming out of Latin culture, as well as Afro-Cuban grooves and hip-hop beats. Their gigs were romps, with Sun Ra Arkestra–style processions through the audience, cowbells clanging, trumpets blaring.

After our rechristening as Sonic Youth, it seemed as if a fresh critical interest was in the air about us. With Richard at the drum kit, we attained an instant connection to the bands he was more attuned to: Liquid Liquid, Dog Eat Dog, Mudmen, as well as Konk themselves. These were bands with a more East Village flavor, what a few local journalists referred to as the "naive rhythm" scene. The musicians Anne, Kim, and I connected to—Glenn, Rhys, Chinese Puzzle, Red Decade, Y Pants—were coming more from the SoHo art noise world.

But we were all part of the same larger community. We all strode the same streets.

For our second gig, at the beginning of June, we found ourselves on a prestigious bill with Branca's ensemble at Great Gildersleeves, a club a block north of CBGB on the Bowery. Our set seemed to go over fine, though all attention was on the new music Branca would be presenting, which had become increasingly explosive and elaborate.

And loud.

Glenn would talk of volume being its own essential aspect in his compositions, an almost tangible element to be employed. It became as central to the work as any musical notation. The high output brought with it unexpected harmonics—ineffable, indefinable moments along the sonic spectrum. The sounds were seemingly out of human control, even though they were created by it. The experience drove Glenn to ecstasy. To be responsible for this transformative noise would visibly affect him, as he succumbed to its otherworldliness. He would extend his arms to the ceiling and unleash an unbridled shout, swept into a mystic vortex by blasting amplifiers.

Lee Ranaldo, whom I had bumped into just before he auditioned for Glenn, had been touring the U.S. and Europe with the ensemble since 1980, the group becoming only more ferocious and mesmerizing. Unlike Glenn's earlier, smaller groups, the current ensemble seemed hell-bent on executing his precise sonic visions. It tore away at the fabric of reality, creating singular moments in which musicians and audiences could—when the alignment was just right—experience extrasensory, soul-shifting explosions.

I had been rebuffed when I'd auditioned, but still I dreamed of being a part of it.

Kim had been asked by the director of White Columns, a gallery way west on Spring Street, to curate an art exhibition. White Columns originally existed in SoHo as the eponymously named 112 Greene Street, founded in 1970 by, among other artists, Gordon Matta-Clark (a year before he created FOOD). Relocated to Spring Street, the gallery was renamed for the stately white columns at the building's front. The director, Josh Baer, was the son of the acclaimed minimalist painter Jo Baer, and he had been raised in the heady New York City art universe.

Josh, sensitive to the fact that Kim and I were subsisting off pennies, put a bug in her ear about the possibility of our new band playing at the gallery sometime. The invitation would gradually evolve into a grander idea: for me to curate a succession of musical evenings there.

I took the opportunity and ran with it, turning it into a full-on exposition of downtown musicians—artists who I felt had been marginalized by the attitudes of many club owners. A few of the prominent local music venues, inspired by the pioneering and popular CBGB and Max's, had begun to cater mostly to new wave audiences. The music was more palatable, accessible, and, crucially for club owners, commercially viable, appealing to the growing horde of clubgoers coming from outside of Manhattan—the derided "bridge and tunnel" crowd. One such club, Hurrah, announced that it had no real interest in experimental downtown music. When it closed its doors, the venue's manager declared to *SoHo News*—

"Let's face it, a lot of music has just become *noise*."

I decided to name the event Noise Fest.

27

OUT OF TUNE

Josh Baer's invitation for me to curate began with modest ambitions—perhaps a weekend of shows—but it soon grew into a sprawling nine-day bonanza. I basically dialed up every band and musician I knew (and some I had yet to meet), performers who I felt were creating new and interesting music, whether or not it appealed to the whims of the contemporary new wave. There were friends of Kim and mine (Ut, Y Pants, Avant Squares) and bands we simply admired (Dark Day, Mofungo, Borbetomagus). A few artists who agreed to play were well established (Glenn Branca, Rhys Chatham, Jeffrey Lohn), but most were fairly unknown on the club circuit.

The festival would become a signal event, highlighting the changing nature of downtown music, blurring boundaries between academic experimentalism, rough-hewn post-punk, free improvisation, urban-teen hardcore, and other flavors of uncategorizable noises.

Our gig during Noise Fest would be our third as Sonic Youth, and the first in which I felt some magic momentum had been achieved. The logic of Richard Edson's insistence that we lock in tighter to his minimal grooves became immediately apparent. The ability for us to hear one another onstage, with reasonable balance, allowed our songs to maintain a clear sense of purpose. The audience responded with genuine enthusiasm, encouraging us with their applause and praise.

Headlining our night was Rhys Chatham's ensemble, one of the most remarkable groups on the scene. Rhys's pedigree and legacy were illustrious. He was a native Manhattanite who had, barely out of his teens, apprenticed as a member of La Monte Young and Marian Zazeela's Dream Syndicate ensemble, in which drone music mysticism was married to sonic minimalism.

He would help found the Kitchen, in the actual kitchen area of the Mercer Arts Center, a complex of studios and stalls where boutiques and sundry retail opportunities existed by day, and underground theater and music filled the nights (most infamously the series of concert-parties the New York Dolls presented there in the Oscar Wilde Room, with mind-bending performances from Suicide directly across the hall).

The Kitchen, in 1974, would relocate to the corner of Wooster and Broome Streets in SoHo, only days before the building that housed the Mercer Arts Center surprisingly collapsed into a mountain of rubble.

Rhys, as the Kitchen's music director, would book every progressive "new music" practitioner he crossed paths with—Laurie Spiegel, Éliane Radigue, Jon Gibson, Tony Conrad—as well as present his own work as a composer and flautist.

I first met Rhys sometime in 1980, when Kim and I had first begun our courtship, back when we passed hours upon hours walking through the streets of Lower Manhattan, holding hands, finding each other, young and open to the possibilities of the universe. Rhys was coming out of his building on MacDougal Street. Kim introduced me to him as her boyfriend, to my pleasant surprise. I was struck by the way he carried himself—his enthusiasm and soft-spoken inflections, and how they countered so much of the gruffness you were typically barraged with among the competing noises of the street.

I had attended a retrospective concert of Rhys's electric guitar music at the Kitchen earlier that spring. There, in contrast to his gentle nature, he was every bit the stern-faced and serious musician, his visage seemingly transformed by the raging guitar action filling the space. Each piece he performed involved a changing lineup of musicians, almost every person playing electric guitar (other than the mainstay David Linton on drums, whose high-energy concepts and hard-hitting propulsion defined much of the music's sound).

I was sitting next to Lee Ranaldo at this Kitchen event, and we laughed as soon as the piece entitled "The Out of Tune Guitar" began. With three guitarists tuned to their own "detuning," it was an audacious piece of music from the very first massed double strum of the electric guitars blowing out of each amp. We couldn't help but feel giddy. I could tell that Lee and I both were very much on board with what was happening before us, knowing how cool and special it was.

We had yet to formally play together, but I had a sense, which I think Lee shared, that it could be amazing to someday connect, to create a killer, cutting-edge group together. The idea lay there unarticulated, waiting for the right moment.

〜

Lee and David Linton performed at Noise Fest as a duo named Avoidance Behavior, in which each took a turn playing his instrument while the other recorded and looped it through the front-of-house PA system. Their output was so incredibly loud and abrasive that it forced the audience (at least those who hadn't already escaped to the safety of the street) to sit with their fingers jammed in their ears. As they permeated the air with their sonic destruction, a local resident appeared at the door of the gallery, a look of shell shock on her face. I approached her to see if she was okay, and she yelled at me in disbelief and horror—

"What is this?! I live on the next block, and I thought there was an accident outside! What in God's name is going on?!"

She was shuddering, tears welling in her eyes.

I explained to the woman, dressed in a robe and house slippers, that we were having an experimental music festival. She shook her head, pointing to the people with their ears plugged as Lee and David nonchalantly emitted more and more screeching frequencies, and said—

"They're going to die. They shouldn't be in there listening to that!! What the hell is this?!"

—before ambling home, clearly disturbed by what she'd seen and heard.

Rudolph Grey presented a trio set on the Saturday of the festival (the night centered around Glenn Branca's ensemble performance) with saxophonist Arthur Doyle and drummer Beaver Harris. They were the only Black musicians involved in the series—for all its claims to inclusivity, the no wave scene was still overwhelmingly white—and they delivered a cry of noise unlike much of what was heard during the week. Other than my transformative experience upon hearing the Human Arts Ensemble at A's a couple of years back, I had yet to be exposed much to the profound, expressive magic of jazz.

To stand and watch Arthur Doyle play in the summer of 1981, his legs splayed wide, his body bending toward the floor, his saxophone dropped between his ankles, then up and back over his head, spraying loose a galaxy of colors and spirited abstraction, was to recognize the shared concepts at play between free jazz and the musical language spoken across the downtown experimental music map.

〜

I swung by the *New York Rocker* office at one point to drop off a Noise Fest flyer and to see if we could get someone there to review the event. The editor Andy Schwartz enlisted the photographer Marcia Resnick to take a photo of all the participants, so I put the word out for musicians to gather one early morning outside the gallery. Most gigs in New York City began at ten in the evening and sometimes not until midnight, so going out to a club, it was always assumed that you might not return to your apartment until past three in the morning—just as street sweepers and garbage trucks began doing their business.

Most everyone showed up for the shoot. The looks on their faces were a mix of half smiles and wonder at seeing one another in the unforgiving daylight.

Of all the editors at the free weekly papers, it was Merle Ginsberg, who oversaw calendar listings at the *SoHo News,* who shared the most enthusiasm for what was happening at Noise Fest. Fascinated by the diverse temperaments that were to be on display, she queried me about everything we planned on presenting. Merle gave us a glowing notice, including a photograph of a cute, almost-smiling Glenn, published for its downtown allure.

Barbara Moore, a Fluxus art book and ephemera dealer, had dropped by White Columns one day with two teenage girls: her daughter, Robin, and pal Jill Cunniff—the duo coeditors of a new fanzine called *Decline of Art.* Robin and Jill mentioned they were friends with the Young & the Useless as well as the Young Aborigines, both new punk bands coming straight out of Manhattan. I was curious to have at least one of them play Noise Fest. I located a phone number for Michael Diamond, the singer of Young Aborigines, in hopes they'd perform.

Kate Schellenbach, the drummer for the band (as well as for her and Diamond's new offshoot parody band, Beastie Boys), was part of the same gang as the *Decline of Art* girls. She had her own fanzine, *Cheap Garbage for Snotty Teens.* Kate's coeditor and best friend from Stuyvesant High School was a young lad a grade higher than her named Larry Chua, by most accounts the most radical kid in their clique. Michael Diamond never returned my call, but this kid Larry located me at White Columns one afternoon, handing me a copy of *his* fanzine, *Tribal Noize.* He offered his band, the Primitives, to perform.

Larry looked amazing, with a severely coiffed mohawk, punk and anarchy badges stuck all about his shirt. He seemed no older than fifteen, and I immediately promised him a slot.

I had yet to investigate the local teenage bands then popping up: Heart Attack, the Mob, Urban Waste, Nihilistics. I had seen their names on flyers and in fanzines, but I felt slightly conflicted about them. These new bands were continuing the legacy of 1970s punk rock—not only the Sex Pistols and the Clash, but more subterranean working-class groups like U.K. Subs and Discharge. They seemed out of step with the post-punk experimentation we thought we were furthering with Sonic Youth.

The prevailing attitude among those my generation and older was that punk had died with Sid Vicious. But, for better or worse, that simply was not the case—certainly not for these young upstarts.

The Primitives arrived, all pretty much the same age as Larry, and proceeded to perform a set so completely bare bones that it was almost perverse in its simplicity as well as its earnestness. One song was basically the guitarist and bassist moving from one fret to the next in a 1-2-3-4 pattern and then back again, while Larry (who, in years to come, would find renown as a socially conscious architecture scholar) sang a nursery rhyme about anarchy. It was the only concert during the fest that brought in teen punkers; the gallery had been mostly occupied by self-serious artists, art rockers, and no wave aesthetes.

I would see this particular gang of Manhattan punk kids, a few of whom were children of art-world parents, bombing around the neighborhoods below Fourteenth Street, free and loud, sneaking into all the music clubs. At twenty-three, I had begun to feel caught between these teen roustabouts and the seen-it-all late twenty- and early thirty–somethings I had been bounding around with. For the first time, I no longer felt like the youngest person in the room.

Shortly before Noise Fest began, I received a phone call at our apartment. Having a telephone was new to me at this point, and it was with an incredible jolt that I heard on the other end of the line my rock writer hero Lester Bangs, inquiring about the event for a proposed preview in the *Village Voice*.

"Hey, it's Lester Bangs. Are you the Noise Fest guy?"

"Yeah, that's me"

—I sputtered.

"Well, if what you're doing has anything to do with noise, then I am extremely interested—*noise is my meat.*"

I gave Lester a rundown of the bands, explaining that many of us had felt ostracized by the new wave gatekeepers in town. He sounded enthused, replying that he would try to come down and check it out.

Before he hung up, I offered him a spot on the last night to make whatever "noise" he felt like playing.

With a surprised laugh he accepted the offer. I told him that we would bill him as the Lester Bangs Explosion.

Again he laughed, saying—

"Okay, I gotta go. I'm at a phone booth and I'm out of coins."

Much like me until only recently, Lester didn't have a phone at his apartment, so he had to use the pay phone on the corner of his street to call anyone or conduct interviews. The greatest music writer of my generation, here in New York City, unable to afford his own telephone.

Each night of Noise Fest I would spray-paint the billed bands' names on large pieces of plywood that had been lying among the detritus on Broome Street. I leaned them against the gallery entrance for all to see. On the final night I added the Lester Bangs Explosion to the roster, only hoping the writer would actually appear.

Lester, alas, was a no-show for his purported set. At night's end, we proceeded to lock up the gallery, our gang planning to head east to the Spring Lounge for a celebratory quaff or two. A half block away from White Columns I noticed Lester, jaunty and somewhat swervy, speeding toward the gallery.

"Hey, Lester, it's me, Thurston! We were waiting for you!"

"Ah, nuts!"

—he said.

"I was stuck at this stupid-ass music biz event."

I was just overjoyed to realize Lester had at least tried to make the gig. I imagine he had planned on reading something. Maybe he would have picked up a guitar and played some free noise action? I would never know.

Under his arm Lester held an LP, and he was visibly thrilled to possess it—

"The best thing that happened tonight is I was given the new DNA record. They're the greatest band in the universe right now. This is the real deal!"

I asked Lester if he wanted to join us for a drink, but he said he was eager to go home and listen to the album—and off he went.

I would never cross paths with him again, as he would escape the planet the following April at the age of thirty-three, having downed too much cough syrup mixed with Benzedrine and other gunk. Lester's passing affected the world of music criticism as much as any musician's demise would have. Fanzines became only more prevalent, coming to replace mainstream journalism as the energetic voice of the musical underground. Most of their writers, consciously or not, were informed by and indebted to Lester Bangs and his celebratory, reactionary, rowdy, erudite, gonzo generation of fellow scribes.

I was glad to present the Primitives at Noise Fest as representatives of the new hardcore scene coming of age around Lower Manhattan. I would become more and more curious about the sound of all these teen screamers, their political energy close to my heart and sensibilities. It was a feeling I didn't always share with the community of artists and musicians I prowled around with in 1981. I admired my cool and educated art-rock pals, but the raw power and essential profundity of punk would never fully subside from my bloodstream.

The New York City hardcore scene—more so than the similarly celebrated scenes in Detroit, Los Angeles, San Francisco, and Washington, D.C.—represented itself with a kind of thuggishness. Many of the New York–area hardcore bands originated from the so-called outer boroughs of Brooklyn and Queens, as well as from Long Island, and they seemingly had no time for the poetic explorations of Television, Talking Heads, or Patti Smith, let alone the art-rock no wave of Manhattan-based bands such as our developing outfit.

The music of these more bullyish bands could be astonishing, though I generally connected with the more intellectual, thoughtful wing of hardcore, particularly the Washington, D.C., contingent around the Dischord Records label.

I had yet to hear or see Bad Brains, the most celebrated of the bunch, though I noticed they had played a few gigs a year prior at the Botany Talk House and Tier 3, around the same time as had the Coachmen. I heard rave reports about them: how they had recently relocated from Washington, D.C., and how high-energy they were. I knew I had to catch these guys.

One afternoon I noticed a band of young, cool Black guys wheatpasting a CBGB gig flyer on a lamppost on the Bowery. I walked over to them—

"Hey, are you guys the Bad Brains?"

They smiled, happy at the recognition.

"I heard your band is amazing!"

—I gushed.

To walk into a CBGB matinee and see Bad Brains was to share a room with one of the greatest bands in the history of rock 'n' roll beyond any doubt. They whipped and flailed through furious rhythm changes, offering punk noise and speed-demon thrash, zooming through a half dozen songs, then dropping into a skanking reggae groove, catching their breath, allowing the spirit to settle a bit and for all to wipe their brows, then off to the skies again with a jet-fueled wildcat wail. The singer, H.R., backflipped and kicked midair splits, just buzzing the hell out of the club, the hardcore kids going ballistic—slamming, stage-diving, howling along to their heroes. It was a righteous celebration of hypersonic beauty, a setting in which the pressures of race, family, school, and environment all blew through the rooftop.

The success of Noise Fest, and our performance there, was disturbed by an unignorable reality: Anne DeMarinis and Richard Edson had made it known prior to the event that they would soon be leaving Sonic Youth, each for their own reasons. It was an upsetting development, coming just when it seemed to me that Sonic Youth was beginning to capture people's attention. Anne had been integral to our musical development; her presence had a glow that I knew I would miss. And in just a short time, Richard had shown us what our band could do with focused and inventive rhythmic concepts.

It created a bit of a mystery, for Kim and me, as to how to proceed. But so many promising musicians would come in and out of White Columns over the course of nine days. Could someone in this creative hotbed be solicited?

While watching Lee Ranaldo play with Branca's ensemble at the festival, Kim, reading my mind, sidled up to me and said—

"We should ask Lee if he wants to play with us."

I had been thinking the very same thing. I asked him later on, and he immediately said yes, fulfilling my sense, when we had watched Rhys play not so long before at his Kitchen retrospective, that there was a magical musical meeting waiting on both of our horizons.

28

THE ELECTRIC DREAD

Public Image Ltd, in May 1981, set up shop in New York City. Their idea was not to perform gigs like any other rock 'n' roll group, but to make recordings, books, and films—to be a "company" of sorts, a *brand* as opposed to a *band*.

Less than a year earlier John Lydon and PiL guitarist Keith Levene had appeared on the program *Tomorrow,* a late-night network talk show with an engaging, funny, take-no-guff interlocutor named Tom Snyder. Lydon and Levene attempted to state their case of being an "anti-band" to Snyder, only to become argumentative when he didn't take the bait.

The band had already shaken up the North American airwaves earlier that year by lip-synching on the weekly music show and institution *American Bandstand,* Lydon making no pretense of going along with the pretense, walking among and dancing around the live TV audience, revealing PiL's music to be nothing but a canned recording.

On the *Tomorrow* show, Snyder was surprised, even astounded, at how rude and aggressive Lydon could be. At one point he admonished the punk lord, only for Lydon to accuse the host of having a "tantrum." Lydon and Levene kept getting out of their chairs to lean across the table and cadge cigarettes from Snyder's pack.

The episode was explosive for us, energizing the entire scene in its defiance of the mainstream.

The Ritz nightclub on East Eleventh Street had a cancellation by the London band Bow Wow Wow (who were managed by ex–Sex Pistols manager Malcolm McLaren, whom Lydon was then suing). Lydon and Levene accepted an offer for their new anti-band to play the gig instead, but only if they could perform behind the Ritz's monolithic video screen, touted as the largest in the world. Rolled down, it filled the entire stage.

They had the idea to illuminate the screen and stage from behind with high-intensity PAR can lights, creating monstrous silhouettes, while Super 8 film footage of the group bopping around Manhattan was shown.

The queue outside the Ritz that night was brutal as rain began crashing down, the club refusing to let people in until PiL's unorthodox stage setup was in place. After finally gaining entry, there was an interminable wait for the show to start, the place absolutely jammed.

Eventually some hapless opening act appeared. They were immediately shouted down and booed off the stage (not unlike the opening band for Sid Vicious at Max's three years prior). The audience was there for one thing only: to see Johnny Rotten's latest creation. As it was, there had been no real sound check, and Johnny arrived late, delaying the concert. The audience, by this time, was baying for blood.

Before too long the silhouettes of Lydon, Levene, and their bandmates rose high on the screen, inciting cheers from the audience. The opening salvos of the band's just released album, *The Flowers of Romance,* with Lydon yodeling an unholy atonal yowl, blasted through the PA.

A live feed of the group behind the screen would intermittently cut into the preshot Super 8 footage. Each time an actual image of Lydon or Levene would appear, the crowd would lift its voice in approval, but the effect soon became redundant and annoying.

Bottles began to be hurled as chants of—

"Lift the screen! Lift the screen!"

—filled the room.

People at the front of the room began tugging at a large white tarp that had been placed on the stage, the group's equipment set up on it, the tarp's edge poking out from beneath the screen. As more of the audience began to forcibly pull at it, the band's gear began to move. The drums went askew, confusing and unnerving Sam Ulano, their hired drummer, an aging and respected jazz musician who had recorded with the iconoclastic composer Moondog, and who the band had met by chance in some uptown bar.

Keith Levene ran in front of the screen, waving his arms at the audience to stop the madness, but it was entirely ineffectual as bottles whizzed past his head, nearly braining him. Stagehands ran out to rescue Keith as a pretaped image of Lydon appeared on the screen, warbling and strumming tunelessly on an acoustic guitar, singing a piss take on an old folkie tune—

I've got a hole in my heart

Levene proceeded to put on a recording of *The Flowers of Romance*. He played some kind of feedback guitar with it, which sounded excellent to me—though my appreciation for it may have been in the minority. More chants of—

"Lift the screen!"

—came, mixed with yelling and laughter, bottles lobbed endlessly toward the stage. Lydon again appeared on the screen, this time singing an actual live and in-person version of the same song—

I've got a ho-o-ole in my heart

The audience lost it.

This was not a concert; it was an insane asylum.

With the pulling of the tarp having fully dismantled the band's gear, Lydon's silhouette loomed across the screen as a giant demon, haranguing into his microphone a singsong tease—

"Silly fucking audience, silly fucking audience!"

It was the final straw.

Bottles now rained over the room and onto the stage, splattering, smashing, and staining the screen, the crazed audience grabbing at it, attempting to tear the offending obstruction down. The pride and joy of the Ritz, its world-famous video screen, hung precariously from its moorings.

In an instant all the houselights flared up, a Wizard of Oz voice booming from the PA—

"THE SHOW IS OVER!! EVERYONE LEAVE!! NOW!!"

Furious security guards began to forcibly push the audience out of the room. No one really fought back; everyone was simply too bewildered, too giddy even, at how messed up and chaotic this gig had become. There were laughs and a few shouts of—

"I want my money back!"

Out on the rain-washed street swarmed seemingly the entire downtown New York City scene, along with people from New Jersey, Long Island, Connecticut, Staten Island, Brooklyn, Queens, and the Bronx, wondering what to do after this epic post-punk disruption—and what could possibly be next.

There had to be a next.

29

FORMING

Glenn had been working toward expanding the lineup of his electric guitar ensemble to further extremes, eventually composing "Symphony No. 1 (Tonal Plexus)." It was the first time, after years of watching and studying Glenn, that I would become involved with his work myself; he finally hired me.

The piece was to be presented at the Performing Garage, an independent black box of a theater on Wooster Street in SoHo, for two nights in July 1981. Glenn had prepared idiosyncratic scores for each musician. In our first rehearsals, he led the ensemble methodically through the piece's four movements. But as we began to play and formulate the music, it soon became apparent that the audiences for the concerts were going to be subjected to a sonic firestorm outside of any listener's expectation.

Each night's concert was packed solid. In the first movement, the unfolding musical exploration, the singular chording of the electric guitars, began to open up a collective sense of awe. Even from just those first sounds, the feeling that I was a part of something magical was thrillingly apparent. The piece grew relentlessly, from our signature double strums into a series of slashing strokes. The cumulative sound grew exponentially, driven by percussion, to a point of repetition, then expanded further into another level of volume and intensity. Audience members began to visibly clamp their hands over their ears until a deceptive, hushed conclusion was reached—only for the music to roar back into its ferocious finale.

Glenn had been experimenting with constructing his own instruments, stringing constructions of wood with steel wire and adhering pickups beneath the strings, so as to create more industrial-sounding tools. The second movement had a few of us striking harmonics from our electric guitars, while others clanged heavy and harsh metallic beats on these contraptions, creating a contrapuntal no wave march.

For the final movement, I had been asked to employ one of Glenn's preferred percussions, slamming a two-by-four against the bottom end of a large oil barrel that sat upon its side—aimed squarely at the audience. After my first salvo, the people sitting in front of me jolted up, scurrying off before my next strike could land.

Later that month Kim, Lee, and I sat together in White Columns after business hours with three unamplified guitars. Sonic Youth had been invited to participate in an event at an art space named Just Above Midtown/Downtown, on Franklin Street in TriBeCa, and it was time to rehearse. Kim and I showed Lee the tunes we had, including "Cosmopolitan Girl" and "Teenage Men."

After a couple of other get-togethers, on July 24, 1981 (one night before I turned twenty-three), we made our way, with a few small amplifiers we were able to collect, to Just Above Midtown/Downtown. We presented our set in the corner of the gallery, as people moved about the space checking out the show on exhibit. We played for no more than twenty minutes to a smattering of attention and some curious, bemused looks. This was Lee's first live experience with us as Sonic Youth, and it felt cool, Lee's interaction with Kim and me ringing fresh and open.

Kim and I flew to Los Angeles later that summer to spend time with her family. When I tuned in to *Rodney on the ROQ* on Los Angeles's KROQ radio station, I heard song after song of new California punk, which tore through my brain. Rodney Bingenheimer spun the track "Caught in My Eye," by the Germs, and I sat stunned at the relentless, soul-burning masterpiece of ravaged punk rock.

To my fortune, the Gordons' house in west L.A. was within walking distance of Rhino Records on Westwood Boulevard, a gold mine of new and secondhand records overseen by a staff deeply engaged in collecting. Though I had no idea who was working there when I first traipsed in, I would, in the coming years, become compadres with a few of these deep-cut obsessives, particularly the music writer Byron Coley and the experimental guitarist Nels Cline.

I could afford only a couple of records, so I picked up the Circle Jerks' *Group Sex* and Black Flag's *Jealous Again*. These were enough to completely light a fireball in my head. The cover of *Jealous Again* was an illustration by the artist Raymond Pettibon, brother of Black Flag guitarist

Greg Ginn, depicting two high school cheerleaders having what appeared to be a hair-pulling fight, with toy guns drawn; the back cover showed a high school jock with a gash in his head alongside a cheerleader holding a pistol and demanding—

"Before you die . . . tell me that you'll always love me."

Totally strange in the context of most punk imagery, and yet riveting.

Before heading back to New York City, I returned to Rhino, spending what little money I had left on the Gun Club's *Fire of Love,* having fallen in love with their song "Sex Beat" upon hearing it on Rodney's show. Rhino also carried such fanzines as *Flipside, Negative Army, Damage, Ripper,* and *We Got Power* and a few stapled black-and-white xeroxed art books by Pettibon himself.

By taking this aesthetic and sound to heart, and mixing it with the experimentalism of Lower Manhattan, I felt there was the makings of something explosive. I was ready and anxious to return home, to reconnect and supercharge Sonic Youth with what I'd found in California, infusing the no wave art-rock scene with the sun-drenched hardcore I'd discovered, buzzing toward a psycho-sonic dream I could barely glimpse.

30

PINCH

Sonic Youth and Y Pants (a trio of Barbara Ess, Virge Piersol, and Gail Vachon playing mostly toy-sized instruments) were booked to play at the New Pilgrim Theater on East Third Street between Avenues B and C. The theater stood shoulder to shoulder with the Nuyorican Poets Cafe and a Latin Pentecostal church. In the 1960s, it had been home to the legendary Slugs' nightclub, where Albert Ayler, Sun Ra, and Cecil Taylor had delivered free jazz to New York City.

This region of the Lower East Side was in a state of disrepair and depression in 1981. There were aging, if not crumbling, tenement buildings and ancient, dented garbage cans, trash spilling over onto the sidewalk and into the gutters. Fire hydrants had their caps unscrewed, their spouts dribbling, after having been liberated by someone in the neighborhood with an industrial-sized wrench to unleash gushing fountains of water for the neighborhood kids to cool off and dance around in. Lots would sometimes be filled with the rubble of collapsed or burned buildings, dilapidated chain-link fences ineffectively keeping people off the detonated real estate. Broken washing machines and upended rusting hulks of cars might be dumped haphazardly amid the debris, havens for skittering gangs of rats.

Like our Eldridge Street home, very few buildings had buzzer systems for their front doors. Visitors would yell their arrival, the sounds of—

"Yo, Vinnyyyy!"

"Yo, Julieeeee!"

"Yo, Johnnneee boyy!!"

—echoing throughout the day and night.

Drug dealing and street crime were constant occurrences. The only safe way to traverse the neighborhood was in numbers.

Lee, Kim, and I had been working up new material, which was enriched by the extended plays of guitar action the three of us had been falling into since Lee entered the picture. We constructed new tunes, and it was obvious that our sound was becoming heavier, more indebted to the wooziness of Mars and DNA, with a focus on alternate-tuned guitars, inspired by Glenn and Rhys.

I rang up Richard Edson to see if he would be interested in playing with us again, thinking he might be intrigued by our progression. We met, once again, in his basement studio, and he immediately responded to the advances we had made, as well as the change that Lee had brought to our sound. As Richard had done previously, he offered us helpful commentary, urging us to define sections in our song ideas for the sake of rhythmic and compositional clarity. He agreed to play with us again.

Lee and I headed over to New Pilgrim two nights before our gig to get the lay of the land and check out the Athens, Georgia, band R.E.M. after hearing their single "Radio Free Europe" earlier in the summer, digging its ringing guitar pop. Only their third gig in the city, R.E.M. played until the PA system fell apart, but they were obviously up to something interesting, particularly the singer Michael Stipe, who shook and danced and writhed his body before the microphone, his curly brown locks flopping into his face.

On the night we played, the audience was sparse, though no more so than when R.E.M. played. We presented our new material, our three guitars melding, chasing, and spiraling into one another. Dan Graham recorded the gig on what was then a rather state-of-the-art portable cassette machine, and he was able to capture the earliest moment of us finding our sound with Lee—more slicing, jarring, and intense than we had ever achieved before.

Excited by the music he heard us playing at this gig, Glenn thought we would be the perfect debut for the record label he was starting with financial assistance from Josh Baer at White Columns. He had brought back a huge Swiss flag from his last European tour, with its exact-proportioned white cross set on a red field. He and Barbara had it hanging inside their apartment. While considering the flag with its icon of neutrality, he decided that Neutral would be an ideal name for the record label he had long dreamed of curating.

Glenn arrived at our Eldridge Street apartment clutching four cheap pawn-shop guitars, two under each arm, no cases, announcing—

"Here, you guys can use these."

We had talked about how it was difficult to experiment with different tunings, as we had only a couple of guitars between us, and the constant tuning and retuning put a drag on our playing. Glenn had come to our rescue. A few of the guitars had their rounded heads shaved to spears, something he liked to do to lend a bit of a savage threat to his stage presence.

Rap was beaming down from the South Bronx into Brooklyn, Queens, and Manhattan with ever greater frequency and volume. By the summer of 1981, it wasn't unusual to find a drummer set up on the sidewalk, playing an insistent breakbeat with two or three kids spinning, popping, and break-dancing on split-open cardboard boxes laid out flat on the hot concrete.

Blondie had released "Rapture," the group's love song to rap, at the beginning of the year, Debbie Harry name-checking the hip-hop pioneer Fab 5 Freddy, who would appear, along with Jean-Michel Basquiat, in the group's video for the tune. As this was some months before the advent of MTV, the clip was primarily shown on the TV show *Solid Gold*, which, despite the corny choreography to pop hits, we would all watch with guilty pleasure.

The *Village Voice* had begun slowly acknowledging rap, along with graffiti art and break-dance culture. The photographer Henry Chalfant, who had been documenting the intricate, multicolored graffiti adorning the city and its subway cars, had connected with Fab 5 Freddy and fellow artist Rammellzee, attempting to showcase what they had termed "Graffiti Rock" at a SoHo performance space named Common Ground. The idea was to exhibit Henry's photos of subway-car art alongside break-dance performances from the Rock Steady Crew from the Bronx. But because of territorial issues between a pair of competing break-dance outfits, the event was quickly canceled.

The Kitchen, in early October 1981, decided to present a similar show. I received a call from a staff member there asking if I would be interested in making a little bit of money acting as "security" for this event.

"Why?"

—I asked.

With some nervousness, the Kitchen employee explained that they were concerned after the skirmishes around the Common Ground nonevent—worried about knives, guns, fists, bloodshed. I wasn't sure why I seemed capable to them of warding off a violent street fight, but I did need the coin.

Other than catching break dancing on the streets and hearing some rap music blaring from boom boxes, I had little experience with live hip-hop. It would be a year or two before I became a rapacious collector, buying every rap and hip-hop side available, so in love with the music that I would encourage Sonic Youth to experiment with sampling beats.

But in 1981, I was simply broke and curious.

When I entered the Kitchen that autumn evening to take on this so-called security job, my preconceptions were blown out the roof. I was instructed to stand by the greenroom door and admit only members of Rock Steady Crew and the Swift Kids, Fab 5 Freddy, and DJ Spy.

I proved immediately, and humiliatingly, ineffectual at my job.

The greenroom filled up with the dance crews, and I was struck by their confidence and bravado, pouring as it did from mostly teenagers. The groups were loud and laughing, big smiles, eyes alight with a sense of purpose, ambition, and joy. I quickly realized there was no way anyone approaching this doorway, which I was supposedly "guarding," was going to acknowledge my existence. The graffiti artist Min One, who looked all of fifteen, approached at one point. I attempted to stop him, my skinny arm barring entrance. He yelled past me—

"Yo, Freeze, let me in!"

Freeze shot back—

"It's cool, it's cool, let 'im in!"

The idea was to stop any would-be antagonists, but nobody like that made their presence known. One kid bustled assertively up to the door, and I clasped his arm—

"You can't go in there. It's only for the performers."

Without looking at me, in a voice that suggested there would be no second warning, he muttered—

"Get your hands off me."

I was standing there wearing my old-man's coat, cheap straight-legged trousers, and a pair of beat-up low-top Keds. It was as clear to me as to anyone: if there was going to be an altercation this evening, it would most likely be not from any rival sets but because of my embarrassing attempts to control the passage of these crews.

The evening's event jumped off at full speed, with Fab 5 Freddy and DJ Spy trading off on the microphone, introducing the dancers, freestyle rapping, and playing breakbeats cranked up at high volume, scratching and improvising over the records. The Kitchen was packed, many people sitting in chairs around the squared-off dance area, others standing, jammed in around the sidelines.

Keith Haring and Jean-Michel Basquiat sat next to each other, wide-eyed at the battling crews taking their turns—in solos and duos—"rocking" through similar B-boy dance opening motifs, then each breaker expressing his singular style, for no more than thirty seconds to a minute at a time. It was loud and fun, the dancers' kinetic joy delivering us to a place of brilliance and ecstasy.

I strode home afterward intoxicated, the zapping phrases and beats buzzing in my head. I would try to describe the experience to my friends and family, but, like so many epiphanies with music and art, words could only fall short.

With Glenn's invitation to release a record by Sonic Youth, we decided to lay down what we had been working on—particularly as he had secured some money for the purpose. We decided to go to Noise New York in midtown, as Lee had recorded there before.

Noise New York had welcomed the downtown avant-garde music scene since the studio's inception in late 1979. Its proprietor, Frank Eaton, had the idea of creating an affordable rehearsal studio, with an ear toward recording as well. He quickly found an appreciative clientele among the outliers on the local music scene, particularly those with scant funds.

Lee, Kim, Richard, and I arrived at Noise New York and ran through our tunes with a young engineer on duty. Small portable walls of baffles were situated between the equipment so as to control the leakage from one microphone to another. It meant that we could play together but only by hearing—not exactly *feeling*—one another.

We all had some concept of how to play while wearing headphones, but it was still a learning experience. I quickly learned to pull a headphone cup partly off one ear to permit a bit of organic room noise into my brain and bones. Our songs were all about the melding of guitars into a uni-fied voice, and whatever the ineffable stuff was that made that work, it was diffused by the cold process of the studio. Noise New York had been outfitted with a sixteen-track board along with a one-inch tape machine, both entirely functional. But it was only as good as our performance.

Listening back to the recordings, we heard stiffness where we had thought—or at least hoped—would be magic. The purity of our creative union was somehow corrupted by proper recording technique. We walked away with our cassettes of the session realizing we needed a way to bridge the divide between our live and our studio performances. It would turn out to be a continual challenge in the decades ahead, its rewards mixed with frustration.

Lee, Kim, and I played as a trio soon after at Stilwende, where Tier 3 had sat less than a year prior. The spot had been refurbished to the point that it was unrecognizable from its earlier incarnation—a bit more scrubbed up, as befitted the changing nature of the neighborhood, which was beginning to attract higher rents. The performance area had been relocated upstairs, a bit of a jazz bar/dinner theater setting. From what I could gather, the murals that Jean-Michel Basquiat and Kiki Smith had created downstairs had been painted over.

Our recordings may have fallen flat, but Lee, Kim, and I had come to feel like we could do anything with our music, drummer or no drummer. The affordability of contact microphones—purchased at the electronics stores running along Canal Street, with their chaotic bins of overflowing detritus—allowed us to create amplified percussion sounds by attaching the mics to various cymbals and, Lee's genius idea, an electric drill.

"The Burning Spear," one of the first tunes the three of us composed together, became our centerpiece, due largely to Lee's eschewing the guitar in favor of the drill and also of banging long, cylindrical chimes we had found abandoned on the street one day.

By jamming a drumstick under the strings of my Harmony electric at the twelfth fret, I was able to create two playing fields on the instrument. Strumming and plucking the strings on one side of the stick produced a different-timbred sound from the other. By rubbing another drumstick against the one lodged beneath the strings, a droning, ringing sound could be made. Add enough volume, and harmonics would occur. Tapping and hitting with shifting levels of intensity created a quality of ringing electric bells.

All three of us had been getting into this soundworld during the few rehearsals we so far had had: Lee sometimes stuck a screwdriver beneath his guitar strings, and Kim achieved slide effects with bottles and drumsticks.

The lyrics I wrote—

> *I'm not afraid to say I'm scared*
> *In my bed I'm deep in prayer*
> *I trust the speed, I love the fear*

The music comes
The burning spear

—were inspired by the spirit talk heard in reggae music, as well as my religious gleanings.

I had spun a couple of Black Uhuru recordings for Kim, so she could play the bass along with them. I figured those economical lines were all the tutorial a person could need to realize the soul of the instrument. Kim soon grasped them with her own personal touch.

The three of us would rotate from the guitar to the bass on different songs, a practice that allowed dynamic changes within our set. Lee had been playing guitar since he was a wee pup and he knew his way around the fretboard, far more so than me. Kim had begun playing the guitar only a couple of years before connecting with Miranda. But there was never a judgmental sense among us that one person's expertise was somehow "better" than another's.

For "The Burning Spear," as performed at Stilwende, I attached a contact mic to a crash cymbal, the only drum piece other than a snare that we had brought along. While playing the drumstick-prepared guitar with one hand, I used the other to intermittently smash out a punctuational rhythm on the cymbal and snare, growing progressively more insistent. Kim laid down the six-note, dub-centric bass line, while Lee cranked up the electric drill. I leaped at the microphone, falling into the people standing around us, yowling the lyrics to the song, purposefully creating a bit of physical interplay with the unsuspecting onlookers.

It was the first night that we truly clicked.

By the second week of December, when Glenn booked Sonic Youth a new recording session—this time at Radio City—we were far more greased and ready to roll than our earlier attempt at Noise New York.

We had been practicing at various spaces, such as U232 on lower Broadway and 240 Grand Street between Bowery and Chrystie Street. Other times we would rent a room at the Music Building on Eighth Avenue and Thirty-Ninth Street, a sprawling warren of various-sized studios. Walking through the halls of the Music Building was to be surrounded by the clashing sounds of bands playing each and every sort of music, creating a clamor as noisy as the honking, screeching, rumbling city outside. Television, Patti Smith, and Talking Heads had all spent hours rehearsing there, along with hundreds of other groups, some camping out in the rooms at night, tossing sleeping bags down onto the floor, then making themselves scarce as bands began blasting through the day. Madonna, barely three weeks younger than me, had famously resorted to crashing there.

At Radio City that late fall, we recorded all the material for our first record in one day, laying down vocals the following day. The evening after we completed the session, we attended a release party for Barbara and Glenn's collaborative LP *Just Another Asshole*, an anthology of artists and musicians presenting short audio pieces, held at White Columns.

Just Another Asshole offered a cavalcade of diverse utterances, tunes, voices, and noises coming from small apartments and studios all over the post–no wave New York scene. Lee delivered a guitar piece entitled "Shift." Kim offered "Working Youth," a guitar and bass duo with Miranda. The title was an extension of *Men at Work,* an artwork in which Kim had overlain that particular phrase upon a black-and-white photo of guitarists in Glenn's ensemble at "work," with their serious visages, the dot matrix of the image blown out and grainy, lending it an evocative depth.

With Lee's assistance, utilizing a reel-to-reel tape deck he had been making tape-noise experiments with, I put together "The Fucking Youth of Today"—a piece in which I asked Kim to speak a bit of snatched conversation, whereupon I would tickle her, causing her to laugh at the end of the phrase. I hoped the line would sound as if it were lifted from a film. The track romps into a repetitive bass and guitar riff, soon superimposed with police sirens and the recorded barking of our dog, Egan. It ends with my voice, bored and sneery, declaring—

Well, you know how I feel about scenes

These three miniatures from Lee, Kim, and me would showcase the sound and rhythmic connections linking us together, even at this very early stage of Sonic Youth.

I always thought that the first sound I would release on a record would be an amplified open low E, struck once on an electric guitar, ringing and resonant. That, to me, seemed important, a heralding of the purity of my rock 'n' roll intentions. My track on *Just Another Asshole* (the first vinyl appearance for both Kim and me) precluded such a wish: the piece began with Kim's voice.

It spoke to an internal evolution, though. The gathering energy of Sonic Youth and the growing intimacy of my relationship with Kim had subsumed my earlier ideas of what my life and my art should be; I was perfectly happy with such an exchange.

There would be no E-string stroke announcing our debut Sonic Youth release either. The band would sequence "The Burning Spear" as our lead-off track, introduced by Richard Edson's cymbal crash. Still, I felt that particular sound was just as significant—the drum, after all, was the heartbeat of music both ancient and universal.

The following day, a cool and grey Sunday, we played a three-dollar matinee at CBGB with the bands Dark Day (led by ex-DNA keyboardist Robin Crutchfield) and Don King (founded by ex-Mars musicians Connie "China" Burg and Mark Cunningham). This was our debut appearance at CBGB as Sonic Youth. With Lee fully integrated into the band, and with Richard Edson returning on drums, this was to be a key performance for us. We would be playing alongside bands we felt most descended in lineage from.

The other groups tended to be rather staid onstage, but we continued to ramp up our energy, pushing our instruments harder, becoming more intense as a unit.

Any great musical collective recognizes the intangible magic that occurs when they play together, creating original colors and dynamics, forging a group personality. Kim and I innately sensed the way we could exchange musical ideas. There was no need for discussion or analysis.

With Lee, it worked the same way. We would all fire up our amplifiers and begin effortlessly playing off one another's actions, decisions, responses, vibrations. It wasn't a matter of our technical abilities. Anne's skills had been more pronounced than Kim's and mine, but the group we formed never gelled in the same way. Kim, Lee, and I pulled from a less traditional canon, were more open to musical structures identifying themselves organically, in the moment. Lee's singing was clear, refined, and natural. Kim and I tended to unleash our voices in disregard to key; it was raw utterance that we channeled.

The three of us quickly recognized the importance of one another's contributions, the way our diverse emotional temperaments added to the music. We agreed that our creative collaboration was as exciting as any we had yet experienced. We allowed the enchantment to reveal itself to us, and us to it. There was an ineffable chemistry to it already, the kind that had always kept me entranced by groups I'd seen and loved onstage.

Not every band could claim such equal participation, even the ones I had worshipped. The Patti Smith Group was inarguably focused on Patti's supernova presence, regardless of how cool or capable her loyal guitarist

Lenny Kaye and space-boy pianist Richard Sohl were while flanking her. Blondie had their "Blondie Is a Group" campaign in the late 1970s, but while it may have assuaged the egos of the boys in the band, it would always be Debbie Harry front and center, the incomparable icon.

The original Ramones had it: Joey, Johnny, Dee Dee, and Tommy were a unit from the start. The Stooges, despite the human firestorm that was Iggy, was a solid quartet of equal measure. The New York Dolls spoke in unison what was at the center of their collective hearts: rock 'n' roll as spiritual epiphany.

The Dead Boys had it.

The Sex Pistols had it.

DNA had it.

In the 1960s, Ornette Coleman's and John Coltrane's quartets more than had it.

The Sun Ra Arkestra had it beyond the cosmos.

Sonic democracy. It was all I had ever desired. Finding Kim and Lee— and Kim and Lee finding me—I felt as great a devotion to music as I'd ever had, my heart, consciousness, and pleasure fully open and alive to its possibilities.

31

I TRUST THE SPEED,
I LOVE THE FEAR

The music was always new.

The group-mind of four people inventing, pushing and pulling against one another, deciding to create—or resist—alliances of sound, heads down, eyes surreptitiously glancing over at one another's fingers on fretboards, moving through passages that could grow into lumbering, then soaring shapes, before dropping into fractured, searching, savage spaces, energy momentarily dimming, then coming back to the world for a pause, to light a cigarette, have a sip from the sweet, cold, milky coffee procured from the bodega on the corner, before starting again.

A song would come into being, always with room for the composition to breathe, to grow, to be nurtured by the feedback it received from ears, eyes, bodies rubbing up against each other. The music would be created above and below the streets, and it was taken back out to the streets, at times piled high with snow and ice; in springtime, with breezes blowing from the Hudson to the East River, carrying scents from bakeries, hot dog vendors, car exhausts. In summertime the music would echo off the age-beaten redbrick tenement buildings, the humidity wetting every human pore; in autumn, it would touch the ears above the collar of a thrift store jacket pulled tight around the shoulders, the city at once a village.

The music, the work, the play—all of it was a gift.

1982 arrived with buckets of rain drenching New York City, the air chilled, though not enough to crystallize into white stuff. A snowfall this early in the season, even if only flurries, had the ability to conjure romance and magic. Winter rain was hardly so welcome, its icy tears dropping from ominous grey clouds in sunless skies.

We mixed our first record fairly quickly at Radio City during the first week of January, proud of and awed at the results. The next day we met with Glenn at our Eldridge Street apartment. He sat listening intently, obviously taken with it, balling his fist, punching the air as the cassette tape blasted forth our new tracks.

We asked the photographer and graphic artist Al Arthur to shoot some photos of the four of us. After developing the pics, we sat together moving the various images around on top of white pieces of paper demarking the twelve-by-twelve-inch parameters of a record jacket. We eventually arrived at the idea of using two of the group photos with no clear delineation between them, as if the band existed in duplicate or we were, maybe, at a quick glance, an octet. The "mirroring" was a nod to the work of our upstairs neighbor Dan Graham, who had been performing stage pieces with mirrors facing the audience.

Kim had chosen a typeface from a Letraset sheet. It was clean and formal, all the letters equal-sized, lending an industrial quality to the art, no undue emotional energy or typical rock 'n' roll quirkiness to it. The strangeness and unease of the two joined photos was offset by the typeface's stateliness.

I could sense Kim's creative eye at work with the cover, though Lee and I offered input. I had imagined a graphic with a bit more hard-core vitality—some noisiness to it. But I recognized the aesthetic sophistication of the design, its own edge, and I trusted Kim's touch. It looked cool.

Glenn and Josh Baer had set up an office desk in the front area of Josh's loft space on Lafayette Street. They had a telephone, a lined yellow pad, and a ballpoint pen. They asked me to come by to see if I had any interest in being Neutral Records' first employee.

They must have figured that, having curated Noise Fest, I had some semblance of the skill set needed to run Neutral's day-to-day business. It was all very straightforward, Glenn told me. I had to simply phone up record stores and distributors around the country to see if they would be interested in carrying our products, which, initially, were Sonic Youth's self-titled mini-LP, records from Y Pants, Jules Baptiste's *Red Decade*, and a soundtrack album to the no wave auteurs Beth B and Scott B's film *Vortex*, starring Lydia Lunch.

Agreeing to their offer, I began to arrive at the Neutral "office" each day. I rang up record stores first in Manhattan, then in other U.S. cities, having received a list of them from New Music Distribution Service, which was situated close by in a building over on Broadway. NMDS had been working with artist-run labels since its founding in 1972 by the avant-garde jazz composers Carla Bley and Michael Mantler. The service was a godsend to the experimental music community in the twenty-plus years it existed.

The fact that Neutral was the new artist's label in town pricked a few ears. Curious musicians began to buzz Josh's loft to solicit themselves to record for us. I would phone Glenn to tell him there was a free improvising saxophonist from San Francisco in the office wanting to record an album for Neutral. He'd respond—

"No, tell him to leave!"

—which I would sheepishly attend to.

Josh had commissioned the graffiti artist Lee Quiñones to paint a mural in the main space of the loft—a gorgeous, vibrant work that looked all the more astounding for being off the street. Quiñones, a couple of years younger than me, was raised on Manhattan's Lower East Side, and he had been tagging trains since he was a teenager. His elaborate works ran across multiple train cars. They were rarely defaced, a statement of respect from other "writers."

Anne DeMarinis had recorded much of Noise Fest on a reel-to-reel tape machine with the idea that a live album might be produced. Rosetta Brooks, an art theorist and magazine publisher newly arrived from London, and Josh Baer offered to produce a cassette of Noise Fest in an edition of one hundred copies, to be released by Rosetta's magazine *ZG*.

When the duplicated tapes arrived at the Neutral office, I proceeded to send one to each musician listed, holding on to a few for myself. The tape was our very first recorded document under the name Sonic Youth, and the only one to feature Anne. I tossed the remainder into a large trash bag, which I flung across my shoulder as I walked from record store to record store to see if any of them would want to carry it. Other than offering to take a copy on consignment, there was barely a whiff of interest.

Glenn would fall by Neutral each day to see how things were going, and, well . . . nothing was going. I may have curated Noise Fest, but I didn't have the wherewithal or, frankly, the motivation to help keep an independent record label afloat. My life then was devoted to playing guitar, scouring the streets for secondhand books and records, seeing gigs and films—anything else was a distraction.

So I was at first surprised, but then somewhat relieved, when Glenn and Josh introduced me to Peter Wright, an English gent who had worked for New Hormones, the Manchester label that had released the first Buzzcocks record in the dawning days of punk. They told me he'd be taking the helm at Neutral going forward.

The label would go on to become important and well recognized under Peter's watch. He had vision and expertise when it came to artist and label management, but also a passion for music in radical defiance of the pop charts. His biting English wit lent a new spike of flavor to our small circle.

This meant, however, that I was jobless once again.

And though I could hardly manage to get out of bed before two in the afternoon most days, the light of being a twenty-three-year-old guitarist alive in New York City, having found love and intellectual communion with Kim, sharing our dog, Egan, and cat, Sweetface—it was, in and of itself, perfection—whether I knew it then or not.

32

GOD IS DEAD

Shortly after recording and mixing our first album, Sonic Youth was asked to perform at the Language/Noise Festival, which would take place at the Public Theater on Lafayette Street, the sweeping landmark Romanesque structure a block up from Josh Baer's loft. Joseph Papp, the renowned theater director, had founded the Public in 1969.

Sitting in our dressing room prior to our set, joined by Glenn and Barbara, we were feeling anxious, overwhelmed by the majesty of the building, as well as the sold-out audience that sat, formally, in a raised semicircle in front of the floor where we were to perform our new music. This was not CBGB.

Just as Mr. Papp himself popped into our dressing room to kindly welcome us to his institution, I was joking with Glenn that I planned to announce one of our songs with—

"This next number goes out to Joseph fucking Papp!"

The evening was introduced first by Papp, followed by the playwright Richard Foreman, with later readings from the poets Charles Bernstein, Bruce Andrews, Hannah Weiner, Ray DiPalma, and others. Sonic Youth performed our set somewhere in the middle of it all. Our playing was bare bones, focused and direct. I thought better than to make my dedication. I decided, actually, to say nothing at all, in contrast to the hyper-verbiage of the event.

The Language/Noise Festival would turn out to be big news on the downtown scene, with such radical events as Peter Gordon and Kathy Acker's "noise/theatre work" *Birth of a Poet* being presented. Two days later, a wicked snowstorm raged up the East Coast, downing a commercial jet into Washington, D.C.'s Potomac River, killing most of the passengers. Throughout the week, the tonnage of snow that dropped onto Manhattan was plowed into high embankments of dirty white sludge, capped with street filth and exhaust. Cars and taxis splashed chunks of shredded ice onto anyone unlucky enough to step too near their trajectories.

The March 1982 issue of *New York Rocker* published a review of our December CBGB matinee gig. The piece was written by Mark Coleman, and it would be the first proper consideration of our band in the press. I felt an altogether new and strange flush seeing the accompanying photo of us. The first lines read—

What's the best way to play guitar with drumsticks? Well, when Thurston Moore jammed one up the neck of his electric during Sonic Youth's Sunday afternoon set at C.B.G.B., it sounded great.

It got only better from there, describing our sound in colorful detail before offering this enthusiastic summation—

A week later and I'm still not sure what hit me, but I know I loved it.

The piece acknowledged Richard's "street-funk smarts" and Kim's "utterly simple, forward bass," recognized our connection to Branca, and finished by declaring us a "revelation." It nailed just about everything I felt we had going on. The fact the commentary came from the highest-profile New York City music paper was a huge encouragement.

We had played CBGB again that early winter, as well as a couple of gigs at Tin Pan Alley, a notorious bar run by women artists aligned with the downtown punk and art world. There, we mixed it up with Times Square locals, denizens of the night in all their rainbow-gender joy, and drug dealers and pimps taking breathers. When performing on the Tin Pan's tiny stage, incredible creatures would stroll up and past the drum kit; the only access to the much needed toilet involved stepping across our playing area. Tin Pan was an amazing and soul-soaring place, where New York City's marginalized communities of creativity could comingle with love and respect.

It was a wild and fertile time in the city. Myriad hopped-up happenings could easily explode on the very same night. On the evening of our CBGB gig, Negril, a small club on Second Avenue downtown, would host one of its first rap events, with the DJs Afrika Bambaataa, Jazzy Jay, and Fab 5 Freddy featured.

At the Mudd Club, Heart Attack and Misguided, two of the bands that would define New York's early hardcore scene, would call forth to the new guard of barely-beyond-teen punks to come join their slam pit.

The writer Hubert Selby Jr.—who had, in 1964, penned the infamous *Last Exit to Brooklyn*—was a featured reader at a tiny literary joint in TriBeCa.

Another writer, meanwhile, was earning himself a well-deserved conviction for manslaughter.

Jack Henry Abbott, a career criminal since the mid-1960s, had been walking the streets of Manhattan in the summer of 1981, after the celebrated author Norman Mailer had convinced the penal system (as well as the literary social establishment) of Abbott's true calling as a writer. He was residing at a halfway house on East Third Street, a stretch populated by lost and damaged souls, its desperate characters hustling any hapless person who found themselves in the vicinity.

Abbott had been out of prison for only six weeks when he sauntered into the always-open Binibon restaurant on Second Avenue and Fifth Street. A modest café, it was as much a gathering place for the Lower East Side music, film, and art scene as Kiev, B&H Dairy, Leshko's, Odessa, or Dojo. Binibon felt more "locals only" than those other spots, though, a bit off the beaten path of any bridge-and-tunnel tourism. Open at all hours, it was a perfect wind-down zone after a night at Club 57, CBGB, Max's, the Mudd Club, the Pyramid Club, or the Saint.

As at many New York City eateries, the toilets weren't available to patrons. When Abbott was denied access, he asked Richard Adan—the restaurant proprietor's strapping son who, at five in the morning, had been working as both waiter and night manager—to step outside for a word. Abbott plunged a knife through Adan's heart, killing him instantly.

The night of the murder, Lee and I had been with Glenn, playing his "Symphony No. 1"—Kim in attendance—at the Performing Garage in SoHo. Thankfully we didn't choose to go to Binibon for a post-gig bite.

Many of us would later read *In the Belly of the Beast*, a collection of Abbott's letters, the murder and the author's association with Mailer giving it a certain transgressive frisson.

Jack Henry Abbott would be apprehended and receive a prison sentence of fifteen years to life. The day of his conviction, on a cold winter night in January 1982, we played CBGB. Leaving the club, we headed east to grab some grub at Kiev. Binibon wasn't an option anymore; it had shut its doors almost immediately after the killing, never again to reopen. The murder was a nefarious watershed of sorts, as the East Village would soon succumb to a changing tide, slowly redefined by money from a new populace that, like so much dull bandaging, would attempt to cover the previous generations' scars of passion and poverty.

33

SIGNALS, CALLS, AND MARCHES

Danceteria, the queer-powered new wave nightclub on West Thirty-Seventh Street, had been shut down by police in 1980. The proprietors, Jim Fouratt and Rudolf Pieper, resolved to reopen the enterprise with live music at its forefront, sharing space with party rooms, dining, lounging, loving, laughing, dancing, drinking, spanking, and seducing. It would be fabulous and fun for everyone who knew the score.

The new Danceteria opened its doors at 30 West Twenty-First Street in February 1982, welcomed with the buzzy, jangling pop of R.E.M. Lee and I had run into R.E.M. singer Michael Stipe on the street the previous afternoon. We walked around for a bit, smoking cigarettes, before leading him to a vegetarian restaurant near St. Mark's Place.

We all arrived for the opening night blowout, but it was so overrun and nuts that we bailed pretty quickly. I returned the following night to hear the Boston band Mission of Burma, who were becoming a rather hot ticket on the new band scene.

Mission of Burma fully caught my attention. Guitarist Roger Miller and bassist Clint Conley raged into sonic overdrive, with some similarity to Glenn and Rhys's open-ended guitar roar, as well as what we ourselves were mining. The band had been together since 1979, with a reputation for amped-up blasting. Their first single, "Academy Fight Song," was a stomping, passionate miniature epic.

I sidled over to club proprietor Jim Fouratt to voice my encouragement, pointing to the stage—

"These guys are amazing!"

Sonic Youth played the third night of the opening week. Lee and I returned twelve days later to perform as part of Glenn's ensemble.

Soon joining the scrum of downtown music hot spots was Pyramid Bar, located at 101 Avenue A, between East Sixth and Seventh Streets.

The Pyramid stood across the street from the A7 club, where hardcore bands had been getting their scene together. From its opening night in December 1981, the Pyramid became the most significant spot in the East Village, with an inclusive atmosphere in which a new queer aesthetic could be seen as an essential element of punk. The club would host drag revues, off-the-rails theme events, and downtown "new music" bands, including ourselves. As the decade progressed, everyone from Deee-Lite to Babes in Toyland to Nirvana would play early gigs there.

Jack Henry Abbott's 1981 killing of Richard Adan had horrified our neighborhood of artists and musicians; so too did the murder of Michael Stewart, a twenty-five-year-old Black artist who had worked as a busboy at Danceteria in the early 1980s. Leaving the Pyramid one night in September 1983, Michael was apprehended by a transit cop on the First Avenue L train platform while spray-painting a graffiti tag across a wall. Michael was on his way home to Clinton Hill in Brooklyn, where he lived with his parents (his father, ironically, was a maintenance worker for the Metropolitan Transit Authority). He tried to run off but was nabbed and thrown into a police van, where he would struggle with his captors, all of them white men. En route to the police station at Union Square, they beat him unconscious, then hog-tied him. At booking, it was decided that he should be taken to nearby Bellevue Hospital for evaluation.

He arrived at Bellevue after three in the morning, comatose, handcuffed, his legs bound, cuts and bruises across his body. Thirteen days later he would die from a brain hemorrhage.

An all-white jury, two years later, acquitted the eleven cops (as well as the MTA itself), though Michael's family was able to win a civil action suit against the NYPD two years after that. (The police never confessed to any wrongdoing.)

It was a galvanizing moment for all of us on the downtown scene. Before the incident came to light, I had never spared much thought for the cops in Manhattan. They were hardly present in the streets when I'd lived in Alphabet City, unless some serious street crime had taken place. As a tall white kid bounding around town, I never felt the glare of suspicion from a cop. But it was plain to me, whether the police would admit it, that the murder was racially motivated. It was an assault on the Black community. But it was also an attack on the diversity that so many of us prized.

Few residents of the Lower East Side were immune to the random violence that permeated its streets. But with the slaying of Michael Stewart, it would become apparent to all of us moving between Club 57, Mudd Club, Tier 3, the Pyramid, A7, and Danceteria that it was the New York police who were to be feared most of all.

34

JACK ON FIRE

Sonic Youth's contemporaries, in the spring of 1982, would mostly morph into other groups or slowly fade away, their members' lives switched onto other tracks. Newer groups appeared, sidling up to us, finding an allegiance in our common sound and approach. Notable among them were Swans, Rat at Rat R, Bag People, Live Skull, and the recently returned Lydia Lunch, who quickly saw Sonic Youth—and, soon enough, Swans—as her new partners in crime.

Lydia had reemerged from a musical sojourn through Europe and the UK, where she had connected with the band the Birthday Party and the Berlin group Einstürzende Neubauten. Lee had been talking about Einstürzende Neubauten since having seen them while on tour with Glenn in Germany in 1981—how amazing the group had been, utilizing metal constructions for percussion, employing street noise as compositional elements, and being altogether influenced by New York City no wave.

Lydia had recorded with both groups and was now back in New York City looking to put together a band. Richard Edson, who was acquainted with her too, thought I would be the ideal bass player. The three of us met to talk about it at an apartment Lydia had been crashing at on Rivington Street, close to where Kim and I were living.

Lydia led Richard and me into her temporary room, which had black lace flowing off the bedposts, air scented with flowers and dark-toned perfumes, and the Holy Bible sitting next to a few pairs of spiked high-heeled leather shoes. Cheerful and warm, fueled with a bit of marijuana, she was altogether agreeable to my involvement. She asked if I would meet her the next day at a rehearsal basement on Grand Street.

I was psyched to work with Lydia, who was considered one of the most radical and significant inspirations in a scene rife with experimental creativity. She had a style wholly her own, influencing what the English press would herald as "goth," alongside her British friends Siouxsie Sioux and Steven Severin of the Banshees.

Arriving at the space the next day with bass guitar in hand, I asked about the music she had been thinking to make. She responded with one word—

"Slow."

She asked if I wanted to dance, shutting off the single overhead light bulb. I was surprised by and hardly prepared for the request—I was beyond shy. But I submitted to it, dancing for a bit, slowly, nervous and gawky, my height towering over her comparatively diminutive body. She began to laugh, then flicked the light back on.

She started humming musical lines close to my ear, which I understood I was to transpose to the bass. I did, though in a woozy state of shock.

After this introductory session, we would meet again for more rehearsals, with Richard at the drum kit. Our compositions became a bit more studiously put together, Lydia cheerful throughout, focused on making sure the groove and temperament were exactly what she required. I attempted to turn her onto the new hardcore bands on the scene, playing a mixtape I had made, thinking she might be responsive to, possibly, Black Flag. But she was unimpressed—

"It's too fast. I only like slow music, T-Stone."

While attending classes at Otis Art Institute in the late 1970s, Kim had met Michael Gira, who had been bombing around the Los Angeles scene singing in oddball groups and publishing a punk-centric art newspaper. Burned out on Los Angeles, Michael and his partner, Susan Martin, relocated to New York City.

One night Kim invited Michael and Susan to see our band. After being introduced, I realized he had been the lead singer of the band Circus Mort, the wheatpasting guy who had clashed with the Coachmen outside of Tier 3 a year prior. Michael, beautiful and intense, had disbanded Circus Mort shortly thereafter to create a far more demanding outfit he would christen Swans. He had rented a makeshift studio—a windowless space with two dank rooms on East Tenth Street between Avenues A and B, an impoverished block—as a rehearsal room, the concrete walls holding in his amplified roar, as well as a place for him to write and make art.

We quickly made peace and shared a laugh over our earlier altercation, and he invited our band to share the rental with him. It made financial sense. Sonic Youth could rehearse there, and I could bring in Lydia and Richard Edson for the music Lydia had been creating. She would soon invite Bush Tetras guitarist Pat Place to join us too, along with Jim Sclavunos to play saxophone, naming the project In Limbo.

Simply getting to Michael's rehearsal space was always a bit of a hairy prospect. Low-level heroin dealers skulked about the neighborhood, solicitous and threatening. We deduced that the rehearsal space had once housed a Haitian church of some kind. One afternoon, Michael found hanging from the door handle a bag containing a sliced-off chicken head. It led him to affix multiple heavy-duty locks to the door.

The second room, separated by a steel door, was where the shared equipment for Swans and Sonic Youth to rehearse had been set up. While Michael was searching for a permanent bassist, I would be enlisted to play Swans' very first shows, which meant that, with the three projects, I found myself spending quite a bit of my waking hours in this windowless dungeon of noise and haunted chicken heads.

Inspired by the fanzines I had found at gigs and record stores, I decided to create my own. It would intersperse images with writing on musicians who I thought shared the same energy, whether they were hardcore, no wave, noise, art rock, or avant-garde. I titled it *Killer,* and my first act was to interview Jeffrey Lee Pierce of the Los Angeles band the Gun Club, whose record I had bought at Rhino in L.A. and who were playing their debut New York City gig at Peppermint Lounge on the first of May.

After their performance, I headed to the dressing room to introduce myself. Some artists might have had a semblance of security, but bands at Gun Club's level (and our own) did not, and anyone with the right degree of gumption, whether a friend, fan, or foe, could sashay into that zone of privacy without much obstacle.

I approached Jeffrey and asked if I could record a short interview on my cassette deck. He agreed, albeit with some hesitation. He laid his body atop a bench, sphinxlike, as I asked my first question—

"Is it true you were the founder and president of the Los Angeles chapter of the Blondie Fan Club?"

I don't think Jeffrey was expecting that one. I was genuinely curious after having read the tidbit in *LA Weekly.* He explained how much he truly adored Blondie, still did, and always would.

I loved this. Blondie was the rare act that could chew bubblegum while reading *Naked Lunch*. They had creative musical output and savvy. I recognized this marriage alive in Jeffrey Lee Pierce as well.

Kim and I were hanging around one day at 99 Records when a young couple entered the store. The fellow excitedly, loudly whispered to his female partner—

"Ohhh, it's Sonic Youth."

This was the first time I was recognized in that way. It took me aback. I approached the couple, saying—

"Have we met?"

"No, no"

—they said, the woman snuggling a miniature schnauzer pup in her arms.

"We just really like your band."

Catherine Bachmann and Nicolas Ceresole were their names, and they had arrived from Rolle, Switzerland, that year. They were renting an apartment way north on the Upper West Side of Manhattan, and they wanted to immerse themselves in New York City's punk, post-punk, and no wave scene, Catherine documenting live gigs as a photographer.

"We have photos of your band at Danceteria and Mudd Club"

—she said in a throaty Swiss-German accent—

"and photos of Glenn Branca and Rhys Chatham and Lydia . . ."

We exchanged telephone numbers, and the two soon invited our band, along with Barbara and Glenn, up to their apartment for dinner and to look through Catherine's photographs.

We took the long subway ride uptown. Catherine had prepared an astounding feast for us, cooked entirely on an electric hot plate in their tiny kitchen area. Nicolas was a ravenous record collector; he had nearly every new release coming out of the underground, with copies of albums from all over the world by the most arcane bands and labels, from the farthest recesses and outposts of recorded sound, all of them stacked against their stereo system.

We sat around puffing on European spliffs of hashish and marijuana listening to and having discussions about these new and different bands. They were particularly drawn to the ones creating harsh, industrial soundscapes. Devoid of rhythm, soul, or decency, these bands' records were seemingly inspired by Throbbing Gristle (a group Nicolas had all extant recordings of) and noise fetishists such as The New Blockaders and Whitehouse.

Our visit would lead to a series of noise-salon dinners, at which we threw these albums on the turntable, one after the other. As the tumult spilled into the small apartment, I would watch Glenn, smoking his filterless cigarettes on the couch, staring down at the floor, listening, puffing, thinking, only for him to look up, scratch his head, and announce—

"Who the fuck listens to this shit?"

Well, we certainly were.

Dinners at Catherine and Nicolas's became an almost weekly ritual, with Sonic Youth, Swans, Lydia, Glenn and Barbara, Martin Rev of Suicide, and, eventually, touring European bands coming through town attending, for the lure of like-minded company and a free and fantastic meal. These two Swiss angels helped feed us starving artists, offering us nourishment of the stomach and of the mind.

The dinners would soon turn into weekly sounding boards. We would bring our most recent demos and live tapes to play and discuss. Michael would throw on a new Swans recording, playing it as loud as possible. Lydia would be rat-a-tat talking with assorted guests, but Michael would insist on full attention to his new music, yelling across the room—

"Lydia! Listen!"

And she'd shout back at him, louder—

"I can't help but not to, Michael!"

Daggers scorched across the smoke-filled apartment.

35

WE DON'T NEED FREEDOM

I had been cutting my hair short to the point where it was very nearly back to the crew cut of my childhood, though never so shorn as the skinhead look of the hardcore kids. I was becoming more aggro onstage—maybe the short hair was an encouragement, but so were our new songs. I began bringing more speed and thrash into the music.

Even playing the first song of ours, "The Burning Spear," I began to wail way harder on the guitar when it came time for my drumstick-beneath-guitar-strings bell tones. What was once cool and exacting had become savage and unleashed, sometimes to the point that I'd fall onto the floor of the stage, recklessly extending the guitar in front of my body, whacking it to within an inch of its life, then getting up and dramatically taking the microphone to yowl—

I'm not afraid to say I'm scaaaaared!

Glenn Branca's demonstrative thrashing also began to inform our stage energy, Lee and Kim ramping up their bashing and wailing.

Michael Gira was becoming more and more of a kindred spirit, though he was less impressed by some of the West Coast records I played than I was, such as those by the Germs, Black Flag, and Flipper. Michael wasn't interested in revisiting punk rock. He saw Swans not as an act of defiance against musical norms but a forum for personal catharsis, using sound to explore absurdity, lust, hope, dreams delivered and dashed, guilt, pleasure, and profanity. Swans was to be personal reckoning as public performance.

I invited Michael to catch Black Flag at a venue called My Father's Place out on Long Island, a not-too-distant train ride out of the city, but he demurred. Kim came along, though, as did Dan Graham. We arrived a little early and waited outside, standing in line with every hardcore kid I had ever seen in New York City, as well as a few hundred others from Connecticut, New Jersey, and beyond.

The show was a can't-miss for me, as Minor Threat and Saccharine Trust were also on the bill. Saccharine Trust had just released *Paganicons*, a record driven by hard rolling bass lines, a sputtering hyper-dexterous guitar style, and pleading raspy vocals, like those of a preacher falling to his knees. Minor Threat was the unadulterated voice of hardcore. It would be the first time I'd see them live. Vocalist Ian MacKaye, a slight shade of a mohawk sprouting across his skull, led the band into song after song, a circle pit of slammers raging in front of the stage that a horde would skank through, then dive back into the dancing delirium, everyone leaping up to grab Ian's microphone to sing along—

We're just a minor threat!

Saccharine Trust–Minor Threat was a one-two punch of punk rock, the rumors of its death in 1977 evidently exaggerated. It was where my heart was, right at that moment, and it would detonate into full bloom when Black Flag hit the stage.

The band began ripping out all the material from their most recent album, *Damaged,* bassist Chuck Dukowski, his instrument hung to his knees, swinging and battering it, his face a mask of rage and angst. Singer Henry Rollins prowled from one side of the stage to the other, drawing energy from the crowd, then spewing it back a millionfold. The snaking guitar lines of Greg Ginn and Dez Cadena wrapped their tendrils around us, with kids crawling across the stage, leaping into the crowd, then getting back up and doing it again.

I left the concert convinced of the truth of Black Flag. We hopped on the train back to Manhattan. I was in a beatific daze, my senses flooded, my heart and soul fully inspired.

We saw our name in print again, this time a review of our appearance at the White Columns benefit in the *Aquarian Weekly* newspaper. The writer, Sukey Pett, was less enchanted with us than Mark Coleman of *New York Rocker* had been. "One Bad Moment in a Night of Fun," the story was entitled—

There is no way in hell I can recommend this band, or even tolerate be-ing in the same room with them . . . Sonic Youth is/are dentist drill drone music.

It was a blow, but we didn't allow it to affect our self-regard. There was a bit of delight, even, in how strong a negative reaction we inspired. We would use the line "dentist drill drone music" in our first press kit, which we would send out to other journalists.

The summer of 1982 found Sonic Youth, more and more associ-ated with Swans, wanting to crash forth from the measured confines of the downtown art-rock scene. Black Flag was becoming a greater inspiration, as was the utter onslaught of the Australian industrial noise group SPK, who had come to town from Sydney. Attending their first New York show, an early June evening at CBGB, we watched as films of surgical evisceration were projected onto a screen at the back of the stage. SPK, with tribal markings streaked across their faces, beat on slabs of metal junk, accompanied by distorted, shouted vocals and tapes of nefarious noise blowing out of the sound system. It was ridicu-lous and awesome. We could only look at each other and shake our heads at the audacity and ear-shredding weirdness crashing around the club.

For many of us, the most remarkable event that summer was the an-nouncement that DNA would be performing their final shows, a two-night showcase at CBGB. Here was the one band that exemplified so much of what the experimental downtown New York City aesthetic was about, where art rock, punk, no wave, and jazz merged. And now DNA was call-ing it a day. Attending those final DNA shows, the future of music felt at once unpredictable and open to trailblazing.

It was the same feeling I would have that autumn as I moved through twenty-one-year-old Jean-Michel Basquiat's show at Fun Gallery—the paintings, as if torn from the streets where they had resided previously, leaning against the walls or else sprawled across the gallery floor, the promise of his work glimpsed at the *New York/New Wave* exhibition, just one year earlier, now in full fruition.

Madonna, meanwhile, would become a lit-up presence on the floors of Danceteria, her eyes sparkling and gorgeous, everything about her stunning (not unlike many of the people gracing Danceteria). The music was hardly our thing, but she was a striking figure amid the coterie of coolness.

Michael Gira was delighted, if not a little surprised, to share with us that he had a little bit of a thing going on with this buzzing sprite. I was happy for him as, hanging out one night in the lounge on the second floor of Danceteria, Madonna moseyed over to where we all were to sit on Michael's lap. He introduced her to Kim and me, a smile on his face. Madonna, sweet but with a studied distance, gave us a hi, then flew off.

The dalliance proved to be short-lived. Michael would become quite bored talking and hearing about it, after Madonna's metamorphosis into a global superstar. At the time it was just kind of funny. We'd ask who was playing downstairs at Danceteria, and the answer would inevitably be—

"Madonna"

—and we would skip away, feeling too cool for her *popular* music.

Kim and I flew out to California again for a couple of weeks that August to see her family and visit friends. She played for me her old John Coltrane and Charles Mingus albums. In the months and years to come, I continued blasting every new hardcore album I found, but Kim would bring jazz into my life, a portal of endless wonder.

Back in New York City, I became friendly with Tim Sommer, the New York University radio DJ. He introduced me to his cohost, Jack Rabid, who edited the *Big Takeover,* a fanzine he had been hawking at punk gigs, and played drums in a band called Even Worse.

The original lineup of Even Worse had broken down, and Jack was keen on keeping it going. He had enlisted Tim to play bass, and the two asked if I would be interested in joining them as a second guitarist. I responded with an immediate yes. They joined Sonic Youth, Glenn Branca's ensemble, Lydia Lunch's In Limbo, and Swans as the bands I was, to varying degrees, involved with.

The first gig I played with them was at a club named Tramps on East Fifteenth Street. I had to play bass with Swans at CBGB earlier the same night, the set intense, brutal, and loud, the summer heat soaking through our T-shirts and ratty trousers. I then hoofed it over to Tramps to whip through Even Worse's set, before heading back down to CBGB to reconnect with my friends.

We all went over to Leshko's to sit around into the late night, drinking iced coffees, eating plates of stuffed cabbage, pancakes, French toast, cheeseburgers, kielbasa, and eggs, going over the night's highlights and lowlights as locals stepped in and out of the café—poets and punks and lowlifes, sometimes coming by our table to ask for some coin or a cigarette. We offered what we could so that they too might find a moment's solace, here on Planet Manhattan, in a cup of java and a summer-evening smoke.

36

NO IDOLS

Glenn gathered his ensemble to fly out to Chicago for the fourth annual New Music America festival in early July 1982. New Music America was a big deal. The festival had a direct connection to the Kitchen, where, in 1979, it had been first launched to gather the most active practitioners of the avant-garde, of so-called "new music."

The hoopla surrounding New Music America 1982 was intense, drawing swarms of the curious and the serious, all of them moving about the grandiose Navy Pier, alongside the city's mayor and John Cage, undoubtedly the figurehead of twentieth-century experimentalism, who was being feted for his seventieth birthday.

It was the first time I'd be stepping out of my city to perform. For as much as the music of the downtown scene was exalted in my mind as some of the most exciting stuff happening anywhere, it also felt intimately associated with New York City to me. In Chicago, it felt like the whole world—and not just the world below Fourteenth Street—was listening.

We played our set, and as we prepared to depart Chicago, word spread that John Cage had been in attendance. Interviewed on the radio the following day, the composer spoke for close to twenty minutes about how disturbed he'd been by Glenn's music, connecting it to "evil and power" and suggesting that it "resembled fascism."

These words would haunt Glenn for years, but they would also define him (whether he liked it or not); a patina of glory stuck to him, as he had, in effect, been dubbed new music's ultimate bad boy.

After I returned to New York City, Sonic Youth would play a few shows with Swans, Live Skull, and a number of newer groups on the downtown scene, including Mon Ton Son, which featured the artist Christian Marclay wearing a modified turntable around his neck, slapping on records that he would play, scratch, and scrape.

At a time when hip-hop DJs were cultivating radical new techniques, turning their turntables into instruments of performance, Christian entered the dialogue from a wholly other direction. He was an art-school turntablist, and he would progressively expand his idiosyncratic sound palette, which would in turn inform his visual work, including sculptures, installations, graphics, and film.

Rap concerts were becoming more prevalent, though, and so was hip-hop style. On Sundays, Delancey Street would be packed with shoppers, mostly hip-hop enthusiasts, seeking out deals on sneakers, coats, records, tapes, and boom boxes. Store proprietors, primarily older Jewish men, sold the latest in hip-hop fashion: leather jackets with an eight-ball icon patched to the back, brown suede jackets with a bit of hanging fringe and an optional faux fur collar, high-top sneakers, Kangol hats, Run DMC–style Cazal eyeglass frames, gold chains with links the size of curtain rings. They stood outside their doors competing for attention, inviting people in with promises of "a nice price."

I would head to Bate Records on the south side of Delancey, as it stocked the newest rap twelve-inches, perusing the bins wondering what each new record sounded like, as many had no cover graphics. I would then head to J&R Music World near Wall Street, followed by Sounds record store on St. Mark's Place, in search of discounted sides.

Kim and I had little cash to spare, and I attempted to be frugal in my purchases, knowing the money would be more responsibly spent on groceries and utility bills. Noticing a record bag under my arm, Kim would give me the hairy eyeball. She tolerated it, although I think she harbored a glimmer of hope that I would someday grow out of such things.

New York City heat waves take no prisoners, and that summer was no exception. Before Kim and I had the means to purchase something as extravagant as an air conditioner, we would sit in front of our one box fan, propped in the window, drinking iced tea and smoking mentholated Newport cigarettes. We lay in bed in T-shirts and undies, listening to the complex of street noise: grinding garbage trucks; neighbors gathered in cliques, leaning against cars and talking loudly; car radios blasting salsa; once in a while a boom box with someone's mixtape of homemade hip-hop distorting out of the speaker—the pleasure of the hot city creating a sense of being in the only place on Earth.

Lydia booked a Halloween show for In Limbo that fall at Peppermint Lounge. She outfitted herself in flowing black lace. Guitarist Pat Place arrived wearing cat ears and a tail, becoming "Cat" Place for the night. This was enough of a concession to Halloween for Jim Sclavunos, Richard Edson, and me to forgo donning anything other than our usual civvies. Peppermint Lounge was fairly jammed, with many in the crowd dressed up for the costume contest, to be judged by Joey Ramone.

The songs we performed were mostly based on the musical ideas Lydia had hummed into my skull—all slow, droning escapades, dripping with salacious lyrics. One tune was built on a bass line I had previously considered using with Sonic Youth but got sucked into In Limbo, with Lydia's vocals a yowling cry of despair.

This number, which threatened the jovial atmosphere of Peppermint Lounge with a call to mass suicide, was the final straw for some people in the audience—including Joe Strummer from the Clash, who happened to be in attendance. With my head down and my eyes staring at Lydia's feet to hold the molten rhythm, I could hear his bellowing from the middle of the club—

"Bollocks! Bollocks!"

37

CRUCIAL POINT

After countless shows in New York, and having gotten a taste of playing elsewhere, specifically Chicago, I was ready for something more. Kim, Lee, and I had the idea that we should head out with Michael and his band to play clubs on the East Coast between New York City and Atlanta. With the list of phone numbers Lee had gathered while touring with Branca's group, we dialed up various clubs, inquiring about having Sonic Youth and Swans play.

Our most pressing issue was that we had no drummer at the moment. Richard had decided to focus primarily on playing trumpet with Konk, the band he obviously felt the most creative intimacy with. We had tried a few people out, but nothing stuck.

I xeroxed a few flyers, scrawling—

SONIC YOUTH NEEDS DRUMMER

—across them along with our phone numbers and wheatpasting them everywhere below Fourteenth Street.

We received one call. It was from a young gent across the Hudson River in Hoboken, New Jersey, named Bob Bert.

Bob met us at Leshko's restaurant in the East Village. He was quiet, a bit hard to read. He didn't stroke our egos about how great we were, nor did he make any obvious pleas for us to hire him, other than advertising the fact that he had actually bought our first record.

He had seen us too, with Richard on drums. He liked what he had heard. It was enough of an endorsement, alongside his enthusiasm for the no wave scene, for us to consider trying him out.

We had been working up songs that had a far more rambunctious edge. At our first rehearsal with Bob, he listened, offering pretty straightforward moves. These developing songs had a few crazed changes in them; I can only imagine they must have been confounding beyond the wires connecting Lee, Kim, and me. We three were already in a zone, trusting one another's playing, allowing our music to possess a unified voice.

We attempted to articulate to Bob what we were doing, or at least thought we were doing. It was all in-the-moment experimentation within the loose confines of a song. We would establish a part of a composition, which would be altered by a new contribution from one member, and we would stop to exclaim—

"Wait a minute, that was cool, let's try that again."

I think Bob could sense that songs were gradually taking shape, but he could have only been overwhelmed by our unconventional language, unsure even how to involve himself.

He was a very tribal drummer, less of a typical rock player than any drummer we had worked with—even Edson, with his Latin-inflected rhythms. After a couple of rehearsals, we got a slightly better idea of who this New Jersey boy was, with his bushy black hair and slightly distant countenance. It belied a refined intellect and no small amount of street savvy. He let on that he had been coming to New York City since 1975, to see bands such as Television and hear Patti Smith read at small poetry events.

This résumé sold me immediately. Bob was invited into the band.

Our first gig with Bob was at CBGB in early November 1982, on a bill with Swans and Don King. It was a coming-out for Swans and Sonic Youth, as we brought new intensity, volume, and action to our sound.

Michael Gira had added a young woman named Sue Hanel as guitarist. She created roaring shards of metallic guitar noise against the pummeling bass of Harry Crosby, locked into the percussive wallops of Roli Mosimann and Jonathan Kane's drumming. Michael continued playing guitar as well, but he focused more on his guttural vocals. Swans was a harrowing experience for some in the clubs, particularly sound engineers. Michael would become almost impossible to work with, uncompromising in how he thought Swans needed to be heard and felt (or more often to be demolished by).

By comparison Sonic Youth was tame, though we were attacking the songs now, inspired not only by Swans but hardcore and industrial music.

Michael owned a monolithic speaker cabinet with six twelve-inch speaker cones, powered by a 100-watt Peavey amplifier head, which he let us use for our bass. My brother, Gene, always encouraging, had lent us his Acoustic amp and speaker-bottom setup, with with four ten-inch speakers. It didn't benefit from our cranking it as loud as it could withstand; the speaker cones eventually shredded. Lee would play through a couple of different Fender combo amps, one for his guitar and the other for an electric zither. At the edge of the stage, Lee set up the large hanging metal chimes that we had found in the street.

For the most part, our clothes for the night were muted and worn: faded dungarees splattered with paint and ink stains and with holes from fallen cigarettes; drab T-shirts beneath unbuttoned thrift store flannel; weathered sneakers with big toes cutting through the front, the heel all but scraped away. Kim wore a white dress with stockings and motorcycle boots, her hair stylishly shorn.

We had a new song entitled "Confusion Is Next," a bit of no wave greyscale that faded into a field of noise, then returned as thrash as I sang lyrics inspired by reading Henry Miller—

> *I maintain that chaos is the future and beyond it is freedom*
> *Confusion is next and next after that is the truth*

—bent over and screaming into the microphone, channeling Alec Mac-Kaye from the D.C. hardcore group the Faith.

Lydia asked me to join her for what would be her first spoken-word performance at a place called Lucky Strike, a late-night bar for downtown darlings situated in a second-floor walkup on Stuyvesant Street. The evening had been advertised as "Sex Stories." The one Lydia had written and shared was a purported eyewitness account of a girl being assaulted. The idea was for me to offer simple, bewildered responses, presumably to underscore its intimate voice: *"What?"* or *"Really?"* or *"Oh no!"*—the straight man, more or less.

Lydia was adored by this hip crowd, who could enjoy her subversive text in the safety of their cocktail lounge. I felt a bit shy, if not embarrassed, for having submitted to this performance. Not because I had any issue with Lydia's writing—her work was always truthful and captivating—but because of the way her fan club might be eyeing me as her latest boy toy.

I knew Lydia didn't see me that way, some kid to consume and forget about. We came to our friendship on equal footing, with a shared fascination for radical music and literature. She and I would become very close throughout the early 1980s, to the point that it began to threaten my relationship with Kim. Lydia wasn't proprietary over me in any way, or anyone else for that matter. She embraced the freedom to find pleasure, letting bodies fall where they may. Her spirit was seductive, to be sure, but she knew as well as I did how profound my connection to Kim was. Lydia was a remarkable friend, someone both Kim and I would work with in various projects, including Sonic Youth.

We had been adding new songs to our set—"Confusion Is Next" but also "Inhuman," "The World Looks Red," "Making the Nature Scene," and "(She's in a) Bad Mood"—focused on playing them for this first tour we had planned. "Inhuman" and "The World Looks Red" were informed by our communion with Swans, with driving, minimal bass figures ravaged by guitar clangor. (Indeed, the lyrics to "The World Looks Red" were written by Michael.) "Making the Nature Scene" was a text piece of Kim's, which she thought to recite against a throttling and percussive bass move that I'd constructed. It gave Lee a canvas over which he could employ his various guitar noises. Bob recognized in the song's groove something he could really add to, and he proceeded to lock right into it, offering a pounding jungle stomp. Kim's lyrics seemed to be based on her readings of postmodern architectural theory. Her lines sounded fantastic, her pronouncements unwavering and furious. The lyrics to "(She's in a) Bad Mood" had been written in homage to Lydia, who could be at once cantankerous and hilarious—

> She's in a bad mood
> But I won't fall for it

The song served as a call for self-awareness on my own part: not to be caught up in whatever chaos Lydia might lob, like a hand grenade, into my daily life.

The singly named Chassler, a local poet and musician, agreed to drive both bands and all our gear (in an attached U-Haul trailer) down to Atlanta and back. Michael Gira would refer to it as the "Savage Blunder" tour, a name that would prove unfortunately apt. There would be a total of ten people in Chassler's van: two in front and eight in the windowless back, huddled together, plopped on sleeping bags, sleeping in rows as we rode through the night.

Our first show was at a club named Cat's Cradle, then located in Chapel Hill, North Carolina, a modest room that attracted no more than a dozen people, curious to hear some new music on a Sunday night in November. After the ten-hour drive from Manhattan—rolling down Interstate 95, staring at each other, laughing, arguing, drinking beer, smoking cigarettes—we were all a little shell-shocked. We decided that Sonic Youth should play first, as Swans was a tough act to follow with their punishingly loud amplification.

We played, and the smattering of people there seemed to be having some semblance of a good time out, clapping and hooting after every song ended.

"*Whoo-hoo!*"

—a few yelled.

"*'Free Bird'!*"

It was as comical and perverse a heckle as we could receive.

With the sparse audience primed and ready for some more weirdness, Swans proceeded to annihilate any conversation in the room with their deafening roar. Within ten minutes, only three or four people remained, one of them a girl named Bambi who, with her small gaggle of friends, invited us to sleep on her floor ("My folks are out of town"). We accepted with muted gratitude. Asking for or accepting places to stay was pretty much the only option we had outside of sleeping in the van. After playing, hanging out at the club until closing time, loading the gear back into the U-Haul, then following someone's car to their house, we would be beyond exhausted. One person would have to sleep in the van to ensure it wasn't broken into or stolen. The others would scout around for corners of the house to unroll sleeping bags in, with some opting to stay awake to continue smoking, drinking, and chatting.

Most of whatever money we made, either from a guarantee or collected at the door or both—or as often neither—we would spend on gas or use to pay Chassler's daily driver's fee. The two bands would split the rest, when it existed, using it for food and cigarettes.

The next night we played the Pier in Raleigh, North Carolina, less than an hour away from Chapel Hill. A few more people showed, after a long and painful sound check in which the soundman at the club got into a war of words with Michael. The guy had asked Swans to turn everything down. The group pretty much turned everything up instead. Michael went to the soundboard and cranked all the faders as high as they could go, telling the sound guy to leave them there. This did not go over so well. The room that night was blazing with noise and shattered vibes. A few kids showed up thinking two hardcore bands from New York were in town, only to be stunned to find our cranked-up art rock.

As we drove farther south toward Georgia, we played the cassettes of the two North Carolina gigs we had recorded on a portable Radio Shack tape recorder. Listening to the music in the back of the van allowed us to hear the strengths and weaknesses in our performances, all of us exchanging commentary on what had worked and what had not.

The 40 Watt Club in Athens, Georgia, was not exactly bustling on that mid-November Tuesday night, but Michael Stipe—whom Lee and I had met in New York City earlier in the year—and his R.E.M. bandmate Peter Buck came by to check us out.

While Swans played their set, the audience retreated to the walls as if the music were flattening them there, though some brave souls ventured into the thick soup of sound. A couple began dancing in a new wave fashion. Michael was having none of it. After a few minutes, he leaped off the stage and began to push his sweat-drenched torso, guitar still strapped on, against the dancing boy, until the two were sprawled on the floor. Returning to the stage as their song sputtered to a stop, Michael explained that it was simply impossible for him to focus when people were dancing in such an inane manner.

The next night we played to a somewhat healthier turnout at the 688 Club in Atlanta, with some of my nearby southern relatives attending. My aunt Peggy, younger sister to my late father, invited us all to spend the night at her ranch house.

The next morning, as we were enjoying welcome cups of coffee and plates of toast and eggs, she looked at us with a face of concern. Michael had yet to enter the kitchen; she asked me if he was okay. I told her he was fine, just a little intense. Michael had performed in his usual attire the night before: threadbare trousers, a distressed white T-shirt, bare feet. My aunt said he reminded her of an escaped convict. To her and my relief, Michael sauntered into the kitchen, freshly showered, with a beaming smile, graciously thanking my aunt for the accommodation and the delicious coffee.

Our next gig was at the celebrated 9:30 Club in Washington, D.C., though we had a day off after Atlanta to cover the mileage. By this point, the complicated dynamics of ten people traveling together in a tight van were becoming clear. One night, Michael had made the decision to mess with the settings on Sue Hanel's guitar amp. The two had a blowout in the dressing room, a few chairs tossed about. The dressing room had a door, though, which allowed the rest of us to duck out. The van, as it sped along the highway, offered no such escape.

At some point during our drive, a war of words erupted between Michael and Swans drummer Jonathan Kane, to the point where the two began throwing fists and wrestling, with nowhere to fall except on top of the rest of us, sitting with our backs against the van walls, our legs stretched out in rows. As the two tussled, we yelled and screamed at them to stop. Drinks, cigarettes, books, magazines, newspapers, cassettes, and shoes flew everywhere.

Chassler pulled over at the next rest stop, and we all went in and sat around while Jonathan and Michael cooled out. Chassler basically told them, and all of us, that if anyone was going to fight in his van, they would have to walk the rest of the way.

Some kid at the Marble Bar in Baltimore, with his arm draped around his girlfriend, thought he would show off by heckling me while we played—

"Hey, where'd you get that shirt? Greenwich Village?"

He was referring to a long-sleeved button-down thrift-store rag I had been wearing every day on the tour. My nerves were frayed after long days of touring. I responded into the microphone—

"Why don'tchoo go home and watch TV where you belong, fuckface."

It brought a bit of an unpleasant edge to the room as well as to the stage. The heckler skulked off, his girlfriend's wrist clasped in his hand.

We were becoming surly and defensive. Both of our bands knew that the harshness of our music was pretty much off-the-grid when compared with what most groups in 1982 were presenting. A few people had responded with interest at these first forays outside of Manhattan, but mostly we felt like we were screaming into a void.

We spent our time back home winding down from the tour—the intensity of it, the personalities all jammed together in confined spaces. The laughs, the shouting, the smells. The tiny bits of money to get through the days and nights. The sleeplessness, the cold germs, the cigarette smoke. The enforced distance from the world we knew. It was draining but also a thrill to know we could survive such an excursion. We began to process the frustrations inherent in trying to garner attention while being wholly obscure, the ideas on how our music could be made and how it could progress.

During this tour and after, though, I began to feel unmoored. The band wasn't functioning the way I thought it could. Fairly or not, I fixated on the drums. I felt we needed a more solid and propulsive energy behind us. I became bitchy and resentful toward Bob.

It wasn't just him. I took aim at Kim too, whenever she played something that, I thought, wasn't the same as when we had first rehearsed it or whenever I felt like she wasn't locking into what I considered the proper rhythm. It would upset her, to the point where she wondered whether it was too demoralizing to remain in the band with me. That was enough to bring me to my senses—for me to recognize that I was being an ass, not fully appreciating the way her wholly distinct approach to playing and performance was essential to our band. I offered my attempts at apologies and promised not to fall into such obsessive selfishness in the future.

Michael was excited that a friend of his from Los Angeles by the name of Tom Recchion would be visiting New York City, with an idea of possibly relocating there.

Tom had cofounded the Los Angeles Free Music Society in 1973. LAFMS became one of the most historically significant underground music collectives on the West Coast and beyond, influencing like-minded groups from damp and dirty basements in Detroit to tiny noise-drenched dens across Japan.

Michael had been extolling Tom's percussion skills, right when my kvetching about Sonic Youth's need for a new drummer was at its height. Tom came by to play with us and was, instantly, pretty great—hard-hitting, playing perfect fills. I wanted him in, but I was afraid to make the call to Bob. I sat in Michael's rehearsal space, whining, spinning my wheels, until Kim picked up the phone and took care of it. She told us Bob sounded hurt.

I felt like a simp, but I had persuaded myself: starting with our next gig, we were going to present a brand-new, piledriving Sonic Youth to whoever was paying attention.

We had been booked to appear at the Mudd Club with Swans. Jeffrey Lee Pierce from the Gun Club was hanging about the room before we played. I reintroduced myself as the guy who had interviewed him for my zine and invited him to join us for a version of the Stooges' "I Wanna

Be Your Dog." He knew Tom from L.A., and he coolly accepted the offer, scurrying up onto the stage and singing along with Kim.

After our set, Swans gave us the thumbs-up: Tom had thrashed away magnificently.

Despite the tension that our East Coast jaunt had inspired, we all agreed to jump in Chassler's van again for a second leg of the Savage Blunder tour, this time out to the Midwest and back. Tom was on board to join us, at first, but a few days prior to leaving, he called to say that he didn't feel ready—nor was he particularly eager to cram into the back of a window-less van with nine others, only to trudge out to the stormy Midwest with no promise of money.

His reasoning was sound enough, though I was still of the mind that anyone should want to drop everything they had going on and take off down the road with a bunch of other penniless musicians, some of them aggressive and confrontational, to play gigs in freezing clubs that may or may not contain a few paying guests, only to load up gear at the end of each late night and sleep at whoever's pad was on offer.

What could be the problem?

As consolation, Tom agreed to play one more gig with us, at Maxwell's in Hoboken, the night before we were due to take off. It turned out to be a freezing night of rain. Bob met us after the show. I had asked him, shame-facedly, if he'd consider returning to the fold, and, generously, he agreed.

So, loading our gear into the van, we bid farewell to Tom and shot off into the cold black night toward Michigan, Bob once again huddled in with us.

As we set up for sound check at Joe's Star Lounge in Ann Arbor, the pro-moter mentioned that Stooges legend Ron Asheton was planning on being there, joined by his bandmate and girlfriend, Niagara. Ron appeared decked out in a leather jacket and teardrop eyeglasses; Niagara was rail thin and astounding, her black hair teased exquisitely across her shoul-ders, her eyes and smile glowing out from her translucent face.

After our set, we hung out with those two, a tremendous thrill as Ron Asheton was the guitarist I had lionized more than any other. When he complimented the band on our take on the Stooges' "I Wanna Be Your Dog," I melted. He said he would gladly play it with us next time we blew through town, a promise he would not break.

Chassler drove us through a wet and savage blizzard en route to Minneapolis, the van slipping and sliding through the blackness of the Illinois night, slowing down at times to a ten-mile-per-hour crawl as huge tractor trailers sped by, spraying torrents of slush and grit against our windshield. He eventually decided to pull off onto the shoulder of the highway for a few hours with the hazard lights blinking while we all attempted to sleep, listening to the storm battering the vehicle, shivering as we wore every stitch of clothing each of us had.

Michael would later recall how completely and utterly dispiriting both legs of the Savage Blunder tour had been, as if every ounce of creative energy and sweat he had invested simply fell into a clangorous abyss, each and every night, hardly a peep of constructive response from anyone other than ourselves.

For the most part we found strength in our camaraderie. By the time we returned to Manhattan, though, Jonathan, having tussled with Michael one too many times, would opt to depart Swans.

For our part, Michael and I would remain friends, bombing around the seedier parts of the city together: investigating the demoralized destitution of Times Square, watching slasher-film triple features in rank cinemas tucked inside scummy buildings. But within a year, as the bands followed their individual aspirations, we would slowly drift apart. Swans became only more intense—a solitary hangman's noose would become their sole piece of stage set design. Sonic Youth would, conversely, further our interest in communitarian ideals, investigating more positive-minded noise action—drawing from the spirit music of free improvisation and the trance-drone sonics of psychedelia.

It turned into a bit of a Rolling Stones versus Beatles thing, with Swans and us. There was never any animosity; we just took different roads, made different friends. Through it all, though, we would appreciate the history we shared in our early days, those weeks and months of living on top of each other, filled with wonder at where we could all be headed.

After returning from the frozen Midwest, we, once again, let Bob go. It was a cold thing to do, but for good or for ill, Sonic Youth was the nucleus of Lee, Kim, and me. An unstated feeling existed among us that whoever was drumming was there only as an invited guest, at least until some kind of established membership was offered.

Bob must have felt taken advantage of by the band in our time of desperation—and justifiably so. While it wasn't unusual with fledgling groups such as ours, this shedding and gaining of members as we negotiated our youthful way into the world, he was right to feel hurt by it.

Still, we needed a drummer. I rang up Jim Sclavunos to see if he'd be interested. After performing and recording with him in Lydia's In Limbo project, I felt he'd be an excellent addition. Jim's playing was more subdued, a less bombastic approach than Bob's. I knew it might not be the exact right energy for Sonic Youth, but I was willing to give it a try if he was.

We would debut with Sclavunos at a gig at the Kitchen. I decided to go wild. As we tore through "Confusion Is Next," I barreled through the audience members sitting on the floor in front of the low-rise stage. As much as the Kitchen crowd welcomed noise, this kind of physical interaction was new. After Iggy Pop and James Chance, everyone felt more or less safe from such invasions of their space by the performers they paid to see.

Bob graciously attended the show, and I was happy to see him there. He was upbeat, excited by our set, breaking down the ways Jim had been excellent on some songs and citing others that he thought he had played better himself—which I had to agree with.

Jon Pareles of the *New York Times* was in attendance, and he reviewed the gig in its venerable pages—

Sonic Youth gets most of its noise from up to three rapidly strummed electric guitars, which compete with shouted vocals by Thurston Moore or Kim Gordon . . . Like Glenn Branca's symphonies . . . the music focuses on texture and the "resultant melodies" each listener picks out of a complex drone.

Pareles pointed to my "stage moves" too, which he said owed a debt to Iggy Pop and John Lydon. It was far and away the most significant recognition we had gotten from the press so far. We were beginning to feel critically validated, and we were unabashedly thrilled.

It was around this time, at a Swans gig at the Ukrainian National Home on Second Avenue downtown, that I met a smiling gent by the name of John Erskine. He looked a few years older than me. As he critiqued the acoustics of the room, and how a band such as Swans could succeed in such a space with the right sound engineer, I took careful note.

He claimed to have witnessed a few Sonic Youth shows and offered us his sound services, writing his phone number down on the back of a matchbook.

I proceeded to introduce John to everyone: Michael, Lydia, Glenn, Rhys. He was soon manning the front-of-house controls for all of us, managing the sporadic levels of personality disorder we all threw at any sound technician whom we felt was at odds with our music-making.

Michael, who had once explained to an aging sound guy that he wanted Swans to sound as if the audience were being slammed in the chest by slamming his own hand hard into the sound guy's chest, was relieved to have some consistency, an engineer with an understanding of such demands. We all were.

Tod Jorgensen, whom we knew from A's and who had been manning the color Xerox machine at Jamie Canvas, the art supply store in SoHo, struck out on his own to open Todd's Copy Shop on Mott Street, between Spring and Prince. He acquired a state-of-the-art color copier, which would attract all the color-hungry artists in the neighborhood.

Kim was offered and accepted a job working the machines. The film-maker Sara Driver was already employed there. The shop soon became a daily hangout for Kim, Sara, Jim Jarmusch (Sara's filmmaker beau), and me.

The interior was small, the color copier sharing space with a black-and-white machine and a tabletop for organizing and stapling. Local artists and musicians hung around for all-day streams of neighborhood chitchat. Dan Graham, Richard Prince, Michael Zwack, Jean-Michel Basquiat, Kenny Scharf, Barbara Ess, Kiki Smith, Keith Haring, and Lawrence and Alice Weiner would all pop in to catch up on the latest gossip, to make copies of flyers for shows, or to create color elements for their work.

Eventually I began sharing shifts with Kim. It had the added benefit of allowing me to run off copies of my *Killer* fanzine when Tod was out, though he became suspicious when reams of copy paper were found to be missing.

Sara, auburn-haired with smart, glowing eyes, was always cheerful next to Jim Jarmusch, his voice a wry, curious tenor, his bushy white hair stacked upon his head. Sara and Jim had created a buzz with a 1980 film they had worked on together entitled *Permanent Vacation*, the first feature-length project Jim wrote and directed after arriving in New York City from Ohio in the early seventies. The film followed a young man in his early twenties moving about downtown, the first depiction on-screen, for many of us, of something that resembled our own lives.

The two were now in the process of producing a film about three other New York City characters, brought together incongruously and soon to become fish out of water as they leave Manhattan. Titled *Stranger Than Paradise,* the film would feature our first drummer, Richard Edson, in a colead role with John Lurie from the Lounge Lizards and Eszter Balint, the young actress from the Squat Theatre who had gotten me that forty-dollar DJing gig a year earlier.

Stranger Than Paradise would become a sensation, at least in the world of independent cinema. It would take Sara and Jim away from the worka-day Todd's—right around the same time that Sonic Youth would spirit Kim and me away to our own vistas of surprise.

38

CHAOS IS THE FUTURE

Confusion Is Sex would be our first proper full-length album, as opposed to our self-titled debut, which had been designated a "mini-LP" because of its brief running time. It was recorded in December 1982 at Fun City Studios, the newly rigged recording basement constructed by the ex–Theoretical Girls and A Band drummer Wharton Tiers.

Glenn and Josh had made it clear that Neutral was cash poor and unable to invest in any other sessions until further notice. We took this in stride, never really expecting that a label would be some kind of continued benefactor of our music—that kind of relationship never even occurred to us. We were simply grateful for what Glenn had done for our band. But we knew that we needed to record the new songs we had been playing and developing all year.

The records I was most enamored with were still the hardcore singles I had been collecting—each produced with a pride of economy, usually manufactured in editions of no more than a few hundred. It wasn't about exclusivity; they struck a balance between what a band could actually afford and how many they thought they could reasonably sell.

I thought the coolest record we could possibly make just then would be a single of our song "Confusion Is Next," which was our personalized take on hardcore, though through the prism of downtown art rock. Wharton invited us over to his studio to get started. Kim, Lee, Jim Sclavunos, and I ran through the song a few times and it sounded great. We also recorded a version of "Inhuman," thinking it would be the perfect B side for the single.

We played the tapes for Glenn and Peter Wright, the new head of Neutral Records, who had dropped by for a listen. Everyone agreed: we needed to record *all* our new tunes. The session was totally on fire. So we asked our Swiss friends Catherine and Nicolas if we could borrow a few hundred dollars for more tape, as well as to pay Wharton, and they graciously agreed. Wharton had a four-track reel-to-reel recorder. We ganged it with another rented reel-to-reel in order to have eight tracks to work with—and we were off.

For all the musical chemistry, there was at times a weird vibe pervading the session. Jim Sclavunos seemed to feel at odds with what we were doing. It's possible he was losing interest in Sonic Youth and wanted to call it a day, to focus on what he was up to in his other projects, the bands Trigger & the Thrill Kings and T-Venus. Whatever the reason, when it came time to record "Making the Nature Scene," it soon became frustratingly apparent to Kim, Lee, and me that the tune just didn't move and groove the way it did with Bob Bert's jungle pound.

We asked Jim if he would be okay with us inviting Bob over to record, and he complied with what came across as understanding. But it definitely introduced a fissure between us. Jim's playing on the other material had been great and swinging, bringing an elegance to our messy sprawl—but he would soon depart Sonic Youth.

Bob, twice jilted but full of good spirit, bounded into Fun City. He had good reason to resent us. Instead he nailed "Making the Nature Scene" in one take.

We were able to record everything in a few days, once in a while skipping out to the corner bodega to fetch cigarettes, drinks, and snacks. Each time I pulled open the refrigerator doors where the cold drinks sat, I marveled at the gorgeous hum coming from inside. After dragging everyone over to check out this subsonic drone, we decided to record it with a portable cassette player, still a rather new machine to have access to. We named the resulting piece "Freezer Burn," splicing a section of it—which we would overdub with bare-bones guitar feedback—onto a live cassette recording we had of us playing the Stooges' "I Wanna Be Your Dog," at the Pier in Raleigh, North Carolina, on the Savage Blunder tour.

Such cassette recordings would become critical to the album. After creating a rough mix of the song "Shaking Hell"—which Kim had written the lyrics to for *Rock My Religion,* a new film of Dan Graham's focusing on the parallels between rock music as a means of transcendence (as exemplified through Patti Smith's rock 'n' roll idolatry and the dancers circling in the slam pit at a Minor Threat gig) and the ritualistic trances of the Shaker communities dotted around New England in the 1800s—we transferred it to a cassette so we could listen to it at home. We realized we could never mix the tune to sound as cool as that rough take. But when we got back to the studio, we found that we had somehow erased the original reel-to-reel recording. So we ended up transferring the cassette dupe *back* to the reel-to-reel, and it sounded hot.

The only two songs we recorded that we hadn't performed during the tours with Swans were "Protect Me You," the only track on which Lee would play bass guitar in the entire course of the band's history, and "Lee Is Free," a reel-to-reel recording Lee had made at his apartment with overdubbed gamelan-like guitars playing off each other, tape speeds shifting, distinct in each channel. Lee had brought the tape in for us to hear, and we immediately decided to include it to close out the album. It jibed with the elemental experimentation running through the session, bringing it to a meditative closure.

I wanted to title the album *Confusion Is Sex* for no other reason than how it rolled off the tongue, playing off the title of the song we had instigated the recording with. Sexual expression held a conflicted place in the downtown scene. It could be either explicitly acknowledged in the work, as with Lydia Lunch or the writer Kathy Acker, or more muted, as with no wave's taste for the androgynous, its scenesters draping themselves in rags that were deliberately nonsexual. Our album riffed on that division. The graphics that went with it were more savage than the stately typeface from our first release, the band name and album title hand-rendered in black Magic Marker, evoking rock 'n' roll noise and energy.

The album was released in February 1983 after hectic splicing and sequencing of tape, some of which had been eaten and crinkled by the reel-to-reel tape machine, some that had been doused by a toppled can of Coca-Cola. But it all survived, more or less, as Wharton, John Erskine (our soundman now in assistant engineer mode), and the band learned together how to make a record, drawing as much from the takes as the mistakes, all of it adding to the momentous energy we collectively had captured. It felt as though we had taken a fire and alchemized it into a fat ferrous oxide strip of magnetic tape.

During the second week of February, a snowstorm rampaged along the East Coast, burying New York City in what the newspapers would refer to as the "Megalopolitan Blizzard." The city would stop—no work, no school, no cars or buses; the subways barely functioning—only a lone taxi sloshing and sliding adventurously along an avenue, its tires wrapped in chains, or else a cop car or fire engine once in a while attempting to save someone's day.

Blizzards such as these allowed a communal reprieve from the hectic life in the city, its millions of citizens huddled into whatever shelters they had at their disposal. There were times, during the winter months, when I would jump onto the Metro-North Railroad to Connecticut so I could see my family, only for the entire train to stop, its electricity shut down, the steel wheels frozen to the rails, and I would sit there trapped in the dark of the car, shivering, with no means of communication, at times for hours.

But for all their inconvenience, the whiteouts of deep winter were gorgeous and romantic in their silence, gleaming and cold, the yellow lights of bodegas coloring the silver air, a few bodies traipsing clumsily through the embankments, sometimes running into each other, maybe recognizing a friend beneath the woolen caps and scarves and coat collars upturned about the neck, smiling at the wild reality of nature's majesty.

39

WHAT MAKES A MAN
START FIRES?

The band that was the greatest focus of my obsession in the early months of 1983 was the Minutemen, a trio from San Pedro, California. They were at once outside of anything else happening musically while being wholly informed by just about *everything* that had been going on musically, from their faraway hero Richard Hell to their Southern California compatriots, including Saccharine Trust, Black Flag, and the Urinals—even the heady excellence of pre-punk acts like Blue Öyster Cult, T. Rex, Creedence Clearwater Revival, John Coltrane, and Funkadelic.

The band was on tour with Black Flag during the springtime of 1983, and Kim and I made sure not to miss them when they played their own gig (their first in New York) at the Wednesday night Music for Dozens series at Folk City. From their first song, we were transported. Every tune was an economical construction, allowing for evocative lyrics, sometimes serious and sometimes comic, calling out the poisonous threat of fascism and even the absurdity of having to make such a musical commentary. "If Reagan Played Disco," "Bob Dylan Wrote Propaganda Songs," and "A Political Song for Michael Jackson to Sing" as song titles alone were wildly inspired.

Guitarist-singer D. Boon was a portly dude who ripped at his guitar with fleet spurting leads, all treble, cutting through the hammering low-end runs from bassist-singer Mike Watt, the two totally locked into the thrashing drums of George Hurley. The songs were one or two minutes at the most and featured rousing chant-alongs, each a miniature manifesto.

I wanted what they had for Sonic Youth—the sound and attitude, the eagerness to effect change through community action. They made you want to run to your practice space and *play*.

Five nights later, Lee, Kim, Michael Gira, and I headed to Great Gildersleeves to see their show with Black Flag. The club was jam-packed with punks, artists, straight people, weird people, old people, young people. During Black Flag's set, while the band went spiraling into an extended version of their tune "Scream," Henry Rollins, already lacerating the blasted fabric of the club's atmosphere, disappeared from my view. Standing three-quarters of the way toward the back of the club, I could see certain sections of the audience ebb and flow as if a river of snakes was slithering underfoot.

A minute or so later, I realized what was happening. Henry, shirtless, clad only in dirty trousers and a pair of beat-up black leather shoes, had been writhing across the club's wooden floor, a primordial hunk of muscle and bone. His body was gashed with scrapes, burns, grime, and spittle, broken glass, shards of plastic, and cigarette butts sticking to his skin, his arms wrapped around his head and his mouth yowling a silent scream.

This was hardcore theater. This was raw, eviscerating reason and raging at every inner phantom. I wasn't the only one who was impressed. I could see how it was blowing Michael's mind. We were awed by Black Flag's power and urgency. I knew then, with absolute assurance, that I needed to channel not only the Minutemen's power of musical and lyrical conviction but also Black Flag's unbridled deliverance and possession into my own music, no matter where it took me.

The author in 1987, closing in on
thirty years old and keeping it
clean at City Gardens in Trenton,
New Jersey

BOOK FOUR

40

JIGSAW FEELING

Branca booked a tour of Europe in order to perform his newly composed "Symphony No. 4 (Physics)," and I was invited to join. The ensemble, in addition to Lee and me, would include eight musicians. Lee and I were the designated tuners for all the guitars. With Glenn's tuning system and an oscillator the size of a small suitcase, I would dial in the tones and Lee would tune the strings to them.

Kim had initially been invited to join the ensemble but had been cut from the roster before any rehearsals. It became an issue for us, as we had decided to book some Sonic Youth gigs on the tail end of Glenn's tour, for what would be our first shows in Europe. The fact that Glenn might facilitate the three of us being in Europe at once would be a huge help financially. But it was not to be.

Lee and I met with Glenn in an office space he had been renting downtown, where he sat with stacks of papers and folders of score notation, along with an array of guitars in varying states of radical modification. Some of them had been strung with piano wire, others had thick screws acting as nodes along the fretboards, and a few had had the frets stripped out of them. Most of the guitar bodies had been physically altered from their original state and re-created as idiosyncratic works of art.

Lee and I asked Glenn if he would reconsider, but he was resolute. It was strange; he and Kim had had a good association for some time— certainly more so than a few others in the touring party. It's possible he felt less comfortable being in a dictatorial role over her than the others in the group, which included Wharton Tiers and Margaret De Wys (both of whom had been members, with Glenn, of Theoretical Girls) and his partner, Barbara Ess. They were perhaps more familiar with Glenn's propensity for megalomania. It's possible he feared that having both Kim and me, a couple, in the ensemble might interfere with the overall dynamics.

Whatever the reason, he wouldn't budge. It was not going to happen.

Despite this setback, we went ahead and booked a few gigs starting after the end of Glenn's run, with the hope that we could pick some more up while on the road.

As ever, our next concern was who to have sitting at the drums. It led us, once again, to Bob Bert. With the promise of him not losing money on the venture and that we wouldn't kick him out again after it was finished, Bob signed on.

Before Lee and I departed with Glenn, Sonic Youth was booked to play Speed Trials, a series of gigs happening at White Columns at the beginning of May. It was an event much in the spirit of Noise Fest, this time curated by members of Live Skull. Bob mentioned prior to the show that he had not only been practicing quite a bit but had been playing with a few local Hoboken bands. The difference was immediately apparent—and exhilarating. At Speed Trials, his playing was more fluid, with a more energized and engaged spirit.

We were slotted to play the opening night of the festival, joined by Manchester punk legends the Fall. Unlike the agitated stage presence of most first-generation punk bands, the Fall exhibited a dour, workmanlike attitude. They prowled into the room, plugging their guitars in with drab expressions on their faces and running through their set on the gallery floor. Their sound, though, ran in stark contrast to their visages—it was exploding, raging, and thrilling.

Vocalist Mark E. Smith held a burning cigarette in one hand, a microphone in the other, the two drummers behind him establishing an aggressive field of rhythm, the bass and guitar jamming repetitively atop it all. Smith's nonchalance was the band's defining vibe. He doused the cig in an ashtray on the floor, stuck his hand in his trouser pocket, then recited a monotone stream of prose, steeped in his Mancunian brogue. It was imperious and seductive in its bored delivery, once in a while spiked with a high-pitched squeak, as if he were a scabrous English schoolboy raising his voice to make a point.

With my first-ever passport rubber-banded to my plane tickets, I packed a large rucksack full of underwear, socks, a few books, and the score I had prepared for Glenn's music. Having never traveled abroad, I kept it light and simple.

Kim and I had been inseparable since we first moved in together. My shooting off to Europe for a few weeks was uncharted emotional territory. She had our dog and cat, Egan and Sweetface, of course. But this would be the first time we were apart, and we kept hugging goodbye. I promised to send postcards. Kim wanted to make sure I had everything I needed. She kept handing me a pencil, her eyes welling up.

Flying overseas for the first time felt as if I were jetting to some other planet, particularly as we stopped off in Iceland for a few hours to change planes. The view from the Keflavík Airport looked out over what seemed to be a lunar landscape. The Fall had been on the same flight with Lee and me, though they would deplane in Iceland to gig in Reykjavík, while we went off to do the Branca dates.

The beauty of the European countries we would see was both overwhelming and sublime. There were the base pleasures of beer, food, wine, and hashish, not to mention the grandiosity of the museums, cathedrals, and landscapes, all of them more ancient and profound than what I'd known from our colonized North America.

Our concerts were held either at established venues such as Munich's Alabamahalle or in alternative spaces connected to the European art world—these would prove to be the main financial support for our unwieldy productions, Glenn's music extremely marginal even here in Europe, where there was seemingly more appetite for such experimentation. The German artists Isa Genzken, Gerhard Richter, A. R. Penck, and Martin Kippenberger would all make appearances in Cologne and Düsseldorf.

Often Glenn was frustrated and irascible as he and soundman John Erskine attempted to achieve the desired volume in the acoustically dead rooms, the sound systems woefully unprepared for his onslaught. During an interminable sound check at Alabamahalle, Glenn decided, after caving in to the club's sound limitations, to push all our amplifiers to the lip of the stage and to have all of us musicians stand behind them. The confounded audience entered the venue only to be met by an assault of guitars blaring out of the phalanx of amps, each one cranked as high as it could go. They would jockey around the front of the stage to peer between the amps so as to glimpse Glenn conducting us.

During one section of the concert, Glenn became more and more agitated, spurring us on to dig harder into the music. I began strumming my guitar so forcibly that the strings began to snap off one by one. Afterward in the dressing room, Glenn looked at me with a scowl, sweating profusely, a threadbare towel around his neck. He threw a nasty invective at me.

It was then that I realized: I had no interest in being a hired musician—in Glenn's or anyone's project. I loved the camaraderie, but I bristled at the authority.

When we played at the Riverside Studios in London, Lydia happened to be in town, and she brought along her friends Siouxsie Sioux and Steven Severin from the Banshees. The room we played in was fairly sterile, the audience all seated. Us musicians sat in metal folding chairs, and as Glenn prepared to cue the ensemble into a section, I felt the need to readjust my body, scraping my chair slightly forward in the dead quiet—once, and then twice. Glenn shot me a quick glare of annoyance.

Afterward, I met up with Lydia and her London pals in the lobby. I asked her what she thought of the concert. She meowed with delight—

"More chair scrapings, T-Stone!"

Between cities and gigs, we often found ourselves waiting together at train stations, each one a work of art. I would take pictures with a disposable camera and buy postcards to send home to Kim, remorseful that she was missing the rich beauty of these places, the majestic sweep of the landscapes rushing by.

Boarding our trains, we would attempt to commandeer an empty passenger compartment so as to sit together. More often we would all just scramble to find any seat available to avoid being relegated to standing in the train car's walkway.

Barbara, Glenn, and I scored a completely empty compartment on one trip. I proposed that we pretend to be zonked-out junkies, so no other passengers would want to enter. At each stop, Glenn and I scrunched down in our seats, making sure our hair was fully messed up, with shirts untucked and shoes off, our bodies doubled over as if nodded out. For the most part it didn't succeed at anything other than earning us strange looks from the local travelers—they didn't care if we were dead or alive; they just needed to sit down.

The concert we played at the Holland Festival, the most prestigious of arts festivals in the Netherlands, was in the Muziekcentrum located in Utrecht. It was scheduled to be filmed for national television. During the sound check, a debate over the level of our amplification nearly canceled the event. We ultimately performed, though almost the entire audience vacated the building, unable to withstand our din.

Lydia, also appearing at the festival, was one of the few remaining souls in the room, along with her confidante Jessamy Calkin, an astute London journalist and gothic doppelgänger to Lydia who had been employed by her to bang on pipes and break glass onstage while backing tapes of our In Limbo sessions were played. Jessamy and Lydia were sitting with Xaviera Hollander, the Netherlands' infamous and celebrated "Happy Hooker." As I approached this unholy triumvirate, they sat with grins on their faces, appreciative of Glenn's refusal to play nice.

It was hard not to fall in love with Holland, its towns of cobblestoned streets running along flowered canals and lined with hashish cafés and museums filled with old-world masterpieces, its cheerful people who embraced experimental music, punk rock, and free improvisation.

Lee would introduce me to his friend Carlos van Hijfte, whom he had met while touring Europe with Glenn's ensemble in 1980. Like seemingly most Dutchmen, Carlos was tall and broad, alert and funny, exuding a centeredness that came with residing in one of the most forward-thinking countries in the world. He had been instrumental in introducing Lee (along with his Fluks bandmate David Linton) to a young, experimental singer-songwriter named Truus de Groot, who had been performing under the name Plus Instruments. Truus lived in Carlos's hometown of Eindhoven, where a wild underground music scene flourished. She relocated to downtown Manhattan in early 1981, and she, Lee, and David played gigs (still as Plus Instruments) along the Tier 3—Mudd Club axis.

By the time we recorded *Confusion Is Sex,* Plus Instruments had (after a few lineup changes) disbanded, with Truus and Jim Sclavunos subsequently becoming a musical—and romantic—couple, performing for a while as Trigger & the Thrill Kings.

Carlos was booking shows at De Effenaar, the main arts center in Eindhoven, where he had been witness to the Sex Pistols and Joy Division, capturing them on his movie camera. In the months and years to come, he would assist us as Sonic Youth took our first baby steps across the continent, becoming one of our most intimate associates throughout the band's history.

At last Kim flew to Paris, joined by John Erskine's wife, Shelly. The two boarded a train to Poitiers, France, where the Branca tour was coming to a pause. I was bristling with anticipation to see her. It had been almost a month that we'd been apart. Entering the rustic hotel lobby, the day blue and sunny, I saw her at the front desk retrieving a key to our room.

Glenn's tour had been so overwhelming—the interactions and the dramas, the rampaging sound checks and concerts, the anxiety of travel, waiting for trains, seeking food, dealing with snoring roommates, every moment a constant engagement of the senses with no room for escape or meditation—that for a flash I didn't recognize this person from a previous world, the back of her hair now cut short, streaked with a subtle gold, and her body smaller than I remembered.

She turned, her eyes and smile connecting with mine, and the distance fell away. I showed her to our room, the windows opened to the French sunshine, trellises of flora, and birds serenading the day.

41

SHAKE THROB THRASH SWITCH STROKE SWEEP SLAM BRUSH

Catherine and Nicolas Ceresole were staying at Nicolas's family's house in Rolle, Switzerland, a small town overlooking Lake Geneva on the Grand-Rue, up the street from where the great nouvelle vague film director Jean-Luc Godard resided. The couple invited Glenn and Barbara, Lee and Amanda Linn (a dancer and choreographer engaged to Lee at the time), and Kim and me to stay in the large abode, its backyard stretching out to the docks on the lake.

The two days we spent there were passed sleeping late, then slow hours of doing nothing but sitting around a large wooden kitchen table, slicing into huge loaves of crunchy baked bread accompanied by cheeses and local white wines, smoking fat hash joints, and taking rowboats out to the middle of the lake. Whatever tension existed between Glenn and me quickly dissipated, his innate charm and humor winning over the atmosphere.

In the second week of June 1983, Sonic Youth played our debut gig in Europe at the Grand Salle d'Entre-Bois in Lausanne, Switzerland, less than an hour away from Rolle. Bob spent his twenty-eighth birthday flying from New York City to Paris, then boarding a train to Lausanne.

We had already sound-checked without him, and we were due to go onstage by the time he had been brought to the club, straight from the Lausanne train station. Lee, Kim, and I had acclimated ourselves to the time difference; we were well rested from the Ceresoles' spa-like accommodations—unlike Bob, whom we welcomed with glee, but who was obviously jet-lagged, unwashed, and utterly fried.

He halted when he saw the drum kit that awaited him. It was a massive black Staccato set, the toms and kick drum having oversized, curled shell bottoms that protruded out instead of down, said to be the loudest kit on the market. The only drummers known for playing such monstrous assemblies were Billy Cobham (who played with Miles Davis), Keith Moon of the Who, and John Bonham of Led Zeppelin. Bob shook his head at the insanity. He sat down to begin the series of crashes that began "The Burning Spear."

We knew things were going to be different from our experiences in the U.S. when we saw that the fifty or so people who had shown up at the gig were mostly straight-up punk rockers—a plethora of dyed mohawks and leather jackets with studs and Crass badges. They crowded to the lip of the stage as we delved into our set, then began shouting, pogoing, slamming into each other, passing bottles of beer and whiskey around, huffing huge spliffs. One kid wrapped a cellophane bag around his head and banged up against the stage, a hyperventilating lunatic.

Our sets were still played in the downtown New York style, which usually meant they lasted for no more than thirty minutes. When we finished and walked to the tiny dressing room off to the side of the stage, the kids weren't ready for us to be done. They went nuts, slamming bottles on the stage, barraging the room with chaotic screams and howls. It was as though, I thought, our music—rife with clanging noise, buzzing feedback, and stomping rhythms—had set them off to a maniacal place.

We had never, ever received a response like this back home.

Lee and I had at least three guitars each. Kim had brought her bass along, and we used whatever amps and drums the clubs would supply. It was always a crapshoot whether venue-supplied amps would work the way we needed, each of us having to contend with ripped speakers or low-powered output, the sound often muffled and muddy.

John Erskine recommended that we turn our amps down in order for the vocals to be heard in the mix. As it was, we rarely could hear the vocals ourselves; the monitors seemed never to be able to compete with our guitar noise. Kim and I were fairly challenged in the singing-in-key department. Not being able to hear our own voices onstage must have created some ear-bending moments for our audiences.

The train system in Europe prided itself on running on time. We bought Eurorail passes and decoded the timetables at each train station, usually with the help of a local promoter. Sometimes we had to jump on a train as it was moving slowly out of the station, barely getting the guitars on board. More than once a couple of us shoved guitars through open windows to the others inside, as the locomotive began to chug forward, then leaped aboard, huffing and puffing, wondering what would have happened if any of us had been left behind.

This was the beginning of us, as a band, falling in love with the world: meeting people for a day or two, our similar interests binding us, the diversity of personalities all in service of music and experimental wonder.

Arriving at the club Loft in Berlin, we were met on the street by Blixa Bargeld, the singer in Einstürzende Neubauten, the band Lee had raved about after seeing them while on tour with Glenn a couple of years earlier. Blixa looked astounding, tall and whip thin, his black hair shooting up like wild growth, exposing a pale white face with wide eyes and a slightly devious smile. He was outfitted in a black leather one-piece suit with a priest's collar around his neck.

We tumbled out of our rental van in our own finery: my white button-down shirt yellowed from being unwashed for a month and a half of touring, Lee in a checkered short-sleeved shirt, Kim wearing a bootleg Minor Threat *Out of Step* T-shirt, all of us in torn dungarees, Kim's with streaks of glitter glued to them. We couldn't have looked more different from Blixa and his all-out display. He welcomed us to Berlin and helped us load our gear in.

Loft was run by an amazing woman named Monika Döring who, in 1983, was forty-six years of age, which, for bands such as ours, seemed unfathomably old. She and her husband, Heiner, had the idea for a venue that would cater to all the new avant-garde post-punk bands rising up. Loft became the center of Berlin's underground music scene.

Monika had a shock of blond hair sprouting from her head, her face glowing with wild swatches of colorful makeup, her clothing a postmodern couture of leather and feathers accented with multiple bangles, beads, large constructivist earrings, and an assortment of glittering necklaces. She smoked cigarettes in a long ceramic filter with one hand, a glass of champagne in the other, always talking, laughing, and absolutely loving every second of her life.

Heiner wore stately and dapper suits, smiling, never saying too much, though obviously in crazy love with his genius partner. They gave dignity to all the freaks coming into their zone, be it Branca, Lydia, James Chance, Johnny Thunders, Sonic Youth, Swans, the Birthday Party, or Bad Brains. To enter Monika's light was to find yourself in a charmed space.

At the tail end of June we played at De Effenaar in Eindhoven, connecting again with the club's booker, Carlos van Hijfte, and his partner,

Moniek, all of us meeting up with Remko Scha, whom we knew from New York City.

Remko was a fascinating experimental musician known for hanging amplified guitars from ceilings, which he would strum, stroke, and beat using mechanized elements that he would control with levers from a tabletop in the middle of the room. I had first seen and heard this incredible phenomenon at a 1980 Tier 3 performance, when Remko had shared a bill with Branca, the two men great enthusiasts of each other.

Remko was already in his mid-thirties, and he cut a glamorous figure, sporting punkish mohair jackets. His erudition, as a professor of linguistics, was countered by his love for rock 'n' roll, which he would call "our own living tradition."

We all met at Het Apollohuis, an arts center founded in 1980. It was amazing to stroll in to find an entire wall of record albums and, on the floor, an array of PVC pipes, kettle drums, metal sheets, and other percussive noisemakers. Remko explained that the San Francisco percussionist Z'ev had been coming in and out of town, using the space to rehearse. Peeling through the records, I was astounded to see every punk album I knew of side by side with art music, jazz, classical, and folk recordings— the most extensive record collection I had yet come across.

Someday I'll have a wall like this, I thought dreamily, *a library of sound.*

Soon enough it was time for us to return to New York. We flew home from Amsterdam's Schiphol Airport, my mind racing with thoughts provoked by our time in Europe. I wanted to gather the forces of Sonic Youth, Swans, and Lydia in service of a new epoch of creativity. It seemed to me that with our collective inspirations, we could forge a world of our own, distinct from anything that had come before us; a movement energized by its own visions; an intellectual forum for art, literature, music, and cinema.

Catherine and Nicolas returned from overseas too. They began to have us all up to their apartment again for food, drinks, and smokes. On one occasion, Lydia, also back in the States, sat next to me on the couch along with Bob, Lee, Kim, Swans guitarist Sue Hanel, Michael Gira, Martin Rev, and Branca collaborator Rudolph Grey. On the other side of the room sat Nick Cave and Rowland Howard of the Birthday Party and Blixa Bargeld of Einstürzende Neubauten (both bands playing gigs in New York just then). The three were huddled together sporting skinny-legged black leather trousers and debonair yet disheveled suit coats, an air of junkie chic dripping from their gorgeous, wasted faces.

Lydia whispered in my ear—

"Over there"

—nodding toward the gothic trio—

"rotten fruit in a rubber suit. Over here"

—jabbing her elbow in my side—

"Sonic Death Rockers."

42

ARCHITEKTUR & GEISELNAHME

Peter Wright of Neutral Records had arranged for a couple of young English girls visiting New York City to stay at our apartment while Kim and I were overseas, to look after our pets. One of the girls, Pat Naylor, had been part of the Manchester scene around Joy Division and the Buzzcocks and their record labels, Factory and New Hormones.

After returning, we put Pat and her friend on our guest list at CBGB, which we played shortly after we got back. Hitting the stage, we felt flush with new energy from the tour, the swaths of sound more defined as our confidence grew.

After our set, we headed out to the Bowery to find a modicum of relief from the intense July heat. My heart lifted when Live Skull bassist Marnie Greenholz ran over to us, clearly lit up, exclaiming how amazing she thought we were. No praise from any media could ever come close to how good it felt to have this kind of validation from a fellow musician.

That summer of 1983, we played shows at the Sin Club and Folk City, both with the trio Ut, whom we were becoming more and more bonded with. The three members—Nina Canal, Jacqui Ham, and Sally Young—shared an aesthetic with Sonic Youth in free-form guitar exploration. These gigs would also be where we'd debut such new songs as "Kill Yr Idols," "Early American," and "Brother James."

"Brother James" had come about as I sat in our apartment with my guitar, strumming it open while rotating the tuning pegs tighter then looser, listening and closing in on the open-stroked sound that had the beauty, warmth, and glow my brain desired. This would be my first move away from either the standard or the loosely defined tunings we had been using for our initial clutch of songs. As it turned out, the three notes I centered on—G, D, and D#—hit a cool, hypnotic spot. "Brother James," as with so many of our pieces, was the result of investigation into such tunings; the only method was to listen, feel, reveal, and refine.

Lyle Hysen, drummer of Misguided and editor of the *Damaged Goods* fanzine, came to the Folk City gig at the suggestion of his girlfriend, Susanne Sasic. They brought along their friend Jesse Malin, the teenage singer of the band Heart Attack. Jesse asked me if I had seen the Dead Boys in the 1970s. I acknowledged that I had, and he just shook his head, as if it must have been the most radical thing ever. It was, indeed, but this was the first time I could remember that a younger person had referred to those ground-zero punk times as a sort of good old days.

"It really wasn't that long ago"
—I ventured.
"Yeah, but I would've been six years old."
I definitely wasn't the kid in the room anymore.

Susanne, meanwhile, was a vision, with long red hair, gleaming eyes, and an understated style. She became a mainstay of our shows, standing always just off to the side, bopping to our noisy weirdness. Eventually she would hop into the tour van with us, first to run the merchandise table of Sonic Youth T-shirts and records, then, after commenting on how the lights were always kind of lame at our gigs, designing and orchestrating our visuals.

Lyle invited us to be part of a benefit show for the Vancouver Five, a Canadian activist collective who had been jailed for bombing nuclear weapon manufacturing facilities, ecologically threatening substations, and porn video emporiums known to stock snuff films. One member, Gerry Hannah (aka Gerry Useless), was the bassist of the Vancouver punk band Subhumans. His incarceration would inspire a spate of defense fund benefits in punk communities across North America.

The New York City show was to be held at the Charas New Assembly Theater on East Tenth Street between Avenues B and C. I knew this audience was going to be mostly people into hardcore, and I decided to go completely off, showing that our band was beyond any punk noise they had heard. During "The Burning Spear" I wailed so hard on my guitar with a drumstick that I nearly took my left thumb off, blood (yet again) shooting out across the stage as I ripped off the strings.

I had been sending copies of our *Sonic Youth* mini-LP and *Confusion Is Sex* album to various fanzine editors around the U.S., along with issues of my own *Killer* fanzine. Most would reciprocate by sending their newest issues to our Eldridge Street apartment. My favorites were *Sick Teen*—a hilarious hodgepodge of images slamming into each other with bonkers word balloons and reappropriated newspaper headlines, and live show and record reviews, irreverent and ripping with Midwest teen energy— and *Touch and Go* from Lansing, Michigan, coedited by Tesco Vee, a guy who appeared to be nearly as old as myself—ancient by hardcore standards, though the local kids seemed to idolize the guy. *Touch and Go* printed manic layouts of live band shots, interviews, and Tesco's gonzo-voiced revelations. He would pen one of the only reviews, and glowing to boot, of our eponymous release from 1982. It meant something to me, coming not just out of the jaded downtown art-rock sphere but from a more distant music obsessive whom I admired.

We scored a gig at the legendary Storyville club in Boston, where Billie Holiday, John Coltrane, Duke Ellington, and Charles Mingus had all played many years ago. David Bowie's Serious Moonlight tour was in town the same night at a local stadium, which may have explained why only twenty people showed up to our gig.

Still, I was happy to see Gerard Cosloy, the editor of *Conflict,* one of the smarter and more engaging fanzines on the scene, manning the DJ booth. I had crossed paths with the teenage Gerard at 99 Records earlier in the year, when he had come to drop off a few copies of his zine, and we exchanged phone numbers. I offered to distribute future issues of *Conflict* around town for him, which Gerard sent me from his family's suburban Massachusetts home.

After we played, the club owner claimed not to have enough money to cover the guarantee we had agreed to. He offered to send us a check later in the week. We told him that we were not leaving the building until we were paid the promised fee. It inspired a kind of Cold War, as he couldn't very well lock us in the venue, and the few employees remaining there really wanted to call it a night.

We stood our ground, telling him to call the police if he wanted to so we could explain how we were being ripped off. We had a signed contract. As the clock neared five in the morning, someone finally arrived with an envelope of money, which we took, driving off into the dawn for the four-hour ride back to Manhattan.

Getting paid at gigs would always be the most contentious part of touring, especially before we had help from managers. Glenn Branca confided in me that the European tour that Lee and I had played with him was the first time he had actually been able to promise musicians a guaranteed fee. Musicians on the downtown scene routinely played for each other without any clear promise of compensation. Money in these settings rarely existed.

In mid-September, the *Village Voice* published "Sonic Youth's Beat Goes Off," a review of a CBGB gig we had with Ut and Rat at Rat R. It panned us for being too loud for our own good. Music editor Robert Christgau had assigned a writer named John Piccarella to cover the gig. He commended Rat at Rat R, who were indeed very on that night with their slipping, sliding rock. But he took us to task for being, he thought, nothing more than loud and bombastic.

The review was humiliating, our band trounced in the most widely read arts paper in the city. Piccarella accused us of being offshoots of the Glenn Branca nexus, but to trifling results. This made me see red. There was no question that we were influenced, inspired, and informed by Glenn's work, but also that of myriad others. I wanted nothing more than for Sonic Youth to be perceived as singular, more than just another downtown New York City art-rock band.

I wrote a letter to the editor, which the paper published, criticizing it for, among other things, its pitiful coverage of the local rock scene, especially as it celebrated English bands. I would take things a step further, writing a new song in the same tuning as "Brother James," calling it "Kill Yr Idols." It opened with the couplet—

> *I don't know why / You wanna impress Christgau*
> *Let that shit die / And find out the new goal*

I felt a certain giddiness in being the art-rock brat. The song concluded—

> *Kill yr idols / With sonic death*
> *It's the end of the world / And confusion is sex!*

Guitars furiously strummed behind the bridges created a sound like a zillion screaming electric birds, the bass and drums stomping a Neanderthal beat.

꙼

While on tour with Glenn in Europe, Lee and I were introduced to Burkhardt Seiler, who had a Berlin-based record store and label named Zensor. Glenn proposed that Burkhardt—an affable gent with a look of hard-partying fun in his eyes—license the albums we had done for Neutral for the European market. Zensor agreed and asked for an exclusive EP too, which we quickly recorded and assembled at Wharton Tier's studio. We tracked three new songs: "Brother James," "Kill Yr Idols," and "Early American."

"Early American" was a strange and unfolding song based on an improvisation we had found ourselves falling into. Kim intoned lyrics inspired by the literary criticism of Leslie Fiedler, whom Dan Graham had turned us onto. When we began to play this song live, I could sense audiences really listening, becoming engaged by the buzzing strangeness of its groove, hearing something quite unlike the music of any other band.

Lydia invited me to be part of another project she was incubating, this one called Immaculate Consumptive, which furthered her interest in the spoken word. The group she proposed would include Nick Cave, Marc Almond (from the UK group Soft Cell), Clint Ruin (a nom de plume for Jim "Foetus" Thirlwell), and me.

It was an exciting prospect, and I was sorry not to partake in it. But with a European label now, Sonic Youth was ready to head back overseas to tour through Germany, Austria, Switzerland, Italy, and the Netherlands. This time we had more confidence in ourselves as a working unit. Bob Bert brought to the band a sense of solidity as a quartet, infusing us with a more seasoned energy, ready for the wonders of the Continent.

We traveled first to Munich, then to nearby Schwindkirchen, and then again to Loft in Berlin, once more welcomed by the effervescent Monika and catching up with Blixa Bargeld and the Einstürzende Neubauten boys. People we had met on our previous tour would reappear at these gigs, some of them musicians, others writers, artists, filmmakers, or journalists. Many we would continue to connect with for years to come.

Blixa, after our gig at Loft, invited us to Risiko, the infamous bar he had been working at, where drink, smoke, amphetamine, and conversation could be had with the wild night owls of the city. Heading out from Risiko to find our way back to our cheap hotel, we traipsed by the Berlin Wall, the Communist East that had previously existed for us only as an alien world now just yards away.

Many venues across Europe were reconstructed factories, where artist studios existed with the support of state arts councils—a situation foreign to us North Americans. Gigs were organized by collectives of young people, and visiting bands were regularly fed by caterers and cafés within such complexes, at times offering them sleeping accommodations.

Pulling up to the Rote Fabrik in Zurich, we found a sprawling structure set against Lake Zurich. It had been a factory once, and socialist youth organizations rallied throughout the 1970s to preserve it as a cultural center. Musicians, dramatists, artists, and stray punks surrounded our van to assist in moving our gear up the stairs to the space where we'd be performing, and doing the reverse at the end of the night, all in gratitude for our travels. These venues were where the creative impetus of 1980s Europe thrived, and each time we returned, I felt as if I were reentering a wonderland of shared dreams and responsibilities.

In Amsterdam we played the legendary Paradiso club, probably the largest stage we had encountered to date. The reason for that was that we were supporting Public Image Ltd, who were launching their first proper European run. PiL had once been the most important contemporary post-punk band to me, but they had recently morphed into a different, almost unrecognizable animal. After the departures of Keith Levene and Jah Wobble, the group was basically John Lydon and the drummer Martin Atkins, the rest session musicians Lydon had corralled from parts unknown.

PiL's stage set this night included rather large and imposing white barriers, sectioning off areas of the floor, Atkins's drum riser unusually high above them. Bob was left to set his kit up at the front of the stage, and Lee, Kim, and I found real estate between the barriers, hardly able to move.

After our sound check, we went on the obligatory hunt for the perfect *frites,* the version of French fries that only the Dutch could master, particularly with their mayonnaise-like *fritessaus* or peanutty *pindasaus.* Belgium went toe to toe with the Netherlands on *frites,* but the Dutch had the good sense to accompany theirs with Chocomel (a more delectable version of Yoo-hoo) or Fristi (a frothy, delightful yogurt drink). Belgium's trump card, though, was of course its Trappist monk ales.

Our tongues and tummies sated, we headed back to Paradiso—only to find someone had stolen our rental van. It was our good fortune that we had cleared most everything out of it. Still, it was a shock.

Lydon shouted from his dressing room as we trundled by—

"Heard you had your van nicked! Bloody shame."

His concern sounded genuine, which I took as a good sign of his humanity, though he didn't interact with us at all otherwise.

We hit the stage upset and cold. Our dressing room had been unheated, freezing and clammy like just about every other, with only a tray of cheese and cold cuts with a crusty hunk of bread and, per usual, a crate of local beer.

Despite being constricted on PiL's stage, we played a great set, connecting with a Dutch audience that welcomed new surprises. The local newspapers praised us, even as they snorted at the watered-down version of PiL.

We had been sleeping either at Carlos's Eindhoven apartment or on the floor of Het Apollohuis after each Netherlands gig, but after playing Paradiso we were invited to stay at the Ex's house in Wormer, an area just north of Amsterdam. The Ex was a band founded in 1979 by three punks steeped in the DIY ethos. With their hard-line anti-war and pro-anarchy declarations, they would become a primal voice for radicalized and politically charged youth across Europe.

But we didn't know any of this as we entered their large house, nestled between two rivers and surrounded by marshy grassland. They had squatted in the building to save it from being torn down. About a dozen people welcomed us, and we were shown to different rooms to throw our belongings in, then invited to join everyone for dinner. All of us sat around a long table with a huge cooking pot placed in the middle, filled with piping-hot potatoes and vegetables that were ladled into bowls for each of us and accompanied by huge slices of freshly baked bread.

The camaraderie and joy of the Ex house was unlike anything I had seen in the U.S., and I fell in love with everything they were up to: producing their own records, booking their own shows, making sure everyone in their community had a place to sleep and something to eat—punk rock socialism in full effect.

Jacqui Ham of Ut connected us with Scott Piering, an American who had been heading up the promotions and press department at London's Rough Trade Records. Scott was slightly older than us, with a bit of heft to his girth, and he wore teardrop eyeglasses and exuded a rather manic, sweaty-browed energy. With some momentum now behind us, he arranged for Sonic Youth to play our first-ever gig in London, at a spot named the Venue. We were billed between a singer named Danielle Dax and SPK, the audacious Australian band I had seen at CBGB a year earlier.

The Venue was a rather large room with heavy theater curtains draping the front of the curved stage.

I was hip to Danielle Dax, as she had been a member of Lemon Kittens, a group Lydia and Jim had turned me onto. Danielle's solo debut, *Pop-Eyes,* had just been released and was getting some positive attention in the UK music weeklies. Danielle thought she belonged second on the bill instead of us.

We didn't agree. We confronted her as she stood in front of her dressing room mirror, teasing her bodacious hair, her face painted wild with color. We explained that though we had never played in London, regardless we had been promised the second slot already. But she had orchestrated the change with the concert promoter. She argued—

"Well, you lot have been abroad, and I haven't."

Scott from Rough Trade tried to reason with her, as did the promoter, but she dug in her heels. We were demoted to being the first act and instructed to play for no more than twenty minutes.

Heading out to the stage, we found a setup entirely unlike the rest of our European dates. The British audience—all of maybe thirty people at this point in the evening—stood far from the stage, keeping close to the bar. Scott had rented some amps for us, but they were ridiculously feeble for our needs. All we could do was crank every knob as high as it would go. We began playing our set, feedback squalls dividing the songs, the audience offering zero response, zero applause.

As we played "The Burning Spear," a couple of young boys ventured to the lip of the stage and gazed up at us with wide eyes and smiles, obviously shocked at the sight of a guitar with a drumstick behind the strings being smashed away at and Lee's power drill fuzzing out his amp. The amp reached a point where it could take no more abuse; it soon began to emit flames out its top, smoke billowing from the grille, the speaker cone obviously ripped to shreds, the tubes burning, melted plastic, glass, and filament stinking the room up. Lee threw his hands in the air, laughing at the absurdity of it. Meanwhile Bob's drum kit began to fall apart, the wobbly stands utterly unsuited to their modest task.

This scenario delighted the two lads to no end, one of them yelling—
"*Bloody brilliant!*"
—as the heavy curtains began to close. Our time was up.

I realized this gig, which I had hoped would turn all of London onto our group, had been a total bust, so I proceeded to throw my body between the heavy curtains, whomping my guitar against the deadweight of the fabric, creating an amplified *thump thump thump,* until our stage power was completely shut off, the houselights turned back on, and the DJ filled the room with music far louder and clearer than what our band had produced.

We were booked on a flight back to New York City the next day, but without a place to sleep that night in London, we figured we would just stay out and then catch the first train to Heathrow in the morning. We stuck around the Venue and caught a bit of SPK, mostly out of curiosity after hearing that they had moved on from the harsh industrial clang I had witnessed the previous year to a more dance- and synth-oriented sound.

Sure enough, the group was far less threatening, particularly without scenes of mutilation and evisceration projected behind them. We split after about ten minutes, depressed about our gig, and caught a tube to Victoria station before the Underground shut down at midnight. It was cold and desolate at the station, and we bundled up with as much of the clothing that we had in our suitcases. We surrounded ourselves with our ten or so ratty guitar cases and took turns attempting to doze before the train could trundle us to the airport.

Within a week of being back home, I headed to Gem Spa and picked up the British music papers *NME, Sounds,* and *Melody Maker.* To my shock, Gay Abandon, a journalist at *NME,* reviewed the Venue gig. She pooh-poohed both SPK and Danielle Dax, but her review of our set was an out-and-out rave—

Sonic Youth were mind-blowing, psychedelic . . . The best thing on eight legs all night.

Such a bummer of a gig, and yet, lo and behold, we got a smashing review out of it. England was weird.

43

SUN IN YR EYES

According to George Orwell's 1949 literary vision of dystopia, perpetual war, and totalitarianism, 1984 was the end of the world—or at least the end of the world as we knew it. All I knew was that, for all the European warmth and the occasional critical support we'd received on either side of the ocean, Sonic Youth was entering this ill-omened year with no real future prospects.

Our first two records had been released through Neutral in the U.S. and Zensor in Europe, but we had no actual contract with either label. I wrote a letter to Glenn and Josh decrying Neutral for not showing us any of their accounting.

"Rip us off, you have to . . ."

—it began brattily.

Glenn wasn't too happy. He was already annoyed at Lee and me for graffitiing SONIC YOUTH in every dressing room and on the guitars we were playing while on *his* European tour. But calling him out for deceptive business practice was going too far. I must have come across as an ingrate.

Glenn's fervor for what our band had been exploring and creating was genuine. He never diminished us, as some critics had, as a simple extension of his musical vision. He recognized us as four individuals complementary to one another, with the potential to be both radical and popular. He saw that we could galvanize the mainstream with our underground credibility, pandering to neither sphere.

In this he turned out to be right. But it was that very eventuality that would ultimately take us away from Glenn and his world.

∽

As the year commenced, Lydia Lunch and Jim "Foetus" Thirlwell became more connected to my and Kim's (and to an extent the entire band's) artistic sensibility and trajectory on one side, with Lyle Hysen and Susanne Sasic on the other—almost as if one couple were the devils on our shoulder, and the other, the angels. Lydia and Jim spoke to our interests in the nefarious and the subterranean, from industrial music to the perversity of Charles Manson. Lyle and Susanne, meanwhile, would join us in our embrace of new American guitar rock excellence, leading us into the world defined mostly by the soon-to-come Seattle-based Sub Pop Records, as well as the bands celebrated by Gerard Cosloy, then of Massachusetts but soon to helm New York's Homestead Records.

Sonic Youth would act as a kind of bridge between those aesthetic poles, Lydia's post–no wave danger married to the coming flood of what would be known as alternative rock. Black Flag and Butthole Surfers would likewise appeal across those borders, both bands becoming very close to us.

But all that was still on the distant horizon. As one calendar year led into the next, my focus was on songs and a new way of approaching them. Despite my long-held inclination to turn up the energy, as with the slamming scorch of "Kill Yr Idols" and "Brother James," I found myself drawn now to a more refined mode of songwriting. I still stood at the altar of the Feelies and Television, those masters of guitar-based music who prioritized melody but had an urban, almost primal edge.

So, moving away from the hardcore, high-energy, and decidedly male noise I'd been making, I began to focus on deliberate chord concepts, picking at notes rather than wailing on my instrument in the way that had so far defined my playing in Sonic Youth. I still deployed various tunings to create unusual resonances, though. One that came into play consisted of, from low string to high, two low F#s, two middle F#s, a middle range E, and a high B. It allowed for a more straightforward drone than even the unusual tuning I'd arrived at for "Brother James."

"Brave Men Run (in My Family)"—titled after a poster of an Ed Ruscha painting we had hanging in our apartment depicting a clipper ship listing upon a windswept sea, the text laid across it as salient as the image itself—was the first song I constructed in this tuning. It began with a cyclical picking pattern, before moving into a swooping chordal gesture, as if, I thought, soundtracking the artist's vision. Kim would pen stirring lyrics to accompany it—

> Brave men run in my family
> Brave men run away from me

I found that moderately hammering down on the low F#s and then up on the B and E in a proto-grungy rhythm made for a great rock riff, not unlike ones used by Blue Öyster Cult or MC5. I kept introducing it at our rehearsals, now held in the basement of Giorgio Gomelsky's Plugg Club in midtown, the song soon developing into "Death Valley '69."

Lydia had asked me to join her for an interview, as well as an impromptu piano duet, at Columbia University's WKCR radio station. Afterward, we decided to take a city bus all the way from 218th Street to the Lower East Side, a solid two-hour journey that spanned nearly the entire length of Manhattan. I talked to her as we rode about how I wanted to write lyrics for this song that referenced my current fascination with Charles Manson.

Various weirdo paperbacks had been coming in and out of our home, most of which I procured from the secondhand bookstores along Broadway below Fourteenth Street and the various street fairs that popped up on weekends. I had become enthralled by *The Family*, the 1971 account by Fugs and Peace Eye Bookstore founder Ed Sanders of Charles Manson and his LSD sex cult—dune-buggy assassins who had misread the lyrics to the Beatles' *White Album* as a demented message to start a race war in order to subvert the American police state.

This historical lunacy was close to Lydia's heart, with her own intense interest in murderers, serial killers—criminals of nearly every stripe, actually. She had read and devoured *The Family* too, and she began excitedly shouting on the bus—

"Charlie is now! Charlie is wow!"

—a phrase the Manson girls had notoriously chanted. I shared with Lydia the lyrics I had written for the chorus—

Coming down
Sadie I love it
Now now now
Death Valley '69

It was an allusion to Sadie Mae Glutz, the pseudonym of Susan Atkins, an all-American girl who had notoriously fallen headlong into Manson's web.

Lydia pulled out her dark purple pen and bloodred notepad, and we began to write lines together, which would, when recorded, turn into a back-and-forth recitation between the two of us during the tune's middle breakdown section.

The song would also have Lee and me employing a snaky guitar line that I had gleaned from *John Thompson's Modern Course for the Piano,* a simplistic manual that was part of a series published from 1937 to 1942, its large red cover adorning our family's piano since I had been old enough to climb up onto the bench. The single-note exercises in this book, familiar to many who have taken piano lessons throughout the years, were some of the first musical imprints on my brain, and I would continually mine them for melodic inspiration.

Kim and I spent that Christmas and New Year's in Los Angeles. We connected with Lydia there, as she was staying with her friend Marcy Blaustein, a fixture on the L.A. punk scene since its mid-1970s heyday.

Marcy had invited Henry Rollins to come hear Lydia read at Beyond Baroque, an arts center in Venice. He'd come, taking the city bus from where he had been staying, the "shed" behind brothers Greg Ginn and Raymond Pettibon's parents' house in Hermosa Beach. Lydia was excited to relay this to me, as she knew I was in awe of Black Flag. She told me that Henry had split immediately after her reading without even saying hello ("Which I liked," she remarked). The two did, however, soon connect. Lydia raised the idea with Henry of presenting a theater piece to be performed at midnight at Fetish, a Hollywood goth joint on Melrose Avenue.

Lydia was the only real goth person I had any time for, and I didn't exactly see her as "goth" anyway, particularly since goth style had largely been gleaned from her in the first place. Henry Rollins was as far removed from goth as could be imagined. And yet here he was, hanging out with Lydia and Marcy in Hollywood. His hair was now shoulder-length, looking more like 1968 Charles Manson's (whom, like Sonic Youth and Lydia, the Black Flag and SST Records faction had been giddily revisiting).

When I met Henry, he shook my hand with a grip I thought would fracture every bone and sever every tendon. We were hanging out on Marcy's front porch in West Hollywood. He sat down, silent and scowling, gripping a white cue ball. I asked him if Black Flag was taking a break.

"Nah, we don't take breaks. We rehearse every day. When I'm not rehearsing I work at SST. When I visit Washington, D.C., I work at Dischord."

That didn't explain what he was doing in Hollywood with Lydia, who came out to the porch with a lit joint, offering me a puff, which I took. I knew Rollins most likely didn't partake in such nonsense, his peers celebrating their straight-edge inclinations. I wanted to show that I didn't blindly adhere to anyone else's rules. The weed was insanely narcotic, though, and it messed me up.

Rollins told me—

"I really liked that Sonic Youth version of 'I Wanna Be Your Dog.' Not many people can get away with covering the Stooges." He then flipped the cue ball up into the air, caught it, and disappeared into the house. I stayed put on Marcy's porch, speechless and irretrievably blitzed.

After Kim and I returned to New York, Gerard Cosloy rang me up with news. He had been asked by Dutch East India Trading, a record distributor, to oversee Homestead, its in-house record label. This would allow him to move closer to New York City, with a salaried job, and to release records by bands he loved.

He sounded a bit on the fence, as it would make him someone else's employee, anathema to many of us. He was still quite young; it would also mean leaving his parents' house in Massachusetts. He added that if he did take the reins at Homestead, he hoped to release the next Sonic Youth album.

I told him I thought he should go for it. He could always quit if it didn't pan out.

Gerard had already released, on his own Conflict label, *Bands That Could Be God*, an amazing compilation of Massachusetts-area groups. It featured great tracks by Moving Targets, Sorry, the Outpatients, Busted Statues, and Deep Wound. Deep Wound and the Outpatients would soon converge to become Dinosaur (later Dinosaur Jr.). Gerard had whipped out a demo of Dinosaur when visiting our apartment, exclaiming—

"This is probably the greatest group in the world right now."

I began to hang out more and more with Lyle and Susanne, watching Lyle drum with his band Misguided at a CBGB hardcore matinee at the end of January. Like a few other first-wave hardcore bands, Misguided had been shifting course into other musical realms—in their case psych-pop, though many other hardcore bands began to incorporate heavy metal into their sound.

Boston powerhouse SS Decontrol certainly did this, as did Black Flag, Henry defying the skinhead uniform he had once been a poster boy for with his grown-out hair. The next time I went to see his band, a skinhead contingent at the front of the stage hooted—

"Cut your hair!"

Henry pulled his cock out of his pants and responded—

"I'll grow my hair down to here before I satisfy *you*."

Black Flag had then been promoting a Los Angeles metal band named Saint Vitus, who likewise had long hair and who affected a menacing, macho stance. When Saint Vitus played the World, a club deep in the East Village, Rick Rubin, whom I knew from the New York University–based punk band Hose, yelled in my ear—

"These guys are amazing!"

For his part, Rubin had recently connected with the Beastie Boys, just as they were turning toward rap. Around Christmas 1983, before Kim and I left for L.A., the Beastie Boys performed at the Kitchen. They ended their thrash set with their then four members rapping to a programmed beat, reading lyrics off printed paper, all of them smiling at one another, a bit shy at the audacious prospect of rapping in front of an audience. They had just released their "Cooky Puss" single, a song that was nothing more than a series of crank calls to a local Carvel ice-cream shop. I thought "Cooky Puss" was funny, and the record became a sensation.

It was a remarkable time of fluid boundaries, when hardcore and art rock and heavy metal and rap comingled, when the dead serious and the comic sat alongside each other, strange and easy bedfellows.

One convert to metal was Swans guitarist Sue Hanel. I visited her at her apartment to listen to and marvel at the band Venom's *Black Metal* album. She became excited, saying she wanted to start a group where she could play Venom-style thrash with noisier art-rock intensity. I could see she was serious, and I told her to count me in.

Venom had played a gig on Staten Island with some new group from the West Coast named Metallica opening up. While I was somewhat interested in seeing new metal bands, I opted not to make the trip. A day later, while riffling through the secondhand bins at Sounds on St. Mark's Place, I noticed a slew of Venom records traded in. I thought maybe their gig didn't go over so well. Rick Rubin sidled up next to me and confirmed my suspicion.

"Yeah, they kinda sucked"

—he said.

"Have you heard Slayer? *Now that's the band.*"

I checked out Slayer's *Show No Mercy* album, though I didn't think it was any better or worse than Venom. Within a couple of years, though,

Rick would produce Slayer's *Reign in Blood,* an impeccable metal master-piece, and the Beastie Boys' *Licensed to Ill*—an unprecedented one-two punch. I was in awe of his Def Jam record label, envious of its high profile, but unwilling to compromise Sonic Youth in order to gain similar attention.

As for Sue's metal project, it would never materialize. Not long after I visited her, she would seemingly disappear, never seen again by any of us who were close to her.

44

SING NO EVIL

Gerard Cosloy wanted to release our next album through Homestead, but I had been approached by a young cat from Los Angeles named Michael Sheppard, who had sent a package of albums he had just released on his Iridescence label. It included new music from Half Japanese, which alone made his offer very interesting, as Half Japanese was among the most radical and charming outsider groups out there.

I convinced the band to spend a day at Wharton's studio to record "Death Valley '69" (with Lydia coming in to sing our lyrics together) as well as "Brave Men Run." I sent Michael the mixed reels of the two tunes, along with a seven-inch sleeve mock-up that featured the 1976 painting *Vesuv,* by Gerhard Richter, depicting a mountain range, solemn and mighty in the golden tones of twilight.

Kim and I had received a postcard of *Vesuv* from Gerhard himself, writing how nice it had been that the two of us had dropped by his studio in Düsseldorf when Sonic Youth had passed through there the previous summer. Isa Genzken, Gerhard's artist paramour at the time, had driven us to the studio, bristling with energy. She told Kim not to spread herself too thin, to focus on either art or music.

I sometimes wondered whether Kim would have preferred to continue as a visual artist, to be recognized in the company of those artists she connected to—whether Isa Genzken, Mike Kelley, or Richard Prince. I knew the instant feedback and engagement that came with musical performance offered her a certain gratification. But at least to my mind, the conflict remained. She could only have wondered what course her life would have taken if she had dedicated herself solely to visual art.

〜

On Easter Sunday 1984, Kim and I sat on my mother's couch in Bethel. She suggested in a matter-of-fact tone—

"Maybe we should get married."

Kim's feelings tended to be conveyed in such measured, controlled ways, but I could always feel the undercurrent of emotion within them. It was visible in her shoulders, raised and slightly on guard. From time to time she'd unleash the feelings more freely, overwhelmed, tears breaking loose from her well; but here she was all composure.

"You want to?"

—I asked, my heart unfolding.

"I just feel like I need to make an adult decision in my life right now."

To appease my family, Kim and I agreed to be married at St. Mary Catholic Church in Bethel. She understood that such a wedding could only take place if we sat with a Catholic priest for a few premarital discussions. We went to the church nearest to our Eldridge Street place, Kim more or less impassive, having been raised in a nondenominational household, though she respectfully acknowledged the obligation.

We were just there for formal permission.

Wayne, Althea, and Keller Gordon flew out for our wedding. We invited Lydia and Jim Thirlwell, as well as Lyle and Susanne and Bob Bert. Jim appeared with his hair sprung wild, up and out, and his eyelids tinted with kohl, wearing tight black jeans, black motorcycle boots, and a cutoff T-shirt.

"I felt like I walked into church with my pajamas on!"

—he said, laughing.

Lydia had her red-tinted hair brushed out, a vision from another world. Bob, Lyle, and Susanne played it a bit more conservative, which suited the setting.

I had asked Harold to be my best man. We had been in touch much less often in the preceding years, as my life with Kim and the band had blossomed. But I held a deep affection for him, and he remained one of my oldest friends. I was honored when he accepted.

Harold arrived at the church swish and fabulous in a sheer shirt with the top three buttons opened, a silk scarf loosely tied around his neck. Before we went to the altar for our vows, the priest asked that Harold button his shirt up.

Harold refused.

I looked at the priest—

"It's okay."

Kim was resplendent in a beautiful wedding gown, wearing the mod-est ring we had chosen together, looking happy, both of us lit up and in the moment.

We had the reception in my mother's backyard, the day smack in the middle of a wicked heat wave, temperatures burbling around ninety degrees. Kim and I changed into more comfortable attire, mine featuring a T-shirt of the D.C. hardcore band Void. We cut the tiered wedding cake, smearing it in each other's faces as tradition demanded.

To mark the occasion, in lieu of a wedding band, I chose to get a tattoo. Lydia had recommended the Los Angeles–based tattooist Leo Zulueta. I made an appointment at Leo's studio that fall, bringing in a piece of scrap paper on which I had drawn, in black pen ink, a simple cross with hand-rendered words scrawled along the top—

SONIC LIFE

45

BOP KYLIX (DEXTERITY)

Lydia was back in New York after a sojourn abroad, this time to stay, her romantic relationship in London having come to an end. She and Jim Thirlwell would soon become a hot and heavy couple, the two of them moving into an apartment way up north from us in Spanish Harlem and then into a large, industrial building deep in Brooklyn, always inviting our entire clique to visit for nights of food, drink, smoke, talk, and laughter, sharing each other's exploits in far-out collusions.

Lydia was a master at locating new blood in the streets, people who shared her persuasions. She announced that she was presenting a reading at the Pyramid Club with Richard Kern, Tommy "Bloodboy" Turner, and David Wojnarowicz.

I was aware of David from the group 3 Teens Kill 4 and had already heard him read from his journals at various small clubs, his dry tenor depicting runaway days of male hustling and reportage of *mano e mano* moral dyspepsia, the words nonchalantly spilling from his cigarette-smoke-filled mouth, his long, serious, rough, and beautiful face holding eyeglasses crooked upon his nose, his torso lanky and tall, dressed in dungarees and a T-shirt, looking as if he had been wearing the same clothes forever—a couture I could personally relate to.

Richard Kern, recently transplanted from North Carolina, was news to me. He presented Super 8 film footage he had been shooting of Lower East Side post-punk oddballs (including Wojnarowicz and Lydia) performing over-the-top simulated (for the most part) sex-and-violence acts in his apartment, scenes at once hideous and glamorous to the point of comic exaggeration. His inspiration was the sleaze of mid-'70s Times Square scuzz porn, along with the current wave of grade-Z gore and slasher films (1981's *The Evil Dead* our new *Citizen Kane*). The result was a cheap and entirely debauched aesthetic, purposefully devoid of any real commentary, interested more in the art of shock as it smacked head-on with hilarity. Along with a few other filmmakers, particularly provocateur Nick Zedd (sometimes Nick Zodiac)—a boy my age with natty red punkoid hair and a bone-white face, his near-translucent eyes conveying humor, bedevilment, and a palpable hate for all authority—Kern would become a central figure of the Cinema of Transgression, a collective making the previous no wave era's Super 8 cinema scene look absolutely quaint.

In the film footage Richard shared, I recognized Lung Leg. She had been video artist Tony Oursler's assistant when we had played at Minneapolis's Walker Art Center two years earlier during our Savage Blunder tour with Swans. Tony, who had known Kim through Mike Kelley, was teaching video art nearby, and he had brought Lung Leg, his student (then known by her actual name, Lisa Carr), to film our performance. In Kern's *Submit to Me,* she scowled at the camera, her stringy hair falling into her crazed eyes, wearing nothing but a dirty slip and acting as if she were a child escaped from a ward and landed in an East Village slum apartment.

In the middle of Lydia reading a new piece she had written, offering a purgative take on an apparent incest, a shout rose from the audience near where Kern and Wojnarowicz were standing. Tommy "Bloodboy" Turner ran out from between the two of them and leaped onto the tiny stage, yelling—

"I can't take it anymore! You want real art? This is real art!"

—before pulling out a small axe and chopping off his hand, blood instantly spurting across the faces of everyone standing in the front.

It was all fake, of course, but it looked and sounded real. After a few breathtaking beats, we all just looked at one another and laughed.

These were Lydia's new friends. They would soon be ours.

The area north of our apartment on Eldridge Street would become an open market of crack cocaine and heroin, dealers calling out—

"Yo, we got the White Lady, we got the Brown Crystal, yo, we got the Black Eagle, yo, the Mexican Horse."

It was a phalanx of death, and I found it safe to traverse only with Egan, a dog causing considerable fright to the already uptight dealers and junkies. Crackheads scurried at the sight of us, looking over their shoulders, eyes darting everywhere, their existence defined solely by paranoia and scoring the next hit.

In direct opposition to this contingent was a scourge recently descended on downtown Manhattan: the "young urban professionals," or yuppies.

They were an upwardly mobile demographic who, not wanting to follow in their parents' suburban footsteps, would relocate to cities for the promise of good times—vying for jobs in the financial sector, willing to slum it in the East Village but with the means to avoid its riskier corners. Soon enough, the city's real estate industry would cater to their whims, pricing out artists first from the East Village and, in ensuing years, from much of the city itself.

The days of Lower Manhattan as a punk rock playground were numbered.

The set of new songs we had been writing in early 1984 would first be performed at Maxwell's, across the river in Hoboken, New Jersey, in late May. We decided we needed to tackle the restless air and dead space happening between our tunes, as we changed and retuned guitars. Our solution was to utilize cheap portable cassette machines that could record, play, and transmit AM/FM radio stations. As we tinkered and adjusted, I would blast through a tiny amplifier various songs ("Not Right," by the Stooges; "Sex as a Weapon," by Pat Benatar; "Jam-Master Jammin'," by Run-DMC) that I had recorded onto cassette tapes, or else I would dial in a local radio station while Lee cranked up the "scream tape," a cassette recording of us all howling in a German wind tunnel that he had made during our last jaunt through Europe.

With Neutral out of the picture, we considered the options for our next album. There was Gerard Cosloy, who had offered to release any new recordings on Homestead, and Michael Sheppard, who had expressed similar interest with his Iridescence label in Los Angeles.

We also considered releasing the album ourselves. Along with editing and publishing *Killer*, I had been inspired to start my own label. I called it Ecstatic Peace, from a line in the novelist and cultural critic Tom Wolfe's widely read *The Electric Kool-Aid Acid Test*, a book that investigated the wigged-out world of Ken Kesey and his Merry Pranksters.

The first Ecstatic Peace release had been a cassette entitled *Hard Rock*, featuring Lydia and Michael Gira each reading a piece of their writing. It was followed by *Sonic-Death*, a pastiche of live snippets, sounds, noises, and conversations that I had spliced from the various tapes we'd made on our second European tour.

Each label held its unique appeal. We mulled our options.

Lydia had curated a program entitled Acts of Emotional Terrorism at Danceteria at the tail end of June 1984, with both Swans and us invited to perform. She would join us for our first live rendition of "Death Valley '69."

The stage was filled with our growing array of sonic totems: Lee's oil can lid, the word "RISE" painted across it, which he would suspend in the air with a chain, clanging away at it with a drumstick, swinging it in front of his face; a rack of tubular chimes (which would soon disappear after we accidentally left them on the street while loading out of a gig at the Pyramid Club); and Kim's large Ovation Magnum bass guitar case, festooned with stickers from Black Flag, Necros, Void, Poison Idea, *Destroy LA* fanzine, and a chaotic cavalcade of others, a sort of message board of 1984 underground rock poetics.

With a nod to my background as a Catholic boy gone astray and to Patti Smith's *Horses* album cover, I wore a white button-down shirt, on the pocket of which Lydia had drawn a crucifix, "ARISE" scrawled atop it and "ONLY BLOOD CAN WASH AWAY BLOOD" below. Kim had "DEATH VALLEY 69" writ large on the back of her white sleeveless T-shirt.

Nick Cave & the Bad Seeds had played Danceteria the night before, and Jim Thirlwell (as "Clint Ruin") had presented his Scraping Foetus Off the Wheel project two nights before that. This delirious troika of Nick, Jim, and Lydia weaved its way around Sonic Youth. We found ourselves riding along with the glamour and post-punk celebrity of it all. But we still felt like what we were doing was wholly distinct from and almost at odds with their fascination with swamp-drenched gothic gush.

Wanting to record our songs as an unbroken stream, replicating the way we'd been presenting them live, with cassette tapes bridging the tunes, we checked out OAO at John Erskine's recommendation. OAO was a recording studio founded in 1981 by Martin Bisi (a member of noise-music improvisers Material), located in the Gowanus area of Brooklyn, then a desolate no-man's-land of dilapidated industrial buildings situated, lost and lonely, between Carroll Gardens and Park Slope.

We took the F train out to the Smith–Ninth Streets stop and trudged over to the studio. Other than a couple of vagrants, some dodgy-looking street thugs, a few scurrying rats, and a roving pack of wild dogs, the walk was unremarkable.

Martin welcomed us, a solidly built chap with long brown hair parted down the middle and hanging just below his shoulder blades, straight and shiny and held in place by a Native American–looking headband. He had an alert demeanor, positive and responsive, as he showed us around the studio (which he had recently renamed BC). It was not much more than a large basement with a twenty-four-track console, a reel-to-reel mix-down machine, ravaged stone walls, and overhead wood beams.

It was rough, yet obviously ready. Martin displayed a row of album covers, leaning against the wall, that had been engineered in the space, including Herbie Hancock's *Future Shock,* the recording that had introduced hip-hop turntablism—via Grandmixer D.ST—to the ears of mainstream America.

He seemed intrigued to work with an actual rock band; most everything he had had his hand in was decidedly non-rock. He seemed to make us for a straitlaced folk- and psych-influenced outfit. He was in for a surprise.

Kim and I still struggled to make ends meet. We worked from time to time as painters, painting the interiors of wealthy apartment dwellers in uptown Manhattan. A woman named Peggy had organized this job for us, also employing Roddy Frantz, singer of the Washington, D.C., band Urban Verbs (and sibling to Talking Heads drummer Chris).

One Sunday afternoon we all gathered at Peggy's Brooklyn apartment for a day-off brunch, and one of her good friends, the artist Moki Cherry, was there. Moki was married to Don Cherry, the trumpet and world music maestro who had come up alongside the iconoclastic jazz composer Ornette Coleman all through the 1960s.

Moki, Don, and their children, Neneh and Eagle-Eye, had been living in a large farmhouse in Sweden, where music events happened all day and night. At this juncture, in 1984, the family was also spending time in a loft building situated in Long Island City, Queens.

I had been toying with an idea for an album cover after seeing illustrations of flaming jack-o'-lantern pumpkins on a Misfits single. I wanted to construct a scarecrow with its head an actual jack-o'-lantern set on fire. This image, to me, would draw together the iconography of the rural and the urban, with a ritualistic quality too. I realized it would be difficult to pull off such a shoot in the streets of New York City and had begun scouting for spots that offered both cityscapes and fields. Moki mentioned that behind their building in Long Island City was an open grassland of sorts, stretching down to the East River. It seemed like a promising setting for such a shoot.

Kim had recommended James Welling, a CalArts grad living in New York City, as a photographer. James took the job on with good nature. One early evening that fall, as the sun began to set, he began to take photos of the scarecrow we had constructed, with and without us four band members surrounding it.

When we finally lit the scarecrow, the head shot into perfect flames, fire licking out of its eyes, mouth, and open top. James snapped photo after photo, and as the flames began to sputter, Kim, Lee, Bob, and I danced around the burning figure, carried away by the ceremonial energy—first as if we were in a slam pit, then joining hands to create a circle, a sonic body, spinning in a ring.

46

BACKSTAGE PASS

While at Kim's parents' house in west Los Angeles that fall, we met up with Michael Sheppard, whose offer to release, on his Iridescence label, our "Death Valley '69" / "Brave Men Run" single we'd accepted. The record would be a one-off—particularly since we had agreed for Gerard Cosloy at Homestead Records to release our next proper album.

Michael arrived at the Gordon home smiling and barefoot. He was infamous for having presented Throbbing Gristle, in 1981, at their only live concert in Los Angeles. He was also friendly with everybody around the SST Records scene, soon bringing Kim and me headfirst into that orbit.

Since the Los Angeles contingent mostly comprised L.A. and Orange County natives (unlike New York, where it was largely us émigrés), there were a lot of kids who had crossed paths during their high school years at various surf, skate, and music events. A quality of teen rivalry pervaded their social circles, even as those youngsters entered their twenties.

The L.A. people we became involved with—other than Kim's older friends, such as the artists Mike Kelley and John Knight—were a singular and inspired clutch of characters, from the filmmaker David Markey, who would document the L.A. scene in his hilarious and wild Super 8 films, to Jeff and Steve McDonald, the irrepressible brothers behind Redd Kross, a band whose infectious devotion to all things groovy, from *The Partridge Family* to the Manson family, had a weird, mystical, maniacal edge.

I admired the way the SST artists continually disregarded the established standards of hardcore, such as they were. Bands like Meat Puppets and Saccharine Trust made highly idiosyncratic music compared with their peers. Even Black Flag, the label's flag-bearer, would forcibly push boundaries, not only taking inspiration from heavy metal but referencing the stretched-out jamming of the Grateful Dead—the historically *least* punk band imaginable.

In L.A. that fall, Michael Sheppard alerted Kim and me to a show Black Flag was playing later that day at a place somewhere in Long Beach. We drove out to find a prototypical suburban home. Walking in, we soon saw that Black Flag was in full battle mode.

Entering through the kitchen, we encountered people our age just hanging about, drinking, smoking, laughing, yelling in each other's ears. The music emanating from the living room was cranked and roaring. I could see through the archway from the kitchen to the living room, with its predictable interior decoration for such a suburban home (massive color TV console, large leather couch, comfy easy chairs, framed family photos perched upon a mantel).

On the other side, Greg Ginn was whipping his sweaty black hair around on his skinny neck and torso, shredding spastic notes from his translucent Ampeg Dan Armstrong guitar. Bassist Chuck Dukowski had recently decided to call it a day from Black Flag. This midday gig would be one of their first to feature his replacement, Kira Roessler, who had been in the notorious late 1970s all-female group Sexsick. She clocked in tight and focused, her Rickenbacker bass large against her small, muscular frame.

I sat up on the countertop in the kitchen and watched as Henry writhed his way into the crowd, the band winding through a lengthy repetition that allowed Greg to just burn against the rhythm section of Kira and drummer Bill Stevenson. Henry wore nothing but a pair of shorts. He was slick with sweat, his long hair matted and dripping, occasionally whipped around to clear his eyes, the moisture spraying anyone within twelve feet of him.

With a psycho glare, he crushed his body up against any of the dudes in the room, attempting to solicit some pushback. He didn't get it, each potential victim unnerved though smiling, moving out of Henry's way with their beers and cigarettes held high over their heads. He slid up against the women in his path, all of whom got the hell out of this maniac's sweat-soaked trajectory.

He moved up against Kim and Michael Sheppard's girlfriend, motioning in a way that suggested he wanted them to follow him into the adjoining bathroom. It was totally crazy. They stood there holding on to each other, nervously laughing. He then made his way into the kitchen and saw me sitting there, skinny and out of my comfort zone, draped only in ripped dungarees, sockless PRO-Keds sneakers, and my beloved white Void T-shirt (the same tee I had worn for my wedding reception).

He began to aggressively tap me in the chest, gesturing at me to come down off the counter. I only stared back, a forced look of amusement on my face, unsure how to respond to this squirming, musclebound lunatic. I leaned over and yelled into the side of his head—

"Leave me alone!"

I'm not sure he even heard my request. He then reached over and squeezed my skinny arm, mouthing the word—

"Weak."

Then banged his fist into his chest, yelling—

"Strong!"

To my relief, he quickly spun back into the living room after this alpha display, rejoining the band to finish singing "Nothing Left Inside," their latest molten dirge of despair and angst.

The Alley Cats set up to play next as I scurried out to the backyard, where I noticed members of Redd Kross, the Nip Drivers, and Saccharine Trust hanging around. Kim was talking to a thin, lanky guy, his face serious, conveying a depth of beautiful sadness.

"Thurston, this is Raymond Pettibon"

—she said excitedly.

I knew Raymond as, among other things, the brother of Greg Ginn, who had been wailing on the guitar inside. Since I'd started coming to Los Angeles with Kim, I had been picking up any Pettibon art zine I could find, stacks of them at the bottom of the music magazine racks in record stores ranging in price from fifty cents to two or three dollars. When I showed them to Kim, she recognized a curious and genuine artist at work.

Raymond, and by extension SST, would tap into the raw intellectualism that sometimes found a home in punk, hardcore, and post-punk. His drawings in these self-published, photocopied zines touched on the conflict between culture and subculture, blurring the line between hippie and punk, idealism and capitalism. He drew from the language of exploitation paperbacks, classic literature, and comic books. The work was, and would continue to be, loaded—at once intimate and inscrutable.

As we talked, Henry came over, toweling himself off and smiling.

"I didn't realize that was you in there"

—he said, recalling our fleeting introduction through Lydia the previous winter.

He launched into how SST was working on releasing an album by Charles Manson, recorded in his Vacaville prison cell. Henry and the L.A. punk-outlier collective he associated with shared Sonic Youth's interest in the imprisoned cult leader. Pettibon had made much commentary on Manson's infamy in his drawings, and Redd Kross had a blast covering the Charlie-penned tune "Cease to Exist."

Much of our fascination with the nefarious figure could be chalked up to the puerility of our age. The fact that the lunacy surrounding Manson in 1969 was at least in part defined by his antagonism toward the Vietnam War and the social structures established in Eisenhower's 1950s America made it hard not to find parallels with the sensibilities of punk rock. But even though Manson had informed our "Death Valley '69," there were limits to our interest in the man. A slavish allegiance to *any* individual was anathema to us, and certainly not to one who had engaged in violent mind games and physical cruelty.

Suffice it to say that, even in 1984, I had no real desire to come too close to the evil personified by Manson in the real world.

Or any world.

47

ANSWERING MACHINE

We decided to name our new album *Bad Moon Rising,* in reference to the tropes of Americana that we felt were reflected in our songs' lyrics and in the burning jack-o'-lantern scarecrow cover. The title was an appreciative nod to Creedence Clearwater Revival, whose song title we blatantly appropriated; the band's front man, John Fogerty, was a rock 'n' roll balladeer who had mined the voodoo mysticism of the Deep South through a West Coast prism.

Kim and I were at her parents' home in Los Angeles in September when I received a phone call from Paul Smith in London. Paul was working as label manager for Doublevision, an imprint he had set up in 1982 with the Sheffield electronic punk rock pioneers Cabaret Voltaire. At the suggestion of Lydia (who had already convinced Doublevision to release the *In Limbo* album I'd contributed to, a good two years after we recorded it), I had posted to Paul a cassette of our finished *Bad Moon Rising* session. I sent a few to other labels we admired as well—4AD, Some Bizarre, Mute—but only Paul responded.

On the phone he enthused about the album, but he told me that his Cabaret Voltaire cohorts had no real interest in releasing a record by a noisy, guitar-centric foursome from New York City. *In Limbo* had seemingly been enough.

Before we spoke, Paul had reached out to Pat Naylor, one of the two young British women who had stayed at my and Kim's apartment during our last European tour. Pat had seen Sonic Youth play at CBGB, upon our return, and Paul wanted to know what we were like as a live act. Pat reported that we were an exciting, noise-strewn mess, with weird and great songs, adding that we kept getting tangled up in our guitar leads.

Striking out with Doublevision, Paul took it upon himself to traipse about London encouraging other labels to listen to our cassette. He ultimately took the advice of Peter Walmsley, who had been running Rough Trade's international department. Walmsley suggested Paul start his *own* label, separate from the Cabaret Voltaire gang. Rough Trade would then put his new releases in its distribution stream.

So, emptying whatever money he had in his bank account, that's just what Paul did, creating Blast First, a label named after the opening line of a satirical manifesto of cultural criticism written by Wyndham Lewis in 1914: "BLAST First (from politeness) ENGLAND." He invited Pat Naylor and her sister, Liz, both young women with experience working in the punk music scene around late-'70s Manchester, to become Blast First's in-house publicists.

I had been keeping a folder of any press clippings on Sonic Youth that I came across. With a sense of anticipation, I made a color-copied set and sent them off to Blast First's UK address, hoping for the best.

Before Kim and I left Los Angeles, Michael Sheppard introduced me to his friend Stuart Swezey. Stuart had had the visionary idea of promoting punk gigs outside of the L.A. club circuit by presenting bands in the Mojave Desert, a place where there were no cop cars in sight, nobody threatening to spoil the party or bust open any punk rocker skulls. He had arranged for Savage Republic and the Minutemen to play, in April 1983, on a remote dry lake bed, utilizing gas-powered generators and hiring school buses to escort the modest number of attendees to the location.

Learning from this experience how to deal with the cold, the wind, the sand, and the challenging acoustic space that the Mojave presented, Stuart set up another desert gig a year later, this time with Einstürzende Neubauten and the San Francisco noise-performance iconoclasts Survival Research Laboratories. With only the barren environment between the performers and audience, and with both acts employing actual TNT-grade explosives in their performances, this would be a concert unlike anything else happening in the punk rock universe, a show that would be talked about for ages.

Three months later Stuart booked the Minutemen again, along with the Meat Puppets, a neo-surf instrumental group named Lawndale, and an experimental noise collective named Points of Friction—only this time to play on a chartered whale-watching ship cruising around San Pedro Bay.

Like anyone else on the West Coast, Stuart had a limited awareness of Sonic Youth. We had gotten some modest exposure there. The day

Michael received copies of our "Death Valley '69" single, he delivered one to Rodney Bingenheimer on L.A.'s KROQ-FM, where the song would receive its first public hearing. Rodney's show, *Rodney on the ROQ*, had caught my attention the first time I'd traveled with Kim to California, his heart-pounding playlist a litany of new California punk and hardcore. I was thrilled to learn he'd be featuring our song. I sat by the radio in the Gordons' house waiting for it to play.

The record was a seven-inch single, so it stood to reason that it should be recorded at 45 RPM. But due to the five-and-a-half-minute playing time, we cut it at 33⅓ RPM, for better fidelity. When Rodney mistakenly played the song at 45 RPM, it sounded like *The Chipmunks Play Sonic Youth*.

Still, despite our relative anonymity, Stuart was excited to invite us to perform at a third desert show, which he was going to name the Gila Monster Jamboree. It would also feature Redd Kross, the Meat Puppets, and a band called Psi Com fronted by a singer named Perry Farrell. It was to take place the first week of January 1985.

I told Kim we needed to bring Lee and Bob out to Los Angeles to do this gig. With luck, we could even book a few other shows on the West Coast. This felt like an undeniable opportunity.

Making my usual pilgrimage that fall, I hoofed it over to Rhino Records. I wanted to introduce myself to the music writer Byron Coley, who I knew was working there at the time. I had very little scratch on me, but I found a cheap copy of Norman Greenbaum's album *Spirit in the Sky*. I had it in mind for Sonic Youth to possibly cover the title song. When I took the record to the counter, Byron slipped it in a paper bag, handed it to me, and, with a smile, said—

"Gratis."

Byron got together with Kim and me for beers and tacos a few times before we split back east. He told me about how he had lived in New York City during the late 1970s, writing for *New York Rocker*, sleeping on the couch in the office there or on park benches on warm enough nights. He had become friendly with a lot of people on the no wave scene, particularly George Scott when he was in 8 Eyed Spy. Byron even wound up as tour manager for them when they played dates across the U.S.

It wasn't just him at Rhino with such colorful stories. The guitarist Nels Cline and the jazz pianist Richard Grossman both worked there. But when it came to records, Byron's knowledge was by far the most formidable, and he had the ability to recall reams of arcana regarding any artist, label, year of release, or country of origin you could think of. And that was to say nothing of his attention to the history of recorded sound. I would soon realize it wasn't just music: he was just as attuned to literature, from hard-boiled mysteries to science fiction, poetry, and underground comics.

Byron had spent some time helping out the loose nuts over at SST Records (sleeping beneath desks at their offices for a while too). But he told me he was ready to move back to the East Coast with his fiancée, Lili, their sights set on Boston, where Byron had plans to join up with *Forced Exposure* fanzine editor Jimmy Johnson. Byron and Jimmy would soon turn *Forced Exposure* into one of the most critical and controversial music journals of the second half of the 1980s, though Byron confided to me his main reason for heading back east—

"You can find more jazz records there."

Sure enough, later that fall after Kim and I had returned to New York City, Byron and Jimmy reached out asking if they could drive down from Boston to spend a couple of days interviewing us for the next *Forced Exposure*. They wanted our band on the cover.

We were excited for the coverage, but we had a few other things to take care of first, such as planning to somehow get to Los Angeles to play the show in the desert and also, critically, pulling together the artwork for *Bad Moon Rising*, which would be released by Homestead in North America and Blast First in the UK.

The front cover would of course be one of James Welling's amazing shots of the scarecrow on fire. For the back cover, we had the idea of including a photo of each of us personally chosen from our pre-punk years: Lee with long hair, smoking a pipe, jumping out of a hippie van; Kim sitting on her teenage bed in a flowing Joni Mitchell–style skirt; Bob hanging out with some New Jersey kids drinking beer and smoking Marlboros; and me with my hair long to my shoulders and wearing a double-knit silk disco shirt (a photo Harold had taken).

Gerard Cosloy at Homestead didn't seem to mind our cover ideas, allowing for the artist to have the final word when it came to an album's visuals. But when we sent the layout to Paul Smith at Blast First, who needed it early to get the ball rolling on the UK release, he marveled at the Welling photo, then pulled out the back cover layout and gasped at how utterly *wrong* it looked.

If he was going to promote us as a band of the future, these early photos of us were just not going to cut it. With some understanding, we sent Paul a photo of us standing around the scarecrow holding hands, which Paul laid out a bit more tastefully than we had. Gerard later received the finished artwork from Paul for his Homestead release, never getting to see our original back cover. That version would later be lost in transit, never to resurface—none of us ever to peep its collaged wrongness again.

While vamping as a slinky and dark guitar figure during sound check before a gig at the Pyramid Club in October, Kim began improvising lyrics inspired by her experience at Black Flag's set at that suburban California home a few weeks earlier. She explored her emotions in real time—those of a woman confronted by a maniacal performer, raging and possessed (taking the form of Henry Rollins), and is seemingly caught in a vibratory state between theater and actual psychosis. We all realized that a sexy, amorphous new jam had just come to life. We began our set with it that night, the song written less than an hour before, naming it "Halloween."

The only other song we had composed since recording *Bad Moon Rising* was "Flower," an open-ended drone that undulated and grew into a series of rushes, stops, and starts. The lyrics to it were inspired by a calendar for the dawning year of 1985 that I had received for free at a local bodega. The calendar, somewhat torn, depicted a young and somber Puerto Rican woman dressed in nothing save for a pair of sheer panties, the lone word "ENTICING" printed tiny in the corner.

With a black ink pen, I wrote on six strips of paper a series of lines that I placed alongside the image—

> *SUPPORT THE POWER OF WOMEN*
> *USE THE POWER OF MAN*
> *SUPPORT THE FLOWER OF WOMEN*
> *USE THE WORD:*
> *FUCK*
> *THE WORD IS LOVE*

I hung the modified calendar on our kitchen wall by one of the back windows. Kim seemed to acknowledge my punk art, though she didn't talk to me about it. At our next rehearsal, while the band rocked through the instrumental part of "Flower," she recited the words I had written, only as shouted pronouncements, before adding her own rejoinder—

There's a new girl in your life
Long red wavy hair
Green, green lips and purple eyes
Skinny hips and big brown breasts
Hanging on your wall
One end slit, the other ripped

I could see how the sexualization of women in photos such as the one I'd displayed (images primarily generated by men) could be seen as disrespectful, insipid, potentially even abusive. And yet I couldn't deny my attraction to the nude calendar girl. I thought that I could acknowledge the photo while turning it, with my lines, into a statement of feminist solidarity and a guiltless sublimation of beauty.

It was a precarious attempt. Whatever feminism I might have tried to impose on the image was countered with Kim's line—

Hanging on your wall

—not *our* wall. There was no violence intended by my creating and displaying the work. But as Kim wrote, there would always be—

One end slit, the other ripped

The feminism I was being informed by at the time—mostly through Kim, but also by our friends and peers—made it clear to me that exploitation and indignity were an everyday reality for women. I hoped that Kim's taking inspiration from my bit of verse, in which an erotic suggestion existed alongside a statement of feminist alliance, meant that I was being exonerated from any aggression that might have been implied by the gesture.

But the two of us never talked about it outright, only through our songwriting. It wouldn't be the last time that music was the mode of dialogue in our relationship. With Kim as the vocalist on "Flower," most listeners would never recognize the dynamics at play in its writing, the assumption generally being that Kim was the sole writer as opposed to it being a lyrical collaboration.

48

STOP SPINNING

In the first week of 1985, Kim and I picked Lee and Bob up from LAX, our first order of business to take them to a local Fatburger to sample some of L.A.'s finest fast food. A few days prior, Stuart Swezey had taken me on a run through Los Angeles and Orange County, hitting every record store from Santa Monica to Hermosa Beach to Torrance to San Pedro—from Toxic Shock to ZED to Moby Disc to Licorice Pizza—so we could hang posters for Gila Monster Jamboree.

Stuart and Michael Sheppard drove the band to a large house somewhere north of Hollywood, where a clutch of L.A. punk artists was living. We wanted to check out drums for the gig, which all the other bands would share with us. Perry Farrell, the singer of Psi Com, was living on one of the floors. He welcomed us to see his pet tarantula.

He wasn't kidding: we walked upstairs to find a massive spider perched inside a terrarium. It stopped me in my tracks, my fear of spiders since childhood freezing my blood. Perry lifted his friend out and placed the creature on his chest. Taking a steely stance, I reached out slowly to feel its fuzzy body, beautiful and exquisite. But I could take only a moment of it before retreating downstairs.

Drums sorted out, and with a detailed map in hand, we drove out to Skull Rock, the site of our show, a knoll in the Mojave Desert less than ten miles from the city of Joshua Tree. Attendees would follow a different map to the town of Victorville, where, in a designated parking lot, they would receive further instructions on how to find the location.

Kegs of beer, jugs of water, baskets of fruit, sandwiches, and a coveted supply of cigarettes were available for us as a crowd of nearly five hundred people began arriving in their packed cars. Word had evidently spread among them that the best way to really experience such a gig was to be dosed on LSD. I hadn't heard it firsthand, but I did notice a lot of levity and bliss rising up from the crowd. The cold desert air soon became frigid; most attendees had had the foresight to bring along blankets, sweaters, coats, gloves, and hats.

Psi Com began their set, playing gothic groove rock, Perry Farrell barefoot and moving about the sand, trying to connect with the crowd. But the open desert acoustics were washing away the tense rhythm of the group, and the music wasn't connecting.

As we plugged in our guitars, it soon became apparent to us that the entire gathering was utterly dosed. They were growing only more flipped out and wild-minded as the lysergic tentacles embraced them. With our feet planted in the desert sand, Bob clicked us into "Brother James," Lee and me double strumming the high strings, down into the darker middle ones, then hammering hard on the whammy-barred G strings. Kim and Bob kept the undercurrent pummeling before Lee and I ripped into a flurry of high notes, the whole band at once crungeing into the verses, Kim belting out—

> Take my hand, he said to me
> Follow now or you'll be damned

We followed with "Kill Yr Idols" and our new *Bad Moon Rising* songs, including "Death Valley '69," ending with a savage take on "The Burning Spear." By the end of the gig it was clear that the crowd had just been ravaged by noise, our psychedelic heavy metal no wave rainbow spiraling into their ears and hearts.

Playing in the desert while tripping was nothing new for Phoenix, Arizona's Meat Puppets. After releasing one of the most iconoclastic records yet for the North American hardcore scene, the Meat Puppets had moved on to exploring their love for ZZ Top–style shuffling rock, even as they spun out psychedelic guitar sounds, the harmonies from the two brothers in the band, Cris and Curt Kirkwood, melding together like sugar and sand.

Redd Kross arrived late to the event after getting lost on the desert roads. They at last appeared, resplendent in big fake fur coats and spandex trousers, their platform shoes ill-suited to the desert terrain.

I found it difficult to believe that Redd Kross's glam-punk thrashing could chase away the dreamy vibes put into place by the Meat Puppets' set and the savage noise of ours. But when they proceeded to blast out their glittering originals and covers, with Jeff and Steve McDonald and rhythm guitarist Robert Hecker pulling out every classic rock move, the three windmilling their hair together à la Gene Simmons and Paul Stanley, and drummer Dave Peterson twirling his sticks over his head—the kind of gimmickery that we art and punk musicians would never stoop to—it put a collective smile on the audience's faces. The crowd screamed, danced, jumped, shouted, and fell into the sand dunes holding on to each other, rolling around like dogs at play. Beer and acid sluiced through their bloodstream beneath the glowing full moon.

It was an orgy of delight and insanity. I could only stand with Bob, Lee, and Kim in laughing admiration. It was a beautiful night, our entry into the creative miasma that was L.A.

Gerard had rung up Ray Farrell, whom he knew from the underground music pipeline, to see if he could book us a few more gigs while we were in California. Ray, originally from New Jersey, had had a similar musical coming of age to mine, drawn to records coming out of the margins in the early and mid-1970s—Blue Öyster Cult, Iggy & the Stooges, *Nuggets*—that lured him to CBGB as early as 1974, where he would witness the baby steps of Television, the Ramones, Patti Smith, Talking Heads, and Mink DeVille.

Moving to San Francisco in 1976, he landed a job working at the legendary Rather Ripped record store in nearby Berkeley, which prided itself on carrying all the coolest records. Patti Smith performed a poetry reading at Rather Ripped in November 1974, around the same time her "Hey Joe" single was released. It was a galvanizing event for those fortunate enough to have been present.

After Rather Ripped folded, Ray worked in Rough Trade's first U.S. distribution office, also located in Berkeley. Along with hosting radio shows on Pacifica Radio's KPFA, one of the first, most daring free-form listener-sponsored radio networks in North America, he began working closer with underground bands looking for gigs in the Bay Area. After Gerard's outreach, Ray was able to score Sonic Youth a few post–Gila Monster Jamboree shows.

We would meet Ray for the first time at a gig he booked for us in Santa Cruz, California, at a small spot named Club Culture. Only a handful of people showed up to the gig, and those who did were disappointed that neither Sonic Youth nor Slovenly (an artful and interesting group Ray had been working with just then) weren't straight-ahead hardcore acts. We finished the night with less than thirty dollars in our pocket.

"That comes to a dollar a minute. Not too bad!"

—I exclaimed to Ray. It was just enough gas money to get to the next night's gig in San Francisco.

We then returned to Los Angeles to play at the Anti-Club. As a massive Minutemen fan, I was anxious and thrilled to see D. Boon and Mike Watt in attendance. I wondered how to approach them, but I didn't have to consider it for too long, as Watt barreled up to me holding a copy of *Confusion Is Sex* and the "Death Valley '69" single, jutting a pen into my hand and asking if I would autograph them.

D. Boon split after the gig to get back to San Pedro, close to an hour's drive. Watt stuck around, wanting to talk more about music, joining us at an Asian eatery, ordering a plate of squid and multiple beers as we rapped into the night. Watt loved what we were up to as a band, our delirious experiments with over-amped sound, without completely abandoning the essence of a rock 'n' roll group—four people with guitars, bass, drums, and vocals.

The Minutemen were riding high on the 1984 release of *Double Nickels on the Dime,* their double LP, which was a deliberate response to *Zen Arcade,* Hüsker Dü's double LP. Both were monoliths issued by SST, and they became major statements in the contemporary post-punk landscape. Mike Watt, like many outlying musicians of the new underground of the 1980s, was a one-of-a-kind personality, a force of nature. To connect with him in person was flattering and filled my heart. The two of us bonded in mutual appreciation for each other's work and would remain lifelong compatriots.

Double Nickels on the Dime, like many recent SST and New Alliance Records sides, had been recorded at Radio Tokyo, a Los Angeles studio located in a tiny house near Venice Beach. We booked two days there to record "Halloween" and "Flower," the first time we would create music outside of Lower Manhattan.

The studio was run by Ethan James, noted for being the keyboardist in heavy metal blues pioneers Blue Cheer during the early 1970s, and he welcomed us in from the glaring sunshine. We proceeded to enter a trance of sorts, the songs almost playing themselves, channeled from somewhere mysterious within. We went deep.

As we bounded around Los Angeles in our final days before departing, Byron Coley, now living in Boston, filed from across the continent a full-page feature on our band in *LA Weekly,* which he titled "Youth, Sonic." He wrote that we had—

> *blown more minds and eardrums than any krappy Kraut noisers ever will . . . When it crashes just right it's not too diff from the churning*

holocaust that's been poured by such guit-bubs as Ron Asheton and Sterling Morrison and Jeff McDonald. It's a highly flammable brand of R&R solvent.

The association with the triumvirate of Redd Kross's Jeff McDonald, the Stooges' Ron Asheton, and the Velvet Underground's Sterling Morrison was intoxicating to us, only more so coming from Byron.

As it happened, our final L.A. throwdown was with Redd Kross at Club Lingerie in Hollywood. Henry Rollins stood front and center in the crowd, writhing, fully engaged in every peal and pulsation of sound spraying like liquid metal from the lip of our stage.

Before splitting town, we met a twenty-one-year-old photographer named Naomi Petersen, who had been documenting the musicians and artists moving around the nucleus of the SST scene. We walked along the Santa Monica Pier with her one afternoon as she took photos of the band. Naomi would appear often in our lives throughout the 1980s, on both coasts, her camera in hand, her eyes wet with being alive in the moment, in love with the underground scene and its music.

Our last appearance on the West Coast was in Seattle, Washington—driving north from Sea-Tac airport on Interstate 5 past miles of stately evergreens, the Pacific Northwest majestic, shining, open, and lush. The gig would take place at Gorilla Gardens. We were to be joined by U-Men, who had been around for a few years, and Green River, a new group in town made up of young gents from various local punk and hardcore bands.

We came out and played to one of the largest audiences we had yet to see. As we raged through our songs, the vibe in the room was like fire in the sky, people's eyes lit up, a sense, I thought, of new musical doors swinging open in their minds.

After our set I jumped into Green River singer Mark Arm's car to fetch some beers and cigarettes at a local food mart. I wondered how this feral pup could see the road, the long sweep of his bangs constantly falling in front of his face, which he'd swoop out with a shake of his head every two seconds.

The year was 1985. Sonic Youth was on the cover of the newly founded, tastemaking *Forced Exposure.* Our album *Bad Moon Rising* was ready to drop in the early springtime. Soon we would be heading back over to the United Kingdom to meet our new pal and label boss, Paul Smith, who would help us inject our noise rock into the critical heart of post-punk London—looking for a kiss on a one-way ticket to God knows where.

49

ON TOP OF A HILL

The only flights we could afford to the UK were on People Express, a cut-rate airline that flew from Newark, New Jersey, to Gatwick, nearly two hours from Central London. This gave us time to meet and get acquainted with Paul Smith, who greeted us at the airport, bristling and skinny, with scruffy facial hair and a glint in his eyes.

He asked us if we wanted to exchange our dollars for British pounds. We figured if we pooled our money together, we would receive a better rate. With about fifty dollars between us, all we were able to manage was twenty-something pounds—enough for cigarettes and a couple of candy bars to get us to wherever we were going. Paul asked us when our return flights were. We had to admit that we'd bought one-way tickets. It was all we could afford. Paul could only smile and shrug, taking the measure of his new act: knapsacks slung across our shoulders, guitars packed in taped-together gig bags.

We jumped on a train and headed to King's Cross station, which was close to the Rough Trade offices on Collier Street. It was great to see Pat Naylor again, along with her sister and fellow publicist, Liz, the two of them bright and cheerful as ever, particularly among most of the glum personages at work there.

We were beyond exhausted when Paul took Lee and Bob off to his tiny flat in Bethnal Green. Kim and I followed Pat to where we'd be staying in Stoke Newington, both areas situated in London's northeast. We rode the 73 bus for forty-five minutes, walked the final quarter mile to the house of Richard Boon and his partner, Deborah Cohen, on Oldfield Road, then plopped on their front-room couch, barely keeping our eyes open as Richard served us a pot of steaming English tea.

Realizing that we were too far gone for any continued niceties, our hosts escorted us upstairs to a room with a bed, which swallowed us up, the house cat purring like a lawnmower as it pushed its entire torso beneath my stomach, an American cave of warmth away from the damp and grey drizzle of England.

Richard Boon turned out to be an erudite and witty gent. He held the distinction of having released the first Buzzcocks record, financed the first recording session for the Fall, and offered Stiff Kittens as a band name to his four mates, who would soon change it to Warsaw before settling on Joy Division. He had been there at the beginning of UK punk, with an interest in the more experimental aspects of the scene, releasing sides by such acts as the Diagram Brothers, Biting Tongues, Ludus, and Gods Gift.

The Naylor sisters, in their capacity as publicists, had passed on a test pressing of *Bad Moon Rising* to Edwin Pouncey, a music journalist at *Sounds* and also an artist and illustrator under the nom de plume Savage Pencil. Edwin filed a five-star review of the album, saying it was—

where ancient ritual meets modern meltdown . . . "Death Valley '69" squeals like a poisonous embodiment of The Jefferson Airplane meeting X, with guest singer Lydia Lunch coming over like a creepy crawly Exene/Grace Slick soundalike to the rattle of all-electric death throes. Sacrificial slaughter never sounded so good. Just one of the curious hallucinations to be heard on this wonderful record.

Julian Henry at *Melody Maker* would write—

Listening to Bad Moon Rising *is like swallowing a cup full of hydrochloric acid . . . Comparison to The Fall, early Pil and Neubauten may head you in the right direction. I listened to* Bad Moon Rising *once, took it off the turntable and smashed it into little pieces. It was the best new record I've heard in a long time. Can somebody send me another copy please?*

These reviews, coming on the heels of similar coverage in the U.S., put wind in our sails. After five years playing together and struggling to find traction—after many dismissive early notices and badly attended gigs—it finally started to feel as though we were getting through. They would be responsible for a considerable spike in sales too. The five thousand copies Rough Trade had pressed began flying out the doors.

At the end of March, we were set to play a radical new independent music series at the Institute of Contemporary Arts. I knew this concert would be a proving ground for us. During sound check, Paul had the idea of having an array of lit jack-o'-lanterns around the stage, in reference to the *Bad Moon Rising* artwork.

Before showtime, we went to cool out at a pub nearby. It was only as Kim and I walked back to the ICA that my nervous system began to attack me. All at once I lost my breath, clutching at the pain streaking through my stomach, cold sweat falling from my brow. Kim held on to me as I leaned against phone booths and trash bins for support, slowly making our way to the concert. I hobbled to the backstage area and sat shivering, nauseated and with a slamming migraine. Whether it was nerves or some bug that had gotten into my body, I couldn't say. I wrapped myself up in every item of clothing I had brought with me. Fortunately I had deliberately packed extra shirts, along with a sweater and a winter parka.

On the bill with us was the industrial music duo of Frank Tovey and Boyd Rice. When they began their set, it was as if four megatons of explosives had been detonated, huge pummeling roars of noise and crushing waves of rhythm that shook the space, the ceiling above the dressing room (which was situated directly behind the stage) threatening to cave in, ancient London dust falling down, creating mounds on my parka and trousers. I thought I was going to black out.

The assault subsided. I was wondering how I was going to pull my sweating, cramped body together to actually go out and play when I heard Kim say—

"Thurston, Michael Stipe is here, he wants to say hi."

I was with it enough to register Michael in the dressing room with me, him suggesting that maybe I should have some tea with lemon and honey. I felt embarrassed by my pathetic state. Eventually it came time for me to struggle out of my folding chair and limp to the stage, where the jack-o'-lanterns awaited, ablaze and glowing.

Lee and Kim plugged in their instruments, and I followed suit, my torso massive from the multitude of shirts, sweater, and parka wrapped around it. As we began, I plucked out the doleful opening notes to "Halloween" while the others expanded into its semi-improvisatory journey, Kim's vocals filling the room—

It's the devil in me
Makes me stare at you

As the music faded away, the audience seemed unsure whether to applaud. Not waiting for them to decide, I launched into the repetition that introduced "Death Valley '69," Lee joining in, the buzz much more stretched out than on the recording. I eventually turned to Bob and Kim and gave them a barely perceptible nod, a cue to click in the one-two slam of the rhythm, and then we were off.

Something within me changed. I could feel the energy racing up from my toes into my stomach into my chest into my shoulders into my neck into my face and warming the roiling synapses in my brain. That night, music proved itself to be a healing force more nurturing than any medicine.

I tore off my coat for "Brave Men Run," then stripped off my sweater for "I Love Her All the Time." During "Ghost Bitch," as Lee waved his contact mic'd acoustic guitar in front of his amplifier, creating howling swaths across the room, I began to remove my shirts, Kim intoning—

Slowly pour the liquid down . . .

Before setting off from New York City, we had walked along Canal Street purchasing multiple cheap bootlegged T-shirts of Bruce Springsteen, Madonna, and Prince to wear onstage. In a way we were "taking the piss," but we also wanted to remark on how mainstream pop musicians such as these created work that was of no less value than that of artists like, say, Boyd Rice.

As "Ghost Bitch" wound down in its spiral of guitar noise, I began to methodically pull off each of the T-shirts: first Madonna, then Prince, then Bruce, then another Prince, and another Bruce, until I was draped, happy and sweating, in just a single skimpy Madonna tee.

I felt reborn by this gig, the set ending as we smashed the jack-o'-lanterns with our guitars, Paul Smith and the Naylors' faces at once grinning and shocked. Richard Boon, Savage Pencil, the girls from Ut, a coterie of jaded music lovers from Rough Trade, and all our new London pals had been swarming around the room. Their praise, while muted in the English fashion, lifted us up, instantly validating us as a force to be reckoned with.

Paul set us up with a couple of other London gigs, including one at the legendary 100 Club where all the heavies had played since the 1940s and '50s (Louis Armstrong, Bo Diddley, B. B. King, Muddy Waters) as well as the 1960s (the Pretty Things, the Who, the Kinks). It was where the first ever UK "Punk Festival" had been held in 1976, with the Sex Pistols, the Buzzcocks, the Clash, the Damned, and Siouxsie and the Banshees featured.

After our 100 Club set ended, we hung out with the various punters in the room. Kim pulled at my arm, pointing—

"Isn't that Ian MacKaye?"

It definitely was. What was he doing here, so far from Washington, D.C.? I walked over to him—

"Hey, are you Ian?"

"Yeah."

He began telling us how much our gig had kicked ass, mentioning that we reminded him of the Butthole Surfers—a major compliment. He told me he was in town working with John Loder at Southern Studios. As we were jawing away, I noticed Nick Cave bounding in across the beer-and-sweat-drenched floor. He was unmistakable as ever: tall and pale, his hair piled high, clothed all in black, unkempt and lit up.

"Have you played yet?"

—he asked in his sexy Australian brogue.

"Yeah, we just ended."

I introduced Nick to Ian, who was visibly thrilled by the interruption. He told Nick how much the Birthday Party had meant to him. Nick took the compliments with grace, then looked around at the post-gig fallout. Spying a few starry-eyed punkers heading his way, he scooted off to the devil knows where.

We took the ferry over to the Netherlands and met up with Carlos van Hijfte, who had organized a few shows for us there. We were due to perform with the writer Kathy Acker in Rotterdam at a music and literary festival of sorts. She had come to one of our shows in London, seemingly intrigued by our forthcoming gig together. But without alerting anyone, she stood us up.

Making the most of her absence, I stepped out onstage holding a copy of Kathy's *Blood and Guts in High School,* written in the 1970s though only recently published. The book had been instantly polarizing, with its descriptions of incest and rape, its dream journals, illustrations, and pages of horrific banality.

I announced to the audience—

"Hey, uh, we're called Sonic Youth, and I don't know how many people know this, but Kathy didn't show up . . . she's not here. Nobody knows where she is. So if anybody out there knows where Kathy is, you should, uh, probably, uh, keep it to yourself. This is Kathy's book. So, I'll leave this, like, right here."

Lee chimed in on his microphone—

"If you want to you can come up and rip a few pages out to take home with you."

We trudged through our set, but our songs were falling apart, as if some disturbed energy permeated the space. We ended the set by playing a mess of "Satan Is Boring," a song we had written in response to news of a Long Island teenager killed by another teen purportedly under the influence of acid and literalizing Black Sabbath lyrics. I stepped to the microphone to sing a new song we had been developing titled "Green Light"—

> I kneel before the green light of her singing crayon eyes
> And then I kiss her stomach and it's then I realize
> Her light is the night
> I'm not blind, I believe in you
> I see a green light

It led into Lee moaning into his microphone as he played cassette-driven tape loops, Bob pounding away on his drums, Kim reciting from Kathy's book—

> She dreams she's fucking someone . . .

Kim handed the book to me, and I began tearing pages out, flinging them into the crowd. It elicited little more than low-level confoundment, the audience seemingly uncertain what we were trying to convey. We had little clue ourselves.

I would never learn why Kathy hadn't made the Rotterdam show. Maybe she sensed the evening's potential discombobulation and it had scared her off. Our paths never crossed again.

Mick Harvey had seen our epic show at the Institute of Contemporary Arts and thought we would be a good supporting act for Nick Cave & the Bad Seeds, the newly rejiggered version of his former band, the Birthday Party.

It was only a five-date tour, but these gigs would be critical in introducing us to an English audience. Each show we became successively tighter and more together, the model of the Bad Seeds offering us all a lesson in stage presence. We went out each night before them, offering feedback-drenched noise rock infused with rock 'n' roll, and the audiences, while not exactly sure about us, knew that we weren't just some run-of-the-mill opening act.

One young punker girl who came to every show was always perched front and center, studiously lighting Nick Cave's cigarette between songs. She approached us outside after the first couple of gigs and told us how she and her coterie of Cave devotees appreciated what we were doing. His was a notoriously tough crowd, and while we didn't see ourselves catering or pandering for their acceptance as such, we felt well pleased to hear that we were cracking through.

The final gig of the tour was at the Hammersmith Palais in London, where the media would be out in force, curious how the ex–Birthday Party lads were faring in their new incarnation. We rose to the occasion, fully on fire. It was Kim's thirty-second birthday, and we were in high spirits. We killed it, the audience reflecting our energy back onto us in even greater measure, Nick and his paramour, Anita Lane, smiling and congratulating us.

Bad Moon Rising would peak at number three on the *NME* independent music charts. It was the kind of recognition I had only dreamed of, albeit thousands of miles from our home. Seizing the moment, Paul had us release a twelve-inch single of "Death Valley '69." On the record's insert, I included Kim's and my address on Eldridge Street, in case anyone wanted to send us mail. For some time I had been writing to punk and hardcore bands at their home addresses, which many would print on the inserts of their single sleeves. It was a directness and intimacy that I admired and wanted to emulate, the de rigueur way for underground bands and their audiences to communicate. I didn't think about any potential repercussions.

It meant that as Sonic Youth's profile expanded, Kim and I would sometimes head downstairs from our pad only to find waiting outside our building's front door some lone pup wanting to meet us or asking for a record to be signed. Sometimes it was more disconcerting, even threatening, as when a boy appeared each day, nervously pacing outside our building, then following behind us muttering—

"Why are you playing games with me?"

It wasn't just unexpected visitors. We began to receive letters, mostly benign, though some were scribbled missives on crumpled paper containing lengthy, psychotic rants. I learned to hold fan letters up to the light and shake them in case unidentified objects were enclosed, a lesson I'd picked up after opening one only for a mess of dead flies to fall out onto my lap.

Throughout the UK and Europe, we reacquainted ourselves with what were now becoming familiar spaces with familiar faces: Rote Fabrik, Melkweg, De Effenaar, Vera, Sputnik. The audiences, whether fifty people or a few hundred, now began to show up with more of a preconception of what Sonic Youth had to offer: the promise of some musical intrigue.

Long days of unloading our gear, working through sound check, attempting to find sustenance, playing the gig, loading the van back up, then seeking places to sleep. It became ritual, and through it all we began to find a true sense of camaraderie, even as we found ourselves on top of one another each day and night, the rigors of touring challenging but also feeding our devotion as a creative collective.

Our shared experience discovering rich veins of European life was heady and profound, rough and beautiful, from the momentous to the banal, etching everlasting memories into each of our psyches.

Gathered at the Rough Trade offices before heading back to the U.S., Paul Smith conveyed how he needed us to return before the year was up. He wanted to capitalize on the band's momentum. We had become extremely close with Paul since meeting him at the airport over a month prior. He had earned our respect as a thoughtful champion of our band. He had also come to see that we weren't the dour junkies our music or haggard appearance may have suggested. Sonic Youth, it turned out, was all about fun, music, art, absurdity—life.

I had written down a list of North American bands for Paul to consider releasing on Blast First: Butthole Surfers, Big Black, Swans, Live Skull, Rat at Rat R, Killdozer, Tar Babies. He stared at the names with an incredulous smile.

Before we left the office, he shared with us his vision for the band. We could become, in his estimation—

"As big as the Birthday Party."

This was heady stuff, but, hey, who knew? In that moment, riding the high off our UK and European shows, anything seemed possible.

It was while I pondered this fantastic scenario that Bob piped up—

"I'm not coming back."

All of our heads turned toward him—
"*What?*"
"I'm quitting the band. I don't want to be away from home so long. I'm married and it's a drag being away."
He paused, before adding—
"And I'm tired of sleeping—or *not* sleeping—in freezing record store basements and beds full of cat piss."
Absorbing the sudden news flash, we assured Paul that we would survive, but I could see how crestfallen he was. He had expended so much energy, taken us so far already—only for it all to come crashing down?
Paul saw us the way we had come to see ourselves, as a four-headed entity: me, the outspoken instigator; Kim, the brooding intellectual with the booming bass; Lee, the high-performance guitar thrasher; Bob, the gentle, restless, primal drummer. How could this unity of art-rock majesty be shattered?

We didn't waste much time dwelling on it. The previous December I had attended a CBGB hardcore matinee featuring the Lansing, Michigan, band the Crucifucks. I had been sending away for various hardcore cassettes, the Crucifucks "demo" the one I was most curious about, if only because their name was so ridiculous. The cassette was utterly genius, with such incendiary, anti-authority, anti-fascist tunes as "Hinkley Had a Vision," "Cops for Fertilizer," and "Democracy Spawns Bad Taste."
I had encouraged Lee to accompany me to check out the band, who were obviously a bit worn down, having been on the whirlwind Rock Against Reagan tour with the Dead Kennedys. They were still pretty hot, though. I had struck up a pen pal communication with their drummer, Steve Shelley, who had sent me a copy of a single from a new project he was involved with named Strange Fruit. It was a wonderful, reverb-smacked dub-punk excursion.
Bumping into Lee and me at the show, he was happy to see us. We exchanged phone numbers, and the three of us talked with some frequency over the course of 1985, the idea at one point bandied about that Lee should produce a Crucifucks session at Wharton Tiers's studio. But it would come to naught, as Steve would soon leave that notorious group.
During one of our phone calls, Steve mentioned that he and bassist Marc Hauser had been considering a move to San Francisco. They had friends around the Dead Kennedys camp there. Lee and I told him to forget San Francisco and to come to New York City instead. There

were plenty of bands in search of a drummer here. Plus Sonic Youth was headed off on our UK/Europe tour, and Kim and I could really use a pet sitter for Egan and Sweetface. He took us up on the offer and, with Marc along for the journey, drove his Chevy van from Michigan out to the Lower East Side of New York City, where the two decamped at our apartment to take care of the animals.

We returned to our Eldridge Street place in early April, suddenly short a drummer. Steve and Marc walked into the apartment from whatever crummy day jobs they had landed that long month in the city while we were on tour, appearing a bit startled to find us standing there with our beat-up guitar cases and luggage. I introduced Steve to Kim, following with—

"Hey, you wanna play drums in Sonic Youth?"

50

HORSE SINGS FROM CLOUD

We began our first rehearsals with Steve in a basement on West Houston Street, the dividing line between the West Village and SoHo, across from MacDougal Street, where Bob Dylan and poets Gregory Corso and Anne Waldman resided.

Playing with Steve was a new beginning, his style completely different from both Richard Edson's and Bob Bert's. Despite his slight, still-teenage-looking build, he wailed and throttled the kit, leaping from his seat when landing a wallop, his timing impeccable, urging us three stragglers to tighten up. There was elasticity to the groove, but also an insistence in his playing that demanded we stay in line.

It was obvious from day one that our sonic engine had been recalibrated. All rockets were set to launch, new planets on the horizon.

"I like the way he shakes his head"

—Kim remarked as we walked home from that first rehearsal.

And then all at once our lives took on the rhythms of a working, touring band, one with, it seemed, a still small but growing audience.

The Butthole Surfers came to town the first week of June 1985, bringing along their Austin, Texas, pals Scratch Acid. We all went to check them out at Danceteria, Lydia dancing, fully into the thumping buzz of Scratch Acid. Buttholes singer Gibby Haynes came out with a dozen wooden clothespins snapped into his hair, which he violently shook, the clothespins projecting into the crowd. The two drummers, Teresa Nervosa and King Coffey, stood and whammed away in tribal catharsis, their skinny bodies falling to the ground between songs. Paul Leary ripped away at his guitar, his face contorted as if he were on some burning acid trip.

We invited the Buttholes to come play with us at Folk City later that week. Our idea was to have a night in which both Steve Shelley and Bob Bert would play drums together, along with tape recorders playing sound events through small amplifiers set up near the bar and in the toilets. Richard Kern would bring in a couple of film projectors and screen his works of perverse gore and sex play onto the walls.

As our set began, we turned all the interior lights off and started into "I'm Insane," a charging, pulsing song from *Bad Moon Rising* in which I recited a litany of non sequiturs cribbed from vintage exploitation paperbacks, then "Ghost Bitch," followed by a new piece entitled "Secret Girl," which consisted of a looping piano repetition I had recorded on a portable cassette deck using the rather detuned stand-up piano in the Gordons' Los Angeles house. Kim composed a recitation to go on top of this cassette loop, with lines that spoke to female consciousness, identity, invisibility, and emotional manipulation through advertising. Onstage during "Secret Girl" would be just Kim and the cassette, the rest of us catching our breath, ready to play one other new song, "Expressway to Yr Skull," which I had introduced on our first rehearsal day with Steve.

"Expressway to Yr Skull" was based on a vocal melody, the guitar chords in simple support, the lyrics bidding an overdue goodbye to West Coast Manson mythology as well as offering a bratty take on the Beach Boys' sun and fun—

We're gonna kill the California girls

The song resolved in a pause before a flurry of chording, the guitars ascending slowly up the neck until they could move no further except into space, at which point Kim, Lee, and I allowed our amplifiers to fade away, just knuckling the backs of our guitar necks to elicit drones, Steve coloring the sound field with cymbal wash.

This was how we ended our night at Folk City.

Steve flew out to Michigan to retrieve his blue-and-white Chevy van (which his ex-Crucifucks travel companion Marc Hauser had since driven back home), and, again with Gerard Cosloy's diligent assistance, we hit the road to play any and every club, college cafeteria, and Veterans of Foreign War hall across the U.S. that would have us. Lee outfitted the van with wood panels across the inside back, to better accommodate our gear. It wasn't first class, but this was a long way from the bodies piled on top of one another that had characterized our Savage Blunder tours a few years earlier.

Our gigs were often riven with conflict before they even began. We were at war with the soundpeople of America, who claimed they had no room in their front-of-house systems for our guitars, which were cranked too loud. Our vocals would be buried, they told us. The bass was far too loud to begin with; they wouldn't even bother mic'ing our amps. Et cetera, et cetera. Some sound checks were more difficult than others. We strained to hear vocals in the monitors, often replaced by honking or screaming feedback, our eardrums snapping shut to their fatal frequencies.

Tinnitus rose and subsided in our heads as Steve's van tooled through the midwestern nights—long, long patches of sameness, the miles endless; windows cracked to let the cigarette smoke out; coins counted to fill the gas tank, to buy a bag of Fritos and a Dr Pepper or Mr. Pibb to keep the body happy; tall cups of gas station coffee repurposed as ashtrays; the huge boom box cassette and radio deck (which I purchased on Delancey Street with the band's money for this express purpose) like a fifth member straddled between the two front seats, playing Steve's mixtapes of country blues records or jamming all the new tapes from our compatriots: Killdozer, Tar Babies, Meat Puppets, Butthole Surfers, the Minutemen, Scratch Acid.

In Chicago, we met up with the front man for the band Big Black, Steve Albini, for a barbecue in the park near his house, then were off to the Sonic Youth gig he had promoted at the Smart Bar. We then connected with Die Kreuzen at Stache's in Columbus, Ohio, their blitzkrieg thrash like a hurricane, the singer Dan Kubinski hanging off his microphone stand like a skater in a blizzard, long hair wet in his face, his high-pitched howl like ice through the bloodstream.

Then Detroit to play with Laughing Hyenas, a new band featuring John Brannon, the intensified singer from Detroit hardcore heavies Negative Approach, and his partner in crime Larissa Strickland on guitar, burning treble-shredding notes. Also on the bill was Rites of Spring, a new outfit from the Dischord inner sanctum of Washington, D.C., looking to further the ur-language of hardcore that they had authored, the songs ablaze, guitarist Guy Picciotto overwhelmed after their set, kneeling before his broken guitar, head in hands.

There was a script we came to follow, as we drove for hours on end, from town to town, city to city, club to club. First we arrived in the general area

Drumstick guitar mania, amped up on tour with thrashers Die Kreuzen and Laughing Hyenas—Somerville, Massachusetts, October 1988

By the end of the eighties, the band would utilize dozens of guitars, mostly bargain-basement pieces, and then, with a little more coin at our disposal, Fender Jazzmasters, Jaguars, and Mustangs, which were still relatively afford-able before collectors began raising their values through the roof.

Yoshimi from the Boredoms makes sure I receive enough sustenance before heading out onstage in Tokyo, early 1989. The Boredoms and Sonic Youth would become close confidants in the art of musical chaos.

Reading Festival, England, summer 1991. Nirvana played fourth on a nine-act bill. They completely stole the day, as they unwittingly prepared to rule the universe.

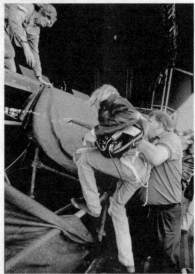

Summer of 1992 at CBGB, playing with percussionist William Hooker. These forays outside the band would shape Sonic Youth's development into the next decade. John Olson of Wolf Eyes pointed to this gig as the spark for a new noise generation.

Producer Don Was gathered together an "alternative rock" supergroup to record rock 'n' roll standards as a soundtrack for the 1994 film *Backbeat*. It would be the first music Dave Grohl would engage in after Kurt's passing that April. Left to right: Greg Dulli of Afghan Whigs, Don Fleming, Mike Mills, Dave Grohl, and me, at thirty-six

While on tour with R.E.M. in 1995, all of Sonic Youth (with one-year-old Coco) and Michael Stipe went to visit William Burroughs at his modest home in Lawrence, Kansas.

Bomb magazine flew me from NYC to Boston with Lenny Kaye, in the autumn of 1995, to file a story on Patti Smith. We spent a day traversing the cemetery where Jack Kerouac is buried, laying flowers (and a pumpkin) at his grave.

Touring the Pacific Rim in 1996 with the Beastie Boys, Bikini Kill, the newly formed Foo Fighters, Beck, Pavement, the Amps, Jawbreaker, and a host of others. We brought my mom along to help care for Coco. She was in seventh heaven. Clockwise from left: Nate Mendel, Eleanor Moore, Pat Smear, Ione Skye (partial), Ad-Rock, and Steve Shelley

In the zone at the Tibetan Freedom Concert on Randall's Island, New York City, summer of 1997, sharing the stage with A Tribe Called Quest, Beastie Boys, Foo Fighters, Biz Markie, Radiohead, U2, Patti Smith, and others

Standing with two pillars of radical guitar action: high-energy maestro Ron Asheton of the Stooges and free improvisation genius Derek Bailey. One of many amazing nights at Tonic, one of NYC's greatest experimental music venues, 2001

Jim O'Rourke enters the sonic stream, 2002.

Reflecting forward. New York City, 2006

Coco Hayley Gordon Moore at ten years old, the light of love, Northampton, Massachusetts, 2004

It was our good fortune that bass player Mark Ibold joined our group after Jim O'Rourke's departure, while Mark's group Pavement was on hiatus. Rehearsing in the Gordon-Moore Northampton basement, November 2008

Yoko Ono invited me to tour with her as a duo across Europe in 2013. Here we're performing my "Guitar Hug" piece, where two guitarists, their instruments at full volume, walk toward each other before embracing, their guitars rubbing and scraping feedback.

A spray of shattered glass and wet noise. Our final gig in New York would be outdoors on the Williamsburg waterfront in the fall of 2011. I had just turned fifty-three, with the realization that radical change was on the sonic horizon.

Finding happiness, love, and our own positive mental attitude, Eva and I make a friendly stop at Dischord House, Washington, D.C.

Stepping into solo world at the Liverpool Sound City festival in 2015. England would become a new home, revealing itself as an island of both welcome and enlightenment.

of a gig, located a pay phone, and called the promoter, the club, or, if all else failed, Gerard back on the East Coast, to receive more detailed directions. Our maps were fine for long highway hauls, but the inner grids of the towns and cities we visited were foreign to us. If we saw anyone who looked close to being a punk rocker, we might yell out the window—

"Hey, which way to Stache's?"

I rarely communicated with my family back home while on the road, lost in the other world of travel. On the rare occasion I did ring my mother, she would say—

"Oh, you're alive."

She wasn't the only one I had grown distant from. As touring had taken me farther and farther afield and I became more deeply entrenched in my life with Kim, the band, and our mutual friends, I had grown apart from my first close musical connection, Harold, to the point where he gave up on me as a best friend.

Setting out on tour with our newly modified lineup, the band stopped in Bethel to stay the night at my mother's place. The four of us went to Harold and his older boyfriend's house nearby to hang out. We sat around and watched TV, having a few drinks. Harold seemed to bristle at my constant sarcasm and snarkiness, honed after nearly a decade of living in downtown Manhattan, only amplified here in Bethel with the band by my side.

I didn't realize the change in my attitude affected him as much as it had. The next morning, as we clambered into the van in my mother's driveway, I noticed every Sonic Youth record I had given Harold stuck beneath the windshield wipers with a note attached—

> Here's your records back
> Give them to your snotty friends

I was stung, shocked even, though Harold had always invested a lot of emotion in our friendship. Somewhat embarrassed in front of the band, I decided to put the incident out of my mind. The wound of our split would stay repressed, the demands of touring day and night overwhelming my consciousness yet again.

We hit Los Angeles for a few days, staying at the Gordons' house in Rancho Park, playing an afternoon gig out on the loading docks of a downtown building with the Minutemen, Savage Republic, DC3, Lawndale, and Saccharine Trust. Then we were off to Texas, ripping hard with Scratch Acid at the Continental Club in Austin.

It was there that we met Terry Pearson, the first sound engineer (other than John Erskine, who had become busy in New York manning sound for everyone from Branca to Elliott Sharp) who was actually on board with what we were up to. He said he really enjoyed it, comparing us to when he had seen the 13th Floor Elevators and Velvet Underground in his youth. We asked Terry if he would ever consider touring with us. His response was a straight-up—

"Hell yeah."

We were set to return to the UK at Paul Smith's behest, this time with Steve Shelley on the skins, but first we would spend the month of October wailing through the European continent, our Dutch confidant Carlos van Hijfte at the wheel, making sure we got from one point to the next, meeting up with friends Butthole Surfers and Nick Cave & the Bad Seeds at the Pandora's Box Festival in the Netherlands.

Another day, another festival, this one Futurama in Belgium with Scotland's the Jesus and Mary Chain, a group we had been reading about in all the British music papers. They were said to be some new noise-drenched Sex Pistols, their gigs cut short by drunken chaos, purportedly by the band as well as their rowdy audience of spotty-faced punters. We saw the four lads walk toward their small hovel of a dressing room, pale, skinny, dripping with petulance. Lee and I went over to say hello, the boys responding with surprise, as if we'd broken some boundary of propriety.

Instead of the rioting we had hoped to witness, the Futurama show was tame, the crowd standing attentively, watching, listening. Lee and I did too, loving the sound of William Reid's guitar scorching through his amp, the reverb-swamped notes surrounded by feedback, his brother Jim's vocals a crooning whisper, also drowned in a universe of reverb. Bobby Gillespie, who played his snare drum and crash cymbal standing up à la the Velvet Underground's Moe Tucker, and bassist Douglas Hart preserved the music's time and space, sensitive to its sonic minimalism. After their set, we seemed to frighten the group with our accolades and compliments.

Paul Smith had put together a gig for us, the first week of November, on the sands of Brighton Beach, just south of London. He had hired a couple of buses to transport ticket buyers, Rough Trade employees, and invited journalists to come check us out in this off-grid location.

An English equivalent to the Gila Monster Jamboree in the California desert, Sonic Youth performing on the pebbled beach of Brighton was Paul's pure visionary genius, drawing attention to our band by having us step outside of the typical showcase at a typical venue. The rickety, jerry-built stage and sound system, planted into the rocks, were sufficient to the task of blasting our audience with sound, though they were raised rather high up and a trifle fearsome. Still, we ripped through our *Bad Moon Rising* set, the onlookers chilly, their backs against the cold water spitting at them from the beachfront, but nonetheless smiling at the sight of these New Yorkers blasting away in a zone where mods and rockers had clashed over twenty years earlier.

Paul had been concerned for the band when we lost Bob Bert, but his anxieties were quickly put to rest. He was astounded by Steve Shelley's input, and his enthusiasm for taking us to our next chapter only grew. He had been tap-dancing across the desks of the English music press, convincing them that Sonic Youth was worthy of their further, serious consideration. Longer-in-the-tooth critics grumbled a bit at our brashness, but it helped that we delivered the musical goods, our connection informed by years (in the case of Kim, Lee, and me with Sonic Youth, and Steve with his previous bands) of relentless rehearsal and touring.

The venerable critic Simon Frith muttered in his writing about us being "clever people playing stupid music," but even he recognized the way we were embraced by many of his colleagues (some of whom he thought should know better). There was always a danger in being the critics' darlings, which we were most definitely becoming. If the critics turned on you, for whatever reason (being too "rockist," being not "proper" rock stars, being guilty of starry-eyed pomposity, or otherwise rubbing the journalist intelligentsia the wrong way), the foundation for your success could shatter beneath you, bringing the edifice that you had carefully constructed down to the ground. With *Bad Moon Rising* and now our live shows lauded by the likes of *NME, Sounds,* and *Melody Maker,* we felt a mixture of pride and trepidation.

Our whirlwind wasn't over. Within a week of returning to the U.S., Sonic Youth and Swans flew out to Los Angeles yet again, this time to play a show downtown in a vacated furniture warehouse on the twenty-first of December. Michael Gira hadn't seen us play for some time, and hearing us with Steve, he remarked on how different we had become, noting that Bob Bert and Steve were both great but utterly distinct drummers. In the years to come, Steve would establish within the band his own vocabulary of experimentation, eventually becoming a solid mainstay of Sonic Youth.

We played "Ghost Bitch" that night, and I turned and watched as Steve left his kit to sit on the floor and play various pieces of metal, creating an improvised clangor in support of Kim's creepy-crawly recitation at the song's head. Lee was in a full state of noise meditation, playing call-and-response feedback measures against my slow punctuations of electric strum.

Lee was using an amplifier kindly lent to us by D. Boon, though the Minutemen guitarist was not in attendance at the concert. That night, just three days before Christmas 1985, he was on his way home to San Pedro from Arizona, asleep with a fever in the back of a van as he cruised along with a few friends and loved ones, riding a straight shot west along Interstate 10. It was deep into the early hours of December 22 when the van's rear axle snapped, flipping the vehicle over into the remote landscape and dry winds of the desert. D. Boon's life was whisked away in the tragic space of a single, terrible moment.

51

IT'S ALWAYS A HEADACHE
THE SIZE OF A TOW TRUCK

1986 would be when we truly learned to tour, to work, to play, to deal with all the savage inequities and gracious epiphanies that we shared in the intimacy of our newly purchased van, bought used from a family man out in Queens near JFK Airport, 747 jets roaring overhead as we made the transaction.

Greg Ginn, founder and guitarist of Black Flag, rang me up early in the year asking if Sonic Youth would like to release records with his SST label. It was a phone call I could have only dreamed of; SST was at the vanguard of rock, as I saw it. For Sonic Youth to be the labelmates of Black Flag, the Minutemen, Meat Puppets, Hüsker Dü, and Saccharine Trust—it was a wish come true without parallel.

I had sent *Confusion Is Sex* and *Bad Moon Rising* to New Alliance, the Minutemen's personal imprint at SST, and I had received an encouraging, if cryptic, postcard back from Mike Watt. He mentioned to me, on another occasion, that one of the people overseeing operations at SST had been reluctant to sign bands outside of SST's local and familial zone and had further said, in a subtle dig at me and the band—

"Record collectors shouldn't be in bands."

It cut me a bit at the time, making me wonder whether there was an impurity in being a fan as well as an artist. I knew for a fact that Henry Rollins was a big-time record collector, as were Barry Henssler and Corey Rusk from Necros, Don Bolles from the Germs, Jello Biafra—even pop icon Elton John celebrated his record-collecting mania in the pages of *Creem* in the early 1970s. I soon recognized the argument for the hogwash it was.

But it meant that I could only be wildly happy to receive the call from Greg out of the blue. Maybe record collectors could be in bands after all. His offer was too special to refuse.

But it came at a cost. Gerard Cosloy had been a patient and loyal advocate of our music, and his Homestead label had helped put Sonic Youth on the map. We sat down to talk to him in the wake of Greg's call. He well understood why we would jump ship to SST, though he understandably wasn't too happy about it.

In the UK and Europe, Paul Smith would continue to work with us, saying that he would gladly cooperate with SST, a situation that would soon prove nearly impossible to get an articulate take on, as the business of releasing records, booking gigs, and promoting bands—everything SST was built to do—could sometimes be hazy, to say the least.

Ray Farrell, our friend and tour connection from Rough Trade's U.S. distribution setup in Berkeley, had recently accepted a job offer from SST, essentially becoming its first paid employee, with the inviting offer of a desk (and a place to sleep beneath it). More than any other individual at the label, it would be Ray who would become our point person.

We had a new label and, with it, a sense that the wind was at our backs. It was time to make some new music.

We found ourselves rehearsing together in a tiny back room just east of Tompkins Square Park in the East Village. We were approaching our songwriting process more studiously now, aware of the critical attention awaiting us and the time and money both Blast First and SST were investing in us.

Kim had become, without any real discussion, the designated bass player in the band. Where before she, Lee, and I had once traded off with the various guitars, the three of us began claiming some of them as our own jurisdiction. Kim picked up the bass more often than not, it eventually becoming her instrument of choice. This would be one more step toward our establishing a more typical rock-band stance. Rather than feeling like a concession toward normalcy, it gave us consistency, stability.

Her ownership of the bass didn't mean that she was immune from my criticism. As newer songs developed, I would sometimes vent frustration at Kim, telling her she wasn't playing parts the way I thought she should. We were both untutored guitarists, but she approached the bass more visually than I did, seeing parts as patterns, her playing propelled by a kind of sense memory. I identified with the method, though I was somewhat more attuned to which notes related to which frets. It led to testy exchanges in front of the band, as I attempted to influence her playing but without a shared language to draw from; it would, at times, bring us to a bitter impasse. Lee, whose knowledge of musical notation surpassed both of ours, would thankfully step in, and the music would arrive where it should. But it would leave me grumpy, and I was sometimes slow to realize the way my insensitivity was hurting my bandmates (and, in Kim's case, my wife). After a tempestuous rehearsal, Kim and I walked home together in discomfited silence, only to be broken by her saying, not for the first time—

"Maybe I should leave the band."

It allowed me to see the way I still sometimes failed to effectively communicate with her in the context of our band—and the harmful impact it was having on our relationship.

Like every creative collective, ours was a constant journey of learning, acknowledging, and allowing for the magic of each person's input to be trusted and regarded with equal measure. It wasn't always easy. All four of our heads would butt, and our emotions would often roil. But more often than not we respected and enjoyed one another's company and that extrasensory interaction that took place among us, which I had recognized first with Kim, then with Lee, and soon again with Steve, the magic becoming the defining feature of our ensemble.

We returned to BC Studios in the nether regions of Brooklyn in the springtime to record our new music, titling the album *EVOL* after a video made by Tony Oursler a couple of years prior, a short piece featuring his artist pal Mike Kelley in which a psychosexual dreamworld has been enacted, the camera frame replete with flooded color and fantasy sequences that utilized cardboard cutouts.

Mike Watt contacted me, as he had just driven across the country with his love, Kira Roessler, who had left Black Flag and Los Angeles to study at Yale in New Haven, Connecticut. He was curious to come down to Manhattan and see us before heading back west. I hadn't talked to Mike since D. Boon's passing, and I enthusiastically invited him to our apartment.

Mike drove into Manhattan, parked God knows where, and hoofed around the streets before ringing us up—

"*Thurst!* I'm in your town!"

I relayed directions as specifically as possible, then peered out our front window until I saw him loping down Eldridge Street picking up two-by-fours scattered among the trash and windmilling them in Pete Townshend fashion as if they were guitars.

"*Yo, Watt!!*"

—I yelled, and threw down our apartment keys. He clambered up. Mike wound up staying a few nights on some blankets that Kim and I had spread out for him. He was astounded by the way our pad was essentially one long hallway, the only door in the place leading to a tiny toilet and sink enclosure, the bathtub situated in the kitchen with a slab of plywood atop it so it could function as a table. It meant that, unless alone, bathing would never be a private affair.

I invited him to the studio to hang out while we recorded, and Lee asked him to track a bass guitar line to a song he had constructed entitled "In the Kingdom #19." It was the first time Watt had played after the shock of D. dying. While Lee overdubbed his vocals, much of it spoken, I thought to introduce a bit of mischief, throwing a string of lit firecrackers into the vocal booth. The explosions utterly unnerved Lee as he yelled and jumped, the smoke and ashen paper filling the small space, choking off any further recording.

My prank didn't go over too well, and I could only apologize for it. We left the explosions and yelling in the mix, though.

At another point, Watt handed me a poem about when he worked as a meter man, and I recorded it, also for "In the Kingdom #19," appearing as the track wound down—

I never gave a damn about the meter man
Until I was the man who had to read the meter, man

Watt would also play on a cover of "Bubble Gum," a song I loved from Kim Fowley's 1968 LP *Outrageous*, an inspired, lunatic concept album of stoned-out hippie life and police paranoia.

He seemed taken aback by our loose working methods in the studio, two dozen guitars in varying states of disrepair lying around in every corner, song arrangements allowed to formulate and breathe as we went along. The Minutemen, apparently, entered a recording session with the material tight and ready to track and mix—in and out, boom. We liked the idea of the studio becoming its own instrument, its own element, yet another member suggesting ideas.

The songs on *EVOL* were a bit tamer than our previous recordings, flirting with qualities of such bands as the Replacements, though still played through our alternate-tuned guitars and refracted through our idiosyncratic prism. For the album cover we used a still from a recent Richard Kern film, *Submit to Me*, which featured his most infamous "actress," Lung Leg, raving at the camera.

We hit England with the album's early reviews well in our favor. Critics were responsive to our songwriting taking a more melodic focus. Dave Haslam in *NME* called *EVOL* "mesmeric." We then hooked up once more with Carlos van Hijfte, who sent us across Germany in a van driven by a young woman named Jeanette Bleeker, a German music promoter running on manic energy and who worked closely with Nick Cave, the two of them creating chaos wherever they appeared.

Her reputation as a force of nature preceded her: clubs became tense as soon as her bands, be it Psychic TV or Swans, straggled in for their sound checks. When one German venue came up short on cash to pay us at the end of the night, Jeanette walked behind the bar and began to throw bottles, one by one, across the room, glass exploding everywhere at 3:00 a.m. as she yelled—

"Pay me! *Now!!*"

—not stopping until she got what she came for.

Jeanette drove at ninety miles per hour along the autobahn, one hand on the wheel, the other attempting to paint her toenails, her bare foot stuck out the driver's-side window. Somehow she would also be smoking a cigarette and rasping in a husky, sleep-deprived voice about her love for Nick Cave and how he frustrated her so by continuing to "lose" his passport.

The mantra of the die-hard performer, whether in music or sports or otherwise, is to always bring your A game no matter how small the audience, how Podunk the town, how low the stakes. You get up there and give those few people something glorious, something they'll always remember.

But, in 1986, a month shy of turning twenty-eight, arriving in a hard-seated van to Treviso, an Italian city just north of Venice, burned to a crisp from having spent five days and nights playing across Germany, I looked at the outdoor stage—only barely supported by metal stilts, outfitted with a low-powered PA system, with about ten punky kids milling around it—and I groaned.

Dark clouds were coming in. Rain had already slicked up the streets. There came the question of whether we should play the gig or cancel. There was good reason to think we could be electrocuted if we played. Alternatively, we could race to unload the van, quickly set up, rip out a killer set for the curious people who had bothered to come, and be on our way before the worst of the storm came.

We chose to cancel.

The promoters were understanding, though still unhappy with our choice. Rather than feeling relieved ourselves, we all just sat around eating cheap pasta and feeling like losers.

Exhaustion begat depression. Learning how to confront those feelings would be extremely important in our continuing perseverance. Touring and playing gigs for multiple nights in a row could be utterly taxing in its repetition and monotony, each band member's peccadilloes becoming more and more irritating, competitive positioning in the tiny social fabric of the group becoming psychotically wearisome and sometimes playing out onstage, negative energy deadening the miraculous gift of being able to see the world, work, eat, play, meet incredible people (some of whom would become lifelong friends and associates), discover foreign lifestyles and new political ideas; to bask one day beneath the Portuguese sunshine, the next day in the mystic beauty of a Norwegian snowfall.

While in the thick of it, though, with money scarce and personal hygiene challenged, you could be driven to your wit's end. The survivors were those who found successful strategies for meditation, relief, and release.

Being in an avant-garde noise rock band wasn't for everyone.

52

CHOOSE ANY MEMORY

When we returned from Europe, Mike Watt's dictum rang in my ears: *When you're not playin', you're payin'.* Whether or not you have an album to promote, it's your job as a musician to hit the road—playing was *work*.

It was in that spirit that, within days of returning to the U.S., we loaded our van up and set out across the country for another round of shows. Carlos van Hijfte flew over from the Netherlands to be our tour manager. He would join our soundman Terry Pearson, lighting designer Susanne Sasic, and the band in the van as it towed a rented U-Haul filled with amps, drums, guitars, and suitcases.

Carlos was tasked with the unenviable job of collecting gig money at the end of each show, anywhere between $30 and $300. He usually didn't have much trouble, except on a night at the Mason Jar in Phoenix, Arizona, where we shared the bill with Saccharine Trust and Sun City Girls. The club claimed it couldn't pony up the full guarantee, due mostly to a less-than-expected turnout. Carlos argued to no avail.

"I used every English word I knew!"

—he told us after returning to our van. Still, he persisted with them.

In the meantime, we called our SST booking agent, Chuck Dukowski, close to two in the morning at a pay phone on the street, the air swarming with dust, heat, and bugs banging audibly against streetlights, giant cicadas serenading us with sonic chirps and staccato clicks, the phone booth speckled with age and rust, Saccharine Trust lying about on the sidewalk in front of the club, both our van doors wide open to let some air in and out, singer Jack Brewer on an acoustic guitar, attempting to learn our tune "I Love Her All the Time" before Carlos reappeared from the back door of the club looking stricken. He was being led out by a grimacing thug, the pistol stuck inside the waistband of the man's trousers assuring us that we would not be collecting our guarantee.

We decided to get the hell out of Phoenix.

As we roamed the country, we played gigs with the regional groups that seemed to be sprouting everywhere, bands that played by no rules, making music that was surprising and inventive: Math Bats, Agitpop, Squirrel Bait, the Leaving Trains, Viv Akauldren, Appliances-SFB, Hell Cows, Happy Flowers. Out of all of them, it would be Dinosaur that we'd find ourselves most connecting with.

Dinosaur, by tour's end, had become one of the most galvanizing groups any of us had ever experienced. The communication between the three musicians—J Mascis, Lou Barlow, and Murph—was seemingly telepathic, hardly a syllable exchanged, their sets a blast furnace of repressed emotion, Mascis's guitar shredding hitting new levels of dexterity, his cracked voice sweet, sad, and enchanted.

With Lou barreling down on his Gibson Grabber bass and Murph motoring it all into rhythmic cogency, Dinosaur's songs veered from barely discernible strumming to nuclear amp assault at the stomp of a foot pedal. On a summer night in Buffalo, New York, Lee asked J if he knew Neil Young's "Cortez the Killer," and he offered a slight nod of assent. They decided to play the song during Dinosaur's set, Lee nailing the vocals and J taking Neil's lead guitar conceptions into more expansive and mind-melting territories than even Neil himself reached. It was a performance truly outside of space and time, witnessed by no more than forty people, their eyes and mouths open wide, looking around at one another in the din of the room, sharing a collective thought: *How insane is this?*

The level of invention happening with bands such as Dinosaur, Saccharine Trust, Meat Puppets, Laughing Hyenas, Die Kreuzen, and Butthole Surfers during the mid- to late 1980s would become our sole inspiration, displacing almost everything else that had occupied our musical minds before, the creative energy shared at gigs and on recordings wiping our collective blackboards, with new alchemical configurations introduced. There was no more hippie, no more punk, no more art, no more hardcore, no more nothing. Only a ticket to create in a zone of liberation and promise.

People our age who were not so inclined to play in bands but still in thrall to the recordings coming out of the underground found other ways to connect: editing and publishing fanzines, photographing, recording,

videotaping, hosting shows at college radio stations, positioning themselves as record store buyers, booking independent gigs at rogue spaces,
and creating distribution centers to disseminate music from independent
labels—not only the music heard on SST, Homestead, and Alternative
Tentacles, but the wealth of recordings being produced on small blues,
jazz, and folk imprints. By the mid-1980s, this collective, many of them
university students, would play an undeniably significant role in the continued welfare of the underground.

It meant that each time we entered a new town or city, there would
be an invitation for us to be interviewed by a local college radio station
director, and record stores with an interest in underground music could
reliably host us for signings. This collaborative ethos, though we didn't
realize it at the time, would inform the generation a half step younger
than ours, inspiring them to build and expand upon what labels and artists like ourselves were transmitting.

It was a select demographic still, hardly troubling the mainstream
airwaves or *Billboard* record charts. But the number of young people identifying with the music and art of bands such as ours was growing, and it
would increase exponentially soon enough, due first to the singular success of R.E.M., turning the mainstream music business on its ear.

But that wasn't on any of our agendas—it probably wasn't even on
R.E.M.'s at first. We just wanted to play gigs together and write our band
names on dressing room walls, signs that said we were there. On one
such wall in a venue in Germany, I took it upon myself to graffiti in
fat black Magic Marker the names of every contemporary band on the
North American scene, from Scratch Acid to Subhumans to N.O.T.A. to
Stiff Legged Sheep to Bramble Grit to Green River to Black Flag to Live
Skull—on and on and on, a litany of more than a hundred names. During the next few years, I would hear from other touring bands who had
played the same club—

"Everyone wonders who wrote that!"

When next in Los Angeles, Kim and I met Kevin Kerslake, a young skate
filmmaker who had the idea of casting Kim in a film he was conceiving.
Wanting to use the song "Shadow of a Doubt" from *EVOL,* he shot Kim
lip-synching the vocals in oversaturated color, the mood, like the song,
wistful and on edge, her body superimposed atop a train as it made its
way through a tunnel, only for her to disappear as it reentered the frame.

Kevin's full idea for the film would never be completed, but the

"Shadow of a Doubt" clip was sent to MTV, which began broadcasting it in the nether hours, reaching into the homes of people across the country—for most viewers, their first encounter with our music.

Ed Crawford, all of twenty-two years old, traveled from Ohio to San Pedro, California, in early 1986 to solicit Mike Watt and George Hurley—the two living Minutemen, still in a state of despair after the death of D. Boon—to see if they would like to start a band together. A huge Minutemen fan, Ed had gotten wind that Watt and Hurley were auditioning guitarists—not exactly true, but he leaped at the possibility.

Watt, struck by the audacity and genuine exuberance of this Ohio kid, gave him a chance. The trio clicked. They quickly put together a new act they called fIREHOSE, Watt dubbing their new guitarist-singer "ed fROMOHIO."

With SST booking us for a monthlong van tour in December, we asked fIREHOSE to join us.

The entirety of the North American music underground had emotionally shifted after D. Boon's passing; his presence and significance had been immeasurable to the community. So it was with some hesitation that people came to see fIREHOSE, which could easily be seen as nothing more than a compromised version of the Minutemen. But the band came out driving and hot, the songs as interesting and idiosyncratic as anything Watt had previously composed, and Ed's playing and singing rang out charged and confident, his rather modest midwestern physique exuding raw emotion and energy.

Mike Watt lived for the road: touring from town to town, unloading and loading the band's gear night after night. His knowledge of world history was profound, but even more so was his interest in North America, especially given his perambulations around the continent while touring. It was a fascination he had shared intimately with D. Boon. By 1986, he and George Hurley knew every club, every punk house floor, every highway, every diner, and every gas station.

We jumped into each other's vans to break up the monotony of having the same band members constantly on top of one another. George and Ed were down-to-earth, cool, calm, and sensitive to personal space; Mike, however, was a relentless spieler, always pontificating, querying, expounding upon everything from French postmodernism to punk as a political lifestyle, usually in the same breath.

We would play twenty nearly consecutive nights with fIREHOSE, hitting the clubs that welcomed the underground scene into their chambers, each with its own distinct environment—the Blind Pig in Ann Arbor, Mississippi Nights in St. Louis, Liberty Lunch in Austin, Einstein a Go-Go in Jacksonville Beach, and the notorious Outhouse in Lawrence, Kansas.

The Outhouse was a cinder block hunk situated on a desolate cornfield, isolated from civilization, its electricity sourced from freestanding gas-driven generators that rumbled and snorted into the night air. It had originally been a spot for local bikers and frat brats to throw down, but by 1985 it had been commandeered, mostly by students from the University of Kansas's KJHK radio station, as a place punk bands could perform without drawing noise complaints from anyone—especially cops, as the building existed outside the Lawrence Police Department's jurisdiction.

When playing the Outhouse, the perimeter of the building would be surrounded by cars and trucks, kids running around, drinking, smoking, whooping it up, bursting inside to thrash and slam and sweat, then whiling the nights away around bonfires, their competing tape decks blaring out Black Flag and Butthole Surfers jams.

Gibby from the Buttholes booked a show with us and fIREHOSE in San Antonio, billing us alongside his band. He taped flyers up around town that read in huge block letters SONIC BUTT FIRE. We had been hanging out in Austin with the Buttholes at their communal house, deep in the sticks, drinking beer out of empty peanut butter jars, shooting fireworks, playing fetch with their pup Mark Farner, and making friends with local artists like the young, soon-to-be-renowned filmmaker Richard Linklater and visionary songwriter Daniel Johnston.

The night after San Antonio, we played in front of no more than thirty people at a Knights of Columbus hall in Baton Rouge, Louisiana, the young promoter bereft at having lost his shirt on the enterprise, but still thrilled that he had brought bands like ours into town. Between sound check and gig time, we had sat on the warm grass behind the venue where our vans were parked, the windows and doors open wide to the southern summer heat, crickets and crawdads singing loud into the day, all of us a million miles from anywhere else, lost in time to the pleasures of our camaraderie.

One subject Mike Watt and our band found mutual fascination with was the pop genius heard in Madonna's recent music, which Watt had been turned onto by Kira. He recognized the way Madonna had come out of punk rock and incorporated its aesthetic into her success. Still, the idea of heralding *any* pop star, even one sprung from the same no wave neigh-borhoods as us, was met with only sarcastic derision by most people on the underground scene.

Lydia Lunch, in particular, would remonstrate me for talking about Madonna in the press. She considered the platinum-album wonder utterly anathema to what she most cherished: art, music, and literature created in total subversion of authority; the absence of compromise; the rejection of what she saw as escapist-pop pablum. I simply liked the songs as well as Madonna's beautiful energy.

And I wasn't the only one in our orbit who did. Einstürzende Neubau-ten's Blixa Bargeld confided once that he enjoyed a lot of the popular music most of his too-cool-for-school associates abhorred. Our acts were hardly a threat to each other; it wasn't as if Sonic Youth or Mike Watt challenged Madonna's supremacy. But we enjoyed the friction that existed between our music and hers. So much so that Sonic Youth had the idea to package ourselves as Ciccone Youth and cover her fabulous "Into the Groove." We brought a twelve-inch of Madonna's record into BC Studios in Brooklyn, where Martin Bisi transferred it to a track. We each listened to the song in headphones as we played, learning the parts while jamming along to the original record. We then mixed in our primitive renditions with the recording's original finesse, adding a bit of programmed drums to it, all of us pushing faders up and down, dubbing out the experience until we thought it arrived at a kind of cool, reckless collaboration (par-ticularly with Madonna's original vocals blatantly heard in the mix from time to time). We sent the finished work off to Watt. He responded by recording his own version of "Burning Up."

The songs would be released as a seven-inch single by New Alliance, Watt's imprint at SST, with Paul Smith releasing them as a Blast First twelve-inch in the UK. That latter release even flirted with becoming a bit of a club hit across the UK and Europe—if only for a hot minute.

When we played Seattle, Washington, in July—again with Green River—Bruce Pavitt, who was a year younger than I was and who had been edit-ing his *Subterranean Pop* fanzine since the early 1980s, came up to me after our set and confided—

"I just realized that Sonic Youth is a rock 'n' roll band."

It wasn't as unusual as it sounded coming from Bruce, who evinced a dry and spacey demeanor, even as his do-it-yourself spirit bordered on the obsessive. But I loved that he recognized what we were doing as more than just art music informed by industrial noise, that our group's sound was immersed in and had a lineage tied to rock 'n' roll.

In conjunction with his pal Calvin Johnson, Bruce sometimes released compilations of underground bands from across the USA. He asked if he could include our recording of "Kill Yr Idols" on his next compilation, a vinyl LP that was to be entitled *Sub Pop 100*. This was perfectly fine with us. We would stay in touch with him as the years progressed, as he looked for further ways to share his love for the sounds blasting forth from all over the country.

While bopping around with us in New York on another occasion, Bruce raised the idea of having his "Sub Pop" enterprise rove around the country, uncovering and releasing music by all the cool underground locals of a given area. Soon enough, though, he realized that there was more than enough energy radiating from his Pacific Northwest for him to be able to stay put and focus on that one zone—a decision that would have world-changing implications for music culture.

With 1986 coming to a close, we prepared to write new songs. We set up rehearsals in a basement on Ludlow Street, just south of Houston, a space that had been brought to our attention by our onetime drummer Richard Edson and his bandmates in Konk. Other than a modest space to jam in, Geordie Gillespie, one of Konk's percussionists, kept an office down there in a small adjoining room. It was across from a tinier spot still, which had nothing more than a mattress on the floor. Geordie pointed it out to us—

"That's where Jean-Michel sleeps."

I saw a box of twelve-inch records by the hip-hop outlier Rammell-zee and K-Rob, which Basquiat had illustrated the cover graphics for, upended next to a disheveled bed. Geordie handed me a copy, saying—

"Check this out, it's wild."

I added it to the ever-growing assortment I kept at our Eldridge Street home. Whenever enough albums piled up, I headed over to St. Mark's Place and spread a few out on a blanket to sell for some extra coin. The Rammellzee twelve-inch "Beat Bop," which was as cool and crazy as Geordie promised, would turn out to be one of them, selling for a buck or two. A noise rocker's got to eat.

53

JACKED FROM SONIC MATRIX

Sōl-Fuc was one title we thought of using.

So was *Heather Spinning*.

Kitty Magic was another.

Humpy-Pumpy was actually in the running.

Kim and I had a print of a painting by our German artist friend Gerhard Richter entitled *Betty* (1977) of his ten-year-old daughter. I proceeded to lay out a record album–sized piece of cardboard, using crayons to color in around the image, and brought it into the Ludlow Street rehearsal space. I had been thinking that *Sister* could be an evocative name for our new album, alluding to the Richter painting but also to the mythos surrounding Philip K. Dick.

Dan Graham had hipped Kim and me to Dick's writing some years back, and Byron Coley led us further into science fiction, especially the novelists producing work under the rubric of cyberpunk. Lee was a longstanding reader of sci-fi, and we would all soon amass a complete collection of the PKD oeuvre, passing them around to each other and marveling at their inventiveness.

Philip K. Dick lore had long alluded to the author's twin sister, who had died in her first weeks of life. Nick Cave and Lydia Lunch both claimed they had been born alongside a dead twin. True or not, it connected them and their celebrity to rock 'n' roll legend Elvis Presley, who also famously was an only surviving twin.

Steve, Lee, and Kim liked the title *Sister,* but they weren't crazy about using the Richter painting. We decided to create a collage of images instead, featuring postcards we had picked up on the road; a photo of Lee's newborn son, Cody Ranaldo; a Richard Kern shot of his girlfriend, Audrey Rose, lying half unclothed on his East Village apartment floor;

327

and an old color snapshot of suburban New Jersey row houses taken by Dan Graham.

I gathered all the attendant pieces and laid them out on two sides of an LP-sized piece of paper, dividing them by using black and gold Magic Markers to create a cross on each side, the two upside down from each other. I scrawled "Sonic-Youth" on one side and "The Sonic Youth" on the other, for no other reason than to destabilize the central aspect of any group—its name.

The songs on *Sister* were mostly in the three- to four-minute range: lean, succinct, more focused than anything we had created prior. There was no discussion about it, no conscious decision to write in such a way, though touring with bands like fIREHOSE, Saccharine Trust, and Dinosaur had likely steered us in that direction, taking us away from the extrapolations of Glenn Branca in favor of economy.

Inspired by Philip K. Dick's religious themes, I wrote lyrics that investigated my own take on Christian ideology, though always keeping it opaque, knowing that any direct statements of belief might not be representative of the band's.

Having written and rehearsed our new songs, we felt the need to record somewhere other than Martin Bisi's studio so that we might explore new sonic terrain. Mark Cunningham of the bands Don King and Mars had mentioned that the album *John Gavanti* had been recorded at Sear Sound a few years back and that it was a functional and affordable space. *John Gavanti* was an outsider take on Mozart's *Don Giovanni*, orchestrated by Sumner Crane, Mark's ex-Mars bandmate. That record made Mars sound like the Osmonds. That such a freakazoid platter had been recorded at Sear was a selling point.

Hiking up to West Forty-Sixth Street in midtown on an early March afternoon, we entered the Paramount Hotel, which still reeked of the 1930s Jazz Age. It housed Sear Sound on one of its floors. We were welcomed by owners Walter Sear and Roberta Findlay, two individuals who seemed to have existed on the edges of the entertainment industry all through the 1960s and '70s and now into the '80s, both of them carrying an air of having been there and back, offering a dry and perverse take on the world around them.

Roberta was a startling woman, her voice filed down from years of mentholated cigarette smoke, with a wild history of having directed and produced exploitation films that had defined the cinema scourge of Times Square. After a few years during which she fell into directing cheap porn films, she met up with Walter, a brilliant sound engineer who had been dabbling in soundtrack work.

Walter had had an early career as a world-class tuba player and had been a close confidant of Robert Moog, the man who developed the original, monolithic prototype of the music synthesizer. Walter had convinced Moog to add a keyboard to the monstrosity so it could be utilized more readily, completely changing modern music composition. He had also spent time as a door-to-door salesman for the theremin, the hands-free (or hands-off) electronic wave form instrument, which Moog had modified to make portable.

As the recording industry embraced digital technology, Walter heard only sonic compromise. He resolutely built his own recording console, rewiring speakers for truer clarification. He opened Sear Sound at a time when analog was being slowly phased out.

Walter was short with a Buddha belly, and he walked us around the place with a Silva Thin cigarette always lit, peering over the glasses that slid down his nose. He had a gentle, chuckling demeanor—offset whenever Roberta clicked her high heels into the room, all anxious energy, offering us a selection of Entenmann's cakes and bowls of peanut M&M's.

We were smitten—mostly by the notion of recording totally in analog, through microphones reconstructed by Walter, but also by the ambience of the place, which was at once vintage and slightly creepy. Walter and Roberta still had their hands in exploitation films; actors lined up in the hallway outside the studio running lines together, hoping for a big break in Roberta's forthcoming *Blood Sisters* film.

When Paul Smith visited New York City from London that spring, we played him the record we'd made at Sear, the first song being "Tom Violence," with a measured guitar pattern leading into a lolloping rhythm, my vocals contained and straightforward, the song's middle section plateauing then rising, Lee's guitar lead licking flames of fire.

Paul sat quietly before proclaiming—

"I can't believe you made a record like this."

I was afraid he was disappointed; there was a solemnity running through the session that was unusual for us, though there were certainly songs as charged and rambunctious as our previous outings.

He continued—

"It's like you made a New Order record. And I mean that in the most positive sense."

I wasn't much of a New Order listener (at least not the UK band—I was more attuned to Ron Asheton's mid-'70s band of the same name).

Still, I understood Paul's implication; the experimental-pop heart of the post–Joy Division band was not lost on me.

Sister would include a cover of "Hot Wire My Heart" by Crime, the 1970s San Francisco punk group whose members had appeared onstage dressed as leather-jacketed hoodlums wearing police hats and badges. It appealed to me both as a fan of the song and as a dyed-in-the-wool punk rock record collector. The album would be released in June, and we would quickly head back to London to promote it. We were to play at the two-thousand-plus capacity Town and Country Club in Kentish Town, one of our biggest shows to date.

Setting up the day before our show at a rehearsal studio, we got wind that Iggy Pop was practicing down the hall. Barry Adamson, whom we knew from Nick Cave & the Bad Seeds, was Iggy's bassist just then, and he rapped with us a bit that day before both our bands began their day's work.

We had planned on playing the Stooges' "I Wanna Be Your Dog," and as soon as we heard the muffled roar of Iggy's group playing the same song, we raged into ours. Taking a breather, we stepped out into the hallway. Immediately Iggy came bounding out of his room, decked out in leather pants with tiny bells attached to the seams, clinking and clanking as he walked purposefully toward us—

"Hey, you guys Sonic Youth?"

We were all smiles, of course, honored to be in the company of this formidable legend. My synapses were racing as I finally met my number one rock 'n' roll hero. We chatted a bit before inviting him and his boys to check out our Town and Country gig. It was a long shot that he would even come, but it seemed like the thing to do.

The night of our show we came onto the stage on fire, playing what I thought was a tremendous set, though it had its hiccups. During the song "Kotton Krown," I had to take a pause to explain to the audience an occurrence that by now could hardly surprise the band—

"My apologies—I sliced my finger open on my guitar, and the blood dripping into the pickups has shorted out the electronics."

"Kotton Krown" was a raw and melodic guitar number I had constructed. Kim and Steve created a loping rhythm that gave Lee a space to swoop long electric arcs into. The lyrics I had written were an afternoon's meditation on love as spiritual essence. Kim and I would sing the song together in the studio, thinking about Lee Hazlewood and Nancy Sinatra, whose remarkable 1968 LP *Nancy & Lee* we had all rediscovered, Hazlewood's alto basso like warm whiskey next to Nancy's cherubic coo.

But like "Star Power" from *EVOL,* another song we sang together in the studio, I became the sole crooner when the tune was played live. It was too hard to hear each other in the monitors to sing in key, not only with each other but by ourselves. Our singing voices remained challenged.

The last song we played during the Town and Country set was "White Kross," a ripping jammer with a burning middle section, the music still in thrall to the Static and Theoretical Girls, though with an element of thrash baked into it. It was titled after an early-1980s Richmond, Virginia, hardcore band called White Cross, who released a whip-fast rager of an EP entitled *Fascist,* though my song lyrics had less to do with antiauthoritarianism and more with my own Christian reckonings—

> *Burning inside*
> *I cross myself it doesn't help*
> *Because I'm not smart enough*
> *Digging into hot white*
> *Learning not to lie*
> *We cross it out and stay away*

It was on such a note that we walked offstage, only to see Iggy standing by the monitor board, his eyes agleam and wild.

"Good show, good show!"

—he said, as we collected around him. I was already in a heightened state, dripping with sweat, blood streaked across my right hand, as I asked him—

"You wanna play 'I Wanna Be Your Dog' with us?"

After a minute or so of the audience yowling, we sauntered back out and I announced—

"Ladies and gentlemen, James Osterberg!"

—invoking Iggy's earthling name. He shot me a look that said, *Why are you saying my offstage name* onstage? before sidling up next to Kim, our vocalist for the tune. Her hair was dyed blond, and she wore a white T-shirt and glitter-painted dungarees, dressed down but with foxy glamour, a look she artfully evoked as she left behind no wave blankness, ditching her glasses in favor of contact lenses and exploring a range of stage couture with a flair that would attract and galvanize viewers of all ages and genders around the globe.

Iggy could see it.

I could see he could see it.

I went off on the bass, rocking it to the song's broiling conclusion, the amps blasting noise as Iggy lay on the ground, humping the floor, then leaping at the microphone, noticing me on my back as I literally tore the strings off the bass, racing over to me, and kneeling down to slam his hands on the stage in rhythm. A truly epic end to a deliriously unforgettable night.

We stayed at Richard Boon and Deborah Cohen's house in Stoke Newington again that night, and I lay awake next to Kim, who had drifted off to sleep, the Boon cat humming like a washer/dryer as it cradled itself between our two bodies, my entire DNA structure glowing gold.

The fact that we had gotten to the point with our band that the one person who more than any other had defined my musical ambitions had joined us onstage and fully thrown himself into the moment—it was beyond any dream I could have once harbored, not so much unreal as irreal, as though I had simply conjured it. I allowed my buzzing and elated existence to lie there fully awake, whispering to myself—

"Holy fuck . . ."

With support from SST, Blast First, and Carlos van Hijfte, we toured through Europe and then the U.S., Terry still at the soundboard and Susanne still designing visuals, with Lee's wife Amanda Linn and their young son, Cody, joining us from time to time.

With bad diets and a steady stream of cigarettes and beer, our emotional states ebbed and flowed, our personalities at times banging into each other—one person going silent for days on end, an exasperated tension pervading the framework of our tiny, makeshift family. It spilled over into shouting, though never physical altercations, an understanding always preserved that the music was taking us somewhere, and we were duty bound to let it.

Change remained a constant. New songs would reliably bring the band to new realms of creation and connection. New friends too, and the continued thrill of discovering new bands like the Hollowmen from Des Moines, Iowa, playing solid, smart, blasting guitar rock; or Grinding Teeth from Houston, Texas, blowing out inebriated psychedelic squall; or These Immortal Souls, the new band founded by Rowland S. Howard from the Birthday Party, crafting crystallized tunes, literate and woozy, unnerving and beautiful.

Though releasing records through SST had undeniably been a feather in our cap, we were becoming increasingly frustrated and perplexed by the experience of arriving in towns where we were to play and, too many times, not seeing *Sister, EVOL,* or any of our other records stocked in local record shops (which I without fail checked out). Coupled with the fact that the accounting for our sales was in constant arrears, it began to feel like, after lusting over SST's appeal from afar for so long, we were now on what turned out to be a bad date. We began to detect a sense of alienation and erosion at the label, with legacy acts Hüsker Dü, Meat Puppets, and Bad Brains all revolting over financial discrepancies. The sense that we were next became more and more palpable.

After our last gig of 1987, at a small club called the Night Shift Cafe in Naugatuck, Connecticut, we crashed out, burned and frazzled from a year of nonstop touring. Kim and I headed to Los Angeles to spend time with her family and to bang around with our West Coast friends: Mike Watt and Kira Roessler, filmmaker Dave Markey, Raymond Pettibon, Henry Rollins's roommate Joe Cole, Mike Kelley, and some of Kim's friends from when she lived there a decade prior.

With the year 1988 dawning, we had no new songs at the ready, though fragments were beginning to be bandied about. After the attention we had generated from our take on "Into the Groove," we decided to go further in experimenting with sounds and samples, inspired by the harder edges of hip-hop—the aesthetic employed by Rick Rubin in his productions for the Beastie Boys and LL Cool J, as well as that of the first three albums from Run-DMC and Public Enemy's just released "Public Enemy No. 1" twelve-inch. But we also drew ideas from the essence of Sonic Youth— from downtown minimalism and no wave as well as early 1970s German drone rock and electronic noise music.

We booked time at Wharton Tiers's studio, where we had recorded so many of our seminal early songs, with the idea of creating in the moment, allowing improvisation to direct the session, with Wharton's nascent sampling tools capturing sounds and beats from various recordings, ours and others'. We assembled a few surprising pieces by listening, discussing, and running in to record a sudden light-bulb-over-the-head overdub, or else by finding singular sounds around Wharton's basement space, such as the specific thump his couch made when struck with a drumstick.

Kim at first found the unstructured approach frustrating, thinking we were spending too much time and money on improvisatory ideas that wouldn't amount to much. I entered the apartment one late afternoon with a cassette of loose mixes we had put together that day, various odds and sods. She looked at me distraught. She told me she was beginning to feel left out of the band in all this futzing around.

She then took it upon herself to record an audio-video version of Robert Palmer's massive 1985 MTV smash, "Addicted to Love," in a pop-up karaoke booth at Macy's department store, the music canned and cheesy against her vocals. From the huge selection of video backdrops at her disposal, she chose one of soldiers fighting in the jungles of Vietnam. Wearing glitter-glued dungaree cutoffs, holding on to a prop guitar, and sporting a pair of earrings I had bought her that displayed the Pettibon/ Black Flag "bars," she lip-synched through the song, the unknown engineer live-mixing the film images behind Kim's performance, creating slo-mo moves during the instrumental section.

It would turn out to be mind-blowingly perfect for the way it gathered together so much of what interested her and us as a band: the swamp-gas frivolity of MTV; the disturbing imagery of men at war, as if from some distant, terrible past; the tragic hero as entertainment. The song's lyrics—

> Your mind is not your own
> Your heart sweats, your body shakes

—added emotional resonance to the political narrative. It was sardonic, smart, sassy, sad, funny, and fucked-up.

And it had cost no more than twenty dollars to make.

We would release our LP as Ciccone Youth, naming it *The Whitey Album,* a nod to an earlier idea to cover the Beatles' entire *White Album* (which never got beyond us rehearsing "Back in the U.S.S.R."). It was also an allusion to our whiteness as a group, even as we were inspired by and working with vernacular music that originated primarily among African Americans.

The instrumental tracks on the album would take their cues from Can's *Ege Bamyasi,* dub reggae, Rammellzee-style hip-hop experimentation, and David Byrne and Brian Eno's *My Life in the Bush of Ghosts,* in which that duo had created soundtrack-evocative pieces utilizing cut-up fragments from southern gospel radio stations.

Such experimentation was well and good, but Paul Smith in London wanted us to record a proper Sonic Youth album before releasing *The*

Whitey Album, and we agreed. We decamped to the Konk rehearsal space again to see what we could come up with.

Paul's Blast First label had been born to promote Sonic Youth, as well as a few of the bands from the list I had given him at our first meeting in London: Butthole Surfers, Big Black, et al. Three years later, by mid-1988, it had branched out, with Paul releasing records by the UK pummelers Head of David (a forerunner to the celebrated Godflesh), the downtown New York guitar pop experimentalists Band of Susans, and the Sheffield, UK, post-punkers A.C. Temple, as well as a collection of recordings licensed from the otherworldly jazz mystic Sun Ra.

All these releases had drained the company of vital capital, and Paul's relationship with Rough Trade, who had distributed his records from day one, had become strained, in part because of his release of our "Flower" twelve-inch, which featured my nude woman calendar art.

Paul had solicited Daniel Miller at the more established Mute Records in London to take Blast First under his label's wing, but Daniel was apparently turned off by our band. He told Paul that the only way he'd be interested was if Sonic Youth wasn't involved. This was a no-go situation for Paul, who had built Blast First around us. Fortunately, Daniel heard our group the second time we performed at the University of London and had some kind of eureka moment, because the deal with Mute was given a green light, lending Blast First a bit of solvency. It allowed Paul to branch out to the U.S., where he would strike a deal with the West Coast label Enigma (with whom Mute was already connected).

For Sonic Youth to move from the staunchest of independent labels, in the form of SST, to Enigma, which was then an adjunct to the corporate monolith Capitol Records, felt like a precipitous slide into major-label hell. It came with all the embarrassment that such a move heralded for DIY darlings such as ourselves.

But we trusted Paul—the work he and the Naylor sisters had done for us had put us on the map in a way that no other label had, in the UK or otherwise. We assumed he had our best interests at heart. The alternative would be to solicit other independent labels, but after releasing records through Neutral, Homestead, Paul's Blast First, and SST, it seemed like a lateral move for our band at best.

I rang up Rick Rubin, who was flying high on the successes of the Beastie Boys and LL Cool J on his Def Jam imprint, to see if he would be interested in working with us. The four of us met him at a coffee shop near the Def Jam offices on Elizabeth Street between Bleecker and Houston Streets to discuss the possibility. But it turned out Rick was splitting from the label to create Def American, telling us he was "burned out on rap." He mentioned being drawn to the commercial aesthetic of the "hit," gleaned from listening to WABC-AM radio. It was clear to us that we weren't the band Rick was looking to invest in.

Still, I knew we were cooking with gas musically. It was all the more obvious when our new booking agent, Bob Lawton, showed up with Susanne Sasic at our new studio of choice, Greene Street Recording in SoHo, and they sat to listen to a rough mix of our first song out of the gate, "Teen Age Riot." These two could be very cool in their enthusiasms, but I could see how struck they were by the swinging majesty of the tune.

The riff I launched the song from was on a guitar tuned G-A-B-D-E-G, conceived with the personal challenge of locating the essence of what I heard in Neil Young and J Mascis, though the parallel would most likely be difficult for any casual ear to discern. The lyrics came from a similar place, the working title of the song originally being "Rock and Roll for President," an ode to the way the political energy of youth was swamped in commodity culture.

Greene Street represented a definite step up for us as a band, the studio recognized as a state-of-the-art spot. It was also somewhat pricier than what we had been accustomed to (though housed in the same set of rooms that early 1970s artist Gordon Matta-Clark and his coterie had used as art spaces—the rent then being, in all likelihood, a bit more affordable). In 1975, the studio had been called Big Apple Recording, which the composer Philip Glass oversaw. When I first met Pam in 1979, she had been doing some babysitting work for Philip, and we would fall by Big Apple to pick up his apartment keys from time to time.

It meant that I recognized the interior as soon as I entered, though the music being produced at Greene Street (which had taken over Big Apple in 1980) was focused mostly on hip-hop, recording early masterpieces from Run-DMC, Afrika Bambaataa & Soulsonic Force, Salt-N-Pepa, Whodini, and Slick Rick. It was the same studio I had been invited to by Howie at Masterdisk to check out Kurtis Blow recording "Christmas Rappin'," to which I had regretfully demurred.

Philip Glass still recorded projects in the studio, as did many other artists, from John Cale to James Brown. This was all persuasive enough. But when I learned that Public Enemy had recorded a large part of their game-changing *It Takes a Nation of Millions to Hold Us Back* there, I was sold.

We met up with Nick Sansano, the house engineer we were to record and mix with. It was clear he wasn't so versed in who we were (similar to when we first met Martin Bisi of BC Studios). This was hardly surprising;

our audience was growing, but we still existed outside the margins for most, perhaps especially for those working in the more professional world of recorded music.

Nick was welcoming, though. He seemed eager to hear how our rock band—one that didn't look anything like the prototypical rock band—would sound. He became only more interested when we began hauling in case upon case of what appeared to be busted-up guitars.

We decided we were going to make a double album, referencing not just the Hüsker Dü and Minutemen precedents but also Captain Beefheart & His Magic Band's *Trout Mask Replica* and Led Zeppelin's *Physical Graffiti*.

For visuals, we turned to photographer Michael Lavine. A Seattle compatriot of Bruce Pavitt and Sub Pop, he had recently moved to Manhattan, and we met up with him during the summer swelter of August, walking through the streets below Houston, the urban darkness lit by streetlamps that glared dully off brick walls, pull-down metal gates, and the cracked and sometimes cobblestoned streets of SoHo, Little Italy, and the Lower East Side.

While considering Michael's photos, which we would ultimately print inside the album's gatefold jacket, we thought about the cover. We opted to use one of Gerhard Richter's 1983 *Kerze* paintings, which I had come across in an art magazine. Unlike my previous suggestion for *Sister,* this time the selection would be embraced by all four of us.

There remained the question of what to call the album. I had written the lyrics to the song "Hyperstation" one day while walking to the studio from our apartment on Eldridge Street—

> *Falling out of sleep I hit the floor*
> *Pull on some rock tee and I'm out with the door*
> *From Bowery to Broome to Greene I'm a walking lizard*
> *Last night's dream was a talking baby wizard*
> *All coming from female imagination*
> *Daydreaming days in a daydream nation*

Daydream Nation would be the unanimously agreed-upon title of our new album, a four-sided opus to be released as the 1980s neared its close, the next decade almost within reach, wild with wonder.

54

TOGETHER WE'LL NEVER

Daydream Nation established a pattern for how the band would move forward with songwriting. One of us would generally bring in a structural idea on guitar, playing it for the group and sharing any ideas toward what the dynamic could be, then allowing the other musicians to create their own parts, jamming through the sections in repetitive cycles, everyone finding a personal expression that supported the song. We moved in and out of one another's melodic concepts, a true group-minded approach to composition.

Though unsuspecting studio engineers, such as Martin Bisi or Nick Sansano, were often astounded by our arsenal of repurposed electric guitars, they soon realized that our relationship with the instruments was serious and functional. It had nothing to do with novelty or gimmickery and everything to do with sound, defined by the idiosyncratic aspects of each instrument, including their ragged nature.

Lee, who had initially presented more abstract sound ideas—with "Lee Is Free" on *Confusion Is Sex* and later with his solo *From Here → Infinity* LP, which he released on SST in 1987—had recently begun to explore his engagement with singer-songwriters. He had dug deep into Bob Dylan's and Joni Mitchell's catalogs during our last trundle across the States, Walkman headphones over his ears, declaiming loudly (as one sporting headphones will do)—

"Oh my god, these songs are *incredible!*"

Kim felt like she had already gone through her Bob and Joni years. For my part, I was rediscovering heavy metal, through Slayer, and picking up any new rap record I could find. Steve was all about the country blues singers from yesteryear. It made for varied listening on the road, our tour van a hotbed of musical joy and competition, complemented by

Susanne's love for what she heard coming out of the underground scene, mostly through her work at Pier Platters record store in Hoboken, New Jersey.

Pier Platters had been opened in 1982 by Bill Ryan, a sweetheart of a man beloved by the underground scene, his gruff demeanor belying a friendly soul. Smoking cigarettes behind the counter, he turned people onto the latest releases coming out of Sub Pop, SST, New Alliance, Touch & Go, and Blast First. Pier Platters became the indie record store of choice for many Manhattanites, who had fewer and fewer options when it came to finding contemporary sides. 99 Records had shut down in 1984, Midnight Records was more focused on garage rock, Venus Records was a rare vinyl collector's joint, and Bleecker Bob's had become a tourist trap horror show. There were other record stores dotted around town, but nothing with the vision of Pier Platters.

We had found a new space to rehearse in Hoboken, and Steve had moved to that city to a pad of his own. It meant that Lee, Kim, and I would often take the short train ride across the Hudson to get out to Hoboken, and with Pier Platters en route to our rehearsal space, it became our regular hangout.

Since Sub Pop had included us on its 1986 *Sub Pop 100* compilation, the label had been issuing a stream of cool, high-energy rock records from the Pacific Northwest, including those from bands such as Green River, Soundgarden, and Blood Circus. It was exciting to see Bruce Pavitt putting his money where his mouth was, clearly impassioned by the bands he was releasing new music from.

The energy of this class of 1988 was palpable from the jump. When Green River splintered off to become Mudhoney and Pearl Jam, it was as if a fireworks factory had opened up. Mudhoney's first Sub Pop single, "Touch Me I'm Sick," offered an exhilarating summation of what was to come, as totemic as "Anarchy in the U.K." had been. At Pier Platters, Susanne would order as many as eight hundred copies of that record from Sub Pop, covering the entire storefront window with as many of them as she could.

Returning to Europe and the UK to tour, we would cross paths and share bills with compatriot bands such as These Immortal Souls, Die Kreuzen, and Dinosaur Jr. (Dinosaur having rebranded themselves because of a threatened lawsuit from a group named Dinosaurs, which comprised elder San Francisco psychedelic pioneers out of Jefferson Airplane, New Riders of the Purple Sage, and the Grateful Dead).

In London we recorded a John Peel session at the BBC studios while staying at the Columbia, a hotel Sonic Youth would crash in many times over—as would just about every traveling rock act in the 1980s and 1990s. The bar area was reliably inhabited by members of Einstürzende Neubauten, the Bad Seeds, Iggy Pop, Swans, the Cramps, and Hüsker Dü—all in various states of inebriation, but on the road and happy to see each other, pint glasses stacked up across the bar, ashtrays overflowing with cigarette butts. After years of touring alongside these bands, Sonic Youth had become an undeniable part of this fellowship.

In no more than a week's time we were back in the U.S. and loading up our van for a tour across the Midwest, this time with Die Kreuzen and Laughing Hyenas. All three bands were firing on all cylinders at this point, and we began the tour by playing the Ritz nightclub in Manhattan, the place packed. Lyle Hysen, ever the angel on our shoulder, shook his head at the sight—

"It's the Monsters of Indie Rock tour."

Touring for *Daydream Nation* brought a new set of ears to our shows: reps for corporate record labels. They would sometimes introduce themselves, asking if we had any interest in possibly recording for them. Mark Kates, from Geffen Records, sat with us after a gig talking about how he had served time in college radio in Boston, working with bands we knew such as Christmas, and how he loved what he heard from our band and from Dinosaur Jr.

Being courted by major labels was new terrain for us. Other bands were approached about the same time, to mixed effect. Hüsker Dü and the Replacements had already signed deals with Warner Bros. and Sire, respectively, though the recordings they would release didn't seem to make that much more of a critical ripple than the ones previously released on independent labels, the might of the major label hardly supplanting the cool factor of the indie.

For its part, *Daydream Nation,* released on Enigma, would hit the number one sales spot in the college radio industry newsletter *Rockpool,* as well as on a few other independent and "alternative" charts. When Ray Farrell, whom Paul Smith had lured away from SST to join Blast First, called me with the good news, I responded with—

"Cool, what happens when we reach number zero?"

Beneath the blasé facade, I had to admit that I was excited and proud.

Rolling Stone had us at number three in its annual critics' poll of albums of the year, and the UK weeklies had *Daydream Nation* slammed hard into number one on their indie charts. We were gold in our small world and feeling pretty good about ourselves.

For all our confidence and boosted egos, though, our bank accounts were still zilch. Touring was essential but also frustrating; too often we were left with not enough money to buy a donut.

Lee and I had taken it upon ourselves to make a video for "Teen Age Riot," the lead single off our double LP, beginning with performance footage Richard Kern had shot of us in his Lower East Side apartment for a potential video for "White Kross" from *EVOL* that had never come to fruition. Laid on top of it would be snippets from our pooled collection of weird VHS tapes full of bands we had recorded off television or that we'd acquired from tape traders, featuring obscure live footage of Sun Ra, the Stooges, the Beach Boys, and others, as well as bits of video camera recordings from our last U.S. tour. The availability of a video camera had allowed us to record hours upon hours of footage, the camera sometimes set up on the van's dashboard filming the open road, long passages of Middle American nothingness whizzing by, spliced with snippets of other bands cranking out their jams, some backstage vérité, as well as our van crew of Carlos van Hijfte, Susanne Sasic, and Terry Pearson interacting with the four of us, all in states of boredom, ennui, sleeplessness, heat-stroke, and, on one distorted day, mushroom-enhanced mirth.

Our autumn run in 1988 would wind up in Minneapolis, and we then flew to the West Coast to join Screaming Trees and Mudhoney to play in the huge open space of Union Station in Seattle. The empty building probably sounded amazing when trains had come roaring in and out of it. But the reverb turned our guitar amps into indistinguishable washes of dull fuzz, our vocals completely inaudible in the din. The sold-out audience of Seattle kids thought they were going to a gig for the ages, but instead were lost in an echoing hell.

Fortunately I had heard Screaming Trees a year prior, when they were on the road with fIREHOSE. Mike Watt had squeezed my arm at Irving Plaza in Manhattan, exclaiming—

"Wait till you see these guys, Thurst!"

Drummer Mark Pickerel counted the band off into a swirling, raging, psychonautic roar. Guitarist Gary Conner, as imposing as D. Boon had been, leaped into the air, scissor-kicking, flailing toward his amp, his hair whipping around his head. Even cooler was wild-child Donna Dresch, ripping at her bass guitar, locked hard into the drums.

Watt began pointing at each member, still clutching my biceps—

"Thurst! *Thurst!* Check it out!"

In the middle of this fury stood singer Mark Lanegan, tall and growlingly handsome, his long hair refusing to stay tucked behind his ears as he held on to the microphone stand like it was the gear shift of a rocket ship. Caught in the firestorm created by his bandmates, he would thrash his head about, though he seemed to burn more inwardly, his eyes cast down. When Mark sang, you could hear a mix of blood, dust, and honey. His tenor was almost enough to push the music aside with its elegance and control and was, without a doubt, one of the great voices in rock 'n' roll, and always would be.

Mudhoney, meanwhile, was an epiphany in its own way. Touring with them would be like being on the road with a pack of unmuzzled dogs, happy beyond belief to be wilding down the highway in their van, their strapping, high-energy tour manager and sound dude, Bob Whittaker, behind the wheel, his huge head of vanilla-blond curly hair blowing in the breeze, a constant grin beaming across his face. The band would tumble out the side doors of their van looking for beer, snacks, good times.

Mark Arm, Dan Peters, Matt Lukin, and Steve Turner were a rock band loving every second of it, the boys having come together in the tiny slam pits of Seattle, Olympia, and Portland. It was as though they were a supergroup from the very start, tearing it up each night, keeping every tourist awake at every Motel 6 or Super 8 we pulled into after sweat-drenched gigs from Santa Clara to Albuquerque.

The Mudhoney boys would invade our stage and create havoc during our take on "I Wanna Be Your Dog," bassist Matt Lukin every once in a while traipsing around with his trousers and underpants pulled down to his ankles, holding a sloshing plastic pint cup of beer over his head, a huge grin on his face. One of his bandmates or I would inevitably tackle him onto the stage floor, only for a pack of gig-stenched bodies to pig-pile on top of him, to the audience's complete joy.

The cross-pollination of punk and metal would become more fervent in Seattle than just about any other scene across the USA, with bands like Blood Circus, Skin Yard, and, most of all, Soundgarden blurring the once hard line between the genres. Black Flag had certainly begun to kick that door down, as did some of the more metal-minded groups on the New

York hardcore scene, Washington, D.C.'s the Obsessed, and SST group Saint Vitus. Seattle's version would be more fabulous, though, and more contemporary in its themes, even as it harked back to the time of Deep Purple and Led Zeppelin.

For me, at times, it was a hard pill to swallow. When Soundgarden first played CBGB, I listened attentively as they wailed to the packed club, the music chock-full of classic hard rock riffs. It's not so much that they weren't technically brilliant but that their songs felt like a regurgitation of the music that bands like ours had sought to dismantle—the metal of yesteryear, embodied by AC/DC, Grand Funk Railroad, and Aerosmith. Soundgarden ended their set with an encore of Led Zeppelin's "Communication Breakdown," singer Chris Cornell replicating Robert Plant's falsetto without a shred of irony.

I left the club and stood watching the crowd flow out onto the Bowery, seemingly turned on by the big rock act from the Pacific Northwest. Susanne walked over to me, and I asked her what she thought.

"They were great!"

—she said.

"I don't know. It just sounded like junior Zep to me."

Soundgarden would go on to create heavy, beautiful hits, with such modern classics as "Black Hole Sun." No matter how corny you think the trappings around an artist are, you have to admit: a good song is a good song. The arrival of Alice in Chains playing their huge grunge anthems, so far outside of what we were doing with our more experimental rock, was a bridge too far for me, at least at first. Even still, I had to acknowledge the music's emotional resonance.

The conflict that I was unknowingly embodying then, between the purity of expression sought by underground rock acts such as ourselves and the blunter approach taken by those acts destined for the mainstream, would soon become the defining conversation around the scene. Our band would attain its own sort of mainstream consideration in the years to come, though always still at the margins—in part because we couldn't be drawn away from our devotion to experimental music.

If there was any sonic bridge between where we saw ourselves, as 1989 loomed, and where mainstream music was heading, it would take shape through the extraordinary presence of a band named Nirvana.

Opening for Neil Young. Nassau Coliseum, Long Island, New York, February 24, 1991, taking the noise direct to the audience's face, whether they liked it or not

BOOK FIVE

55

RUBEN'S BEARD

We sat with Ahmet Ertegun, the chairman of Atlantic Records, at Mr Chow, the infamous Chinese restaurant and watering hole for the rich and famous on East Fifty-Seventh Street, as he regaled us with stories of the Rolling Stones, Billie Holiday, and the Sex Pistols. A young A&R man at Atlantic had brought us to Ahmet's attention as a potential signing, but when they realized we had no interest in changing our sound to create "hits," those talks abruptly ended.

Later we met with a roomful of men at Columbia Records, including Tommy Mottola, who popped his head in the door to eyeball us for a second. One of the suits told us—

"At the end of the day, the word 'no' does not exist in our vocabulary."

I was very impressed to meet one executive there who talked about strategies to combat censorship, a subject that interested us, since we had no interest in modifying our language, verbal or visual. This guy mentioned it had been his genius idea to wrap Roxy Music's 1974 *Country Life* LP, which had featured two topless women on its sleeve, in green cellophane, so as to defy squeamish retailers. That tidbit alone sold me on Columbia, but after they actually listened to our recordings, they rang to say they weren't interested anymore and to please not call back.

The word "no" certainly existed in their vocabulary that day.

Our U.S. booking agent, Bob Lawton, offered to act as our pseudo-manager in these situations. When A&M Records in Los Angeles came knocking, we all flew out together to meet them. We would also sit down with the folks at Geffen Records, David Geffen himself shuffling in to tell us his label was the only label we should sign to, and to definitely *not* sign with A&M. He added that David Crosby's latest memoir was full of lies, then he was gone.

Stowing away our suntan lotion and sunglasses, we jetted back to cold

New York City, the new year creaking open. Our left-leaning hearts were bummed to watch George H. W. Bush sworn in as president. A week later we set off to tour New Zealand, Australia, and Japan for the first time.

Upon arriving in Tokyo, I immediately felt as if I were an alien creature, my elongated body sticking out more than usual above the hordes as they moved through the city, everyone stopping in regiment while waiting for traffic lights (a social agreement that would never fly in the Western world). Men and women bowed to each other, every shopkeeper greeted each customer with a pleasantry, department stores situated uniformed employees to bow and welcome customers into their emporiums, taxi drivers drove in suits, ties, and white gloves, all with nary another Westerner in sight. It was a culture seemingly in touch with its consumerism but that hadn't lost its spiritual center.

To our good fortune, we found ourselves playing shows with the Osaka band the Boredoms. Their lead singer, Eye Yamatsuka, ran up to me in the dressing room to introduce himself—

"We are Pisshole Surfers! This is P-We!"

—he said, pointing at a young girl, who smiled widely and bowed before saying—

"I am P-We!"

Eye handed me a Boredoms seven-inch entitled *Anal by Anal,* which had an illustration of a Japanese greaser holding a switchblade and a motorcycle chain, the songs titled "Anal Eat," "God from Anal," and "Born to Anal."

I wasn't able to afford records much in those days. The ones I was most interested in tended to come from the bands we had connected with the last few years, all of us trading our releases with one another. As far as I was concerned, Dinosaur Jr.'s *You're Living All Over Me* was as good as anything ever committed to vinyl. But . . . *Anal by Anal*—this was something else.

The Boredoms ran through their set, playing what seemed like at least a hundred tiny songs, each one a short, stabbing, punctuated shock of noise, P-We (her real name Yoshimi Yokota) wilding on her drum kit in precise fury, every once in a while shrieking in a frequency so high I could feel my eardrums sweat.

Soon enough we were back in the freezing February of New York City to catch our breath. We were blown away when *Daydream Nation* appeared as the number two album of 1988 (right below Public Enemy's *It Takes a*

Nation of Millions to Hold Us Back) in the *Village Voice* Pazz & Jop poll of music critics. A *New York Times* review compared us with the Grateful Dead and John Coltrane.

Ray Farrell, working the Blast First phones for Paul Smith, made sure our record was available anywhere and everywhere. Pat Naylor hammered at more press. A young woman named Anne Lehman assisted Paul with his day-to-day workload, and our lawyer pal Richard Grabel advised us on who to deal with and how to handle major-label attention. More than ever, we had a team supporting us.

To add to the fervor, we had been contacted, not too long after completing our *Daydream Nation* sessions, by a couple of bright Irish gents— David Donohue, a writer from Ireland's *Hot Press* music magazine, and James Morris, a film producer who had been working closely with the Pogues—to gauge our interest in a film documentary focusing on the downtown Manhattan art-music scene. The director on the project would be Charles Atlas, a brilliant video artist who had been the filmmaker in residence for Merce Cunningham's legendary dance troupe. We jumped at the opportunity.

Charles was a pleasure to work with, sharing ideas and concepts of how we might be portrayed, his eye for movement artful and dignified. He took us to the abandoned Brooklyn Navy Yard, constructing and lighting a stage where we could run through our newest songs live for his cameras.

John Zorn would be the other main subject of the documentary, with talking heads in the form of Lydia Lunch, Glenn Branca, Dan Graham, Rhys Chatham, Lenny Kaye, Ikue Mori, Christian Marclay, Karen Finley, and *Rolling Stone* scribe David Fricke, as they pontificated on the downtown Manhattan of the 1980s, evolving from its days of recklessness, crime, and grime, yet always defined by the artists who, as Branca would quip (inspiring the documentary's title)—

"Put the blood in the music."

To ours and Blast First's good fortune, *Put the Blood in the Music* was aired in the UK on the high-profile *South Bank Show,* hosted by the erudite, old-school BBC arts presenter Melvyn Bragg—much to the amusement of our London friends, the juxtaposition of our American mayhem next to Bragg's stuffiness an absurdist thrill.

On the night of the broadcast, we were finishing up recording another session for John Peel, this time deciding to create new songs on the fly in the studio—an annoying idea for the BBC's radio control freaks, but a great opportunity for us to continue exploring composition that was defined completely by improvisation, our hands on the faders when they weren't on our instruments, the engineers uncomfortable, no actual band manager in sight. We delivered instant songs such as "Major Label Chicken Feed" and "Corporate Ghost."

At one point, Lee yelled to me in the playing room—

"Hey, what should we call this next song?"

Attempting to restring one of our battered guitars, I yelled back—

"I don't know. I'm trying to string this guitar—anyone got any clippers?"

"Clippers?"

—Lee responded, then announced to the control room—

"The song's called 'Clippers.'"

The irrepressible boys of Mudhoney flew over to join us in the UK for more than a dozen shows, each night the audience filled with kids who had been waiting for this moment to let loose, not in the skinhead stage-diving way I knew from hardcore shows, but in a less testosterone-fueled manner, Kim's presence offering a beacon to women ensuring that our shows would be more welcoming and safe than those of our predecessors. Which isn't to say that there wasn't chaos. Steve would click off a song, and I'd feel Mark Arm whizzing fast behind me, racing to the lip of the stage, then backflipping into the crowd, setting the place off, every audience member soaked in sonic bliss.

The London musician Nick Hobbs had figured out how to bring bands from the Western Hemisphere into the Soviet Union, having had success with the Sugarcubes from Iceland. Paul Smith sat down with Nick at the Rough Trade offices in London, and Nick mapped out for him just how we could make the trip. With the correct paperwork and the right comportment, we could play some shows behind the Iron Curtain without having the government security forces toss us out—or imprison us.

Paul, Ray Farrell, and the music writer Keith Cameron (on assignment from *Sounds*), joined Susanne, Terry, and us on an Aeroflot flight to Moscow. Still anxious about *any* plane flinging me up into the stratosphere, I tensed as the Aeroflot beast shook and rattled, sounding as if its every bolt was coming loose. The flight attendants had offered no safety warnings prior to takeoff. Some of the seats had no seat belts. The plane ascended not gradually but with the nose nearly straight up like a rocket. At one point a piercing alarm began buzzing, red lights flashing in the cabin. I could only presume it was an alert to hold on tight.

Similarly, when descending into the port city of what was then known as Leningrad, the plane simply nosed straight downward before leveling out, then banging onto the tarmac with a series of bounces.

Welcome to the Soviet Union, you post-punk Western brats.

We were set up in a hotel in the city center, the streets clogged with dust and pollution, the cars unbothered by filtration or regulation. A few people our age nervously addressed us in the hotel lobby, asking if we had any dungarees to trade for rubles, a currency worthless outside of the USSR. One kid slipped me a copy of his fanzine, basically two pages stapled together, the words all in Russian with a very faint image of the Sex Pistols. After a bit of halting conversation with the kid, I realized how limited the awareness of punk in Russia still was. The Sex Pistols were still a fairly new discovery in 1989.

Keith Cameron and I went out searching for a record store—ridiculous, as there were no actual stores besides indoor markets, which would open for a select few hours and consisted of tables with hats, gloves, shoes, socks, bread, and apples for sale.

If there was a sense that Mikhail Gorbachev would soon loosen the USSR's control over much of Eastern Europe, leading to the dismantling of the Berlin Wall, it was beyond my ken. All I could think about was how on earth we were going to subsist without our spoiled, Western expectations being met. Eating meant sitting and waiting in cavernous, unpopulated restaurants with menus that listed hundreds of items, the lethargic waiters claiming most everything to be unavailable. Bottles of water tasted of salt, but to drink tap water would be a surefire ticket to dysentery. The available food that arrived after a couple of hours of waiting was hopelessly inedible, comprising suspicious chunks of mystery meat. Fruit and vegetables were simply out of the question.

Still, there was much to take in. We visited museums, ornate and replete with astounding masterworks. The subways were clean and shining, like underground palaces, stations adorned with massive chandeliers.

"Stalin made sure the people had majestic public transport"

—explained one of our Soviet guides.

To hail a taxi, we would raise a hand in the air, at which point any local citizen might pull over, our Soviet promoter leaning into the driver's-side window to negotiate a fee.

During sound check in the hall for our Leningrad performance, we realized the amplifiers we had been supplied had serious issues, mostly in achieving our necessary volume. Vocal microphones were wired through tiny speaker bottoms that sat on each side of the floor. Terry scrambled to rewire the system to create some kind of push, an activity he had become accustomed to while traveling with us all over the world—front-of-house systems many times requiring a full reconditioning—but this was almost beyond help.

We played, and an audience gathered, mostly university students and what looked like their extended families, sitting at tables out for a night of music from Western entertainers. Husbands and wives sat in dinner dress. There were a few grandparents. Some children scampered about. No one seemed outraged or offended by our music. The drumsticks under the guitar strings, the discordant tones and weird structures, the diminished firepower of the sound system—I had the sense we were received as a group who played rock music, just not very well.

We certainly weren't giving them Billy Joel.

On the overnight train to Moscow, I became ill from whatever bacteria had crept into my system, the sleeping car freezing, security men wrenching the door open every hour to ogle Kim's passport and mine. I woke in the middle of the night wondering if there was any way to eat anything at all. An old woman, her head scarfed, her body squat and bowlegged, came by with a bucket, motioning to Kim and me to see what was inside. I peered into the black cauldron, where I saw pale sausages swimming in dank grey liquid. I decided to hold off on eating for another day.

Staring out the train window as dawn breached the horizon, I watched vast expanses roll by, a thatched hut coming into view every once in a while, sometimes with a bent-over old man puttering around it. I wondered what those lives might be like, how remote, with nothing but the cold sky above you and the hard earth below, silence broken by the passing of trains.

In Moscow, a few local bands were on the bill with us. Some of them got into yelling matches with various promoters. Fists were swung, burly men facing off like dogs establishing their rank. The audience in Moscow was not too unlike the one in Leningrad, though the show was better attended and the equipment slightly superior. We let loose, fully focused on playing as well as we could considering the circumstances.

We boarded a train south to play Kyiv in Ukraine, and it was like being delivered into Eden. The sun deigned to shine, and our hosts offered us resplendent trays of fruits, vegetables, pastas, and meats—foods we hadn't lain eyes on in what felt like an eternity. We sat there, regenerating slowly.

We visited the local artist bar that night, and en route I saw RAMONA graffitied on the wall of a building.

"Ramona. That's the title of a cool Ramones song"

—I said to our guide.

"Oh yes, that's the name of our local punk rock girl."

"You have a local punk rock girl?"

As we settled in the bar, he pointed to a girl busy talking to some friends. She had Joan Jett black hair and a black leather jacket peppered with a few badges.

"That's Ramona,"

—he said with a smile.

A dream. A punk rock angel in the wild.

Expecting another nightmare gig, we were relieved to find that the Kyiv venue was geared up with a hot sound system and a decent backline. We came out and unleashed a week of pent-up art-rock fire, the audience immediately picking up on our energy. They pogoed, crowd-surfed, yelled, laughed. They wouldn't let us leave. It was a transcendent celebration.

Years later I would meet the singer Eugene Hütz from Gogol Bordello. It turned out he had been a teenage boy at this gig, his brain and heart activated by what he'd seen and heard. He told me how transformative that night had been for him. After Boris Yeltsin and his party began to withdraw restrictions on travel to the West, Eugene would race off to New York City in search of his own sonic heart.

56

STAIN

Susanne Sasic proposed we check out a group Sub Pop cofounders Bruce Pavitt and Jonathan Poneman were fired up about, an act called Nirvana. They touted the boys as the next new thing, hot on the heels of Mudhoney, Screaming Trees, and Soundgarden.

Sub Pop, at the end of 1988, had released Nirvana's first single, in which they covered "Love Buzz," a 1969 song by Netherlands psych-pop hitmakers Shocking Blue. This alone had sparked my curiosity; I had always loved the Shocking Blue album, released stateside in the early 1970s after the global success of their hit song "Venus." Who were these youngsters from the wilds of the Pacific Northwest covering such an obscure Euro-pop tune (and eschewing one of their own songs) for their debut release?

On a summer evening in July 1989, Nirvana was set to make their first visit to Maxwell's, the Hoboken club that had become as important to us in the late 1980s as CBGB had been earlier in the decade. Bruce Pavitt had asked Susanne to create the label graphics for "Love Buzz," and he telephoned her from Seattle asking if she could round up troops to go and support the guys when they landed in our neck of the woods.

So Susanne, Kim, J Mascis, and I trundled onto the PATH train in Manhattan. As we cruised beneath the Hudson, Susanne told us that the band might not be as great as Mudhoney, whom she adored, but we were only too happy to do right by her and our good buddy Bruce.

Reaching Hoboken, we walked the fifteen-minute trek from the PATH station to Maxwell's. The New Jersey streets always offered a bit of a decompression from the everyday chaos of Manhattan, and it was an unusually pleasurable stroll that July, the evening timeless and perfect, its sultry energy propelling us forward toward we knew not what.

Nirvana was billed with labelmates Tad, a Seattle band founded by a bear of a musician named Thomas Andrew Doyle. They were heavy into heaviness, their sound crushing and dark-blooded. Nirvana was booked to play first, and they had just hit the stage as we entered the venue. Maxwell's was fairly popular with locals as a bar and restaurant. We gig-goers skirted that part of the place—aromas swirling about as diners chattered, released from their nine-to-five—to reach the back area where a tiny stage sat facing a smallish room.

The space that night seemed to be populated at about a quarter of its capacity, forty people tops, mostly regulars whom we were mates with: Steve Shelley, who lived nearby; Maxwell's proprietor, Steve Fallon, who loved nothing more than to stay up all night with bands like the Replacements, getting totaled, laughs all around; and the effervescent Julie Panebianco, who delivered good vibes and adoring assistance to every artist in her zone, working with, among others, R.E.M., Hüsker Dü, and New Order.

The modest turnout this evening wasn't unusual; it was preferable, actually, as it allowed for easier viewing of the musicians, crowded onto a stage that stood no more than a couple of feet from the ground. I always preferred to be as close to the stage as possible, so I could really immerse myself and study the musicians.

Nirvana, that night, arrived as a four-piece: Jason Everman, guitar; Chad Channing, drums; Krist Novoselic, bass; and Kurt Cobain, guitar and vocals. It took all of an electric flash of a second to see how incredibly beautiful they were and how soul-shredding the music was. I strode to the front of the room, pulling toward the side of the stage. I stopped, agape and transfixed.

Kurt was center stage with Jason on his right and Krist to his left, looking rather tiny flanked by these two larger boys, particularly the towering Krist. Jason was raging, his long curly hair whipping across his face. His amp's Marshall logo had been replaced with the word "NIRVANA," and the speaker bottom was reconfigured to "MASH ALL." His and Kurt's guitars sounded hotter than holy hell, cranking through the tunes they had recorded for their *Bleach* LP, which Sub Pop had released only a month prior.

I had yet to hear *Bleach*, but the songs they played that night—and Kurt's voice, like a swarm of bees buzzing around a hive tucked into the eaves of a suburban garage—drove into a hot spot in my cranium. His nondescript appearance—ripped jeans, battered sneakers, a ratty, unbuttoned flannel shirt over a sweat-drenched tee—belied the force of nature within him, blasting through and past his bandmates.

If Jason looked like a kid ready to drop everything and join Megadeth,

Kurt, Krist, and Chad came across like characters out of Stephen King's "Children of the Corn," disoriented to find themselves in a land of East Coast big-city know-it-alls. Kurt jumped and fell to his knees, thrashing a scratched and beaten Univox Hi-Flier Phase 3 guitar, racing up to the microphone where he sang, rasped, yelled, and bled—

> *Gimme back my alcohol!*
> *Gimme back my alcohol!*

His stringy hair was a mottled curtain falling into a face of high-boned cheeks, softly angled beneath old-soul eyes, blue and fierce.

Everything I had adored in hardcore was on display that night, fused with a sense of melodiousness I had rarely found in that music, sweet tones mixed with sour-tongued thoughts, themes beyond simple joy, anger, sex, or sadness. It was as if the essence of what rock 'n' roll had once been—from the moment Ike Turner and the Kings of Rhythm recorded "Rocket 88" in 1951—was now germinating in the soul of a straw-haired boy dripping with desire, intelligence, and emotion.

J Mascis appeared next to me in front of the stage, similarly enthralled by what he was hearing. Of course J got it; the same lexicon of punk and hardcore that had inspired me had fueled his own music.

When the band wailed through their song "Dive," I noticed how Kurt moved his barre chord, ascending from one fret to the next in a methodical rise to the chorus—

> *Dive, dive, dive*
> *Dive in me!*

They were musical steps toward electric bliss, a modern-day punk equivalent to the fretboard climbs I had heard from Tom Verlaine a dozen years prior, moves I had been infusing into Sonic Youth tunes. Now this unwashed, wild-voiced kid from God knows where was slaying my soul with the same such climbs.

The set ended with "Blew," Kurt repeating—

> *You could do anything*
> *You could do anything*
> *You could do anything*

—as the band broke into noise and chaos.

Krist began to spin his skyscraper body in a mock pirouette, his hands over his head, bass feeding back. On such a small stage, he carelessly banged into Kurt, who responded by barreling back into Krist, wiping out the microphone stand, which, along with the monitors, spilled off the stage onto the audience's sneakered feet.

I stood there amazed, the small crowd around me whooping at this sudden detonation. Krist whipped his bass up and off, diving headfirst into Chad's drum set. Chad, looking like Kurt's country cousin—the same stringy, unkempt hair falling across his face; a few unruly teeth; a flannel shirt straight off the fifty-cent rack at the Aberdeen Goodwill—sprang up from his drum stool, leaning back against the wall so as not to get smacked by flying pieces of his decimated kit. Krist, looking like a six-foot-six-inch human fuselage, lay sprawled on top of it all.

Jason, meanwhile, stood splay-legged before his amp, cranking out rising torrents of feedback as Kurt began to smash his electric Univox on the wooden stage until the instrument broke into irreparable chunks, tuning pegs and strings scattered among the detritus.

Out on the road, perpetually skint, making barely enough money to buy gas or a pack of cigarettes or a Coke, the only actual currency a band had was its gear. I later heard that Nirvana had been winding up their sets each night in pretty much the same way, busting up their equipment beyond repair. It was as if each night's gig might be their last, and if so, then who cares about your gear?

Total nihilism.

Sub Pop was canny enough to recognize that this bit of mania, surely inspired by the Who's famous destruction of their instruments, could create its own underground buzz. Bruce and Jonathan made sure the band had new amps and guitars for their next gig. But the Who had been international rock gods. Nirvana, in the summer of 1989, were hardly as well-known as labelmates Swallow or the Fluid.

The theater of destruction was, without a doubt, wild fun. But what set it apart from gimmickery was Kurt and Krist themselves, who came across not as miscreants or showmen but individuals called to tear apart the dead-end illusion of the American dream. They weren't wreaking havoc for our amusement so much as screaming into the void for some sign of release, of salvation.

They weren't alone in this feeling. It would soon be clear that Nirvana was articulating something that connected not just with the punks but with the nerds, the freaks, the geeks, the losers, and the weirdos. That first gig at Maxwell's was high-octane proof. In it, I saw the seeds of the coming decade. It was going to be more than just cheap thrills, offering instead a radical reconsideration of musical expression at large. It would present an alternative—a word that would soon take on heightened meaning—to the corporate pandering that had so far defined popular culture.

That movement's progressive, troubled spirit would largely reside behind the glassy blue eyes of Kurt Cobain, anointed as if by some lost angel, an artist destined to shine, scorched and exquisite, if only for a fleeting moment.

57

HEY BASTARD

Before 1989 ended, Sonic Youth would part ways with Paul Smith and Blast First. Paul had been our friend and our champion; his love for the band, his time, and his investment had often been the only things that had kept us going through our most difficult years. But we began to feel frustrated with inconsistencies in our communication with Paul, dealing with what we felt were his idiosyncratic ideas about how our band should progress at his label.

Ultimately we made the group decision to work with Mark Kates at Geffen, signing to DGC, the label's newly formed imprint that was to house its fringier acts. Gary Gersh was to be our A&R guy there.

Gersh brought in a succession of potential managers to work with us, each one cornier than the last, dollar bills zapped into their eyes. We were distressed—until Danny Goldberg of Gold Mountain appeared with his assistant John Silva.

Danny was a progressive activist who had palled around with Patti Smith on St. Mark's Place in the late '60s hippie halcyon days. He became vice president of Led Zeppelin's Swan Song label in the early 1970s and had promoted the legendary No Nukes concert in 1979. He was a bona fide music business legend. But it was Silva who really caught our attention, as he had been managing Redd Kross.

Done deal. For the first time in our eight-year existence, we now had "official" management.

We owed DGC a record, which meant it was time to record again. Don Fleming, a musician who had relocated to New York City from Washington, D.C., and who had a great garage punk-pop band named Velvet Monkeys, had a good ear for what we were up to as a band. We asked him and J Mascis to coproduce demos for what would be our first Geffen release.

We had discovered Waterworks, an inexpensive, tiny studio on Fourteenth Street situated directly above a twenty-four-hour bagel store named Dizzy Izzy's. We set up shop there, running through all the new songs we had been working on.

Kim and I had spent some time the previous summer at the Klamath River with her family and friends. I had brought along a guitar and worked on the structures for what would become "Tunic (Song for Karen)," "Dirty Boots," "Mary-Christ," and "Titanium Exposé."

Lee had a few ideas too, which we worked on at Waterworks, and Kim had written a song inspired by *Sir Drone,* a crazed and brilliant film that Raymond Pettibon had made that year starring Mike Watt and Mike Kelley as discombobulated Los Angeles teenagers in the mid-1970s as the culture transitioned from hippie toward punk. It featured a wayward girl by the name of Goo. Kim was tickled by the character of Goo, a self-realized female punk rocker surrounded by self-obsessed boys having an identity crisis. She wrote the song as if channeling the Pettibon character's mind.

Kim and I returned to Los Angeles before the year ended, spending the last night of the 1980s walking around Manhattan Beach in the South Bay with Pettibon, Watt, Kira, David Markey, Jordan Schwartz, and Robert Hecker from Redd Kross, settling down around a metal picnic table inside a Mexican taco joint. When the clock struck twelve, the kitchen workers came out, cheering and banging away on pots and pans.

I was, as always, on the lookout for any group that pushed boundaries, opened new vistas, exuded fresh ideas, hopes, and magic. Fugazi, a brandnew supergroup of sorts from Washington, D.C., that included Minor Threat's Ian MacKaye and Rites of Spring's Guy Picciotto and Brendan Canty, along with local bassist Joe Lally, was all of that in spades. When they first played at Maxwell's, I made sure to check them out.

Ian was surprised to see me—

"I thought you would be going to see the Butthole Surfers."

The Buttholes were playing in Manhattan, but I had been keen to hear Fugazi, who were as amazing as I'd hoped, driving the underground forward. The rhythms generated a heavy skank groove, but more than anything it was the democratic interplay of the band members that floored me, allowing for one guitarist to lose himself in feedback glory while another writhed across the stage to test and follow his body's liberation, gyrating and dancing, encouraging the audience to let loose however they wished. Fugazi would become one of the first groups from our extended scene to blast us into the new era.

We had been invited to play with them at a D.C. benefit for Positive Force, a punk-based activist organization funding progressive causes. It would be our first concert playing songs that we were set to record for DGC. Much of our material was still tentative, but we knew that to perform the songs live would be critical in discovering what aspects of them worked and what required modification.

When it came time to track, we again worked with Nick Sansano, who chose to record us at Sorcerer Sound, farther downtown, and then took us back to Greene Street for overdubbing and mixing. While at Greene Street, Nick reported to us the fantastic news that Public Enemy was booked for the same time. We would be working in one room while they would be in the other.

It meant that between takes, we got to hang out on couches and chairs in the common room with Chuck D, Flavor Flav, the producers Eric Sadler and Keith and Hank Shocklee, as well as Public Enemy's friends, including Ice Cube, Kurtis Blow, and Sister Souljah. For a devoted hip-hop fanatic, this was the stuff of dreams.

While recording a new song called "Kool Thing," we sent word to Chuck to see if he would improvise over Kim's vocals. He appeared in our room, announcing—

"Let's do it."

"Do you wanna hear the track?"

—we asked.

"Nah, just run it."

He went into the playing room, slipped on some headphones, stepped up to the vocal mic, and, in one take, improvised alongside Kim's soliloquy on female empowerment, his voice like melted butter in the groove of the track.

Boom—there it was. That's all it took.

He smiled in response to our blown-away thank-yous and returned to his work on *Fear of a Black Planet*.

Kim had actually cribbed that album's title in one of her lines for "Kool Thing," announcing, *"Fear of a female planet."* We were aware of Public Enemy's working title at a time when few others were. Chuck had been subtly taken aback, hearing her intone the phrase in his headphones, but only for a millisecond before responding deftly—

Fear, baby!
Let everybody know.

Raymond Pettibon had given me a T-shirt with an illustration he had made of a Joan Crawford–like face, just one of the motifs he would constantly draw. Above the visage he had inked the words "Blow Job?"

I had worn this shirt from time to time, receiving a mixture of looks from people, mostly confoundment. I was wearing it when Kim and I were photographed for the cover of *Option* magazine, the image ultimately censored. We batted it around as an album title for a while, relishing the idea of naming our major-label debut *Blow Job?* It would undoubtedly ruffle a few feathers, push a few buttons. But we also knew it could haunt us in the long run. We would eventually name the album *Goo* instead.

Having Pettibon's art grace the cover felt like it would be a nod to our subcultural family. Plus it felt audacious and radical—if not quite as shocking as *Blow Job?*—to have his work on a major-label release, where there was more expectation of high-color gloss.

Riffling through a stack of Pettibon magazines in our apartment, I chose two images, Scotch-taped them to a white twelve-inch sleeve, then sent it off to Kevin Reagan, the Geffen art director.

When next in Los Angeles, I stood with Kevin at his work desk. He asked me how much he should clean up the image, referring to a few dirty finger smudges on the Scotch tape, which one of my hairs had also been caught under. To eradicate the human elements took away a bit of the playfulness of the cover. It looked like a bedroom-produced fanzine layout—which, essentially, it was. Now, cleaned up, it seemed bland, formal. It didn't look as good.

We decided to keep it dirty.

Having been a band for close to a decade and for the most part managing our own affairs, we now embraced the benefits that came with being under contract with a corporate record label. After nearly a decade in our Eldridge Street apartment—and having a bathtub that doubled as a kitchen countertop—Kim and I decided to move to a new, considerably larger loft apartment on Lafayette Street, just south of Houston Street, across from the building David Bowie had a penthouse pad in and around the corner from the original Knitting Factory.

It soon came time to leave New York, though, to go on our first tour in support of *Goo*. Joining us would be STP, an all-girl band that played knife-edged no wave punk tunes, and Bob Bert's new group, Bewitched. The underground scene, already skewing male since the dawn of punk in the '70s, had become steadily jammed with men, especially with the rise of 1980s hardcore. Women were not entirely invisible in this movement, but any group, like Sonic Youth, with one or even two women was an outlier. It led to much condescension by the media, with its warmed-over "women in rock" coverage.

STP was a welcome ass-kick then, and it contributed to progressively-more-enthusiastic women in our audiences. This was helped too by Kim's stature on the scene—an intellectual and feminist onstage for the world to consider. There were other, similar developments happening further afield. The music and activism of Bikini Kill—three women and a man from Olympia, Washington—were uniquely feminist, inspiring fanzines and instigating workshops under the moniker created by singer Kathleen Hanna: "riot grrrl."

Bewitched headed back to New Jersey before we hit the West Coast. We added Nirvana to the bill. Since seeing them at Maxwell's, I had become obsessed with their album *Bleach* and its singular sound—the purity of Jack Endino's straight-to-the-heart recording and mixing, in service to the impeccable punk pummel of the tunes, Kurt's voice a cross between a twenty-something Bob Dylan and Lemmy from Motörhead.

When we had brought *Goo* in to be mastered at Masterdisk by my old workmate Howie Weinberg, I brought along *Bleach* as an example of what a perfect record sounded like. He played it on an extreme-high-fidelity turntable and stereo system in his control room, and it sounded beautiful and ballistic to my ears. For his part, Howie said—

"There's not much going on there, it's just left, right, center, solid mid crunch, ballsy low-end bass, with the highs nicely placed."

Mastering was about modifying the frequencies of the studio recordings to make them warmer, hotter, cooler; about readying them for transfer to vinyl or compact disc, dialing in the recordings as they filtered through analog gear (a process that would eventually be replaced, with valiant attempts at replication, by digital recording technology).

Howie and I attempted to put words to it, but what we were really hearing that afternoon at Masterdisk as we listened to *Bleach* was what Endino had heard when tracking it at his Reciprocal studio in Seattle, and what, in less than a year's time, the entire planet would hear: Nirvana's ineffable magic.

Having Nirvana and STP play before us each night was like having an electrical cord attached to our nodes. By now Terry knew what it took to make our band roar, regardless of how messed up a club's sound system was, sometimes racing from his mixing board to the PA stacks and microphone setups onstage to rectify any issue. A review once noted that Sonic Youth's soundman ran about the room like a "one-armed taxi driver with crabs."

Terry could only laugh—oh, the glory of recognition.

People at our gigs responded favorably to Nirvana and STP, neither band having too much of a profile outside of a few reviews in local fanzines. Nirvana was better known in the Pacific Northwest, though it was only in Seattle when we played the Moore Theatre that I saw a portent of the manic effect they could have on an audience.

It was a weird gig because the theater was seated, and the audience had evidently been warned not to stand up and crowd the stage after some recent incidents occurred there due to wild stage-diving. When STP played, it was to a bunch of seated, expressionless kids. The band was unimpressed by their reaction. Not knowing anything about the stay-in-your-seats order, singer and guitarist Julie Cafritz, who in the 1980s had been a founding member of Washington, D.C.'s notorious Pussy Galore, began haranguing the audience.

"Oh, so this is Seattle rock city, huh? *What a bunch of boring losers!*"

—she snarled in her microphone, her leg up on the monitor, white panties blinding the front row as she flipped the middle finger.

Nirvana played second, and the locals, who knew what they were in for, decided to just break the rules and charge to the stage, banging their heads, gnashing their teeth, singing along to Kurt's words.

When we played at Calamity Jayne's in Las Vegas, all three bands were huddled together before sound check in the baking parking lot next to the club, waiting for someone to show up and let us all in. Nirvana's lineup was in transition, currently Kurt, Krist, and Melvins drummer Dale Crover (who would wear nothing but a pair of tight bikini bottoms as he masterfully whammed his kit each night).

Sonic Youth and Nirvana each had our vans. STP had a rented car, stuffing all their gear in the trunk and between them. While we stood around, Kurt ambled over and handed me a cassette tape of their new demos, the word "Sheep" stenciled on the tape shell. I had already shared with the guys my love for *Bleach,* so the tape was a welcome sight. Kurt mentioned that the song "About a Girl" from *Bleach* was more of what they wanted to explore on this new *Sheep* material.

We dug the band's new tunes, most of which they had been playing on tour. On first listen of the cassette, though, I wasn't too sure about the recordings. They sounded more garage pop–y, less metal-infused, a quality I missed, even if all the songs were undoubtedly remarkable.

Whatever their next proper record would be, it was sure to be good.

Our final show with STP and Nirvana was in Vancouver, British Columbia. It seemed word had spread about how killer these shows had been, because the audience we found was roiling and ravenous. Kurt and Krist ended their set by destroying the stage, as was their custom. I ended ours by flying into the crowd with my guitar, pushing, slamming, and flattening kids as they in turn leaped on top of me, my amp screaming in feedback bliss all the while, only for me to crawl back onstage, hobble past the monitor board, and sidle up to Kurt, Krist, and Dale, all smiling, a happy, soulful energy in their glistening eyes.

We headed back down toward Seattle, where everyone was to go their separate ways. The line of cars waiting at the U.S.-Canadian border was miles and miles long, our vans sputtering and choking, each car changing lanes at one moment only to become stationary for another hour. Just as we reached mental flatline, we heard shouting and horns blaring. Ten cars ahead of us, we saw Krist running and zigzagging through the lanes, yelling at people to leave their cars and revolt against the customs officers.

"There's more of us, we can take over. This is bullshit, *let's just crash through the borders!*"

—he shouted, jogging past us and banging on our van's hood before disappearing off into the distance.

Onward to Europe. We invited the Minneapolis trio Babes in Toyland to join the tour, and in the UK we hooked up once more with These Immortal Souls, along with a new band named Teenage Fanclub. They offered a fresh take on the artful pop of Alex Chilton's early-1970s band Big Star, stepping almost completely away from the punk vocabulary to compose swirling, jangling, rousing tunes, emphasizing melody and harmony and fearlessly engaging with young male sensitivity.

A couple of years prior, Douglas Hart from the Jesus and Mary Chain had booked Sonic Youth in a small Glasgow space, and he had driven up from London with a new group named My Bloody Valentine. I remembered them playing fairly typical minor-key, post-punk guitar tunes. Lately though I had been reading concert reviews in the music weeklies that crowed about how My Bloody Valentine had sheared heads off like no other band. I found this a bit hard to believe from what I remembered seeing, but I picked up their 1988 LP *Isn't Anything* and gave it a spin.

I needed to sit down. The band's main songwriter, Kevin Shields, had radically transitioned the band to what I was hearing now. It was as if he had melded elements of Dinosaur Jr. and ourselves into his own vision of wholly new electric pop. The sound of Jazzmaster guitars and Bilinda Butcher's swooning voice sent my entire cellular system into a trance, as though from a buzzing mantra.

This was not the band I remembered.

To our good fortune, the group had come to New York City in the springtime of 1989, and we had connected with them, watching and hearing them play in front of audiences of twenty to thirty people but knowing we were experiencing something unique. Bilinda was serene, her head slightly cocked to one side to see her guitar frets, the faintest of smiles on her face as though exquisitely enchanted.

"She's the female J!"

—Susanne yelled in my ear, sharing my delight.

Perry Farrell, whom we hadn't seen since playing in the Mojave Desert with his band Psi Com five years back, had become a hot commodity. His band Jane's Addiction had cracked into the mainstream consciousness of the MTV generation. He appeared at our gig at the Boathouse in Norfolk, Virginia, wanting to gauge our interest in Sonic Youth possibly playing a traveling circus he was putting together for the summer of 1991 with the working title of Lollapalooza.

I shrugged, not quite certain what he was on about. I told him to keep us posted, but we didn't get the call (at least not that first year). We got other news, though, that sounded far more intriguing. Neil Young's management was curious if Sonic Youth would consider supporting the legendary songsmith's tour beginning in the new year.

For this invitation, there would be no shrugging.

We ended the East Coast leg of our tour in Miami, where I had been born some thirty-two years prior. The palmetto trees and bougainvillea, whose scents had once been a calming presence, were now nowhere to be found. The South Miami Beach streets around Club Nu were desolate and strewn with trash, police cameras affixed to streetlamps to record drug deals, the art deco hotels crumbling from neglect, sea salt rotting through their seafoam-green paint.

Aleka's Attic, a band formed up north in Gainesville, Florida, by the twenty-nine-year-old actor River Phoenix and his younger sister Rain, opened up for us, their music sweet and soulful, free from any pandering to Miami's unruly crowd of moshers.

As December waned, we traveled to the Aragon Ballroom in Chicago to play on a highly publicized bill with Public Enemy. The Aragon's acoustics proved to be inferior, and both our groups suffered for it, as did the sold-out audience. But some good music was to be had, and we retired to our dressing rooms to hang with our Chicago friends, beers and positive energy all around—it had been a killer year for Sonic Youth.

I sat on the ledge of the window, a few floors up from the street, as the crowds dispersed from the building. The air was clear, sharp, and winter-cold as I watched a few young people disseminate anti-war literature.

"The Bush family are war criminals!"

—one of them shouted.

"Operation Desert Storm is blood for oil!"

—another yelled out.

I couldn't have agreed more. Soon I saw a few men, dressed casually in muted work wear, address the protesters. In a flash, they began to pound the kids with their fists, knocking them to the ground, then pulling their modest booth over and stomping on it.

"Whoa! Check this out!"

—I yelled. Everyone came over to peer out the window as more men converged on the scene, beating on anyone who looked as if they might be sympathizers. Within minutes it was a melee, and cop cars quickly appeared. Soon the police too began to bang heads—and not those of the instigators.

The club promoters immediately shunted us out of the building through a side door into a waiting van, whisking us away from the mayhem.

58

ARC

I tried to convince Elliot Roberts, who had been Neil Young's manager and right-hand man since Neil split from Buffalo Springfield in 1968, to have our friends Nirvana join us on Neil's Smell the Horse tour, handing him a cassette of *Bleach*. He said that while he liked what he had heard, they had already decided on the group Social Distortion.

I was flattered, if a bit perplexed, that Neil wanted Sonic Youth on board. Elliot claimed that Neil really wanted to challenge his audiences, many of whom were of the age that when they went to a gig, they were seeking a safe night of classic rock.

Well, we could certainly upset that expectation. I asked Elliot who else they had been considering.

"A German band named Einstürzende Neubauten."

I laughed—

"Are you serious?!"

Now *that* would have been a tour.

Minneapolis's Target Center arena, in the freezing January of 1991, would be our first stop—by far the largest stage we had ever set foot on. Neil and Crazy Horse had used up all the allotted time, so we would be refused a sound check. This was jarring. Just as jarring was the fact that we had been given only thirty minutes to play.

When we crept out onto the stage, there was absolutely no response. We plugged in to begin "Tom Violence," the opening track from *EVOL*, and Kim's bass amp blew out, which created downtime and discombobulation as our crew anxiously attempted to figure out what had happened. Precious minutes ticked by.

The audience—the few who had ambled in from buying hot dogs and Cokes, whiling away the time before Neil hit the stage—gaped up at us in confusion. *Who are these oddballs and what are they doing here?*

We became more adept at surviving a set in our new role as opening act to rock gods, but we could only marvel at the lethargy and indifference of the people who claimed their seats early. Going on before us, Social Distortion had even less of an audience. They opted to simply run out and run through their set each night, undeterred by the indifference, then repair to their tour bus and, like supporting bands everywhere, settle in to watch movies or play video games.

We kept cranking our amps up from night to night, playing harder and harder, stretching out the noisier sections to mess with the sensibilities of the classic rock fans in the audience. I responded to heckling—

"You suck!"

"Play some *real* music!"

—by taking off my guitar to dangle it in front of the stage, where it would scrape, bang, and bash against the metal structure, the amplifier shrieking at stun volume.

A few nights, realizing my rig had been set on wheels for easy on/off, I rolled my two 4x4 twelve-inch speaker bottoms, stacked on top of each other, out to the lip of the stage, to bombard the few confounded people sucking on their soft drinks. When that got old, I would use the longest guitar cable I could find and walk among the empty folding chairs, scraping out feedback against them and then across the bodies of some of the people sitting in them, at times flipping the vacant seats into a pile.

This was not a popular move among Neil's road crew, who glared at me.

The tour offered catering, and on that first day in Minneapolis, we stood in line, peering into the warming trays, deciding what free food we would be so lucky to chow down on, when one of Neil's burly crew members piped up—

"Let's get moving, it's not a science experiment."

Immediately we realized: to them we were just young upstarts, brought on the road with a bunch of men who had come up through the rock 'n' roll tour wars since the late 1960s, with their hierarchies, unwritten laws, oaths of loyalty, and brotherhood. Hippie idealism married to biker bravado.

Neil's band would hang in the catering rooms among us, but he himself would never be seen there. He would, on a rare occasion, pop into our dressing room—usually a huge, white-bricked sports locker room, reeking of chlorine and lit by harsh overhead fluorescents—to say hello and to thank us for being on tour with him. He once had Susanne Sasic trim his hair. We were elated to hear him rave about how incredible it was to hear a song like "Expressway to Yr Skull" reverberating each night into his dressing room, the droning hum of the electric guitars singing to his rock 'n' roll heart.

As the tour progressed, Neil began to incorporate longer passages of sustained feedback improvisation into his songs. His audience lapped it up, even if, earlier in the evening, they had disparaged and booed us for offering much of the same. Neil's crew wouldn't dare criticize their boss, but there was a palpable feeling among them that our noise rock was corrupting Neil. And while they might have seen us as a bunch of smarty-pants New York City punks who didn't even know how to play real music, they had to contend with the fact that Neil loved us—to the point where he began to wear Sonic Youth T-shirts onstage.

One night as he wrangled with a long bit of feedback squall, trying to rein it into musical epiphany, Neil stepped up to the microphone to ask—

"How do they do it?!"

I told him at one point that a lot of us would love to hear his feedback improvisations incorporated into his records and that those sections might even compose a dedicated album.

He loved this idea, though Elliot Roberts looked at me with eyes that read—

Really? Thanks. Can you step away from my artist, please?

Neil would invite Kim and me onto Pocahontas, his 1970 tour bus outfitted with vintage Buick lights and portholes, the wood interior carved with hippie feather swirls. Sometimes we traveled with him from one town to the other. One night he passed me a VHS copy of *Muddy Track,* an unreleased film he had made during his 1987 European tour with Crazy Horse. He had set up a video camera on his amp to record the gigs and on the dashboard of their tour bus to document the ups and downs of life on the road.

The film was a brilliant vérité of a group working it out on tour. I couldn't understand why he held back on releasing it. I could sense his resistance to authority, that he would rather bury something than be told what to do with it; maybe he was afraid it would be compromised in some way if it were put out for a wide audience. He would infamously be sued by David Geffen for delivering albums that were inconsistent from one another, as if Neil Young wasn't being "Neil Young" enough.

Our bands would usually connect during sound check (whether we got one or not), members of Social Distortion and Crazy Horse hanging out with us behind the stage playing ping-pong, Neil occasionally cruising by with a big smile. The days were wide open before and after our shows, allowing me to buzz into town to hit every record store and bookstore imaginable, eventually filling up an entire storage bay beneath our tour bus with boxes and boxes of secondhand LPs and books.

I walked onto Neil's bus one evening in Hamilton, Ontario, to deliver a note to his driver from our bus driver in regard to some parking situation at the venue.

"Hey, Thurston!"

—Neil shouted, making me jump. I didn't think he'd be on the bus just then.

He had a huge smile on his face, sitting in the front lounge with three straight-looking guys who were somewhere around his age.

"These guys are the Squires!"

A few days earlier I had shown Neil a bootleg CD I had bought that had a bunch of Buffalo Springfield rarities on it, as well as two songs from 1963 by his first band, the Squires, from when he had been a teenager living in Winnipeg.

The men all grinned at my shocked expression, wondering how anyone might know who or what the Squires were.

"Oh my god, I was just listening to you guys! That song, 'The Sultan,' is amazing!"

They couldn't believe this gangly six-and-a-half-foot-tall weirdo was exalting their early 1960s Canadian surf-rock band—probably not a reaction they received too much. Neil just laughed. I could see he was in nostalgia heaven.

In Toronto I was interviewed by *NOW*, a weekly arts paper. I groused about how our soundman Terry had been prohibited from mixing us any louder than Crazy Horse. In fact, we were told to stay significantly quieter. This sound hierarchy sucked; volume had always been an important component of our music. We began to complain to Neil's management and ours, saying that we were wasting our time on this tour. We had achieved a significant profile in our specific scene; we weren't so ambitious that we would do *whatever it took* to attain rock-star popularity.

Given the staunchness of our independence and our long-cherished self-sufficiency, signing to Geffen had been no easy choice for us—nor did it come without some embarrassment in our world. We made sure not to sign any contract that might dilute our band or what we did. With John

Silva in the manager's chair, proving to be genuinely wise and ethical, I felt free to continue doing what we always had.

Not everyone regarded such decisions as lightly. Our old friend Steve Albini, the front man of Big Black and a soon-to-be legendary record producer, suggested that to sign with any major would be to sleep with swine—a view commonly held in our circles. He published opinion pieces detailing the way once independent bands were systematically reamed by the corporate monster they had signed their lives away to, ultimately destroying the essence of their music. His points were salient enough, and there were plenty of examples to hold up in support of them. But the indie bands in these scenarios were depicted as though they had no agency, stupidly falling into the traps that major labels had set for them.

We were not that band.

Anyway, after the interview, upon my waking up in the tour bus parked outside Toronto's Maple Leaf Gardens arena, rolling my frame out of my too-small bunk and padding up to the front lounge, Lee came bounding in from outside.

"Dude, you're dead!"

—he said with a grin.

It seemed Neil's crew had received copies of that week's issue of NOW, my face on the cover. The interview inside had me venting about the belligerent, almost bullying nature of Neil's crew, and how ridiculous and gross it had been to see them hire a stripper for one of their birthdays, in addition to my laments about not playing at the volume we desired.

I walked into the huge back area of the arena to find a copy of NOW pinned on the wall of the tour manager's makeshift production office, my face staring back at me. It hung alongside a Jamie Reid–designed poster for the Sex Pistols, the words "Fuck Forever" emblazoned across it. I doubt the crew could name one Sex Pistols tune (even though Neil used Johnny Rotten's name in "Hey Hey, My My [Into the Black]"). I figured the guys just thought it was funny and rude and outrageous.

Neil's crew looked at me and I looked at them. I pointed to my picture pinned up next to the Pistols poster—

"Good company."

Eventually we had had enough. We sent word that we were bailing. Neil stepped in, coming to our dressing room to ask what it was we wanted. He then walked over to the production office and told the entire crew—

"Let Sonic Youth play as loud as they want. They're like me, *they're volume junkies!*"

Tensions eased somewhat, though the shadow of our having complained to the boss would never truly leave. We weathered the rest of the tour, playing good and loud, even if we never won over much of the audience, some of whom would sit in their chairs with their middle fingers raised through our entire set. A crescendo of booing rang out when we departed the stage.

We only added more pain to the problem. Bush's Operation Desert Storm was in full effect in the Middle East, and Neil responded by playing "The Star-Spangled Banner," à la Jimi Hendrix, each night. Our reaction was less subtle. I had found a used cassette of Black Sabbath's 1970 album *Paranoid* and, in the middle of our set, would blast "War Pigs" out to the audience. Ozzy Osbourne and Neil Young were odd bedfellows, though they were both activists for peace and love.

Neil wound up canceling our planned Los Angeles shows, claiming he had an ear infection, though word spread that there was some friction with the promoters. Los Angeles was the place we were most excited to play, as it had become a kind of second home to Sonic Youth, with friends accrued by us across a decade. It left us with some free time.

The singer Courtney Love had been writing to Kim, asking if she'd produce her Los Angeles band Hole's first album. Now that we had some unplanned downtime, Kim decided to go for it. David Markey and our friend Joe Cole took us to hear Hole play, opening for Babes in Toyland at Raji's in Hollywood. We thought they were pretty good, with inspired songs like "Retard Girl," "Teenage Whore," and "Pretty on the Inside." Courtney herself was obviously a force of nature. Kim asked Don Fleming to fly out and assist in the production, trusting his ear and aesthetic and knowing that he had a knack for bringing good energy into a room.

With Neil's gigs suddenly vanished, our band decided to play two nights at the Whisky a Go Go before heading off again for eight more shows with Neil and Crazy Horse, from Reno to Vancouver. Reaching the Bay Area's Cow Palace that early March, we had come to expect a storm of resistance and ridicule. That skill would serve us well soon enough, when we found ourselves facing festival audiences.

And the Cow Palace might have been just another disappointing show on this tour, save for one glaring difference: it was general admission. We came out onstage for our set and started up "Schizophrenia," the place packed to the rafters, the entire front section engaged with what we were doing, smiling, ready to hear some cool music. The set just ramped up as it went along. The crowd pushed us forward with their enthusiasm, demanding the only encore we would play for the entire two and a half months we endured our supporting role.

All that was needed to connect with these audiences, it turned out, was an opportunity for listeners to interact, commune, come together. They were perfectly willing to be "challenged," as Neil had suggested. Seated, ticketed arenas had prevented this from ever truly happening. Now here it was—people who were actually curious to hear us, allowed to be up front where the action was.

The Cow Palace concert instilled a renewed confidence in us, something we sorely needed at that point. When we arrived in Seattle to play the Coliseum, we invited everyone we knew from around Sub Pop to be our guests.

The Seattle crowd, with our friends from Sub Pop, Nirvana, and Mudhoney all in attendance, as well as emissaries from DGC up from L.A., was gracious to us—far less vicious than, say, the Hershey, Pennsylvania, crowd, which had bayed for our blood, booing so loudly that at times we could hardly hear ourselves play. It's possible that, after twenty dates that ranged from one coast to the other, we had simply figured it out—learned how to present our weird (to say the least) music to an audience wanting to hear "Cinnamon Girl." It was only just as the tour was ending that we began to offer genuinely successful performances.

For all the ups and downs of that tour, the conflict and disappointment it sometimes brought, the truth was that seeing and hearing Neil Young and Crazy Horse each night had been a rare and tremendous opportunity. To take in Neil's songwriting, singing, guitar playing, and all-around open-mindedness was to be in the presence of a singular genius devoted to rock 'n' roll music.

We had had the good fortune, in other words, of attending a master class. Kim and I felt beckoned back to our home life, as did our bandmates, eager to reacquaint ourselves with our pets, children, significant others, families, and neighbors. But I knew that the lessons we had learned on tour with Neil would serve us soon enough. We would be heading back to Europe to play festivals that summer, this time inviting our pals Nirvana to come join us in the pit.

59

LET ME CLIP YOUR DIRTY WINGS

Kurt and Krist came strolling out of customs at London's Heathrow Airport, Kurt pushing a trolley of guitars and luggage, his head scrunched down between his shoulders, Krist tall and bright-eyed strolling next to him. Their sound guy, Craig Montgomery, a soft-spoken and gentle soul who had been running the mixing board for just about every band on Sub Pop, from Mudhoney to Tad, was also in tow, along with the monitor engineer Ian Beveridge and tour manager Alex MacLeod. Our manager from Gold Mountain, John Silva, would be joining us for this tour; he had already been sold on how amazing Nirvana was after seeing the West Coast gigs we had played together. He enlisted himself as their manager, negotiating a record deal for them at DGC.

The next day we all flew to Cork, Ireland, for the first gig of our tour together, crashing out in some cheap hotel. The following morning I came downstairs to the tiny lobby to fetch coffee, where I found a dude stretched out across the only chair in the room. He had longish black hair streaked with gold and was wearing ripped trousers and sneakers and a weathered parka. He looked as if he had just gotten off a boat, which wasn't too far from the truth.

"Hey, are you Dave?"

"Yeah, hey . . ."

—he said, the jet lag obvious in his face. Soon everyone else came down looking for caffeine and met Dave Grohl. I had seen him play with the Washington, D.C., band Scream one sweaty night in New York City, joined by Detroit hardcore jokesters the Meatmen and Canadian punk legends D.O.A. I just remembered a tumult of punk drumming. I could only hope he was going to be as solid a drummer for Nirvana as Chad Channing or Dale Crover had been.

Standing on the side of the stage that night at Sir Henry's in Cork, I was taken aback anew by the group. They began their set with "Drain You," with its abrupt opening, just Kurt's vocal accompanied by a thinly strummed guitar—

> *One baby to another says*
> *I'm lucky to have met you*

—only for Grohl to raise both his hands straight up over his head and wallop the hell out of the song, swinging like a punk rock Art Blakey, gritting his teeth and thrashing his head. In just those first ten seconds, I was as stunned as I had been when I first saw them at Maxwell's two years prior, but only more so, as Grohl had completely and obviously elevated the group to something utterly other, singing harmonies with Kurt, turning every song into a rollicking, rampaging killer. The crowd, the majority of whom likely had no clue who this band was, were immediately ignited by what they heard.

I had asked our filmmaker friend David Markey to join us on tour to document the ten dates together, as David had become friendly with Kurt and Krist when he had joined us on our earlier West Coast jaunt. We knew that most of the European shows were going to be festivals, and we'd be meeting old pals such as Dinosaur Jr., Gumball, and Babes in Toyland along the way. The idea was to put together a long-form video, something we could potentially sell on our merch table. We were playing mostly songs from *Goo* and a few from the previous albums, as well as three that we had been working on for our next recording: "Sugar Kane," "Orange Rolls, Angel's Spit," and "Chapel Hill."

The first festival date was at Reading in England, Sonic Youth performing right before the headliner, Iggy Pop. Babes in Toyland, Nirvana, and Dinosaur Jr. all preceded us. After having received so much animosity from Neil Young audiences, to see an entire field of people dancing and shouting and having the time of their lives, not only when we were playing but with all the bands—it was amazing to behold. The English skies greeted us, big and blue with late-summer warmth.

Backstage we all rambled about, each band fielding scheduled interviews, usually no more than five to ten minutes apiece. The requests from journalists had grown increasingly frequent, and it sometimes became a game of catch-me-if-you-can. While touring the U.S. in our van, Susanne had taken up the task of organizing interview requests for us, which often demanded that we pull over, locate a pay phone, then feed it with coins so that one of us could talk with a local newspaper or radio station, previewing the show that we were riding into town to play.

But our growing fan base, coupled with the support of a major label, meant that we would soon be heading out on press jaunts—touring *without* playing—a couple of weeks at a time across Europe, England, North America, Australia, and Japan, conducting a dozen or more interviews, junkets that lasted entire days. There were trips to regional radio stations, in which we talked about our lives, our new record, sometimes going deep, other times burning up the hours with silliness and inanities, many times too tired, burned out, hungry, restless, or ornery to offer much of anything at all.

All this self-discussion had an impact on our group ego, sometimes building us up, other times making us feel ridiculous. I found myself seeking strategies to deflect the attention. I always enjoyed waiting for the interviewer's tape deck to start rolling and then, knowing they had thirty minutes before a press officer would arrive to tell them to wind it up, as another journalist was on deck, asking the writer questions about their *own* life, which they couldn't help but answer. I grilled them on which bands and records and books and films they had been digging, letting the conversation lead to anything other than what was on their agenda, which was to extract useful quotes and sound bites from us about Sonic Youth. When their time was nearly up and the press officer gave them the one-minute sign, they would look absolutely stricken, realizing they had gotten nothing for their half hour.

It was a cruel trick, though in truth it worked only some of the time. Seasoned journalists knew what I was up to.

Courtney Love, who was best friends with Kat Bjelland from Babes in Toyland, showed up with them to join our gang at Reading. She couldn't help but notice Kurt, with his trousers ripped apart at the knees and a brown leather thrift store coat across his bony shoulders—we all did. He would leap off the stage with his black lefty Stratocaster (which he could continue to play through a basic wireless setup), only to scramble back onstage, dodging and darting around Tony Hodgkinson, the drummer of the English band Bivouac, whom Nirvana had invited to perform as an "interpretive dancer." Tony whipped around and gyrated, kicking out his legs and arms like a windup doll, going absolutely ballistic. Krist and Kurt tore through "Negative Creep," the audience losing it—*Who the hell are these guys?!*—their song "Endless, Nameless" devolving as it was wont to do, Krist removing his bass and humming it straight into Dave's kit, inspiring Kurt to walk slowly backward toward the lip of the stage, his amplifier howling, then racing to the drums, leaping up, spinning around in midair, and splattering into the kit, demolishing the entire backline, the stage crew freaking and scurrying to rescue their microphones from this feral kid who had arrived from out of nowhere.

Two days later at Pukkelpop in Belgium, we were excited to discover the Ramones headlining. Nirvana was so close to the bottom of the bill that their name wouldn't even appear on the posters; they would go on at noon, the first music the festivalgoers would hear. They cruised through their songs like it was punk rock breakfast, "Endless, Nameless" once again their perfect finale, Kurt leaping onto Krist's shoulders, the two united as a monstrous ten-foot creature, their guitar necks scraping noise out from each other.

By the time the Ramones hit the stage it would be late into the night, all of us fried from a day of shenanigans and warmed-over catering. There had been David Markey shooting footage of Kim and Kurt spoofing Madonna's *Truth or Dare* tour film; someone peeing in London band Ride's champagne bucket while they were onstage; the occasional cracking open of a book, if just to escape social interaction with the same people you spent every day and night with; or else simply drinking all the free booze on tap.

As the Ramones fired off their first *"1-2-3-4!"* I sat with Kurt between the stage barriers and the stage itself, watching Johnny Ramone race from the edge of the stage, then jump on top of a purposefully placed road case—looking nothing but cool, Johnny's moves down, never changing them for anyone, God bless him.

I noticed Kurt's head slumped between his knees, his hands over his ears, his eyes shut as the Ramones drone-blasted at us. He was obviously lost to the world after an endless day of noise. I motioned for our stage tech Keith Nealy, standing not far away, to check out the sleepyhead next to me. Keith broke into a smile, and in silent, mutual agreement, we pigpiled and slam-danced on top of Kurt, the three of us rolling like dogs in the grass, just beneath Joey Ramone as he bellowed—

Hey ho, let's go!

Security guards raced over to request that we leave the premises *immediately.*

It was time to split anyway.

Kurt and Courtney had fallen in love. It became obvious at the festival in Rotterdam; there was a buzz between them. Kim teased Kurt—

"What's going on with you two?"

—but he wasn't saying.

A white lab-coat-looking garment hung in a closet in our shared dressing room, and Kurt decided to wear it onstage over his cutoff dungaree shorts, along with a bit of Kim's makeup, which she applied on his fuzzy face: red lipstick, rouge, and eyeliner.

I sat up in the balcony with Courtney, the room Nirvana was playing in only half full, as there were gigs all around inside the sprawling De Doelen convention center. Nick Cave was performing spoken word on the floor below Nirvana's stage; the band had been instructed not to make noise until Nick finished. Krist and Kurt attempted to perform a reading of their own, from what sounded like fortune cookies, but they quickly became restless, defying the promoter's wishes and playing an at-first-ginger version of "Polly."

We had all been drinking a bit in the dressing room, though Krist and Kurt seemed more inebriated, Kurt especially. He began to grow frustrated during their set, his pedals unplugging and his amp sputtering on and off at times. He seemed more bemused than angry, but by the end of "Negative Creep," he threw his hands in the air as if to say *Enough is enough.* He then ripped his guitar off and torpedoed it directly into Dave's kit, before walking over and climbing across the drums like a kid navigating a scrapyard, the set splayed across the stage. Dave jumped off his drum stool and raced over to Kurt's microphone, where he maniacally repeated—

"Thank you, thank you, thank you very much, you've been such a wonderful audience, thank you, thank you . . ."

—as Kurt picked pieces of the drum kit up and whammed them forcefully into the stage.

The audience *had* been wonderful. The kids in front had headbanged away gleefully to the songs from Nirvana's not-yet-released second album.

Kurt, after fully demolishing the drum kit, decided to ballet prance over to his speaker stack and knock it over, the Marshall 4x4 bottom very nearly braining him. He smashed his skull repeatedly into the speaker bottom's mesh grille. A drunken angel seemed to guide him around the stage as he contemplated, then destroyed. There was an emotional ebb and flow to it, even a humor.

I certainly was amused as Krist rolled onto his back to unbuckle and unzip his long, tight trousers, pulling them off to reveal the tall drink of water was wearing a pair of candy-red bikini briefs. He proceeded to scale the PA stack, which teetered under his weight, standing precariously and fully threatening to fall onto the audience below.

Men wearing the same white lab coat as Kurt came rushing out to detain Krist, pulling him down from the stack and wrestling him to the floor, then surrounding Kurt to halt the carnage. Nirvana's monitor engineer, Ian, bolted over to protect Kurt, who had begun to push back at the stage police, Ian yelling and pointing in their faces, demanding they keep their hands off his friend.

The gig was both terrible and the most beautiful performance I would ever witness. I looked at Courtney, all this time in a flushed swoon since Kurt had locked eyes with her at the start of the set. I said to her—

"I think Kurt needs you right now."

She gave me an intense double take.

"Go on"

—I said with a smile. She lifted herself up from her seat, her torn black lace top fluttering across her shoulders as she sped to join her great love.

Just when we thought we'd get out of 1991 alive, Neil Young and his wife, Pegi, asked us to play at their annual Bridge School Benefit at the Shoreline Amphitheatre, one hour south of San Francisco, near the ranch where Neil, Pegi, and their children lived. Neil and Pegi's son, Ben, had been born with a severe motor impairment and used a wheelchair to assist in his speech and movement. The Bridge School was a charity that aided other similarly affected individuals and their families. For the event, Neil, beloved by the music world, enlisted heavy hitters (Bob Dylan, Tom Petty, Bruce Springsteen), deep-roots legends (John Lee Hooker), some newer faves (Patti Smith, Pearl Jam, the Smashing Pumpkins), and now his favorite band of iconoclasts, the one everyone around him despised— Sonic Youth.

We were informed that the show was to be "acoustic," which as a band we were very much *not*. But we decided to rise to the challenge, prepping tunes to be played entirely on acoustic guitars and acoustic bass, with Steve on loose percussions, as opposed to his traditional rock kit.

We knew something was not quite right, though, when we saw that none of the other performers—including Don Henley, Tracy Chapman, and Nils Lofgren—had similarly confined themselves to acoustic treatments. They all rocked through amplifiers with hybrid electric-acoustic instruments, which wowed the families and old-timers spread out on blankets enjoying the gorgeous late-fall breeze of Santa Clara County.

Even John Lee Hooker sent his guitar through an amp!

We figured that placing microphones in front of our rented acoustic guitars would suffice. We would soon find out how mistaken we were.

We walked onto the stage to an audience largely unaware of us or our music. It became clear that we were hapless fish out of water. An arc of young children in wheelchairs had been positioned on my side of the stage, where the monitor board had been placed. Neil's monitor engineer, who had suffered through our perceived insolence all through the Smell the Horse tour, shot me a sly look and said—

"Have fun out there."

As we began to play "Dirty Boots," we immediately realized something was terribly wrong. There were no monitors at all; none of us could hear the others' strumming. Kim's acoustic bass was strong and booming through the front of house, which lent some semblance of structure to the music to anyone paying attention. But beyond that we were adrift.

We clumsily made it through a few tunes, the audience perplexed at best. A few enthusiasts moved up to the stage to cheer us on, but as our set progressed, we became more and more *un*together, and the crowd began to turn on us. We attempted to play "Cinderella's Big Score," a winding, dark tune with lyrics by Kim about her troubled brother, but we had to halt it to beg the monitor engineer to turn the freaking monitors up. As our second try proved equally impossible, Kim yelled into her microphone a frustrated—

"Fuck!"

—which didn't exactly endear us to the upper-middle-class families in attendance.

Amid the rising boos, I announced—

"You know what I think we should do right here, ladies and gentlemen? Why don't we just do a New York Dolls song, seeing as how we come from New York . . . New York Dolls were a great group, we learned everything we know from them. This song is called 'Personality Crisis.'"

"Can we hear some more guitar?"

—pleaded Kim.

"I know these monitors can hold a lot of power."

She strapped on an acoustic guitar while I grabbed her bass, playing a demented version of the song's opening riff, waiting for some sign that the monitors were coming to life. The audience howled for us to get the hell off the stage.

"We never said we were professionals"

—I muttered into the microphone, a line I remembered Johnny Thunders saying one night long ago at Max's Kansas City.

While touring with Nirvana in Europe, we had been astounded by how many new people embraced our bands and how much punk culture was now being celebrated in the mainstream, from style features in fashion magazines to Hollywood hair metal band Mötley Crüe performing an insipid take on "Anarchy in the U.K."

David Markey could only shake his head at the whole thing.

"1991 is the year punk broke!"

—he quipped. It was at once the moment punk became incorporated and the moment it was destroyed. (It was also what David would title his tour film.)

That idea must have been on Kim's mind at the Bridge School debacle. While we were struggling to kick-start "Personality Crisis," the crowd revolting against us, Kim said her piece—

"Umm . . . this is the year that punk finally broke . . . 1991. If you knew Mötley Crüe are now doing Sex Pistols songs and read about 'modern punk' in *Elle* magazine, you'd know that 1991 is the year that punk finally broke."

It was lost on the audience. We banged our way through the Dolls tune, jeers, boos, and catcalls rising louder and louder.

> *Personality wonderin' how celebrities ever mend . . .*
> *Personality crisis, please don't cry*

—Kim sang. She then raised the acoustic guitar over her head and smashed it onto the stage, wood splinters jettisoning violently into the front row.

As unidentified flying objects began to hurtle *back,* toward our band, I threw the bass down and ran off the stage, Neil's monitor engineer grinning at me, his eyebrows raised. I soon found myself blocked by the phalanx of kids in wheelchairs. I could only hastily scramble through—

"Sorry! Excuse me! Sorry!"

Convening in the dressing room, we licked our wounds in a state of stunned silence. David Markey excitedly told us how insanely punk the whole thing had been. Our head of management, Danny Goldberg, had come along and could only shake his head—

"I can't believe that just happened."

We eventually walked over to Neil's dressing room to apologize and say thank you for having us. He was sitting on a couch with Nils Lofgren, who only stared at us, a thought balloon over his head reading *Losers*. Neil commended our daring-to-be-different-while-being-thrown-to-the-lions defiance. We hadn't planned it that way; I had genuinely hoped to be accepted by this audience, as we played acoustic versions of our avant-garde rock. It just didn't pan out that way.

Neil and Pegi's son, Ben, sat outside the dressing room in his wheelchair. I knelt down next to him to say thanks for having us on board and sorry about the obviously terrible and humiliating performance. Ben stammered into my ear as I leaned in to hear his voice—

"Well . . . what I've learned . . . is that . . . once in a while . . . everybody has a bad day."

60

WHEN ANGELS SPEAK OF LOVE

In late 1991, our friend Joe Cole was murdered by a Venice Beach drug gang as he and his roommate, Henry Rollins, were returning home one night. Henry had escaped by bolting through their house, leaping out the back window, and vaulting fences. Joe ran toward the street, only to be executed a second later on their front patch of lawn.

Joe and Henry were great friends, and he was extremely close to David Markey. Kim and I, after all the time we had spent together in Los Angeles since the early 1980s, had come to love Joe as well, as did just about everyone we knew in the SST universe. Kim and I would allude very specifically to Joe in the lyrics to songs we were constructing for *Dirty*, our next album.

Asking Butch Vig to produce *Dirty* didn't take too much thought. I already had most of the hardcore singles he had recorded at his Smart Studios in Madison, Wisconsin. His recording of Nirvana's soon-to-be supernova *Nevermind* sounded impeccable, a one-two punch of Butch recording and Andy Wallace mixing. (Nirvana had chosen Andy because he had mixed Slayer, which seemed as good a reason as any when making a choice as such.)

While technical expertise is a plus, it's personality and congenial communication that make a great record producer, and Butch Vig had all three in good measure. When Butch came to New York City to meet us, I pulled out the *Acceptance* EP by the early 1980s Madison hardcore band Mecht Mensch, one of the first things he had ever recorded. Butch's eyes widened at the sight. He couldn't believe I owned this obscure midwestern punk side, which had hardly made it out of Madison. He was even more shocked that I was asking for our next record to sound like it.

We had been sending cassettes to Butch while writing and rehearsing new songs, loads of them, in our Hoboken practice spot. He was a bit thrown off by all the weird guitar tunings we employed. He wanted to strike a balance between the lush otherness that our slightly detuned instruments could provide and the vibrational pleasure afforded by finely tuned instruments. Unlike any of our previous producers, Butch was adamant about our guitars always being in tune *with themselves,* at the very least. Kim, Lee, and I would sit in front of him with various tuning apparatuses, loosening and tensing our strings in micro differentials.

A number of bands rehearsed in the myriad small rooms beside ours. The bleed-through from room to room was chaotic, though once we got blasting it hardly mattered. While working out these new tunes, though, we were amazed at what we heard around us. The strains of bands learning the riffs from *Nevermind* permeated the space. Nirvana was quickly becoming omnipresent.

Nevermind had been released in September to generally decent reviews in the mainstream press (although *Rolling Stone* was famously underwhelmed). For their first video, for the song "Smells Like Teen Spirit," they performed in a high school gymnasium supported by goth cheerleaders. It was gold; that was obvious upon first viewing. It was primarily due to how great the song was—the hook, the singing, the playing—but also how Kurt looked on film. He was the everykid, looking as far from the typical, glammed-out rock star as could be imagined.

During the December holidays, Kim and I had dinner with Nirvana's and our manager, John Silva, along with his fiancée, Shana Weiss, toasting the fact that *Nevermind* had reached number one on the *Billboard* sales charts, spurred on by heavy rotation of the video on MTV. Viewers had been requesting the video to such a degree that MTV had no choice but to keep on playing it. People who bought the album found the promise of "Smells Like Teen Spirit" replicated tenfold, each track just as galvanizing.

David Markey was being both serious and ironic when he said that 1991 was the year when punk "broke." But there was no way he, or any one of us, could have envisioned how significantly punk, in the form of our pals Nirvana, would reach the masses. The band went from virtual anonymity to the realm of the Beatles in seemingly no time at all.

If anything distinguished Nirvana from the alternative rock bands that were signed in their wake, angling to become the next big thing, it was that the record industry had, in truth, had very little to do with the band's success. Yes, they were supported by a major label, the same as ours. But the response to their music was organic, and as sales shot through the roof, the label and the band's management scrambled to deal with it, as if lassoing a tornado.

DGC and Gold Mountain were, as to be expected, thrilled by this turn of events, the sky raining silver and gold onto them. They respected Nirvana's eagerness to preserve their relationship with the community that had nurtured them, one that distrusted capitalism and its role in art. At the same time, their act was in the midst of becoming the most famous band on the planet.

A few bands closely associated with us and Nirvana—Meat Puppets, Butthole Surfers, Babes in Toyland, Hole, Soul Asylum, Urge Overkill—would join us in major-label world. Some achieved considerable success, although never coming close to the heights of *Nevermind*.

We could tell something else was afoot, though, when labels began signing bands that many of us had never heard of, let alone played with. There were still those stalwarts of the road making waves with the majors: Jane's Addiction, a Los Angeles supergroup of sorts; Red Hot Chili Peppers, also from L.A., their appeal similar to Jane's Addiction, though they would locate stardom by melding punk with funk and frat-boy fun; Pixies, pop-punk outliers who delivered college rock perfection. It wasn't too much of a stretch to imagine these bands sharing the stage in the 1980s with, say, Tad or Mudhoney.

But when the labels began presenting newly formed groups as the sound of the current alternative rock scene—acts such as Bush, Candlebox, and Stone Temple Pilots—it felt as though they had emerged from some alternate universe, totally unknown to the underground music circuit so many of us had been close witnesses to for at least the last ten years.

Kurt mouthed off about Pearl Jam, lumping them in with this brigade of bands seemingly cashing in on the golden cow of *Nevermind*. But to my mind, Pearl Jam's and, to an even greater extent, Seattle heavy rockers Alice in Chains' only crime was their novelty, channeling inspiration not just from the dinosaur rock of Led Zeppelin and Bad Company but the punk purity of more contemporary acts like Mudhoney.

I think Kurt, like all of us, ultimately realized that these arguments about the worthiness of a band's success—about who *deserved* it—didn't amount to much. As his band began its meteoric ascent, I wondered for a brief moment about whether Sonic Youth might be next. Nirvana wore our T-shirts and sung our praises, giving us the kind of visibility we never expected.

My instinct told me that our music could never be accepted in the mainstream in the same way, but Nirvana showed us that anything could happen, at any level. So we went into recording our next album, *Dirty*, with a view that the sky was the limit.

Our songwriting ritual was evolving and becoming ever more refined, me generally introducing chord structures to the group, not telling anyone explicitly what to play though at times expressing what I thought a song's dynamic should be. Even that could morph into something more or less than what I'd envisioned. After sketching out a song's basic framework, we would all play repetitions of the various sections, each person locating themselves in the mix and the groove. Lee would bring in pieces too, which tended to be more fully formed, though always open to Kim, Steve, and I offering our own input. Kim would present riff ideas in rehearsal, a few times bringing in loose shapes she had readied at home.

Sonic Youth rehearsals truly felt like eight hands pushing paint around, teasing, daring, challenging, connecting, disconnecting, taking left turns—the beauty was that we all felt free and open, confident enough with one another and ourselves to go whichever way the music took us. Any one of us could stop at any time to point out an aspect of a song and to discuss whether it sounded cool or not. My riffs would either be further developed, find their way to the dumpster, or become fused together to create a wholly other piece.

Guitar tunings would define our choices, especially in how Lee responded to my musical offerings. He could either replicate my tuning or introduce some other he had developed on his own. Though I was certainly privy to his tunings, I didn't take any strict note of them, preferring to simply trust his creativity. The academics of it were overshadowed by the sheer state of sentient sound we conjured.

While our use of implements—power drills, drumsticks jammed into and hammering onto guitars—could be seen as what made Sonic Youth "experimental," it was our *structuring* of songs that I always felt made us most unique. Guitar modification was easy enough; it called to mind the grumpy museum visitor contemplating an abstract painting and claiming, "My ten-year-old could do that." The most genuine exploratory aspect of Sonic Youth, I felt, was in how a rock song could function outside traditional rock structure, even as it borrowed rock's established language.

Dirty would be the culmination of Sonic Youth's steady progression into a heavier rock sound, one that was inspired by the Sub Pop warriors of "grunge." Though our love for Mudhoney and Nirvana was enduring, we began to find ourselves more attracted to newer, more introspective artists such as Sebadoh, Royal Trux, Daniel Johnston, and Pavement.

When I talked with Courtney long distance around this time, she mentioned that Kurt too was listening to Sebadoh and Daniel Johnston. Kurt's love for the Pixies, the minimalist pop punk of Scottish bands the Pastels and the Vaselines, and the heaviness of fellow Washingtonians the Melvins would be tempered by his connection with classic country blues, not to mention experimental noise rock.

"Our next record's gonna be more like you guys"

—he said to us out on the sidewalk after their New York City gig the previous September.

Dirty would be critically lauded, though still too far out to be devoured by the mainstream.

"I'm so proud of you guys"

—Courtney announced into our answering machine one day.

"This record's gonna be so huge."

It was nice to hear, as was knowing that Courtney and Kurt were listening. The fact that the album ultimately *wasn't* huge in any commercial sense didn't hurt so much. We were making music that moved us and that connected with a certain audience. We got to travel the world sharing our songs. We had somehow succeeded in not having to work day jobs for years. Huge or not, Kim and I were basically content with our lives in our high-ceilinged loft on Lafayette Street.

We had been booked to play with the Sun Ra Arkestra on the Fourth of July 1992, one of the final performances the great composer of mystic jazz music and art would ever play. The forecast promised stormy skies, a problem for a concert held outside at the Central Park bandshell, free for everyone.

We watched the rolling thunderclouds closing in as Sun Ra Arkestra took the stage before us. Within ten minutes, however, the sun broke through, whooshing the clouds away.

A couple of years earlier I had sat by myself in the small Knitting Factory space on Houston Street listening to Sun Ra Arkestra fill the room with soul tone jazz therapy. The ensemble, per usual, ended the night by parading through the audience, that evening intoning—

Sing the cosmos's song

We all clapped to the rhythms and smiled. As Sun Ra danced by me, his Buddha body draped with glittering scarves and Egyptian pendants, his knit hat sewn from myriad colorful fabrics, he gave me a wink as I sat alone at my little round wobbly table. A second later I felt his two hands gently clasp my shoulders. Before I could startle, he lowered his gleaming face to mine as he singsong whispered into my ear—

"Sing the cosmos's song."

Now, at Central Park, after the Arkestra's cloud-clearing set, I knelt next to Sun Ra's wheelchair. His hair and stubbly beard were dyed a natty orange, his ability to speak diminished, he had to rely on tiny gestures to cue his band as he played the keyboards. I said quietly into his ear—

"Thank you for the music."

61

SECRET KNOWLEDGE
OF BACKROADS

Mike Kelley sent Kim and me a copy of the art journal *XX!st Century*, which featured an image of a ragged rescued stuffed animal, obviously very used, taken from a new series Mike had created entitled *Ahh . . . Youth!*

Mike had taken portrait shots of seven of these creatures and lined the images up on either side of a photograph of himself from when he was a gawky, pimply adolescent, the viewer subjected to the juxtaposition between life and object, and vice versa. It had subtexts of memory, dreams, the purity of infancy, and nostalgia, as reflected through a tossed-away thrift store soul mate, dirtied by love. One such image would grace the cover of our new album, *Dirty*.

Mike also sent an image of a collaboration he had done with the Los Angeles S&M performance artist and poet Bob Flanagan, which depicted Bob and his partner, Sheree Rose, two wild stars on the Los Angeles poetry scene, fully nude and straddling large plushie animals. This polarizing image would appear on the CD version of *Dirty* beneath the slightly opaque disc tray, where it could be somewhat obscured. Perhaps a little *too* dirty, it would be excised from the CD after its initial run.

"All right"

—David Letterman exclaimed, the noise of us plugging our guitars in crackling over the air—

"our next guests are a very popular band, and tonight we are happy that they're making their network television debut with us. This is their newest album, entitled *Dirty*—for the kids. Ladies and gentlemen, please welcome Sonic Youth!"

The show's producers always encouraged bands to have Letterman's music director, Paul Shaffer, and the house band perform with them, as it benefitted the studio musicians moneywise. Not all guest artists felt it appropriate to their music; arguments sometimes ensued, television and union rules invoked.

Not for us, though. We thought it would be a gas to have these hotshot pros deal with our noise rock.

We were fully geared up and ready to burn, knowing we had to truncate our tune "100%" to its shortest length so as to fit it in between ad breaks. Wearing a Royal Trux T-shirt, I scraped out the noise intro as Steve clicked all of us in, and we were off, fully in the thrust of the moment. "100%" would always end with Lee and me pausing our guitars to allow Steve and Kim to establish a bad-motor-booty two-note figure, before we reentered to incinerate it with slide guitar, using drumsticks that swiped wildly across the frets.

For tonight's show, Lee had found a regulation baseball bat in the greenroom and decided that he would use that instead of a mere drumstick. When the section came, he picked up the bat and whammed it along his guitar neck. It sounded tremendous, and I quickly hopped over to where he was in order to have our two guitars clash and clang together. It led to us falling to the ground, spilling over the monitors. I sprang up to end the song before crashing again to the stage floor, punctuated by a final *BLAM* from Steve.

"Are you okay?"

—Letterman asked each of us, thinking maybe we'd had an accident or that Lee and I had some beef with each other, deciding to fight it out on national television.

Stephen Malkmus, the singer, guitarist, lyricist, and cofounder of Pavement, was the first person I met who saw Sonic Youth as a literate band and not just a noise-minded one.

Malkmus and his University of Virginia college pals David Berman and Bob Nastanovich had become smitten in the 1980s with the SST label, not only for the cranked-up post-punk clamor it presented but for the lyrical poetics of Jack Brewer of Saccharine Trust, Mike Watt and D. Boon of the Minutemen, and, he would tell me, Kim, Lee, and myself.

I would be awoken in the middle of the night sometimes by the phone ringing and would lie there waiting to hear the message—*Who the hell is calling at three in the morning, for God's sake?*—only to hear a couple of dudes singing—

We're the Walnut Falcons, hey hey . . .

—blathering further nonsense before hanging up. *Beeeep.*

Malkmus would later confess to me that it had been Berman, Nasta-novich, and himself, who had gotten our unlisted phone number through a friend of theirs who worked at the phone company. Walnut Falcons had been the trio's fantasy group before they became the Silver Jews, which Berman would ultimately oversee, while Malkmus and Nastano-vich joined up with guitarist Scott "Spiral Stairs" Kannberg and studio engineer and drummer Gary Young to become Pavement.

Pavement's self-released 1989 EP, *Slay Tracks: 1933–1969,* had been an excellent, beneath-the-radar, DIY production—the slightly insolent yet educated boy-voice of Malkmus channeling Lou Reed and the Fall's Mark E. Smith, his band sounding smart and loose, their minor-key gui-tars knowing how fun it was to all of a sudden turn a song into a mael-strom of noise.

Gerard Cosloy had split from Homestead and joined his friend Chris Lombardi in launching Matador Records in 1989. They would issue Pavement's debut LP, *Slanted and Enchanted,* which delivered above and beyond the promise of their EP, the album an affecting and infectious collection of songs that pricked up all the hairs of our ears.

Kim, our ex–Pussy Galore and STP friend Julie Cafritz, our book-ing agent Bob Lawton, and I went to check the group out one night at a multi-band show at the Ritz, located in the old Studio 54 in midtown Manhattan. They definitely had it together. They were a curious sight: Gary Young, their slovenly, hippie-inflected drummer; Nastanovich, who bounded smiling around the stage, adding a bit of extra snare drum and cymbal to Gary's swing, hooting vocal responses to Steve and Scott's sing-ing; Mark Ibold, the bass player from DUSTdevils, a new addition to the band. These guys were too cool, and they sounded sweet.

We invited them to join us on our 1992 Pretty Fucking Dirty tour starting in Austin, Texas, that September.

On the road our bands became fast friends. Their company was more reserved than the loose-nut hilarity of Mudhoney or the dark and crazed energy of Nirvana. Like those bands, they were alive and free and devoted to the life of making music, but what distinguished Pavement was how closely they shared our own personal aesthetics—our interest in art, music, and literature—even if we were to some degree their older cousins.

Sonic Youth was older than most of the bands we found ourselves playing with into the '90s, with Kim turning forty in 1993 and Lee and me only a few years behind. Kim and I were aware of how our marriage positioned us as parental figures of a sort to some of the younger musicians we met. Our relationship—a husband and wife in a band—made us unusual, even if it was never something we showed off; we weren't too much into lovey-dovey displays of affection, even in our tightknit social world.

I got jealous sometimes about the way Kim gave attention to other male musicians, men whom it was obvious that she admired, either intellectually, emotionally, or both. She seemingly took in stride my platonic friendships with other women. Whatever feelings may have lingered within us, neither of us ever felt the need to confront the other in any accusing way.

Sonic Youth exuded an overall steadiness, even if it would become apparent to bands touring with us that we butted heads as much as any group. I could become testy and demanding—I was still sometimes guilty of losing patience with Kim, as we worked out a specific section in a song, or sniping at Steve during sound checks to play more the way I thought he should. I could see the way I bummed them out, how it made them feel demeaned, which would bum me out in turn. Lee sometimes felt he was being ganged up on by Kim and me. He might respond by not speaking to anyone for a spell, standing onstage playing his guitar expressionless and sullen. He and Kim developed a more aggressive push and pull, the friction between the two sometimes evident. Not every day was sunshine and flowers.

The band, like most, was truly a family in how it loved and fought—silently at times, demonstratively at others, expressing all the harmony and dysfunctionality that any classic familial unit would. As we grew up and became more mature, some of our rougher edges smoothed themselves out and the discord receded.

Bikini Kill's Kathleen Hanna coined the term "rock star toddlerism." It wasn't unusual to find bands twenty to thirty years into their career acting far younger than their age would suggest. Arrested development set in; groups that started when their members were in their early twenties clung to the exuberance of their youth, even as they progressed into successive decades.

For all the bumps that sometimes surfaced on our own ride, even as we matured, we remained dedicated and thrilled to be on the rock 'n' roller coaster.

62

THE FOREST AND THE ZOO

Through the last two weeks of September 1992, Pavement followed us across Texas, up to Denver, out to Northern California, then down the coast to play an outdoor gig at Castaic Lake, with Mudhoney joining in on the bill. Kurt and Courtney showed up to the concert, having just become new parents to their daughter, Frances Bean, a month prior.

Earlier in the month, Nirvana had appeared on the MTV Video Music Awards. Kurt had hoped to perform his song "Rape Me," obviously a contentious request. He had penned the tune in 1991, a defiant and angry song with a protagonist who refused to be made a victim. Kurt thought it was the heaviest salvo he could throw at viewers, primed to expect something cautious and frilly.

The network refused. It went so far as to threaten to not only never play Nirvana videos again but also any videos by bands associated with Gold Mountain or DGC (ourselves included). Furthermore, they would fire Kurt's friend Amy Finnerty from her job at the network.

The group relented, agreeing to play their song "Lithium." As they took the stage, Kurt began to strum the opening chords to "Rape Me," and I sat watching the television thinking—

Oh my god . . .

But they then switched gears and blasted into "Lithium," the song ending with Krist tossing his bass high up in the air, only for it to come down and conk him hard to the ground.

At Castaic Lake, Mudhoney invited Kurt to play a song with them. As we walked over to our dressing room trailer behind the outdoor stage, I asked Kurt if he wanted to play a solo tune too.

"Sure"

—he said.

"But you have to play 'Rape Me'"

—I joked.

As it turned out, he walked onto the stage wearing the pajama bottoms he'd arrived in, sat in a chair, and announced—

"I'm gonna play a song by Huddie Ledbetter, who was a slave in the South. Thank you."

He strummed out a tentative, then scorching rendition of Lead Belly's "Where Did You Sleep Last Night?"

It was a curious circumstance: Nirvana's stardom had approached supernova magnitude, but many of the young folks in the audience on this night had yet to find themselves caught up in the celebrity stargazing. They chatted and heckled as Kurt played his acoustic guitar while singing out the country blues perennial—a seemingly unfamiliar tune to a large portion of this crowd. Some doofuses thought it was cool to throw coins onstage.

Punk rock takes no prisoners.

The Boredoms came over from Japan that fall, connecting with us to play their first shows in the U.S., their maniacal music zapping everyone's minds. Leader Eye Yamatsuka was still a force of nature, flying around the stage, screaming and backflipping. Drummer Yoshimi Yokota (P-We, as I first knew her) added her high-frequency screams into her headband microphone while playing her furious percussion.

After their first gig with us and Superchunk, on an outdoor stage outside of Raleigh, North Carolina, the Boredoms utterly pulverizing the audience, we began to set up our own gear. Susanne Sasic, adjusting the lighting rigs behind our amps, could only laugh at how fantastic and galvanizing the Boredoms had been. She teased me—

"Now it's *your* turn."

Following bands as interstellar as the Boredoms, or as electric as Mudhoney, Nirvana, and the Jon Spencer Blues Explosion, or as radical and fetching as Royal Trux, was at once daunting and inspiring. It was a gauntlet thrown, a call to deliver a set at full potential, no punches pulled. It was probably the greatest proving ground we could have asked for; it's hard to think how we would have developed as a band without sharing stages with these ridiculously inspired bands.

In November, we took Pavement to Europe, with Sebadoh joining us and the London quintet Huggy Bear jumping on a few shows. Huggy Bear was remarkable: three girls and two boys who played raucous punk rock that dealt with gender identity, feminism, and fun, a British answer to the riot grrrl scene shaking up the underground across North America. They would come to a lot of people's attention when they landed on the front cover of *Melody Maker* after a singular Valentine's Day television broadcast of *The Word* in 1993. It was an amazing performance, raw and direct, singer Niki Eliot burning up the camera with candy-orange hair and singing "Her Jazz"—

> *This is happening without your permission*
> *The arrival of a new renegade*
> *Girl/boy hyper-nation!*

Afterward, as the host began spouting typically sexist crud and American supermodel duo the Barbi Twins were interviewed, Huggy Bear, off camera, began to pelt the host with whatever they could get their hands on, before being chased off by security.

We seemed to have earned some kind of exemption from Huggy Bear's general anti-major-label bias. Playing with them, Pavement, and Sebadoh, I could see how the model of independence, self-governance, and defiance of mainstream standards of success that had defined us since 1981 had become commonplace. It was these new bands—coming up around riot grrrl or else the Pavement axis—that were the underground rock radicals now (musicians who were maybe nine years old when our first record was released).

We traveled across Europe with Pavement for a month and a half in late 1992, the cold coming in harder each day, all of us fed by a catering crew that followed the tour, living again on buses, everyone in each other's way, vying for the stinky toilet or the microwave or the VHS player, attempting to smoke cigarettes without gassing out everyone who didn't smoke, reading crime novels, peering through the front window as the bus driver drove through the long nights, twisting in and out of the Alps or across vast expanses of farmland, the earth and the air emitting new smells as we crossed from border to border.

Touring had now become home.

63

NOON AND ETERNITY

Sonic Youth wound up touring nearly nonstop from June 1992 to March 1993, through North America, Europe, England, Scotland, Australia, New Zealand, Singapore, Japan, then back to the USA via Hawaii. There were more high points than I can count, though our show at the Santa Monica Civic Auditorium at the beginning of March 1993 stood out, a homecoming of sorts.

We were able to sell out, or nearly sell out, the venue, Screaming Trees joining us on the bill. With alternative rock and grunge making head-lines, we had attracted the attention of lots of new people, in the audience and backstage. Gene Simmons of Kiss, Michael Hutchence of INXS, and the film director Oliver Stone all showed up at the concert. With the rise of the MTV alternative rock generation, we were officially on the radar.

Hutchence seemed like a sweet guy, just wanting to say hello and tell us he liked our records. We rapped about the "little band" scene in Melbourne of the early 1980s, mythologized in the great film *Dogs in Space* that he had starred in. The bands around that scene, such as the Primitive Calculators and Tsk Tsk Tsk, were some of the most interesting underground experimental groups of that era.

Gene Simmons, sans Kiss makeup, hovered about. We all gathered around him because he was Gene Simmons from Kiss, for God's sake. He seemed confused that there were no groupies around.

"Where's all the chicks?"

—he asked. I wasn't sure if he was baiting me or being serious. I explained to him that what he was seeing backstage was who we were. The women there were artists in their own right. I told him we came out of punk rock and that he should check out riot grrrl. He nodded his head before asking again—

"Yeah, but where's all the chicks?"

We played one last concert (before a much-needed three-month break) at Seattle's Paramount Theatre with the Hoboken-based band Cell and the feminist punk duo Mecca Normal from Vancouver, Canada.

The entire Seattle and Olympia scene, including Kurt and Courtney, showed up. I asked Kurt how the new Nirvana album session they had just recorded at Steve Albini's Chicago studio was sounding, and he responded confidently—

"Really, really good."

"You got a title?"

"Yeah"

—he said, and with droll perversity added—

"*I Hate Myself and I Want to Die.*"

I paused for a second, thinking he was joking, but he seemed like he had made his mind up. I laughed.

"That's a fucking awesome title."

The night after, before flying home to the East Coast, Kim, Susanne, and I went to dinner at Krist and Shelli Novoselic's house, happily unwinding, Cheap Trick records playing on the turntable. Dave Grohl came by, bursting into the house full of spunk, then drove Krist and me over to the Nirvana rehearsal studio so they could play me a few of the tunes they had recorded with Albini. I was stunned by two astounding songs back-to-back: "Heart-Shaped Box" and "All Apologies." The look on Dave's and Krist's faces told me they knew very well these tracks were musical gems. My exuberance seemed only to corroborate their own wonder.

Another song they played me was "Moist Vagina," with its shouted refrain of—

> *Marijuana!*
> *Marijuana!*
> *Marijuana!*

I loved the sludged-out riff of the tune, the lyrics slurred atop it filled with angst and sex and dope. I said I thought it would be the most radical song to open the album with. It would never appear on the proper album, though. Given Geffen's headaches with "Rape Me," I can't say I was surprised.

We waited for Kurt to arrive that night as he told Krist and Dave he would, though he would be a no-show. We decided to jam out in the meantime. Dave ran to the kit, immediately firebombing out beats as Krist strapped on his bass. I grabbed a guitar and together we ripped through an hour of rock noise before heading back to Krist's pad.

The Geffen brass were apparently bumming out the band, as they had taken issue with Steve Albini's idiosyncratic mixes: the drums and guitars loud and dry up front, the bass tubular, the vocals unadorned, without any noticeable effects, only modest in the mix. However Kurt personally felt about Steve's mixes, it drove him crazy being told by industry people how his music should sound.

After returning to New York and hearing an advance cassette, I rang him and Courtney up. I told Kurt how much I loved the songs and the recording, how it reminded me of what the band the Jesus Lizard was to some degree mining (and whose albums were also engineered and mixed by Albini). I told him not to be concerned about the label's demands for accessibility, to stay true to the band's own vision and progression.

The album that ultimately saw the light of day would be something apart from either *Nevermind* or *Bleach,* a dark and foreboding beast, raging, beautiful—and titled a little less brazenly as *In Utero.*

I hardly spoke to Kurt when Nirvana played Roseland in New York City in mid-July 1993 during the New Music Seminar. Nor did I two months later after Sonic Youth returned from the European festival circuit and Nirvana appeared on *Saturday Night Live* for *In Utero*'s release. I mostly hung out with Courtney there in the NBC greenroom, her exuberance never failing to ignite any gathering, Kurt coming in and out, preoccupied and anxious.

The last time Kim and I would see Nirvana was when they played Miami later that November as part of a proposed six-month-long arena tour for *In Utero.* We had come down to Coral Gables to spend Thanksgiving with my mother in her childhood home, to which she had decided to return, leaving Connecticut behind for a while.

We took my mom along to the concert, which was at a large bandshell amphitheater at Bayfront Park. There we met up with John Silva from Gold Mountain, Susanne, and our guitar tech Jim Vincent, the latter two having been hired by Nirvana. Our band had come to require (and be able to afford) guitar and drum techs; monitor engineers; tour, stage, and production managers; as well as extended lighting crews and bus and truck drivers. We noticed Nirvana kept hiring away our people. We could hardly blame the crew; there was certainly more coin coming from Nirvana's touring world. It meant having to say goodbye to a few of our coworkers, though.

Whenever our band pulled into a town to play, the first people in the venue and the last ones to leave were always the road and production crew. I would walk into sound checks with bags full of records and books I had had the pleasure of hunting out in local shops, as well as a belly full of whatever the best Mexican food in town was. I would realize, guiltily, that these folks had been setting up the stage since 10:00 a.m., subsisting on a communal box of donuts and tepid coffee, while I was off satisfying my cravings.

With two buses and an equipment truck—pretty much the largest touring cavalcade we'd ever experienced—we had become an extended family of sorts, all of us in it together as we traveled across the planet, working whatever hours were demanded, then retiring to the bus to enjoy a drink or two, sharing stories of how insane an audience was—

"Did you see that guy backflip off Lee's monitor?"

"Someone threw a cassette onstage and it hit me in the face."

"I can't believe I broke three fucking strings on the first song."

"Maybe if you point your guitar amp away from the vocal mic, it won't be so loud for everyone."

"Who was that crazy dude from Poison Idea who drank all the beer and ate all our pizza backstage?"

"What month is it?"

Each concert would invariably include a guest list of musicians from local bands, friends met while on the road, fanzine editors, college radio DJs, people associated with the record label, as well as family members who hoped for a little personal time, even though you were basically at work.

"It's like me coming to your office and saying *Hey, let's hang out!*"

—I would explain to cousins, aunts, and uncles, trying to justify why I couldn't spend more time with them.

"So when are you going to get a real job?"

—one of my relatives would ask in all seriousness.

We were carnies. Life in a bus bunk, hurtling across the highways, safe with friends and fellow freaks—it was really the only place I wanted to be.

Miami at that time was the home of Harry Pussy, my favorite group of the moment, featuring Adris Hoyos, a Cuban American drummer and screamer who throttled her drum kit like a speedcore demon, and Bill Orcutt, her partner in crime, who played scrabble-action guitar. The two had released a couple of remarkable, earsplitting singles.

They were playing in North Miami on the same night as Nirvana. At the end of Nirvana's set, I stood next to Courtney by the side of the stage and asked her if she could tell Kurt to announce the Harry Pussy gig.

"*What?*"

—she asked.

"Tell Kurt to tell everyone that Harry Pussy is playing at Churchill's later and that we're all gonna be there."

It wasn't true at all—there was no way my mom would go see Harry Pussy in North Miami, at that time a pretty dangerous zone. Courtney ran out onstage and cupped her hand over Kurt's ear as he sat down to play an acoustic version of the Vaselines' "Jesus Wants Me for a Sunbeam" (which he had just dedicated to the memory of River Phoenix, who had collapsed and died more than a month earlier from a hot shot of bad dope).

He mumbled into his microphone—

"There's this band called Harry Pussy who are playing at Churchill's tonight . . . so you should go and see them."

Hundreds of people heeded the call, hoping to hang out with Nirvana, who, like my mother, Kim, and I, decided to skip the gig.

Kurt, Krist, Dave, and their new member, Pat Smear, the legendary punk guitarist from the Germs, all seemed happy to be playing in front of such huge crowds, their records dominating the charts. They still joked around with each other onstage, saying things most arena rock bands would never dare to utter.

Their Miami amphitheater show was certainly okay, but the band felt divorced from the incandescence I had witnessed touring together in Europe back in 1991. Susanne's lighting was still great, their production eye-catching. But the primal emotion that they had once unleashed had become dissipated—there was too much separation now between the band and the audience, literally and figuratively, for the kind of exchange of energy I had once been enthralled by.

A big, impersonal venue wasn't what I wanted just then. I only wish the Harry Pussy gig might have been easier for us all to attend, and that I could have brought Kurt along with me to check it out. I think he would have adored it.

Frances Bean Cobain was just over a year old at the time. She hung with her nannies backstage in Miami that night, running around, grabbing whatever she could off deli trays, beautiful and full of light, both Courtney's and Kurt's features visible in her expressive face. My mother sat watching as Courtney told Frances to settle down, opened a juice bottle for her, and put her on her lap for a bit of mother-daughter knee-bouncing and laughter.

"You're a very good mother"

—my mom remarked.

Courtney jolted still, taking in my mother, her eyes wide. It was so unlike the accusations that Courtney and Kurt had been dealing with in the press, the two of them always depicted as drug-addled monsters.

Courtney breathed deeply and said an appreciative—

"Thank you."

At the end of the night, my mother, Kim, and I got ready to leave. We stood on the loading dock behind the arena saying goodbye to John Silva. He was telling us about the Lollapalooza festival coming up in 1994, Nirvana headlining, to be joined by Hole, Mudhoney, Screaming Trees, Tad, the Vaselines, Sebadoh—all bands Nirvana had kinship with and that would be along for the ride, earning them significant paychecks too. Sonic Youth would certainly be invited. It sounded great, but there was one hitch.

"We're going to have a baby"

—Kim said to John. He stopped, then smiled a huge smile, Kim's eyes tearing up.

"Well, that certainly changes things"

—he said with a delighted laugh.

64

WINNER'S BLUES

We had already written and recorded *Experimental Jet Set, Trash and No Star,* our next album, by the end of 1993, spurred by a clutch of songs I had written for a solo tour in Japan earlier in the year. Kenji Kodama, a record-collecting obsessive and proprietor of the amazing Time Bomb music store in Osaka, Japan, had organized the tour. It had me playing with guest musicians such as Eye from the Boredoms and radical psych-noise guitarist Keiji Haino. Free Kitten, a trio Kim had put together with ex–Pussy Galore guitarist Julie Cafritz and Boredoms drummer Yoshimi Yokota, and Mosquito, a duo of Steve Shelley with the songwriter Tim Foljahn, were also part of the cavalcade. It meant that, even though it was ostensibly a solo tour, three-quarters of Sonic Youth were present for it.

Soon enough Kim, Steve, and I flew from Japan to Australia to meet up with Lee and our crew, where our band would be hitting the road for the second annual Big Day Out festival with Iggy Pop, Nick Cave & the Bad Seeds, Mudhoney, Beasts of Bourbon, the Disposable Heroes of Hiphoprisy, Helmet, and dozens of other bands. It was a loose affair of music and friends beneath the January summer sunshine, and we were geared up for good times.

The first day in Melbourne commenced, each of us visiting one another's stages to check out the action. We looked forward to when Iggy's band, the headliner, took the stage, eager to see and hear the master at work—the pied piper of punk, our lord of chaos, the man who had started it all. As soon as his band fired up, we charged to our usual vantage point on the side stage; none of us had seen the streetwalking cheetah all day, and we had been tossing back bottles of Australian lager since at least 10:00 a.m. It was time to release the bats, to kick out the jams. But as we reached the ramp that led to the side of the stage, we were stopped by strips of police tape prohibiting our entrance.

What?

We ran to the other side—same thing.

We pleaded to the security guards standing at the top of the ramp to let us up (*"We're the other bands!"*), but they were under "strict orders." I went out to the front to catch a glimpse. Iggy was dancing and flailing and yowling away, as expected. His band was something else, though, a bunch of long-haired Hollywood metal dudes. They played every note perfectly, though with their long leather jackets they looked like they thought they were on tour with Guns N' Roses.

The tour hit Sydney, and Iggy began to mosey out from his trailer to catch some rays and fraternize with his tour mates, though always at a bit of remove. I sensed someone who had spent too many years dealing with lunatics who wanted a piece of him or someone who was competitive with bands that tried to outshow, outblow, and outwail each other onstage. Why he didn't want us other musicians to watch him perform from the side stage, I could never figure out. I loved it when other bands watched us—and vice versa.

All the musicians were put up in the same hotels, the bar areas teeming with good vibes late into the night: Blixa Bargeld and Mick Harvey jawing with Lee and Steve; Kim and me rapping with Steve Turner of Mudhoney as his bandmate Dan Peters lit a cigarette for Matt Lukin, who stood holding a can of Foster's, his trousers nonchalantly down at his ankles.

One night after the day's festivities had wrapped, I walked into an indoor swimming pool area to find the Mudhoney boys already in the water, dunking each other, tossing around beach balls. A few pro skaters had been on the road with the tour, exhibiting daredevil half-pipe maneuvers, and they were at the pool as well. Some of them climbed up the interior walls until they reached recessed windows that looked into the rooms, and from which they leaped, dive-bombing into the water.

A gent working behind the front desk in the lobby entered the pool area, upset at what he was witnessing, especially as the pool was meant to be closed at that late hour. The people whose windows the skaters had been diving from must have phoned down with noise complaints.

"This is against the rules!"

—he yelled at us, livid.

"Everybody needs to leave . . . *NOW!*"

With a collective groan, we began to hoist ourselves up, but not before

Mark Arm climbed out of the pool and ran, wet and sloshing, to where the angry night manager stood. In a blink of an eye, Mark pushed him into the water. We all went quiet before the hotelier popped up like a cork, his suit, tie, leather brogues, and hair soaked to the bone, his face beet red as he bellowed—

"I'm calling the police! I'm calling the police!"

We hastily grabbed our things, Nick Cave striding over to a dripping and grinning Mark Arm to say—

"You, sir, are my hero."

Experimental Jet Set, Trash and No Star was recorded by Butch Vig and coproducer John Siket at Sear Sound, the antiquated studio in the Paramount Hotel where we had recorded *EVOL*. It was released by DGC, though it was a massive departure sonically from *Dirty*. That album had been heavier than any of our music before or since, emerging in the post-*Nevermind* landscape, catapulting itself into the alternative market, which was then welcoming the far more accessible and radio-friendly ministrations of Pearl Jam, Soundgarden, Bush, and Stone Temple Pilots.

I had toured solo on the side stage at Lollapalooza in the summer of 1993, and I could see how young listeners were as informed by MTV as ever before. It wasn't Sonic Youth's *Dirty* that spoke to them so much as the dark metal roar of Seattle band Alice in Chains' similarly titled *Dirt* (which would outsell *Dirty* by a millionfold). Intellectual art-core noise rock had nothing on their brooding, smoldering grunge.

This realization was becoming increasingly apparent. It was easy to see how more direct music could touch a larger demographic. But for as much as a band like Alice in Chains could make my sensors melt with their very human, raging sound, I knew that could never be Sonic Youth's reality.

Pavement's Bob Nastanovich sent Kim and me a bumper sticker celebrating a racehorse favorite from the track that Bob frequented in Louisville, Kentucky. It said—

I'm Betting on BULL IN THE HEATHER

The poetry of the line inspired Kim to pen lyrics likening the racing of a heart when thinking of love to a horse zooming with the wind. Her words rode along a guitar line I composed, stripped of any distortion pedal noise but creating only more tension for it. This song, along with nearly the entire album, would be our effort toward a new minimalism—not exactly what DGC or Silva's office had hoped for, but they could see we were only being what we promised to be: true to ourselves.

It would be our beautiful friend Yoshimi from the Boredoms who would help inspire the name *Experimental Jet Set, Trash and No Star,* as she sat in the back of a New York City taxi one day with Kim and me and some fan ran over to excitedly say hello to her through the window. She didn't at first understand the adoration.

I laughed, saying—

"Yoshimi, you're a star!"

She held one hand in front of her face, the other hand waving negatively—

"No! No star! *No star!*"

"Experimental Jet Set" was literal enough, conjuring a rock 'n' roll band touring the planet but always engaged in challenging music. "Trash" was a gentle nod to the New York Dolls and the glamour they had made manifest, forever inherent in our music and in our work more broadly. Taken together, the phrases evoked a band dedicated to its craft, enjoying the fruits of its labor, but still, as always, riding on the margins.

As new groups began to rise up in solidarity with the more feminist-leaning elements of the scene—first-wave bands such as Bikini Kill, Huggy Bear, Bratmobile, Skinned Teen, and Heavens to Betsy finding support from Fugazi, Beat Happening, Slant 6, Babes in Toyland, and more—Sonic Youth found ourselves in a new position: we had become the establishment act. Groups occasionally took issue with what they saw as our band's outsized influence on the contemporary scene, as in Bikini Kill's song "Thurston Hearts the Who," which says—

> *If Sonic Youth thinks you're cool*
> *Does that mean everything to you?*

Bratmobile had similar fun with punk-boy hero worship in their song "Cool Schmool," taking aim at one of the Pacific Northwest's foundational punk bands—

> *I don't wanna sit around and talk about the Wipers . . .*
> *I don't want you to tell me what's so cool*

Such excitable rants aside, it felt like our band had attained a kind of role model status among younger groups. Both Kim and I found creative inspiration and energy from them, no matter how much they might take aim at us. Kim, in particular, would be recognized as a feminist forebear for the scene, for the female-fronted, queer-positive riot grrl movement.

Sonic Youth booking agent Bob Lawton rang me up the morning of April 8, 1994—

"Did you hear?"

"Hear what?"

—I asked.

"Cobain . . ."

Oh no.

It hadn't been looking good in the preceding months: the overdose in Rome, reports of Kurt missing in action around Seattle, the intervention by his friends and family. Reportedly Kurt had taken his life three days ago, before being discovered by a worker installing security lighting at his Lake Washington house.

Kim was at a photo shoot for the X-girl clothing line that she had cofounded with Daisy von Furth, younger sister to Julie Cafritz, at Daisy's apartment farther downtown. She was nearly seven months pregnant and happy. It pained me to do so, but I called over to Daisy's apartment and broke the news to her—then she went silent.

"Kim?"

She couldn't speak. In the silence, I could sense her weeping. Like every one of us, she had loved the boy.

Before Kurt died, he penned some liner notes for the 1993 DGC reissue of the Raincoats' 1979 eponymous debut album, saying how the band's music had made him feel as if he were—

a stowaway in an attic . . . listening in on them.

The reissue would revitalize interest in the Raincoats, who re-formed in celebration, composing new music and even enlisting Steve Shelley to play drums. Their first gig in New York City was to be the same day we all learned of Kurt's passing. Watching and listening to the beautiful strangeness and genuine heart of the Raincoats that night, I flashed to Kurt's last line in his notes—

Thank you very much for making me feel good.

In early 1994, before Kurt's demise, Dave Grohl joined Afghan Whigs singer Greg Dulli, Soul Asylum singer and guitarist Dave Pirner, R.E.M. bassist Mike Mills, producer Don Fleming, and me to record Chuck Berry and Little Richard songs for the soundtrack to *Backbeat,* a film focusing on the relationship between Stuart Sutcliffe and his teenage buddy John Lennon in early-1960s Liverpool, through to the Beatles' early days in Hamburg, when the lads were basically a rock 'n' roll cover band.

I knew how to play a barre chord and could do a bit of chug-a-lug boogie, but I never really learned to play the classics. I had basically gone straight from picking up a guitar to making my own brand of noise. This project, produced by the inimitable Don Was, would be a crash course in what it must've been like to be in such a band as theirs.

The film was to be released in June, a month before our baby was to be born. It would also coincide with the first MTV Movie Awards. Our *Backbeat* "band" was invited to Hollywood to perform a couple of tunes for the show's live broadcast.

This would be Dave's first appearance since Kurt had passed, all of us acutely sensitive to that fact. Dave was hanging in there, obviously heartbroken but open to rocking out with some pals.

The film's production company put us up in the Chateau Marmont, the most infamous—and desirable—place to hang one's hat when in Los Angeles, the sprawling, ivy-covered complex reeking of Bugsy Siegel–era louche glamour. I was the last *Backbeat* boy to receive his room key, which would turn out to be to the only room they had available: a suite that took up an entire floor. We band members went up to check it out, Don Fleming quipping—

"Well, we know where the party room's gonna be."

Mike Mills had already been in town with his R.E.M. band-mates Michael Stipe and Peter Buck, overdubbing and mixing their forthcoming LP *Monster.* The boys were curious if I would be willing to drop by the Ocean Way recording studio to maybe add some guitar to a track. Walking into the control room, I was surprised to see Courtney sitting on a couch next to Michael. She looked a bit surprised to see me as well.

R.E.M. producer Scott Litt played me a few songs, one of them "Crush with Eyeliner," which I immediately responded to. Instead of guitar, I asked if I could sing a few vocal echoes to Michael's chorus lines, my favorite being—

She's her own invention

At some point Courtney asked if I would take a walk with her, and we went into another studio and sat down. She wrapped her arms around me and wept.

"He loved me, he actually, really loved me"

—she said, the words wrenching from inside her.

"No one had ever loved me before like that."

The awards broadcast had our *Backbeat* band performing on a stage that was essentially metal grating, with lights streaming up from beneath it. We plowed through the classic "Money (That's What I Want)," which Dulli sang before switching guitars with Pirner, who sang "Long Tall Sally." At the end of this short romp, I figured there was no way I could depart such a ridiculous showbiz stage without leaving my mark. I leaped on top of Dulli for a bit of guitar-smash, our bodies rolling into the amplifiers, which came crashing down. As the song went up in smoke, I jammed my Rickenbacker (rented for the occasion) into the metal grating beneath us, inadvertently shearing the neck off.

We all repaired to the massive Marmont suite, where revelers began ordering drinks and food on the film production company's tab. Within an hour, as word of our party spread, close to a hundred people streamed in. Courtney came, along with Michael Stipe, Winona Ryder, David Markey, Mike Watt, Billy Corgan, Quentin Tarantino, and all their friends and hangers-on, people finding the door to a room full of free-flowing booze and weed like cats drawn to catnip.

Out on the balcony overlooking the legendary Marlboro Man cutout that faced Sunset Boulevard, Courtney told me about how an old boyfriend who had broken up with her some years back had scaled up to the tippy top of the iconic billboard, yelling out into the Hollywood night—

"I'm free! I'm free!"

I had a flight back to New York City at eight in the morning, but by four the gathering had yet to break up. I went into my spacious master bedroom, closed and locked the door, set an alarm for two hours later, and crashed out in all my clothes.

When I returned, sleep-deprived and drained, to our Lafayette Street apartment, I rang up our management office to ask if the film people could take care of the taxi receipts I had incurred to and from the airport. The next day I received a response: the producers would comply with my request only after I made good on the $40,000 room tab at the Chateau Marmont, not to mention the fumigation and cleaning expenses they had gotten stuck with. That was to say nothing of the destroyed Rickenbacker.

My Hollywood soundtrack career was put on hold until further notice.

Two weeks before Kim's due date, she sang "Bull in the Heather," her bass resting across her very pregnant midriff, for Sonic Youth's second go-round on the *Late Show with David Letterman*. On the first of July, she and I took a taxi up to NYU's Tisch Hospital on First Avenue and Thirtieth Street, where she gave birth to our baby, a girl we would name Coco Hayley Gordon Moore.

We stayed in the hospital a few days for observation, most of the doctors and nurses away for the Fourth of July weekend, the building empty and quiet as fireworks bloomed outside our window looking over the East River, the colors glowing across Coco's sleeping face.

Life would be different now, changed in profound ways.

Watching, holding, singing to my daughter, tending to her crying, listening to her laughing, immersed in her sounds and smells. We would settle her into a couple of large pillows, her old-soul eyes staring up at us, a perfect Buddha child feeling our love, two people who had had the sweet fortune of bringing to the universe a gift of naked joy, divinity made manifest in the life of an exquisite girl whom I would forever cherish.

65

CREAM PUFF WAR

1994 brought with it changes both wrenching and beautiful.

For Sonic Youth, it came in the form of a sort of slow-motion epiphany. Whatever hopes we might have once harbored that our band could achieve mainstream acceptance had essentially been dashed. Our reluctance to concede to the musical standards of the moment meant that we were destined to remain distinguished outliers.

If we had found ourselves in an alternate universe, one in which we sold millions of records . . . who knows how it would have affected our lives?

All I knew was that we had come to terms with who we were and would always be: an experimental rock band. As 1994 opened forth, we found new liberation.

Kurt's death had been terrible and sad. It brought with it a kind of musical fracturing. Only with his passing could we see that Nirvana's model of success was sui generis. It was something bands might aspire to, but none could achieve. Punk rock would become popularized by MTV. But simultaneously, it would take root in other, more obscure soil, to brilliant effect. With the same excitement I had when I walked into Maxwell's in 1988 to hear a new Sub Pop band, I would now head into a basement in Brooklyn to hear Ohio trio 16 Bitch Pile-Up, Massachusetts group Sunburned Hand of the Man, Michigan trio Wolf Eyes, Connecticut free jazz saxophonist Paul Flaherty, or New York City's Double Leopards and No-Neck Blues Band.

These artists were part of a huge and growing underground scene investigating freshly liberated ideas of drone, psychedelia, jazz, punk, folk, ambient, and electronics, all unifying around a new creative identity. It manifested itself outside of any ambition toward mainstream acceptance—almost in direct resistance to it. Heralded as anything from "noise" to "freak folk," the activity would be global, taking as its antecedents the harsh industrial soundscapes of Throbbing Gristle and Nurse with Wound, the English countryside lamentations of Anne Briggs and Bert Jansch, the Japanese blare of Merzbow and Hijokaidan, and the noise rock of Swans and, certainly, Sonic Youth. To me, the thrill of discovery and invention among this coterie (made up of multi-genre record collectors as obsessive as I) was as exhilarating as it had ever been.

I would reach out to extreme and marginalized recording artists, some of whom had nothing more than a cassette release or two to their names, to open shows for Sonic Youth. At times a free improvising tabletop noise experimenter or free jazz collective would show up at sound check, after I requested a local promoter locate them. I would ask the musicians how many gigs they had played. The answer might be "None, this is the first time I've ever played live." This, before playing a set in front of fifteen hundred Sonic Youth fans. Usually it was fantastic, though performances were occasionally so radical as to polarize listeners, sending some of them into palpable states of confusion.

Through all this, though, a notion hovered over me like a shadow: there would never be anything as beautiful as what my bandmates and I had witnessed while on tour with Nirvana, that month before *Nevermind* hit. Each night was a spiritual communion between musician and audience, each night a reminder of why we chose this life.

We'd been hearing enticing reports from compatriot bands about Doug Easley and Davis McCain's studio in Memphis, Tennessee, and we decided to make the trip down south to record our next album there. It was a record that would introduce our new triple electric guitar sound, eschewing the bass guitar, those frequencies emanating from Steve's kick drum instead.

Kim's recent guitar playing with Julie Cafritz in Free Kitten had opened a new soundworld to her, one that harkened back to the music she had made in 1980 with Miranda, Nina Canal, and Christine Hahn. The instrument seemed more open-ended in her hands now. Our having three guitars in play at once provoked new ideas from all of us.

A Sunday morning in Memphis while we were recording would consist of grits, eggs, and biscuits, followed by a visit to church to hear soul visionary Al Green preach.

"Come in, come in, welcome, welcome, my brothers and sisters! Sit! Sit! Make room for these children of the Lord!"

—Reverend Al would cry out into his microphone to the congregation as we strolled in mid-service. He would beseech, sing, holler, and dance to the live musicians roaring out electric gospel, his emotions seemingly taking him to the brink of passing out.

Al Green's energy galvanized us as we began recording at Easley Studios that early spring of 1995, a session that would be easygoing yet serious—serious enough that when we first started tracking, we bailed on a rare invitation to meet the Grateful Dead.

The San Francisco legends were due to perform at the Memphis Pyramid arena, and we had called John Silva to see if we could get passes to hear the concert. Lee had seen the Dead a few times, but no one else in the group had. The punk bands that I had come up with had a checkered history with the Grateful Dead and their hippie ilk. When Black Flag had declared their debt to the band, it was taken as a kind of heresy. But they were fellow improvisationalists and musical titans in their own right. An opportunity to see them—and meet them—was too compelling to resist.

John rang back and said we were fully hooked up. The Dead said they were excited to meet us too, a cool surprise.

We had hardly gotten to recording our first song when we realized that it was time to split to get to the concert. We continued to burn the clock a bit, debating whether to forfeit the money it was costing us to rent the studio (not to mention jeopardizing our momentum; we were just beginning to track some killer takes) in order to go see the Dead. We decided they would understand if we continued to work, and so we did until the wee hours.

The following morning Silva rang the studio, where we were still at work refining our sounds.

"What happened to you guys? The Grateful Dead were waiting to meet you. I just talked to their road manager, he said they were bummed."

We felt bad, but we figured there would be a next time. To our further regret—and to the loss of the music universe—Jerry Garcia would pass away that autumn.

We decided to name our new album *Washing Machine*. We had contemplated changing our band name altogether to get on a new foot, Washing Machine a contender to replace Sonic Youth. We had been asked by

R.E.M. to play support on some of their upcoming arena shows, and we said sure but . . . can you bill us as Washing Machine?

This didn't fly with anyone outside the band, understandably. We made one last push with the folks at Geffen. Could the album be titled *Sonic Youth,* the debut release by this new band named Washing Machine?

This too earned an unmistakable, exasperated—

"No."

With Coco just over one year old, we went out on the road with R.E.M. knowing that guitarist Peter Buck and his wife's one-year-old twins would be with them as well, a rock 'n' roll nursery situation in effect. The Bucks had a couple of nannies in their employ; we hired our friend Maurice Menares, who had already toured with us a few times, driving equipment trucks and handling merchandise. He was an expert in taking care of the children in his own family and was intensely protective. Coco would sleep in a foldout crib that we set up in the back lounge of the tour bus, the humming, rumbling bus engine as we motored across the country her lullaby.

Mid-tour we would play the Gorge Amphitheatre, a huge and remote open-air venue two and a half hours east of Seattle, surrounded by Native American reservations, the Columbia River roaring behind it. With the next day free, we repaired to Seattle, Kim, Coco, and I kipping at the Bucks' house in the Leschi area of the city so our babies could play together. Unnervingly, the room we stayed in looked out toward Lake Washington and the home Kurt and Courtney had lived in, the greenhouse room above the detached garage where Kurt had ended his life perched before us like a totem of desolation.

Four days later, playing just outside of Lawrence, Kansas, Michael Stipe would join us and our soundman Terry in visiting William Burroughs and James Grauerholz at their modest home. James was the music fan of the two—the man I had watched lighting Burroughs's cigarette at Patti Smith's CBGB gig some two decades earlier. He was aware of how bands such as ours had recognized and name-checked Burroughs.

When James introduced William to us, he perked up on hearing our names, saying he had characters in his novels named Lee and Kim. Thurston he recalled from the magic troupe the Amazing Thurstons. I had walked into the house with Coco in my arms, and she began making a few complaining noises, as infants do. William held his hand up like a wizard and she stopped, her face changing from a grimace to innocent curiosity.

Sitting in their living room, I noticed stacks of magazines devoted to knives and guns. I tried to engage William on the subject, but he could tell I could not give a rat's ass about weapons. He boiled down his fascination by repeating a favorite line of his, spoken like a true-blue American woodsman—

"I like guns that *shoot* and knives that *cut*."

We headed out to his garage to view some of his shotgun paintings, huge pieces of scrap wood that he had blasted with buckshot, splattering wet colors into abstract pieces. In the backyard sat a replica of Wilhelm Reich's "orgone energy accumulator," a wooden box lined with metal and a ratty chair inside for anyone to sit and absorb the ethereal orgone power, which Reich equated with the life force of nature. The contraption in William's backyard was full of weeds and spiderwebs. I sat in it anyway, feeling nothing.

Kurt had visited Burroughs when Nirvana had come through Kansas, the two men supposedly finding genuine connection. William asked about Kurt, looking at me with an almost childlike confoundment—

"Why would anyone choose to take their own life?"

I thought of the blank emotion I felt a few days earlier, peering out at the Cobain greenhouse, my mind unable to draw any significance from the structure, its blackened windows like dead eyes, closed to the world.

I had no answer for Burroughs.

Lollapalooza had become the highest-profile summer concert, its organizers partnering with promoters to only grow the monolith. For its 1995 run, founder Perry Farrell was adamant about maintaining Lollapalooza's original intention, presenting more challenging music, as opposed to some of the more established alternative rock and rap acts that had filled recent bills.

Sonic Youth was asked to co-headline with Hole, and it gave us a chance to present a wish list of bands we'd like to have join us on the festival, most of which were met: Pavement, Jesus Lizard, Cypress Hill, and Beck. They also appeased our requests for regional experimental bands to play the side stages.

After our set on the first night, finding us once again at the Gorge Amphitheatre, I made my way to our dressing room trailer. Inside I saw Kathleen Hanna of Bikini Kill, whom we had invited to come along. She sat in a chair pressing a towel full of ice cubes to the side of her face. I was in an elated state, the gig having drawn thousands of people, a fantastic day in the warm July air. I asked—

"What's going on? Did you hurt yourself?"

Kim explained to me, a look of utter disbelief on her face—

"Courtney punched Kathleen in the face while we were onstage!"

We all knew that touring with Hole brought with it the potential for drama. Her band was huge news at the moment, as there was immeasurable appetite for anything that had come close to touching the legend of Kurt and Nirvana. Courtney was a classic rock 'n' roll troublemaker, but she was also the widow of a beloved icon. This was her life, her time—and she was going to throw punches at anyone who even slightly ridiculed or challenged her.

Kathleen Hanna and Kurt Cobain had been friends before Courtney had entered Kurt's world. I hadn't witnessed this event—I'd been standing some twenty feet away, wailing with the band—so my knowledge was only second- or thirdhand. But the two women had had *some* kind of altercation on our stage that night. According to Courtney, Hole guitarist Eric Erlandson had handed her a bag of candy, telling her she should give it to Kathleen as a peace offering—or possibly as a joke? Kathleen had evidently responded with something that made Courtney see red, because—*boom*—Courtney smacked her in the face, candy flying everywhere.

For her part, Kathleen said that she had just been standing there minding her own business when Courtney struck her.

Whatever the truth was, Courtney's physical response had won her almost limitless attention, especially coming on the first day of a solid month of touring together. She was unapologetically herself, embodying the description she seemed destined to personify: notorious.

Fred "Sonic" Smith had passed away the previous November, and Patti Smith returned to New York City with their two children to live. She had already presented a few sporadic readings around town, which I regretfully missed while on the road, but she had been booked to perform on the second stage at Lollapalooza's stop in New York.

She shared our dressing room trailer, and we contained most of our fawning, though everyone had books for her to sign. I walked her to the stage and listened to her sing "About a Boy"—ostensibly about her feelings after hearing of Kurt's death. Allen Ginsberg stood next to me listening, Coco in my arms as she pushed her fingers into Allen's bearded mouth—pretty annoying for some grown-ups, but not this poet, who moaned a comic *"mmm"* and *"yummm"* as he playfully sucked on her fingers.

Who is this grown-up actually letting me do this?

—Coco seemed to be thinking.

By mid-August Lollapalooza would wind up at the Shoreline Amphitheatre in Mountain View, California, where Sonic Youth had been traumatized four years earlier at Pegi and Neil Young's Bridge School Benefit. The Youngs attended the concert, arriving at the comfortable open-air backstage area looking rested and healthy, with none of the wear and tear that we musicians exhibited from months on the road. The late day was as warm and calm as one could wish for, the general vibe one of joyful camaraderie, even as we processed the news of Jerry Garcia's passing nine days earlier.

Some of Jerry's compatriots were backstage too, and as Lee and I stood around talking with Grateful Dead keyboardist Tom Constanten and a few of his pals, opining about the heart and soul that had been lost with their dear brother Jerry, I caught sight of a woman my age, sleek and willowy, her white skin almost glowing, in a tight black leather pantsuit that crisscrossed over her torso like a bondage X. Her eyes were shining coals, her red-lipsticked mouth blowing out smoke from the cigarette she held in one hand as a drink sloshed in the other. Amid all the dungaree-clad and flowing-skirted hippies, she looked as if she'd come from some other planet.

I noticed her ambling directly toward us, her eyes catching mine. It was then that I realized: it was Siouxsie Sioux of Siouxsie and the Banshees.

The Banshees had apparently broken up the previous month, though it was hardly on my radar, occupied as I was with Lollapalooza. I had not a clue why this amazing creature had descended on this idyllic Northern California venue; she couldn't have been more out of step with her surroundings. Still, Siouxsie was a true star of punk's ground zero, and her presence was enough to set my heart galloping.

And now here she came, infiltrating the ring of Deadhead hippies that had been conversing with Lee and me.

I smiled, taken aback as she said hello as if we knew each other.

The Deadheads seemed slightly perplexed by this catlike presence. I introduced her to everyone—

"Hey, this is Siouxsie of Siouxsie and the Banshees."

She ignored my greeting and clasped my arm, saying—

"Why are you talking to these *dead* men?"

This elicited a few nervous chuckles, the hippies glancing from her to me, hoping for some explanation. I really had no rejoinder. Siouxsie addressed Tom Constanten—

"Aren't you grateful to be *dead*?"

Her voice dripped with British sarcasm; she seemed inebriated and ready to cause a ruckus, but these peaceniks kept their cool. Siouxsie turned and zigzagged away, leaving us at a loss for words. It seemed that punk's animus toward hippie culture was alive and well, at least in some corners.

We dedicated our last Lollapalooza set to Jerry Garcia, knowing how much he had meant to this particular area of the universe. It was a good gig, long and open, the stars aligning. We cruised by the well-wishers backstage, all smiles and congratulatory backslaps, and into our dressing room to pour a cold drink and to collapse on the couch.

Within seconds, though, Siouxsie, still with the devil in her eyes, prowled into our room. She fell backward onto the couch, scrunching me up against the armrest.

"That was bloody fantastic, you lot are fucking beautiful"

—she said, her mouth an inch from my ear.

Kim took in the scene with an amused smile. She knew I was secretly enjoying the attention, Siouxsie a significant figure in my punk rock history book, even if she could tell I was just as uneasy about how to exactly handle it. We eventually fell into small talk, Siouxsie assuming a semblance of propriety, having apparently decided against any further troublemaking. She turned out to be delightful and charming—though she still couldn't help but bristle at all the *hippies* running loose around the place.

They weren't the only ones. It was with a full heart that I watched Coco learn to walk and run and dance during the tour—providence to her boundless future.

I was invited by *Bomb,* a New York City journal of contemporary art and literature, to fly up to Boston to spend a weekend in October interviewing Patti Smith, who was due to read at a couple of poetry events.

I took an early-morning train out to New York City's LaGuardia Airport to catch a tiny prop plane. I spied Lenny Kaye sitting in the waiting area with a guitar case and small travel bag, and I introduced myself.

Lenny was still the tall and skinny guy I had been following since the 1970s in the pages of rock magazines—as well as onstage with Patti—though he had replaced his classic black-framed eyeglasses with, I assumed, contact lenses. His long black side-parted hair was now shorn to a more contemporary, spartan cut.

The two of us landed at Logan Airport thirty minutes later and were driven to the artist Patti Hudson's home—the two Pattis were close friends and confidantes—where our Patti was busy preparing Polaroid photographs for *See of Possibilities,* an exhibition opening in Boston a few nights later.

The photographs were small observations of daily life that had caught Patti's eye. She had notated each image with a line of text around its white Polaroid frame. Her spirits were high and friendly as she asked me to help choose, out of the many images she had, which ones would work well in the show.

I pointed to a shot of an orange basketball sitting abandoned in some weeds by a weather-beaten fence, saying—

"I really like this one."

"Oh yes, that reminded me of Jim Carroll"

—she said, peering down at the Polaroid through her drugstore reading glasses.

Patti wore her hair in two loose braids, one tucked behind each ear, so as to focus on the work in front of her. She wore jeans, army boots, and a simple white blouse, her face pale yet radiant with creative solemnity.

Soon Lenny, Patti, and I threw our things into a car to drive to neighboring Lowell, Raymond Foye at the wheel, Lenny riding shotgun, Patti and me in the back. Raymond, a Lowell native, had been working as a photo curator for Allen Ginsberg. Our event that evening was touted as "Lowell Celebrates Kerouac!" The affair had become an annual gathering of Kerouac family, friends, scholars, and performers. That night would feature Patti, the Beat-era legend Herbert Huncke, and music from Gloucester, Massachusetts, mainstay Willie "Loco" Alexander.

Patti's plan was to read for twenty minutes or so, then have Lenny join her for a few songs: "Dancing Barefoot" (which she would indeed perform barefoot, on a Persian rug) and a new tune she had composed on an acoustic guitar entitled "Beneath the Southern Cross." Since I was along, she asked if I would join them in playing.

Patti showed me the rudiments of the song, and I joined them onstage, Lenny and me on either side of her as she sang—

Oh, to be not anyone
Gone
This maze of being

After the show, Lenny, Patti, and I were taken to our hotel, at which point the three of us gathered in my room to conduct my interview for *Bomb*. But as we sat chowing on room service, I began to develop a seismic migraine—possibly from the travel, dehydration, or simply the anxiety of sitting in a hotel room, thirty-seven years of age, with two people who, more than any others, had kidnapped my senses as a teen, calling me to New York City to investigate a dream of living as a poet and rock 'n' roll musician.

The following day Raymond drove us to Edson Cemetery to visit Kerouac's grave. The four of us rambled along the autumnal brown pathways between where the dead lay resigned, the trees newly bare, their leaves fluttering in scattered piles. Patti placed on Kerouac's grave a few small flowers and a guitar pick.

We then journeyed to Lowell's Jack Kerouac Park, where marble memorial stones were etched with passages from Jack's books. Patti, with her Polaroid camera, shot photos of my hands and hers laid upon the stones, our fingers pointing, as if divined by some Ouija board, to the charmed texts.

Patti and Lenny would invite me to play with them again the next night at a church in Cambridge, Massachusetts. First, though, Patti was to appear at a bookstore signing in Harvard Square.

She sat at a table piled high with copies of *Early Work, 1970–1979*, a just-published collection of her writings. The queue of people waiting for her snaked from the signing table through the store and out into the street, an unusually lively turnout. I hovered about, living out a fantasy of being Patti's confidant and bodyguard. After thirty minutes Patti noticed people were asking her to sign books other than the one she had recently authored. She queried the next person in line about it.

"They sold out, there are no more"

—the fan answered.

Patti's demeanor went from cheer to chill. She announced to the room—

"When I worked at Scribner's bookstore in New York City in the early seventies, I would always make sure that when an author was having a signing that there would be stacks and stacks of their new book piled high around them."

The room went silent, the salespeople suitably chastened. Patti finished up and we all split.

To continue promoting *Washing Machine,* we toured across the U.S., choosing bands to play with us that we had affinities with, particularly Bikini Kill, whose company we all enjoyed immensely. Kim and Kathleen had become quite close, and I was continually blown away watching guitarist Billy Karren shred pure punk guitar excellence with drummer Tobi Vail and bassist Kathi Wilcox.

A year earlier, Bikini Kill had played a gig in a basement space on the Lower East Side, and I had taken along Mike Watt, in town performing with fIREHOSE. Like many of their shows, the audience was primarily female, and with the basement steaming hot, a few young women took their shirts off, baring all, as male concertgoers tended to do without fear or much notice. Watt grabbed my arm and yelled in my ear—

"Thurst, why are those girls taking their shirts off?"

I explained to him in as few words as possible that it was their right to feel free and fearless. The next thing I knew, Watt had shed his flannel shirt, his hairy chest gleaming in the sweat-soaked basement.

"Watt, what are you doing?"

—I yelled, laughing.

"Solidarity, Thurst, solidarity!"

—he called out, his fist raised high in the air.

Playing with Patti Smith at the 1995 Lowell Celebrates Kerouac! weekend in Massachusetts—a wish made manifest

BOOK SIX

BOOK SIX

66

LATEX GOLD

I invited my mother, at the beginning of 1996, to come along with us on tour through Southeast Asia and beyond, where we would be performing alongside the Beastie Boys and Foo Fighters. She had always expressed a desire to travel afar, particularly to what she called "the Orient," and I figured after all she had given me (including: life) it was the least I could do. Kim and I asked her to assist in looking after Coco, then one and a half years old. The musicians and crew all addressed her as Eleanor.

She became quite close to Pat Smear, who had followed Dave Grohl from Nirvana to the Foo Fighters, the new band Dave had recently formed, and Pat would demand that my mother sit with him on all the airplane and bus journeys the three bands shared.

While taking photos from the broiling mosh pit at a New Zealand stop, my mom found herself swallowed up in the audience's maw. Something similar had happened to her when photographing us in Miami a few years back, only this time she got a sprained leg serious enough to land her in a wheelchair. Our tour manager, Dan Mapp, a man who brought daily affirmation and positive energy into every room he walked into, took me aside, saying, regretfully, my mom would most likely need to return to the U.S.; a sixty-nine-year-old woman in a wheelchair was not exactly what the crew needed to be dealing with on tour.

She refused.

She had already garnered a bit of a fan club across the Pacific Rim, intermingling with our audiences, a few of whom were jazzed about meeting Thurston Moore's mom. Some fans would continue to be pen pals with her for years, sharing photographs and memories.

With a day off in Jakarta, Indonesia, we all met in the hotel lobby to be guided over to an inner-city flea market. My mother loved flea markets, as we all did, but she had been instructed to stay in her hotel bed with her leg raised and a bag of ice pressed to her knee.

Heading out the lobby doors, I jolted at hearing Pat Smear's voice—"Wait for us!"

I turned to see Pat as he pushed my mother in her wheelchair, her face lit up with joy and a hint of guilt.

"Look, she's not staying in this hotel by herself while we have fun, *no way*"

—Pat declared. He was a hero to us all for being so sweet with my mother, with a demeanor that promised a swift ass-kicking if anyone got in his way.

Later on in the tour, as we all sat together in a tiny plane circling Manila, the inclement weather bouncing us in the air each time the pilot attempted to descend, the entire fuselage of the cabin began to fill up with smoke. Already on edge from the turbulence, we turned in our seats to find Pat huffing on a cigarette and sweating profusely. He responded to our shocked faces—

"I don't care! We're gonna crash! *I'm smoking, goddamn it!*"

We would trek farther, through Japan, then head back home for a short break before touring across Europe for another two months. Upon returning to New York City, we would be invited to perform on *Late Night with Conan O'Brien*. When the show was broadcast, I watched myself, my head facing down to the monitors where my lyric sheet had been placed, out of sight of the television cameras. I realized how lame it looked.

The truth is that I have always found it nearly impossible to remember lyrics. I could see now how it stopped me from facing out to the listener as I sang, offering a more emotive connection. In David Markey's *1991: The Year Punk Broke*, there are moments in which I simply made up new words to songs such as "Teen Age Riot," in order not to have to deal with lyric sheets onstage. But it just sounded ridiculous, especially to anyone watching who—unlike myself—actually *knew* the words.

I had my methods of coping. Usually for the first week or so on tour, I would employ memory routines to retain lyrics, and it seemed to work. But once onstage, I'd be flustered by everything else—the action on my guitar, the responsiveness of an amp, the interplay with Kim, Lee, Steve, and the audience, everything—and my mind would go zip.

After a couple of weeks, I would pretty much have the songs down, but remembering words was always an annoying challenge. It might be the reason I found so much fulfillment performing instrumental improvisations; they allowed me to fully immerse myself in music-making, unbothered by memory or distraction.

Yoko Ono had always used her voice for something outside of traditional lyrical singing. So had many other "sound poets" such as Kurt Schwitters, Henri Chopin, and Jaap Blonk. But I had never had much interest in expressing myself that way.

Yoko's son, Sean, had become friendly with us, the Beastie Boys, and other musicians in our social sphere. He began to bring Yoko into the fold. She soon invited me to perform a few duo gigs of guitar improvisation along with her free-vocal rumination "Mulberry," a piece she had originally recorded at home, in 1971, with John Lennon. "Mulberry" was a lacerating bit of noise and howling, based on her memories of being a young child in the Japanese countryside, running home from picking mulberries as warplanes roared overhead.

Before actually meeting Yoko, I had been asked to remix a track from her newly released album, *Rising*. For years I had been collecting every Japanese noise cassette I could get my hands on. Sticking a cassette by Masonna, Monde Bruits, Merzbow, Incapacitants, or Hijokaidan into any stereo system, I would invariably be met with shouts of—

"Noooo! Turn it down! Turn it off!"

I loved them all, though—each one a harsh wall of sonic destruction. The sounds blowing off those fat ferrous oxide cassettes transcended the violent provocation of their creation, becoming otherworldly, as if unleashed from radical meditation.

Beyond just listening to these tapes, I had been thinking of ways to *use* them. I had the idea of playing them all at once, each one on a dedicated tape machine, blasting through a singular sound system and enclosed in a soundproofed room to be built inside of a gallery.

While this idea would never come to fruition, each gallery I solicited thinking it was potentially too disturbing, the invitation to remix Yoko allowed me to apply it elsewhere. The wildest, most extrapolated piece on *Rising* was the title track. To my good fortune, it was the one I had been asked to tackle.

I booked time at Greene Street studios and brought in ten cassettes, one each by Aube, C.C.C.C., Hanatarash, Incapacitants, Keiji Haino, MSBR, Masonna, Monde Bruits, Gerogerigegege, and Violent Onsen Geisha. I could hear at the beginning of Yoko's source track an almost imperceptible sound. I asked the engineer what it might be. He cranked the track up as loud as possible, and it revealed itself to be Yoko's breath as she waited for her moment to perform. Recording engineers would typically "spot erase" such indiscretions, even though they'd be inaudible in the mix. To my delight, this spot erasure hadn't been executed with "Rise."

I decided her barely recorded breath was going to be my impetus. I cranked the breathing *way* over the guitar, bass, and percussion, then flooded the track with a mix of the noise cassettes I'd brought, her actual voice entering into the mix raw and naked on top like a goddess tearing through a fabric of chaos.

While on tour in Australia I received a message at our hotel room: Yoko Ono was on the telephone. I was anxious, thinking she must be angry at how I'd destroyed her song. Instead she regaled me with how much she loved it, not only my amplifying her breathing between words, but the rainbow of electronic noise I'd assembled as accompaniment.

This was the beginning of a creative relationship that lasted for many years, as Yoko would invite me to perform concerts with her, at times as a trio with Kim. It culminated years later in duo performances on a tour we had together through Europe, playing museums in obscure regions that had rarely had the opportunity to witness such an uncompromising avant-garde artist as Yoko Ono.

On the road, we discussed the fury she still felt from the public for her involvement with the Beatles. I could only tell her how I thought her contribution to the group made it more amazing, how many of us actually felt the Beatles became significantly more interesting through the introduction of her radical ideas of art and performance, always with the promotion of peace at its heart.

More than fifteen years into its life, Sonic Youth was now fairly established as a band, a subject of critical and public acclaim—as well as debate. Either we seemed to be fetishistically adored or we rubbed people the wrong way. There wasn't much in between—indifference, poison for any artist, had never been much of a threat to us.

We became more active in our side projects, mostly musical, though Kim would return to visual art to a degree she hadn't for the last decade. Her friendships with the artists Rita Ackermann and Jutta Koether, as well as the inspiration Coco added to our lives, brought forth new ideas, new vistas, not to mention new windows of time—especially with our touring life settling down somewhat, as we tried our best to prioritize parenting and Coco's school schedule.

I found myself playing more and more with both younger musicians coming onto the experimental music scene as well as old-school free-music no wavers. I hadn't fully lost touch with my closest collaborators of the previous decade, such as Lydia Lunch, though our paths rarely crossed for a while. The same for Michael Gira, not to mention bands we'd palled around with on the road like the boys in Mudhoney.

Even Bikini Kill and the Beastie Boys, bands I'd struck up more recent connections with, were overshadowed in my life by my involvement with noise experimentalists such as the percussionists Tom Surgal and William Winant, the Los Angeles–based radical guitarist Nels Cline, and, in what would turn out to be a significant development for Sonic Youth, the Chicago experimental musician Jim O'Rourke.

At summer's end in 1996, I raced up to see Patti Smith and her band at the Central Park bandshell, missing the gig but talking my way backstage. Patti's nine-year-old daughter, Jesse, eyeballed me, then ran to her mom, who was climbing down the stairs at the side of the stage after the group's last number.

Jesse whispered in her mom's ear, pointing at me. Patti hustled over—

"Come play our encore with us."

I eagerly agreed, following them all back onto the stage, the voracious audience roaring for more. A guitar tech strapped a Jazzmaster across my shoulder, with Patti imploring me—

"That was Fred's guitar—be very careful!"

She was referring, of course, to her late husband, Fred "Sonic" Smith.

Drummer Jay Dee Daugherty shouted over to me—

"Just go wild!"

Lenny quickly showed me the chords, and soon I stood with Patti, clutching Fred's guitar, his and Patti's fourteen-year-old son, Jackson, smiling at me, his own guitar at the ready as we prepared for the stage. I headed to the amplifier, feedback organically emerging, the identical frequency Patti and Fred had serenaded my teenage heart with back in the 1970s.

Before 1996 came to a close we would visit Israel, Prague, Budapest, and the Canary Islands, stretching farther into the world, discovering the beauty of our planet. New opportunities revealed themselves. Matt Groening, creator of *The Simpsons,* brought us on board to be part of the show's slightly late-to-the-party alternative rock episode entitled

"Homerpalooza." It was the single mainstream cultural event that we'd find ourselves most identified with across the world.

We had asked the producers if we could record a Sonic Youth version of the show's theme song, something of a loaded request, as Kim's ex Danny Elfman had been the song's composer. But they went for it, and our crazed version played out over the end credits.

We had been told many times that our music was very "filmic." But other than working on instrumentals for a little-seen 1987 film titled *Made in U.S.A.* (starring the actor Chris Penn), we had made few forays into Hollywood. Any Sonic Youth music heard on screen had been licensed from our albums.

There had been an offer in 1995 for us to record music for the adaptation of Jim Carroll's memoir *The Basketball Diaries*, a depiction of the poet's teen years in Manhattan as he struggled with heroin addiction while being scouted as a future basketball star. As a representative for the band, I visited Jim at the West Village home of his ex-wife, Rosemary Carroll, and her husband, Danny Goldberg, the former head of our management company. In the years after leaving Gold Mountain, Goldberg would attain CEO posts at Warner Bros. and Mercury, as well as a stint as president of Atlantic Records. For his part, John Silva would remain our lifelong manager, first in partnership with Gary Gersh and then as the head honcho at his own shingle, Silva Artist Management, where he carefully guided the boats of the Beastie Boys and Nirvana.

Jim welcomed me in, his frame rail thin, his disposition quavering, his voice weedy and questioning. The look on his face shifted between bemusement and anguish at the general perversity of the human endeavor.

"Besides Sonic Youth, I wanna have Lou Reed music in the movie"

—he told me at one point.

Just then the doorbell rang, and Lou himself entered the room, sporting a hairstyle that was short around the sides with a shaggy mullet hanging in the back. Before I knew it, I was sitting between Lou and Jim watching a rough cut of the film. A young Leonardo DiCaprio played Jim's character very well, but the movie retained none of the affecting tone of Jim's memoir, more episodic and sensational than what was on the page. Jim wrote as a poet, but the film seemed to diffuse that essential aspect of his work.

As the movie ended, Lou stood up and began to put his coat on.

"So what'djoo think, Lou?"

—Jim asked, sensing something was amiss.

"That was the worst movie I ever saw"

—said Lou.

"That scene where your character is freaking out in the subway and is being terrorized by two mustachioed Christopher Street leather boys—gimme a break. Fucking terrible."

And with that, he split.

Jim was mortified. *What am I gonna do? Lou hates my movie.*

"I don't think it's that bad"

—I offered.

"The actor's great. But maybe ask the director or producers to cut the leather boys in the subway scene."

Just then the telephone rang and Jim picked it up. I could hear him responding at intervals—

"Uh-huh . . . Okay, Lou . . . Ummm, I guess so . . . I can ask."

Lou had apparently decided to ring up Jim from a phone booth with a suggestion. He should demand that the film producers strip *all* the dialogue out of the film and have it replaced with Jim reading his own book as voice-over instead. I was impressed—more by the idea that Lou thought it was a reasonable request to entertain than by the artistic merit of it.

After all was said and done, Sonic Youth never got a call back to record any of the film's soundtrack. The filmmakers ended up having Jim record songs with Pearl Jam, the Seattle band on their way to becoming a post-grunge marquee powerhouse.

Byron Coley, my pal dating back to his Rhino Records days, filed a report for *Spin* magazine on the iconoclastic folk guitarist and polymath John Fahey, an outsider genius and legend of the 1960s and '70s who had issued recordings of alternate-tuned guitar-blues explorations. Lee and I had picked up some of his easier-to-find recordings while touring across America, recognizing the guitar magic they possessed.

Byron's article spurred a renewed interest in Fahey, bringing him back onto stages where he would play with some present-day outsiders. Glenn Jones, of the eclectic Boston folk-psych band Cul de Sac, helped organize an East Coast appearance by Fahey. I was solicited to play shows with the man, as well as driving him from gig to gig in the brand-new white Volvo station wagon Kim and I had just purchased.

With Coco growing fast, we saw our Manhattan apartment, once a vast loft beyond our wildest dreams, becoming a bit crowded. We began to look for larger places in the city. We had been visiting Byron and his family up in Deerfield, Massachusetts, next to where J Mascis lived in Amherst and close to Northampton, the home of Smith College. After renting a couple of houses in the area, we decided to make a full-time move up there, finding a large three-story structure up the hill from Smith.

The car, our first ever, had been a necessary evil.

Fahey landed in Boston, where he was supposed to meet someone to take him to the Iron Horse Music Hall in Northampton, a solid two hours west from Logan Airport. Not finding his ride, he decided to jump into a taxi. He gave the driver the address of the club, arriving there without a dollar to his name. The club owners had to scrounge around so they could pony up the $300 fare.

The guitar John had brought with him was in disarray, so he requested an instrument-repair person to come fix it. When I walked into the small venue, I saw Fahey sitting on the stage, his distended belly sticking out over the dungarees that rested on his hips, his thinning blond hair slicked back. He wore cheap black sunglasses, which he tilted down to peer at me as I stepped up to greet him.

"Well, it's about time. Here, take this and see what you can do with it"

—he said, handing me his guitar.

"What do you want me to do with it?"

—I asked, confused.

"*Fix it!* You're the guitar repair guy, right?"

"No, I'm the guy who's opening up for you for the next five nights."

I had come in with Phil X. Milstein from the Velvet Underground Appreciation Society, who was going to play bowed saw with me in duo for a couple of the gigs, and Ray Farrell, who had flown out from Los Angeles to join us on the road—Ray was an old-time Fahey enthusiast, and he'd be lending a helping hand as we loaded our little amps in and out of clubs.

John peered over at Phil and Ray, asking—

"So . . . which one of you is the guitar repairman?"

With Ray and me in the front of the Volvo, John would make himself at home in the back, his heft sprawled across the seats. He was funny and smart, his chatter veering from Beethoven to how Wendy's hamburgers were so much better than all the others. I threw a CD on of some recent Sonic Youth instrumental music. Fahey chimed in, his voice high and nasal, his vowels elongated—

"Oh, what's *this*?"

"Just some new stuff my band is working on"

—I responded.

"Oh, it sounds like Debussy"

—he said, adding after a beat—

"Only *better.*"

Fahey could be a charmer.

From his lounging position in the back seat, he would balance a Radio Shack cassette recorder on his belly, creating mixtapes of radio, wind noise, and conversation. By the time we reached Boston, the rope securing his dungaree cutoffs had broken, resulting in his having to constantly hike his trousers up over his posterior. I worried, walking along the street with him, that we might arouse undue attention, so we began looking for a new belt, my gift. The only place nearby was an upscale men's clothier, which graciously, though with some curiosity, supplied us with a fine leather accessory.

John's physique hadn't shocked me so much until the day I knocked on his motel door to alert him of our early-morning travels to New York City, where we had been booked to play CBGB. John opened his motel door, and I immediately noticed his suitcase upended on the floor, dozens of his CDs—all in dirty, cracked cases—strewn around. This was his merchandise, which he had yet to sell, or even display, at gigs. Also catching my eye was John himself, naked as the day he was born.

"Oh, do come in. Would you like to listen to some Stravinsky with me?"

"Sure, okay . . . Umm . . . you know you could be selling these CDs on our merch table"

—I offered.

"Oh, I know. Take whatever you want. They're all excellent."

John's playing at the gigs was unnervingly tentative. Occasionally he would find his way into brilliant passages, only to stop and leap out, never allowing the audience to get too comfortable. His thorniness had always been inherent in his work, only now it was full-blown. Suffice it to say that he wasn't pandering to our audiences.

After the tour we would correspond by mail, John writing me bristling diatribes accompanied by cassettes of found sounds, train noises, and various records he had liberated from thrift shops. He could be irascible and demeaning at times, but I could see how much he loved the people who loved him.

I would last talk with this giant of the mystic blues six months before he passed, when he came by to say hello in Portland the summer of 2000. He was accompanied by local guitar aficionados, who looked after his welfare the best they could. John told me how much he enjoyed hearing our music. He was still wearing his cheap sunglasses after dark, a choice inspired by the great bluesman Skip James, who once told him—

"If I take them off . . . *the whole world will burn up.*"

It was hard to believe that David Bowie was turning the ripe old age of fifty in 1997, but time rang its crazy toll. The Thin White Duke decided to throw a birthday bash at Madison Square Garden. We had learned, back when *Sister* was released in the 1980s, that Bowie bought our records. His ear for new currents in music, whether popular or beneath the radar, was well-known, so it wasn't shocking that he had heard of us. Still, it was a thrill when we received a call asking whether we'd be interested in playing a song with him at the event.

We met Bowie at Looking Glass Studios, the recording room owned by Philip Glass, on Broadway just north of Houston Street. His idea was that we would play along with the tune "I'm Afraid of Americans," from the new album he had been working on, to be titled *Earthling.*

It was immediately clear that he was someone who could light up a room, an energy of sublime awareness perceptible in him. He could be controlling of the situations around him, not in a brutish way, though when I began to talk to Steve nonchalantly about some Little Richard tidbit I had recently read, Bowie quickly interjected with a Little Richard story of his own: the rock 'n' roll legend had evidently come to London in the 1960s, and Bowie and his mates had been called upon to be his backing band for a few shows, David playing saxophone.

Before the concert got into gear, we gathered for a group photo, David joined by Sonic Youth, Foo Fighters, Placebo, and members of the Cure, Pixies, and Smashing Pumpkins. I stood in the back (as tall people do), holding two-and-a-half-year-old Coco in my arms. As David got up to leave and get ready for the big night, he turned and began waving to where we stood—

"Hi, Coco! Bye, Coco!"

It was sweet and curious, his acknowledging the one person in the room who had no idea who he was.

For the gig, we set up with his band, all of them playing through high-powered, high-tech amplification systems. We added our scrapes and screeches into the mix, creating the edge that David felt appropriate for the song's narrative of paranoia. We repaired backstage to catch our breath before I headed to the monitor board to watch Lou Reed join Bowie for renditions of "Queen Bitch" and "White Light/White Heat." I reminded myself how incredibly fortunate I was to be woven into this rock 'n' roll dream, before racing back to be with Coco.

67

SILVER BREEZE

Sonic Youth had invested our 1995 Lollapalooza paycheck into outfitting a rehearsal and recording studio, which we would christen Echo Canyon, in a building on Murray Street down by the World Trade Center. By late 1996 we were recording every note we were playing, a process instrumental in defining our newest songs, the music becoming only more focused on experimental structures, with sound concepts not indebted to any specific genre, mostly executed by three electric guitars and percussion.

Though Kim, Coco, and I had transitioned to Northampton, we held on to our Manhattan apartment, constantly traveling the three hours back and forth, never entirely letting go of the big city we came up in, especially with the Sonic Youth studio now situated there. Other than a few appearances (the first Tibetan Freedom Concert on Randall's Island in New York, the Bumbershoot festival in Seattle), we wouldn't tour at all in 1997, the band focusing on songwriting and recording, Kim and I more fully engaged with raising Coco as she entered her school years.

We booked a late-November evening at Avery Fisher Hall to present most of the new music we had been developing for our next album, which we had decided to title *A Thousand Leaves*. It would be all instrumental versions, and we asked Tom Verlaine—one of our great musical influences, certainly for Lee and me—to appear on the bill with us for the occasion.

The title, *A Thousand Leaves*, was nothing more than an English translation of the French "mille-feuille," a pastry better known in the U.S. as a napoleon. I had attempted one morning to order such a pastry in a Parisian bakery, not knowing how to pronounce it. Once hearing it, I thought it charmingly evocative. We considered titling the record *Mille-Feuille*, but the whole *Pretentious? Moi?* aspect of it seemed a little too much, so we opted for the translation. (My alternate album title idea, *Ham Radio,* would have had on its cover a film still of the actress Sally Kirkland riding naked atop a massive hog, taken from the obscure 1969 underground curiosity *Futz*. This, unsurprisingly, got a collective thumbs-down.)

Leading up to the album's release, we created music for the soundtrack to *Suburbia,* a film by Richard Linklater, whom we had first met through the Butthole Surfers in Austin, and adapted from a play by Eric Bogosian, our New York compatriot from the Kitchen. With Echo Canyon up and running, and Wharton Tiers manning the twenty-four-track console and tape machine, we would continue to record every moment of amplified inspiration that came to us.

With so much material now being generated, we eventually decided to create our own in-house label, Sonic Youth Recordings (SYR). It would allow us to release the more improvisational and wide-ranging music we made, stuff we figured Geffen Records wouldn't have much interest in. With the time and freedom that came with having our own space to create, our songwriting became more expansive.

As ever, the assigned singer of a song would take on the responsibility of writing the lyrics. Unlike any discussion of the music being played, there was never any debate about the lyrical content a bandmember presented. Furthermore, we had an understanding among us that Steve's cymbal splash had equal value to one of Lee's lyrical phrases or to Kim's guitar part or to a peal of my feedback. We held on to the notion that our band existed as a forum, a sonic democracy, each of us participating singly but with a unified voice.

Our compositions would always be credited—

"All songs by Sonic Youth."

We returned to touring across the U.S., Europe, and the Pacific Rim for most of 1998, not looking back at our catalog much, only playing the wealth of material on *A Thousand Leaves,* asking audiences always to think of us as a new band, as if this record were our first.

A Thousand Leaves would constitute a "return to form" to many critical ears, the band showing its maturity but still taking risks, looking inside themselves more. It would also be the year when the "Youth" in our name began to ring false to some. Our ages became their own story, me turning forty; Kim, forty-five; Lee, forty-two; Steve a baby at thirty-six.

We had been at it for sixteen years, and for the first time we found ourselves hearing from cub reporters at British music weeklies that Sonic

Youth should consider hanging it up—enough is enough, make room for techno, et cetera. I wasn't put off by it; the music press is always enchanted with the new and the young. I was advanced enough in my career not to feel in competition with the latest thing, but also as open to new sounds and new musical exploration as ever. My musical apprenticeship was ongoing.

Coco would travel the world with us in 1998, four years old, climbing up onto my shoulders for a crow's-nest view or strapped safe into her folding stroller, holding tight to Zoe, her orange stuffed monster friend from *Sesame Street*.

Zoe would escape from the stroller at times, nearly getting lost, such as while crossing a six-lane Bangkok street of nonstop cars and three-wheeled tuk-tuk taxis. I raised my hands in the air, a giant beanpole from North America dodging the maniacal drivers before swooping Zoe up to return her to Coco's tearful embrace, Kim yelling—

"Oh my god!"

We intersected with the experimental Chicago musician Jim O'Rourke when inviting him to join us and an old friend, the Mills College percussionist William Winant, in performing a free improvisation set at San Francisco's Amoeba Music. It would lead Willie to suggest that Sonic Youth record an album of "new music" compositions. Willie recognized our lineage, obscure though it was, to twentieth-century academic composition, from John Cage to Pauline Oliveros. He guessed we might be the only rock band who could perform such pieces in the context of rock without it seeming gimmicky or forced.

We still had to return to Europe, Japan, Australia, and New Zealand, though, for another round of touring. With the FIFA World Cup happening every four years, we were no strangers to competing for audiences, promoters sometimes apologizing to us—

"Sorry, there's not many tickets sold, everyone's at home watching the World Cup."

We had a significant gig scheduled at the Olympia in Paris, the grand theater where Edith Piaf, Serge Gainsbourg, John Coltrane, Miles Davis, the Beatles, the Rolling Stones, and every major light of the twentieth century had performed. On this night, our gig was to coincide with France playing its semifinal against Croatia.

The theater wasn't exactly sold out, though the size of the audience was healthy enough. To appease French fans, I announced the score of the game after each song. With the luck of the football gods shining down on us, France won the match and the Olympia erupted into mad cheering.

We decamped back to our bus, parked on Boulevard des Capucines. The driver attempted to set forth into the night toward our next day's concert in Brest, which was to be an all-day festival with Echo & the Bunnymen, the Jesus and Mary Chain, and about a hundred other bands—but we couldn't budge. Everyone in Paris had taken to the streets, going nuts, celebrating their win, stopping all traffic as the deliriously happy citizenry headed toward the Champs-Élysées to gather.

Our tour bus became a perch, people jumping onto the roof waving flags, swigging bottles of wine, dancing and howling at the moon with the sweet heat of victory. All we could do was peer out the windows at this community of joy until it eventually died down, dawn blinking across the city—then tiptoe our way out of town.

Before breaking for the end-of-year holidays, we would continue with various side projects. One September evening, en route to a gig with percussionist Tom Surgal at the Cooler—a basement club on West Fourteenth Street, just a stone's throw from the Hudson River, lately one of my favorite spots—I ran into Beck.

I had known Beck since 1994, when I first saw him play a leaf blower at a backyard gig in Los Angeles. He had interspersed his noisemaking with acoustic guitar songs that were sensitive and striking. I would subsequently invite him to be a guest on an episode of MTV's late-night alternative rock program *120 Minutes,* which I had been asked to host. Mike D from Beastie Boys was in town, and I had him come along as well.

I'd had the idea that Beck could answer my interview questions with spontaneous gestures, such as taking off his shoe and throwing it against the wall. He, Mike, and I then performed an improvised noise-hip-hop jam, in which I slid a feedbacking toy Marshall amp across the strings of a cheap electric guitar that I'd laid on the floor, while Beck played cassette samples and Mike spat Schoolly D rhymes. It was a short-lived time when, at least after midnight, MTV allowed its guest hosts a bit of imaginative leeway. They even green-lighted me to show live video clips of Harry Pussy and the Japanese underground noise sensation Masonna.

Beck, these four years later, was riding high on the success of his album

Odelay, and he asked me what I was up to. As I had done prior, I invited him to come along and jam.

Tom wasn't quite sure about me showing up with Beck, but he was pretty used to my surprising him every now and again. Beck, recognized by a few in the tiny, crowded Cooler space, gave a nod to his grandfather Al Hansen's Fluxus theatrics by walking around the stage with a guitar that he sometimes hit and wrapping the guitar strap around his head like a headband, as Tom and I moved into our familiar playing field. Eventually Beck began removing pieces of Tom's kit, very methodically, and placing each item somewhere else onstage—behind the back curtain or in the audience—until Tom sat on his drum stool with nothing in front of him.

It turned out Beck had come to town to host a night celebrating the release of the book *Playing with Matches,* a posthumous overview of Al Hansen's wild legacy. The local gallery Thread Waxing Space was presenting an exhibition of Hansen's works. With support from Yoko Ono, it would bring together some of Al's old-school Fluxus pals to create a "happening" at the Roxy. Musicians such as Marianne Faithfull and Cat Power were on board to perform—and I got the call as well.

I knew just what music to contribute.

The Fluxus energy Beck had tapped had been informing a trio I was playing with at the time, a group named FOOT—basically Don Fleming, our pal Jim Dunbar (a rather rogue A&R man at Columbia Records), and me making synth-inspired noise. Jim's apartment, up a long, long narrow stairwell on Canal Street, around the corner from West Broadway, was a gathering place for FOOT jams, guests coming up to wail with us on the synths. I brought Patti Smith over one evening with her bandmate Oliver Ray intending to play a little music.

When all the instruments and amps were fired up, Patti took her clarinet out of the case she had brought along.

"No, no—you can't play that here!"

—both Jim and Don yelled.

"What are you talking about?"

—Patti responded, surprised.

"Only music generated by electric signals are allowed in this room"

—Jim explained.

"Electricity is what separates us from the animals"

—Don added.

Patti didn't know what to say or make of these two, looking at me and then Oliver, who simply shrugged.

"If you want, you can go down to the street"

—Jim said—

"and play the clarinet through the intercom. Then we can put a microphone on the little door speaker up here and record you that way."

Oliver came to our rescue. He proposed walking back with Patti to their place on MacDougal Street to grab an electric guitar—or *some* nonacoustic instrument. Oliver eventually returned, but without Patti. She had obviously had her fill of FOOT.

When Beck invited me to perform at the Al Hansen celebration, I knew FOOT would be the perfect act.

Keeping in the Fluxus spirit, we decided to add a bit of surprise to this particular performance. We often brought in an unexpected guest performer, like when rock 'n' roll cover girl Bebe Buell had shouted through our din one night at the Cooler. Another gig of ours had involved having Tom Verlaine, J Mascis, and Jim O'Rourke all crammed into my Volvo. I had been asked to play a noise event up in western Massachusetts, and for the performance, we sent a microphone cable out from the idling car into the small club, where an amplifier was on full blast. Jim climbed up onto the Volvo's roof and worked out on a yoga exercise ball while smoking a cigarette. Meanwhile, Don Fleming and I held the microphone against the car's speakers, flipping through the radio, also on full blast, while blowing the horn incessantly. Soon enough, neighbors came running out of their houses yelling, and we peeled away, tossing the microphone out onto the street. Verlaine and Mascis sat in the back all the while wearing similar, impassive smiles, hostages to our noise shenanigans.

For the Roxy gig we decided to ask a male go-go dancer to join us.

I reached out to Glennda, half of *The Brenda and Glennda Show*, broadcast on cable access television in the early 1990s and hosted by the radical drag queens Brenda Sexual and Glennda Orgasm. She hipped me to a friend who could guide Don, Jim, and me through the gay nightclubs of Manhattan in search of the ideal go-go boy whom we could hire for our set. We ended up at Splash, a huge space in midtown with fountains of gushing water spraying everywhere and dozens of dancers, all of them super cut and buff, wearing nothing but short shorts as they gyrated and sweated on pedestals. We decided on a Puerto Rican gent named Leo, offering him fifty dollars to come by the Roxy and dance with FOOT.

Unlike the original 1960s Fluxus happenings, the Roxy evening would be populated by supermodels such as Amber Valletta and Kate Moss, along with it-boy Lemonheads singer Evan Dando, the actors Gwyneth Paltrow and Liv Tyler, and a bevy of celebrities that included Lou Reed and Rose McGowan. Most of the performances were by the numbers, a song here and there, interspersed with a few performances by original Fluxus participants such as Larry Miller (re-creating a Dick Higgins piece that involved climbing up and down a ladder; it seemed to only befuddle the glitterati in the room).

Marianne Faithfull and Cat Power played cool sets, and the MC Vaginal Creme Davis was hilarious throughout. But the energy coming off the stage was mostly subdued—until FOOT appeared.

We plugged in our guitars and synthesizers, cranked everything up to nuclear volume, and began to wail like animals let loose from cages. All chatter was immediately drowned out; the audience could only stare at us, our noise-horror blasting the room apart.

We had told Leo to disregard the absence of any actual beat in our "music," just dance as if he were hearing the disco boogie of Splash. He came strutting out, hot in his tight-fitting cutoff shorts. We proceeded to blow more and more noise action from the amps, thrashing guitars across the tops, then slashing them against the hopeless monitors. After a solid five minutes of this assault, we threw everything down and I ran over to Leo, shouting into his deafened ear—

"Let's get out of here!"

—and with that we scrammed offstage.

Yoko Ono jumped up from her front-row table with a huge smile on her face, applauding excitedly—the only person to do so. I could hear her yell—

"*Bravo!*"

On the last night of 1998, Kim and I would be invited to join Patti Smith at the Bowery Ballroom. I was reminded of Patti's legendary New Year's shows of twenty years prior, those nights that had so excited and transported Harold and me.

Before going on, we huddled in the tiny upstairs dressing room with Tom Verlaine; Michael Stipe; Patti's son, Jackson; and her sister Kimberly. Patti's group played their set, took a breather, and, after one in the morning, returned to the stage, Kim and me joining for a barn-burning rampage on "I Wanna Be Your Dog." Kim and Patti went head-to-head, toe-to-toe, two artists on fire, facing off as we all shredded the night into pieces, into the future.

With the winter of February 1999 slamming across New York City, Sonic Youth would head back to Europe, bopping across France, Greece, Portugal, and Spain. The final show of our run would take place in Granada, Spain, on a bill with the Master Musicians of Jajouka, a contemporary faction of the mystic Moroccan Sufi trance musicians.

The original Jbala Sufi group had attained a universal profile with the 1969 recordings that Brian Jones of the Rolling Stones had facilitated. Their musical society, heralded as sacred messengers in their mountain villages, had split into two camps of younger and elder, the former becoming traveling representatives of the holy music. It was with them that we would collaborate onstage at the end of their set.

The following day we boarded a ship with the Jajouka crew to Morocco, to spend some time exploring the Berber city of Fez. We spent hours walking through the medina, where all motorized vehicles had been prohibited, shopkeepers racing through dirt-strewn alleys with mules loaded down with produce, yelling for us to stand aside lest we be trampled.

Coco, now four and a half, clung safely to my shoulders. She watched as children her age toiled with their families or came home from school dressed in uniforms. They stared at her and she stared back, the children smiling and beautiful. Elderly women shuffled over to Coco and me, bowing and then reaching their hands up to caress Coco's golden hair.

After our tour, on April Fool's Day, the band decided to move ahead with the idea we had discussed with William Winant and Jim O'Rourke at Amoeba Music a year back, of performing select pieces from the canon of radical twentieth-century music.

After debating which composers and which pieces we would tackle, we set up a session at Echo Canyon to record compositions by John Cage, James Tenney, Pauline Oliveros, Takehisa Kosugi, Christian Wolff, Cornelius Cardew, Yoko Ono, and George Maciunas.

Both Kosugi and Wolff were invited to the studio to guide us through their pieces, composer and turntable pioneer Christian Marclay performing with us on the Kosugi composition. Coco performed Yoko's 1961 "Voice Piece for Soprano" (the instructions being "scream against the wind," "scream against the wall," and "scream against the sky," all of which Coco nailed in one take).

For George Maciunas's 1962 "Piano Piece #13 (Carpenter's Piece) for Nam June Paik," we needed a piano, as the score called for any number of musicians to hammer nails into each key on the instrument until it was muted (and subsequently destroyed). Adam "Ad-Rock" Horovitz of the Beastie Boys came to our rescue, offering us an old piano his family wanted to be rid of. We would readily decimate it, and Sonic Youth documentarian Chris Habib, whom we had become friendly with through the years after he filmed so many of our concerts, recorded the action for a video adjunct to the session.

We headed out to the West Coast to play a couple of outdoor summer fests with Sleater-Kinney, Guided by Voices, Superchunk, Rocket from the Crypt, Bratmobile, the Boredoms, and a host of others. One night, as we traveled between festivals, we parked our equipment truck and our bus at our hotel off the freeway, as we typically did.

The next morning we woke to find the truck had been robbed of everything we owned and had cultivated since day one: guitars, drums, amplifiers, effects, notebooks, outboard gear, cables, lights. Every single little piece of our live world—not just for us four band members, but for all of our tech people as well—*poof*—gone.

Dumbfounded, we traveled in our tour bus to the festival site, with about two hours to go before we were due onstage. What could we do? We went to each band's dressing room trailer and asked if anyone would let us borrow a guitar or two, and, if so, would it be okay if we restrung and retuned them? We promised to restore each one back to its original state when we were done.

Every group we solicited was extremely gracious; they were as shocked by the theft as we were. We went out to play a set of Sonic Youth tunes drawn primarily from the 1980s—ones we figured were the easiest, rawest, most direct numbers that didn't require very much in the way of sophisticated guitar tech, tunes like "Brother James," "Mote," and "White Kross," many of which we hadn't played in ages.

Being forced to perform our earlier material, through no choice of our own, allowed us to celebrate what had unintentionally, organically become a sort of Sonic Youth legacy. While I would sorely miss my Jazzmaster, which had come to feel like a soul mate, I embraced the liberation of losing things, being stripped of attachments, and recognizing the band as a union of our selves, not just our instruments, gifting us with the challenge to react, regroup, reconsider, rejoice—and reignite.

68

ZEN CONCRETE

A new artist-curated festival in the UK by the name of All Tomorrow's Parties invited Sonic Youth to perform in the springtime of 2000. The event would take place at the off-season Camber Sands Holiday Centre, with invited bands camping out in chalets with beds and kitchenettes.

This first ATP was curated by the Scottish post-rock group Mogwai, the whole affair the brainchild of Barry Hogan, a young, ambitious entrepreneur who had been inspired by a previous event organized by the Glaswegian pop maestros Belle and Sebastian. We had it in our heads—mistakenly, it turned out—that the premise of All Tomorrow's Parties was to have bands present themselves outside their usual parameters, allowing their more experimental aspects to be shared.

I had constructed a twenty-minute electric guitar instrumental, first performed at a solo gig at the Cooler in New York City. After we'd accepted the ATP offer, I showed this piece to Lee, Kim, and Steve. We decided to play it as a group, along with a few instrumental versions of the disparate pieces we had recently composed together.

The day of our set, as the lengthy instrumental got under way, Kim stepped up to her microphone and began a freestyle recitation inspired by a *New Yorker* magazine piece she had read on the airplane ride over from the U.S., exploring the relationship between American poet Sylvia Plath and her English poet husband, Ted Hughes.

In the moment I bristled. I thought the instrumental should be entirely *instrumental*. But listening to the recording on the way back home, I realized how fantastic it sounded, Kim's verbal improvisation taking the music to new heights. I immediately suggested we release it as a twelve-inch.

In this view, I was in the distinct minority. The piece had generally been hated by those present at the gig. By all critical accounts we had stunk up the place. We had been expected to play the hits—*Give us "Teen*

Age Riot" or *"Kool Thing."* Instead we improvised on structures no one was familiar with. Kim actually deigned to play some rudimentary trumpet. How dare we?

NME would review the concert, publishing a photo of me holding my guitar behind my neck. We had recently released our "new music" session with Jim O'Rourke and William Winant, entitling it *Goodbye 20th Century.* The writers at *NME* had a field day with their headline: "Goodbye 20th Century, Goodbye Talent."

By this point in our existence, I had heard way worse. *NME*'s slagging could only be taken as hilarious; we didn't need to prove ourselves to anyone anymore, least of all the journalists at a fading music rag. We would eventually release the ATP performance as an SYR recording, using the "Goodbye 20th Century, Goodbye Talent" clipping for our cover art.

We had already recorded much of *NYC Ghosts & Flowers,* the album we created using new and random guitars that we'd recently harvested from various music stores (as well as from forgotten corners of our rehearsal space). Jim O'Rourke had been invited to collaborate with us on our last two SYR releases, and for *NYC Ghosts & Flowers,* he continued to do so, joining Wharton Tiers in the producer chair, all the sessions recorded at our Echo Canyon studio on Murray Street.

While mixing the tune "Free City Rhymes" one afternoon, Jim looked up from the board and said—

"Would you mind if I try overdubbing some bass guitar on this?"

"You know how to play bass?"

—I asked.

"It's actually my main instrument."

Jim quickly laid down a hip bass line. We liked it so much that we asked him to keep it up for the rest of the album, excited by the prospect of the bass guitar reentering our music. He also supplied a bit of synthy electronics on a stark track entitled "Side2Side." We realized that to perform the song live, without his addition, would be either impossible or vastly inferior to the recorded track.

There really was no question, after all he'd contributed to the album—we decided to invite Jim into the band.

Jim's humor, even when he was grumpy, was smart and sardonic. He made for polite and charming company, though he could be as catty as any of us. We quickly found ourselves bouncing our respective obsessions off each other, from experimental arcana to the likes of Sparks, Bowie, Roxy Music, Velvet Underground, and the universally appealing Beatles.

Our last show as a quartet had been the ATP hate-fest. Our first show with Jim would take place in Paris at the Centre Pompidou, a night of improvisation with Brigitte Fontaine and Areski Belkacem. Brigitte, then sixty-one years old, was a surrealist provocateur, actor, singer, and poet with a history of feminist militancy (she publicized having an abortion in 1971 France when such a thing was considered a crime). The avant-garde recordings she had made with her partner, Areski, in the 1960s had been informed by traditional French chanson, interwoven with free improvisation, world music, and uncategorizable song structures. *Comme à la Radio,* Brigitte and Areski's collaborative recordings with the Art Ensemble of Chicago, had been an essential document among a certain class of record-collecting obsessives.

We proposed a recording session with Brigitte and Areski, which would take place at a studio just outside of Paris and would bring us face-to-face with this woman whose brilliance was not only in her work but in her personality, her fashion, her energy, her mind, her laughter, the way she held her wineglass and cigarette. Everything about Brigitte was otherworldly. She was an aesthete and an intellectual, someone both maddening and marvelous.

The gig had us in free improvisation mode, Brigitte entering only after ten minutes, her legs crooked into the shape of a triangle, her arms stretched out like a cross before she grasped the microphone and steered the music the way only she could.

Our first proper Sonic Youth gig as a quintet would be in Minneapolis at the Walker Art Center. From there we would travel across the country, joined by the space-age UK group Stereolab and the Washington, D.C., band Quix*o*tic. The third gig of the tour, in Pontiac, Michigan, had Ron Asheton and Niagara coming by to say hey.

Steve and I had recorded music with Ron a few years earlier for Todd Haynes's 1998 film *Velvet Goldmine,* in a band put together by FOOT comember and Columbia Records A&R roustabout Jim Dunbar, working alongside music supervisor Randall Poster. Our soundtrack group would also comprise Don Fleming, Mike Watt, Mark Arm, and Sean Lennon.

We dubbed our ensemble Wylde Ratttz (a subtle nod to Bowie guitarist Mick Ronson's first band, the Rats), initially recording Stooges songs for actor Ewan McGregor's faux band in the film. Michael Stipe, one of the film's producers, liked what he heard and green-lighted us to record more, allowing Wylde Ratttz to compose a few originals and to learn a few covers.

The sessions for the soundtrack took place at Sear Sound, and while I thought I knew how to play Stooges songs as well as any blue-blooded punk rocker, sitting across from Ron on facing piano benches, I saw how to actually *swing* the songs—as opposed to using the straight, downstroking style I was accustomed to. It was a guitar lesson I could never have dreamed of as a young lad separating stems and seeds on the gatefold cover of *Fun House*.

At the Pontiac, Michigan, gig in 2000, we offered Ron a guitar, and as I introduced him with "Ladies and gentlemen, Ron Asheton from Ann Arbor," he joined us for a fifteen-minute encore of "I Wanna Be Your Dog." With Jim co-manning the bass guitar and Kim unencumbered, she could really concentrate on her vocals while investigating a new physicality onstage. She had danced openly during "Kool Thing," stunning audiences who had already been entranced by her through the years. During this night's "I Wanna Be Your Dog," she spun, spilled, sprang, and splayed across the stage, yowling without letup on one of the most important compositions in the history of rock 'n' roll.

Pearl Jam, who by 2000 had become one of the world's highest-profile rock bands, invited us to tour with them all through October, likely at the behest of singer Eddie Vedder, who had seen us play numerous times when we toured around with his pals in Mudhoney.

Eddie was a genuine, caring, and curious cat. He was singular for the way he galvanized the attention of both the confident and the dispossessed of contemporary youth culture. Eddie offered nothing too weird, but always with an underlying sense of displacement, a mistrust of authority and rock-god celebrity, and a common-man quality that blended naturally with his feminism. Plus he was a surfer, a Zen-punk model of integrity for a nation of kids fed messages of greed and capitalism.

Earlier in the year, Pearl Jam had found themselves face-to-face with tragedy, while performing at the massive Roskilde Festival in Denmark. With the voluminous audience pushing toward the stage, nine people were sucked into the undertow and crushed to death, all in view of the band. The group had subsequently canceled the rest of their tour, and their North American dates with us were called into question. But they knew they had to overcome the disaster, which had obviously disturbed them.

And so we set off. The first night in Virginia Beach, we stood on the side of the stage with Pearl Jam's crew and security while the band opened their set. The audience, certainly aware of how difficult it must have been for the musicians, scarred by their last concert, showered them with dignified applause. The backstage crew looked at one another with a deep sigh of relief—then back to the grind.

Eddie would find camaraderie with us on the road, enjoying the company of six-year-old Coco, the two spending each day's sound check hours playing games together, drawing, reading, and just generally being best buddies.

By the summer of 2001, we had exhausted our touring possibilities for *NYC Ghosts & Flowers*. We prepared to take *Goodbye 20th Century* on the road, though only through Europe; rock venues in the U.S. weren't too keen on aleatoric avant-garde music. William Winant joined us, and each night we presented this different version of Sonic Youth in concert, all of us sitting in chairs, playing our set of scores by James Tenney, Steve Reich, and others.

Coco usually headed off with her nanny to sleep, either on the bus or in our hotel room, though she sometimes watched us play. She had grown up sitting on the side of the stage, a pair of ear-protection headphones dwarfing her tiny head. At times, while we would be off in some wild improvisation—usually at the end of a set, during either "Death Valley '69" or "The Diamond Sea"—I would look over and see her sitting cross-legged, a concerned look on her face as her parents scraped their guitars against the lip of the stage, her dad jumping into the pit to push his guitar into a cameraperson's lens or to climb up onto the audience's raised hands.

One evening on the *Goodbye 20th Century* jaunt, as she practiced "Twinkle, Twinkle, Little Star" on a piano in the dressing room, someone suggested that we should include it in our repertoire. At first I rejected the idea, thinking it would disrupt our set list in all its controlled austerity. But Coco really wanted to go for it. So at the top of our set, I walked out and introduced her, and she sat at the piano, playing the piece beautifully.

Most European audiences responded favorably to the *Goodbye 20th Century* concerts, though some folks didn't get the memo. They yelled at us while we were loading out—

"What the hell was *that*? You played no songs!"

Performing at Sónar, the vanguard electronic music festival in Barcelona, Jim invited the British electronics iconoclast Peter "Pita" Rehberg to set up and play with us, giving him no directions except to respond to the music however he wished. It turned out to be a strange affair. I figured we would be celebrated for performing these incredible works by titans of twentieth-century composition: Cage, Reich, Oliveros, and Kosugi. Instead the audience milled around the cavernous room, giving us no response at all. We scampered off the stage afterward to their collective disinterest. I could only deduce that Sónar was more about the very cutting edge of modern composition, with techno seemingly its essential element. We had offered what was old and quaint, like showing up at a free jazz festival and playing Dixieland.

Jim worked relentlessly on recording and mixing at Echo Canyon, to the point where he was all but living there, sleeping on the couch surrounded by patch cords, guitars, effects pedals, and stacks of DVDs of obscure films. Our filmmaker friend Chris Habib, who encouraged and facilitated our initial forays into the online world, had helped install a live camera feed for enthusiasts to watch us work in real time on the internet (which Jim diligently disabled in his "off" hours).

Asleep in the early morning of September 11, he was jolted off his makeshift bed and onto the floor. He ran to the window to see massive clouds of white dust filling Murray Street. Another explosion, and he figured Lower Manhattan was being bombed. He grabbed his belongings and bolted down the back stairs to the street, then up to the corner of West Broadway and north toward Chambers Street.

A cop yelled for people to head down into the Chambers Street subway station, which Jim complied with, then figured he might wind up trapped, so he ran back up and farther north to Canal Street. There he encountered people interrupted in their morning commute, looking southward at the hell unfolding before them, dazed citizens trundling forth covered in white soot.

I was at home in Northampton, having just walked Coco to her school on the Smith College campus, a mere two blocks away. Kim was in New York at our apartment, taking care of some business with Daisy von Furth's and her X-girl fashion line. Returning home from drop-off, I flicked on the small television set in our kitchen, hoping to catch a bit of harmless morning programming. I found a still image on the screen, a freeze-frame of an airplane heading straight into one of the Twin Towers, its nose nearly touching the building.

The late-summer morning was bright and blue, and the juxtaposition of this frozen shot and the perfect day outside was odd and unsettling at first. I stared at the set, listening to the stuttering commentary—

"As far as we know, a Boeing 767 jet plane has crashed into the north tower of the World Trade Center."

The picture on the screen sputtered to life, replaced with the north tower engulfed in flames, the news team scrambling for more information from downtown police and fire departments.

My phone rang just then. It was Julie Cafritz, who had recently moved from Manhattan with her husband (and Sonic Youth booking agent), Bob Lawton, to Florence, a smaller town next door to Northampton.

"Are you watching this?"

—she asked.

"How could a plane hit the World Trade Center? It doesn't make sense"

—I replied.

Just then, in view of the television cameras, a second jet roared directly into the south tower.

"This is insane!"

—I gasped.

Julie quickly recognized the implications—

"Oh my god. This is a full-scale terrorist attack."

"I need to call Kim"

—I said, then hung up. I dialed our Lafayette Street apartment, the phone ringing, ringing, ringing, the answering machine clicking on, then me yelling—

"Kim, pick up the phone! *Kim!*"

I eventually heard the clatter of the answering machine being disengaged, Kim's voice asking—

"What's going on?"

"Are you watching the news?"

—I asked breathlessly.

"No, I was just getting out of the shower."

I could hear sirens wailing in the background.

"The World Trade Center just got attacked by two planes crashing into them. You need to get out of there. Is Jim at the studio?"

"I think so . . . I'll call you back."

I rang our Murray Street studio, but there was no answer. In fact there was no tone whatsoever. I tried calling our apartment again, but it was the same thing—dead air. I ran outside and jumped into our car, driving toward Interstate 91 to head south to New York. My frenzied plan involved calling one of Coco's friends' parents to pick her up at the end of the school day.

By the time I reached Springfield, Massachusetts, though, radio announcers stated that all airports had been shut down and that no cars were being permitted to enter Manhattan—the city was in total lockdown.

I turned back, feeling helpless. I dialed the apartment again and again, but to no avail.

At 2:00 p.m. I walked to Coco's school. The parents all looked at one another with similar concern, no one really knowing anything yet, except for what was being broadcast on every station on television, theories and conjecture beginning to emerge. As I walked Coco to our home, I mentioned that Mom might be a little late in returning from the city.

That evening I did my best to explain that something terrible had happened in New York, but that it was being taken care of. I wanted to be sure she heard about it from me. As I sat downstairs later in the night, staring at the flurry of news reports turning up on the TV, Coco crept next to me in her pajamas. I clicked off the screen.

"I'm scared"

—she said.

Kim was eventually able to call from a cell phone while leaving the city with Daisy and her husband, Rob, in their car. She sat in the back seat next to Jim, traumatized, telling me they were snaking their way up north through back roads, as the highways around New York City had all been shut down.

I told Coco her momma was en route. When they arrived, Jim looked stricken. He repaired to our large basement, home to a couch, music equipment, and ten thousand albums, where he could sequester himself from the world outside. Daisy and Rob decamped to Julie and Bob's. Tom Verlaine and his partner, our artist friend Jutta Koether, also arrived at our house, as we'd offered them refuge.

It would be a month before any of us could mosey past the police blockades at Canal Street and then Center Street to enter our studio. All the tape machines were zapped, our recording files sent to digital hell. One of the jet engines from the plane that had departed from Boston, taking its hijacked turn directly over Northampton before heading to its infernal destination, had landed on the rooftop of the Murray Street building.

We soon organized, with Tom Verlaine, a benefit concert for Central American workers killed in the attacks, inviting the poet Eileen Myles to perform, as well as Cat Power and the free jazz duo of saxophonist Paul Flaherty and percussionist Chris Corsano.

That night, Sonic Youth would debut material from our next record, which we felt could only be named *Murray Street*. The song "Rain on Tin" featured the lyrics—

> *We all hope*
> *To signal kin*
> *Rays of gold*
> *Now rain on tin*
> *Gather 'round*
> *Gather friends*
> *Never fear*
> *Never again*

69

KALI YUG EXPRESS

The World Trade Center attacks, coming nearly a year after the contentious Supreme Court decision to instate Republican George W. Bush as U.S. president (after he'd lost the popular vote to Democrat Al Gore), set a pall across the progressive cause in America, an attitude of cynicism taking hold.

The most important job of Kim's and mine was preserving the welfare of Coco, granting her a steady world of school and friends. Our home life in Massachusetts grew more domesticated, offering her greater consistency than we could while constantly uprooting ourselves to tour or to play a noise gig in some remote location.

Visiting Los Angeles, I continued to check in with my old gang there, centered around David Markey's pad. We never much went to shows anymore, usually just a Mexican restaurant or sneaking into a movie theater for old time's sake. Hopping into Mike Watt's van one evening, I commented on the heaps of detritus scattered about the seats. Watt snapped at me—

"Get used to it, Thurst, 'cause as soon as you're off that magic carpet ride, you're gonna be right back in here."

We laughed. The truth was that, though I romanticized that vision of touring across the country in a van the way we had through much of the 1980s, I knew those days were over (or so I thought).

Barry Hogan decided to bring the ATP festival stateside. Our stinker of a performance in the UK must have been so much water under the bridge, because Barry asked Sonic Youth to curate. Taking over the UCLA campus, we had the exploded-candy-store good fortune to bring together, among many others, Cecil Taylor, Television, Destroy All Monsters,

Merzbow, Tony Conrad, the Dead C, and the beginning of a Stooges reunion, with Ron and Scott Asheton playing *Stooges* and *Fun House* songs joined by J Mascis and Mike Watt.

To hear Ron Asheton and Mascis trade off on lead guitar sections was phenomenal. So was Watt's roaring bass against the kicked-back drumming of Scott "Rock Action" Asheton. Scott was one of the unsung highlights that distinguished the band; he never played the drums in a bombastic way, employing instead more of an electric-blues swing, the tiniest hair behind the beat, sitting at the kit as if straddling a Harley-Davidson.

The decade from 1998 to 2008 or thereabouts would turn out to be rich in the kind of experimental basement noise, free jazz, free folk, and weird rock that had long enraptured me. Even the scene around our home in modest Northampton amazed me, allowing both Kim and me endless ways to engage in the contemporary underground, often with artists a generation or so younger than us. Still, we were never made to feel out of place—indeed, as members of Sonic Youth, a band responsible for turning many of these young people onto noise music in the first place, we would be seen as local royalty.

The shows we played as Sonic Youth with Jim O'Rourke elevated us, our sound more refined and mature, though our early propensity for reckless behavior and coloring outside the lines would never completely abate.

Asked to perform a few songs at Waterloo Records in Austin, a typical promotional situation for bands coming through town, we could have stuck to the script and offered a simple setup of three or four songs, then gathered behind the counter to sign discs. We decided instead to perform a different kind of gig, creating a series of noise "events," such as having Lee swat tennis balls across the store toward the stage, where a guitar sat plugged in at blast volume. Every once in a while, a hit was made and then—*Kerblaaammm!* Or we had Steve sit on my shoulders with an electric guitar strapped on as the audience threw chocolate and vanilla MoonPies at him and he batted them away—*Blam! Blam! Blam!* Kim and I performed "Hugging Piece," which I had composed in homage to Fluxus music. The instructions had two guitarists slowly walk toward each other, their guitars cranked. When they were as close as they could be, the couple embraced, the result an electric-noise detonation of strings and pickups rubbing against each other. (I would perform the same piece a number of times while on tour with Yoko Ono in later years.)

Other "events" that day included Jim singing a Rush song, which Lee and I interrupted with intermittent blasts of guitar; Kim and Lee sticking record album sleeves over their hands like mitts and attempting to play their guitars; and each of us performing a solo using only the jack from a guitar cable plugged into an amp—all the controls on ten, naturally. (I played mine by pressing the jack to one of my nipples.) As sound alone, it wasn't for everyone. But it was the kind of off-kilter performance I'd have liked to see from any band, which was always the point.

Iggy Pop had inevitably gotten wind of the fact that we had recorded Stooges songs with Ron Asheton for Todd Haynes's *Velvet Goldmine*. He would hear about Mike Watt and J Mascis playing with Ron and Scott at ATP and a few times after. It began to feel as though the Stooges were back in action—only not with Iggy. Whatever weird vibes persisted among the guys since their fallout of the early 1970s, it was high time for Iggy to reconnect and a proper reunion to emerge.

Soon enough it came to pass. The Stooges' first reunion gig featuring Iggy (and with Watt hired to man the bass) was announced for the 2003 Coachella Festival in Southern California. Thank the gods of high energy, we were on that weekend's bill as well.

I had had the privilege of seeing the various Stooges play from close proximity before. But standing on the overly crowded side stage at Coachella, crammed next to Steve, Lee, Kim, Jim, and members of Hole and White Flag, not to mention what appeared to be every hipster from L.A., was something else altogether. We waited as though for the second coming of punk rock Jesus, a palpable buzzed-out feeling among us, like a firecracker whose fuse was lit and ready to pop off.

Then they hit.

The first block of chords introduced "Loose," and Iggy was, indeed, loosed like a cheetah from a cage, kicking his legs out and leaping onto Watt's bass rig, flipping the bird with both hands high in the air to the audience, many of whom had waited for this moment for way, way too long. He turned to give us freeloaders a second of acknowledgment, making simulated jerk-off motions in our direction. It was animal rambunctiousness, lit up and goddamn ready to save the decade from the shitstorm it was quickly becoming.

Surprisingly, after our notorious disaster thirteen years prior, Neil and Pegi Young invited Sonic Youth to perform once again at their Bridge School Benefit in Northern California. A lot had changed with the band since our first appearance, and it would continue to change—not only for the group as a unit but for each member, time taking its crazy toll on all of us.

The show would present our band as a far cry from what it had been at the earlier benefit. Singly and as a group, we had developed as musicians and performers. We were better prepared to act our age (advanced as they had become), while keeping the youth in our blood and in our heads. Lee, Kim, and I all had children in tow now, ten-year-old Coco finding a young friend to run around with backstage while the grown-ups did their thing.

Paul McCartney stood by the monitor board watching us as we performed, his set to be the last of the night's. As we walked off, he followed us to the outdoor dressing room area. Lee, Steve, Jim, and I peered out as we saw Paul walking over to Kim and starting a conversation.

"Holy moly"

—we collectively whispered, before Kim turned and pointed at us, the boys in the band.

She later explained that Paul had asked her how she had tuned the bass. She told him the bass was the only stringed instrument we used in standard tuning, and that if he wanted to talk tuning, he should speak to us three guitar lunatics.

Paul sauntered over to say hello—all warmth, no imperiousness, just wanting to talk.

Oh, but we had some questions: Were there any unedited, longer versions of "Revolution 9"? Was "Revolution 9" inspired by Cornelius Cardew? Did Allen Ginsberg influence Paul's poems and lyrics? Important stuff.

I had with me a copy of Paul's poetry book, *Blackbird Singing*, which he dutifully inscribed. He talked of how Ginsberg had tried to edit his work by eradicating all the prepositions.

"I told him, 'Allen, then it sounds like *your* poetry, not mine.'"

Jim and I asked about the *McGear* album, which Paul had produced in the early 1970s for his brother, Mike McGear. We were massive fans of the record, with its pure pop experimentation, along with its incredible arrangement of Roxy Music's "Sea Breezes." His face registered disbelief—

"Are you kidding me?"

"No! We love that record. And the Scaffold records too!"

—Jim and I gushed.

Scaffold was the 1960s English pop group that Mike McGear had worked with.

"No one ever really asks me about Mike"

—Paul said, still surprised by our enthusiasm.

"Dude, we know way more about Scaffold than the Beatles"
—I joked (kind of).

A while later I noticed Eddie Vedder, also performing that weekend, introducing Paul to Johnny Ramone's widow, Linda. Johnny had passed away just three months earlier, after succumbing to cancer, and Eddie had been very close to him. Sonic Youth had performed at a benefit concert for prostate cancer research a month after Johnny passed, along with Blondie, David Johansen, Alan Vega, and others. When we hit the stage for our short set, we launched with our first-ever group-composed tune, "The Burning Spear." I dedicated it to—

"All the Connecticut Ramones fans out there."

It was my salute to the very early days of the Ramones, when they would bop into Connecticut and play little clubs and high school auditoriums for budding teenage punk rockers like myself.

Walking over to where McCartney, Vedder, and Linda Ramone were now congregated, I hovered nearby. Eddie flashed me an inconspicuous grin, reflecting how incredible it was that Linda was gabbing with the Beatle. Paul took Linda's hand, told her how sorry he was for her loss, and relayed how touched he had always been that her husband's band had named themselves after McCartney's pseudonym. (He had used the name Paul Ramon in the 1960s when checking into hotels with the Beatles.)

Linda stood silent for a moment before thanking him. Soon after he wandered off, she told us that she had forgotten that detail of the Ramones' history and that it blew her mind.

It blew my mind as well.

I grabbed Coco and told her we were all going out to sing "Hey Jude" with Paul from the Beatles, but she was ten years old and far more interested in hanging out with her new friend, the two of them running around the dressing rooms and playing video games.

"Just for a minute"
—I said. I picked her up and hoisted her onto my shoulders, then walked out onto the stage to join everyone as we sang—

Na na na nananana nananana
Heeeeey Jude

Soon I put her down and smiled, saying—
"Go ahead, I'll see you back there."
She ran offstage to have some fun of her own.

70

FREE NOISE AMONG FRIENDS

We would name our 2004 album *Sonic Nurse,* using cover artwork by Richard Prince, an artist Lee, Kim, and I had known since the late 1970s (Richard having been a guitarist, for a short stint, in one of Glenn Branca's early lineups). He had since become a blue-chip art star, and his new series of paintings, referencing vintage nurse-themed paperbacks, we all agreed were smart and gorgeous.

Jim O'Rourke's integration into the Sonic Youth songwriting process was complete by this point. His expertise as a mix engineer had enlivened us, as had his presence with the band onstage. But by the end of our relentless touring schedule to promote *Sonic Nurse,* he signaled to us that he was ready to leave.

It was clearly a fraught decision for him, informed by his personal life as well as a long-harbored dream of moving to Japan and immersing himself in the country's language and culture. After two shows in Brazil at the end of November, he was gone.

His departure was a blow to us. Jim had been critical to our band as we entered the post-9/11 universe, and we felt his absence. Kim asked me to have a word with him to see if he'd reconsider. His contribution had given her a wholly new space to perform in, and she was reluctant to give it up.

But it was not to be.

It hadn't been all peace and love with Jim in the band, any more than it had been without him. We still brought the typical dynamics of a family to Sonic Youth—the unspoken resentments, unrecognized value, unrealistic expectations. Through the years we had often had to push through uneasy periods of personal discontent, only to resolve them often through a dose of time and reason, a certain amount of wisdom gleaned from our greater maturity.

With our disappointment, however, came a sense of excitement too. We would be returning to our core lineup.

I would turn forty-seven in 2005, and Kim, fifty-two. It had already been five years since I'd written the lyrics to "Radical Adults Lick Godhead Style," a song recorded for our *Murray Street* album—

> *Here comes something: you are Lou Reed*
> *Transformer cracked by the backyard stream*
> *Killer tunes bubblegum disaster*
> *Radical adults lick godhead style*

Even back then, having just reached the big 4-0, I had been contemplating the value of age in rock 'n' roll. The mainstream music of youth culture had shifted toward eroticized Disney pop (Britney Spears being a liberated update of the 1960s buttoned-up Anita Bryant model, more or less), as well as MTV-friendly groups that played a caricatured version of punk.

Rock 'n' roll as a mode of artistic expression had largely become ossified, offering listeners safe, controlled, neatly packaged rebellion. The most radical voices I found were coming either from the basement-noise and freak folk scenes or from artists well into their middle age, such as Yoko Ono, Neil Young, and Patti Smith (to say nothing of the universe of avant-garde jazz and free improvisation still being vigorously investigated by John Zorn, Cecil Taylor, Ikue Mori, and Peter Brötzmann). Within the mainstream, it was only rap in which I found organic, genuine, raw power.

Kim and I connected with a fellow in Northampton named Andrew Kesin who had the idea to produce a film on the radical women in music history, which proved to be as massive an undertaking as its premise would suggest. Andrew and I drove out to Woodstock together to film an interview with the composer Pauline Oliveros and her partner, the poet, playwright, and dream therapist Ione. After that we traveled to a house nearby where the sound artist Maryanne Amacher resided.

Maryanne's house was a classic haunted mansion on a hill, three stories high, all rickety wood slats, with a sloping yard of trees, the wind howling through the branches, dead leaves covering a creaking porch. She had been a legend in psycho-acoustic sound exploration, the tendency of the human ear to perceive otherworldly audio sensations, which

Maryanne attempted to activate and transmit through various means of amplification—usually at bone-crushing volume.

When Andrew and I knocked on her door, she was closing in on seventy, appearing with long red hair streaked with gold, dressed in glittery trousers and scarves, crooking a finger at us to come in and make ourselves at home. She had us sit in front of a pair of massive speakers while she dialed in intense tones, with their resultant harmonics, asking us to cup our ears with our hands in order to modify the transmissions. She laughed excitedly and shouted, dancing from one foot to the other—

"Listen! *Listen!!* Isn't it marvelous?"

And it was; extremely so.

The first decade of the 2000s was a spectacularly fertile period for outsider music, and Northampton turned out to be a welcoming spot for many artists and musicians to perform, usually at communal houses or local record stores. Byron Coley and I oversaw the New Grass Center for Underground Culture, a music and literature emporium. It would ultimately situate itself in an old mill building in Florence, Massachusetts, mostly occupied by artisans and holistic health practitioners. For years, once or twice a week, bills of four to five artists and groups would perform, set up on the floor of a modest-sized room, ringed with hundreds of thousands of albums, books, magazines, and select bottles of whiskey. As host, Byron (the archivist behind all this vibrational ephemera) would prepare massive feasts, only asking that donations be dropped in a passed-around bucket.

It was within this intensely vibrant western Massachusetts community that I would record *Trees Outside the Academy,* my first proper solo release since *Psychic Hearts,* the first solo album I'd put out some twelve years prior. Bringing in Steve Shelley to play drums and Samara Lubelski on violin, I recorded all of it on the third floor of J Mascis and Luisa Reichenheim's house in Amherst, where a functioning recording studio had been outfitted. J and Luisa's house had once belonged to actor Uma Thurman's family, her father being the Buddhist scholar Robert Thurman, and this top floor had been where the Dalai Lama had slept when in town.

Coco, by the time she got into her teens, had begun singing and playing guitar with a group of girls her age, their band going by the name Lightbulb. She performed on a few bills with local noise and teenage punk groups, as well as with some of her parents' experimental music friends and neighbors. It was thrilling to hear the strains of Lightbulb jamming in our basement. I would make sure never to interrupt them; if we needed Coco's attention upstairs, I'd just flick the lights off and on. Walking down there once while they were playing in order to fetch an album, I noticed Coco making vocal noises by switching the on/off button on her microphone, creating an electronic stutter. Of all the cool effects I had witnessed in my days, this one just became the coolest.

She was better aware than most kids her age, or anyone for that matter, of bands with noisier predilections, like Harry Pussy, Wolf Eyes, and Hair Police, all of whom she had watched from side stage. But she gravitated mostly toward the records we had in our kitchen: the Beatles, the Kinks, the Ramones, as well as a few lesser-known acts, such as the 1960s folk rock group Tudor Lodge.

When Coco came upstairs for dinner one night after a particularly raucous Lightbulb practice, she commented off the cuff, with preternatural wisdom—

"Noise is only really good if you're the one making it."

71

DO YOU BELIEVE IN RAPTURE?

Money would both save and destroy the city I loved. The 1990s would prove to be the last decade in which Manhattan could be said to be the epicenter of art created in the margins, the streets, the alleys, the tenements, the lofts, galleries, and cafés. Poetry would keep its vigilance, at the Poetry Project and elsewhere. But all around it, the city had, by the 2000s, become saturated with money to the point that it was nearly unrecognizable as the city I had moved to.

Money cuts both ways: lower crime and murder rates were an unalloyed benefit to New Yorkers. But the infusion of money had also made it next to impossible for artists and musicians of any age to live, work, and grow there, the way I and my fellow creators once had.

We began working on songs, once again as a quartet, splitting time between Echo Canyon in the city and our Northampton basement. Eventually we would be evicted from Murray Street, priced out by the rising cost of real estate situated near the destruction of the World Trade Center, much of it rebuilt to attract high-end residential and commercial tenants.

We would record *Rather Ripped* (the album's name in reference to the San Francisco record store of the 1970s) at Sear Sound, our old haunt, Walter Sear and Roberta Findlay still keeping the place friendly and old-school New York weird. With engineer John Agnello, who we knew from his production work with Screaming Trees and Dinosaur Jr., the songs would step back from the expansive noise and winding constructions we had investigated with Jim O'Rourke, focusing on more clear-cut rock expressions.

We discussed the idea of finding a bass player, or some other "fifth" member, mostly wanting Kim to feel freed up to express herself the way she had while touring with Jim. She said one day—

"I have an idea for the perfect bass player. Mark Ibold."

Of course, I thought. *He would be ideal.* We knew him well from touring with Pavement, and his personality and playing style seemed well matched to our needs, not to mention the excitement it would provoke among those who liked both our bands.

I rang Mark to ask him, and he was caught off guard, thinking it over for fully three seconds before saying—

"I think I should do this."

Our first gig with him would be at CBGB, appropriately enough, in the early summer of 2006, where we presented all of *Rather Ripped.* The songs, while in stages of studious containment on the album, fairly exploded onstage, much in the way of our other recorded music.

Touring this album was exponentially fun: Mark enthusiastically waking early each morning to discover regional food markets; our tour manager, Dan Mapp, always maintaining positive energy and encouraging laughter as a holistic balm; and especially having Coco along, in her preteen wonder, as she became progressively more familiar with the rhythms of touring life. A kind of happy stasis set in within the band.

The music we made continued to challenge, but our audiences arrived prepared for it. The sounds, techniques, and structures we brought forth that had once felt exotic were now part of a common musical vocabulary, from the high profile and commercially accepted, like certain factors of Radiohead, to the fringier offerings of any number of underground up-and-comers. It was enough to make me suggest—as a joke (I think)—that our next album be performed only on pianos and chain saws. It was a wish for change.

I would increasingly find my enthusiasms engaged by poetry—its history and lineage, the nature of its creative work. The poet Anne Waldman would check out my library when coming to Northampton to read at our New Grass space, asking if someday I'd like to teach a class at the Jack Kerouac School of Disembodied Poetics, the summer writing workshop at Naropa University in Boulder, Colorado, that she and Allen Ginsberg had founded in 1974. It was a gracious offer, one I eventually accepted.

Sonic Youth, by 2007, was regarded as a "heritage act"—a gentle way of saying we were long in the sonic tooth. But I liked that. I liked being the older folks in a world where the young and the new constantly took the spotlight. I knew we had made our mark; they called us the "grandparents of grunge," the "sonic pensioners." For all the dismissiveness, I sometimes felt we were at the top of our game.

We performed at Berlin's Postbahnhof, playing encore after encore, the audience howling and chanting their approval, refusing to let us leave the building. We played two shows in China, hordes of young people traveling across the country to shower us in rock 'n' roll deliverance. Young Chinese musicians would later tell me how our concert had subsequently inspired a slew of new bands to form across the country, open to the endless possibilities of experimental rock 'n' roll. These are the gigs I consider our last real moments of sonic adoration, so high was the energy, joy, and love, so rich the appreciation for our music. They were nights to hold close.

Attending an art event in the newly moneyed Chelsea district of Manhattan, my life would forever change. It was an opening for the artist John Miller—the same John Miller who had colluded with the Coachmen in the late 1970s. Set up in the gallery were a couple of amplifiers and a drum kit, John playing guitar with Mike Kelley drumming and Tony Conrad playing violin—art-rock action at its mightiest.

I was happy to see my friend Eva Prinz arrive, as I hadn't seen her around in some time. She came in glowing with happiness, her black hair and dark eyes afire and gleaming, wet with life and laughter. We sat on a bench together to catch up.

Eva and I had been introduced a few years earlier when she was working as a book editor at Rizzoli, the fine arts publishing house. She edited artist monographs, as well as scholarly surveys of the visual art world, such as the ones surrounding the musicians Louis Armstrong and Woody Guthrie. One of the first books she gave me was a magisterial study of the silent-screen goddess Louise Brooks, whose enchanted beauty I had to admit reminded me of Eva's.

She had been freelance editing artist books and catalogs, as well as curating *Radical Living Papers,* a show of historical underground press newspapers and communiqués, which were as radical as the show's title suggested, the walls of the attendant gallery exhibition festooned with vintage counterculture explosions of love, liberation, and resistance to the U.S. war in Vietnam.

She had invited me, a while back, to edit a book for the Universe imprint that she oversaw at Rizzoli, exploring the visual love-letter world of mixtapes—the art of creating personally sequenced cassettes of songs to share between people. I enjoyed the project, which had me contacting dozens of musicians and artists and asking if they had held on to any of their old tapes. I asked those who had to write down why they created it and for whom. The resulting book was titled *Mix Tape: The Art of Cassette Culture,* the cover boards cut into the shape of a cassette.

I continued to meet Eva from time to time in her office at Rizzoli, presenting publishing ideas to her for local photographers I appreciated. She once mentioned a proposed book by photographer Susie J. Horgan, and I smiled—

"Oh, cool, I've known Susie for ages."

Susie had worked with Ian MacKaye and Henry Rollins at a Häagen-Dazs in Washington, D.C., in the early 1980s, back when those two young sticks of dynamite were busy jump-starting the local hardcore scene around Dischord Records. Susie had photo-documented their time together there, as well as in skate parks and punk clubs. With appreciations in hand from Ian and Henry, I worked with Eva to publish Susie's book, titled *Punk Love,* an inside view of the joys, energies, and youthful abandon around that sister- and brotherhood.

In time I would introduce Eva to Jim O'Rourke, the two becoming romantically involved. She sometimes joined Sonic Youth in our tour caravan during Jim's tenure with the band, traveling anywhere from Las Vegas to Istanbul. I was always game for hitting secondhand bookstores, and she leaped at the opportunity to hop in a taxi and explore with me. We became fast friends.

Once in Portland, Maine, she and I visited Strange Maine, the wonderful vintage record, book, clothing, and ephemera emporium, where we discovered a shoebox full of hand-inscribed mixtapes. Our mixtape book still fresh in stores, we decided to purchase the entire box, recognizing them for what they were: totems of one heart speaking to another; the friction of a needle pressed into a groove, relayed to ferrous oxide cassette tape, rolling across magnetic heads to say *I love you.*

After Eva and Jim went their separate ways, Jim sailing off to his new chapter in Japan, I didn't hear from her for more than a year.

Now, as we sat in this gallery, John, Mike, and Tony thrashing away in the next room, I learned she had a new position as a senior editor at Abrams. She asked me if I had any new projects in mind. It would lead me to introduce her to Abby Banks, a young woman who traveled across the U.S. living in and photographing the interiors of punk houses— essentially communal squats where artists could live and work, debate and dialogue.

Abby's *Punk House: Interiors in Anarchy* was followed by a few other books, which we coedited, including monographs by the photographers Justine Kurland and Michael Lavine. I loved working on these projects, and I loved working with Eva. For two more years we worked to bring books into being, traveling to paper mills in Massachusetts, even considering the start of an independent imprint. That last idea would be realized as Ecstatic Peace Library in 2010.

It was around this time that I realized too that I was falling in love with her and that, despite the formidable obstacles to our being together, I had to tell her.

I steeled myself and rang up Eva, telling her I needed to speak to her about something important. I had no idea how she'd react. She was a force of nature, a feminist and an intellectual, and we were both in relationships with other people, mine certainly more famous and public. But her soul had charged every cell in my mind and body—she had completely captured my heart—and I couldn't deny my true feelings.

I drove down to New York, and we met on the corner of Mercer and Prince Streets in SoHo. I didn't mince my words; I professed to her without hesitation—

"I've fallen in love with you."

She seemed genuinely surprised by my pronouncement, but when she blushed with joy, I could tell that my affection was shared.

The difficulty of our being together was unfathomable. We both had family worlds with which we were deeply intertwined, to say the least. We kept our communion to ourselves for some time, before eventually coming out with the news. It was met, unsurprisingly, with gasps among the people close to us—and later from our fans and supporters, deeply invested in the band, whether or not they personally knew us.

For the sake of both of our families, we attempted to stay apart, Eva relocating to England and Kim and I attending marriage counseling in Massachusetts. But it was to no avail. The yearlong absence from each other only made our mutual devotion stronger. We ultimately embraced our truth and our love, finding a home together, seeking distance and some hope of safety from the narratives that had by then made their way into the media, none of it supportive.

The circumstances that led me to a place where I would even consider such an extreme and difficult decision—to leave my marriage to Kim, my partner and bandmate of almost thirty years, the mother of our child together, the adored aunt to my nieces and nephews—are intensely personal, and I would never capitalize on them publicly, here or anywhere. I will simply say, with a clarity of heart, that Eva appeared to me as a vision

I had once only dreamed of—she came into my life as a wish come true. We would, in time, become husband and wife.

Sonic Youth's final album would be released three years after *Rather Ripped*. With all the various side projects each of us had been working on, the lives we had grown into, the unspoken feeling that Sonic Youth was reaching its conclusion—we felt less motivation to crank out yet another record and head out on yet another string of dates, playing to the same-sized rooms or, in some cities, being downgraded to smaller venues.

Writing and rehearsing new music with Mark was a positive experience, the five of us meeting when we could at Echo Canyon West, our new space in Hoboken. John Agnello was elected, once again, to record us, though this time the album would be released by Matador Records. We had fulfilled our final obligation to Geffen by delivering a compilation album of some of the more outré tracks in our catalog, naming the record *The Destroyed Room*, based on the cover photograph by the artist Jeff Wall. It felt like a significant gesture, walking away from the corporate behemoth that our label had become by giving it what was likely our most experimental record, accompanied by Jeff's image, a depiction of an intimate environment artfully disrupted.

Having a new album, our fifteenth, released through Matador was inspiring and invigorating. It had us reconnecting with Gerard Cosloy, cofounder and owner of the label, who had supported our band way back in the early 1980s, releasing our turnabout album *Bad Moon Rising*.

Before John Fahey had passed away, Byron Coley had sent the man a bit of money in exchange for some of his artwork, giving him my Northampton address. A huge cardboard box, falling apart and crushed in transit, subsequently plopped on my doorstep, swirling abstract paintings spilling out of it.

"Take one"

—Byron offered before he trundled the rest to archival safety.

Like the mind and body choosing a crystal, I reached for a small painting with the title *Sea Monster*. I suggested to the band we use Fahey's painting for our new album cover, and, everyone having flashed their green lights, I brought it to Matador's art department to discuss a layout.

As I stood there, shifting the Fahey work into various positions, I spread out a selection of paintings and photographs by friends and artists to be used for the inner sleeves—one of them an image of a psychedelic flower bursting forth from its cusp. It had been illustrated by my brother,

Gene, in his teenage years—he who had turned me onto "Louie Louie" more than four decades earlier and who had gifted me my first electric guitar.

The final line in the credits to the album would be in honor of the person who had created the template of high-energy rock guitar that I had aspired to. It read—

Ron Asheton Forever

Ron had passed away earlier in the year. So had my teenage best friend, Harold, with whom I had experienced the birth of punk rock. The day Harold passed, before I received any news of his death, his spirit had awoken me in the middle of the night, his figure in the corner of my room, one last fleeting moment together before leaving. I was not so much frightened as made curious by what I'd seen, a feeling of peace pervading me as Harold bid me a ghostly goodbye.

"What are you calling the album?"

—the art director prompted me.

I picked up the Fahey painting, its red, black, and white colors like a sentient eye of blood, a swirling nebula of energy, a cosmic portal alive with music and emotion, answering—

"*The Eternal.*"

Coral Gables, Florida, 1950

In Memory of
Eleanor Lillian Nann Moore
(1927–2022)
and
George Edward Moore
(1925–1976)

Cabaret Metro, Chicago, November 5, 1988

Acknowledgments

First and foremost, I extend endless gratitude to every Sonic Youth fan on the planet whose energies I have always depended on for impetus and inspiration. The darkest days can flare to instant luminescence whenever anyone shares with me their appreciation for how Sonic Youth changed their lives, saved their lives, or simply blew their minds. These exchanges will always be an essence beyond any fame or fortune.

I dedicate my heart and soul to my wife and paramour, Eva, who stayed close, strong and supportive, while I processed such personal memories from these bygone days, her scholarly book editor's consciousness allowing me confidence as I obsessed over minutiae. And to dear Isabel and Julian, their love, awareness, and intuitive respect offering me the space and time necessitated for writing.

To converse and work with my editor, Yaniv Soha, would prove a delight; his diligence, understanding, and sensitivity to my initial outpouring of pages ("Have you read *Ulysses*? Well, you've delivered *two Ulysses*!") were always keen to the necessity of economy while retaining a consistent voice, and always aware of dignity as the defining aesthetic.

I reached out to a great number of people, most of whom responded with generous feedback, and all with genuine enthusiasm as I buried myself in Sonic Youth research, attempting to locate specific documents, particularly during the pandemic months when libraries were shut and personal archives had been tucked away with no real answer to how our futures would unfold.

The lovely folks in the periodicals department at Broward County Library in Fort Lauderdale, Florida, where I would eventually spend numerous masked hours scrolling microfiche of their holdings of the *Village Voice* (which, after much research, seems to be the only library to offer a complete run of said publication, one of the most—if not *the* most—significant surveys of New York City art and culture from 1955 to 2017), and the British Library in London, England, who retain hard copies of *NME, Sounds,* and *Melody Maker* (nesting radically alongside Shakespeare's original sonnets, William Blake's illuminated manuscripts, et al.).

ACKNOWLEDGMENTS

I would also like to offer appreciative thanks to my book agent, Luke Janklow; my long-standing representation at Silva Artist Management; and the excellent people at both Doubleday/Penguin Random House (North America) and Faber & Faber (UK).

I had always thought my mother, Eleanor, would someday read her youngest child's memoir, but she would pass away right when the work was coming to its close, on the morning of her ninety-fifth birthday, December 10, 2022, in her home as the first snow of the season fell peacefully, as beautiful as she.

As the final edits of the book were being put to bed, my friend Tom Verlaine would pass away on January 28, 2023, his visionary guitar playing and music so essential to my, and so many others', sonic lives.

A huge thank-you to the Sonic Youth road crew through the years who, for every gig, were the first people in and the last people out—Eric Baecht, Lance Bangs, Doug "Spike" Brant, Bill Caulfield, Nic Close, Matt Crosby, Jerry DiRienzo, David Doernberg, John Erskine, Deanne Franklin, Chris Habib, Dan Hadley, Laurence Kern, Karrie Keyes, Jamie Knobler, Mike Lamb, Jeremy Lemos, Dave "Rat" Levine, Dan Mapp, Maurice Menares, Aaron Mullan, Keith Nealy, Terry Pearson, Bill Ryan, Susanne Sasic, Chad Smith, Luc Suer, Tomoko Tahara, Peter van der Velde, Jim Vincent, Bart Vriesema, Matt Zivich, our booking agents Carlos van Hijfte, Bob Lawton, and Eric Dimenstein, and everyone else who made sure we walked out onstage with unity and confidence.

And to all the labels who ran hard for us—Neutral, Homestead, Blast First, SST, DGC, and Matador; and to our merch-and-destroy design teams at Tannis Root and Bingo Merch.

And to my brother and sister, Gene and Sue, and their growing families— Toni, George, Danny, Katy, Conrad, Alden, River, Tallulah, John, Elle, Kevin, Yves, Louise, Julio, Uma—my cool cousins Anna-Louise, Janie, Katherine, Bob, Greta, Allison, their families—and especially to my daughter, Coco Hayley Gordon Moore, poet and artist.

Illustration Credits

ILLUSTRATION CREDITS

7 (bottom left)   Courtesy of Naomi Peterson Photography by Chris Petersen Images

7 (bottom right)   Courtesy of Naomi Peterson Photography by Chris Petersen Images

8 (top)   Courtesy of Naomi Peterson Photography by Chris Petersen Images

8 (bottom)   Courtesy of Naomi Peterson Photography by Chris Petersen Images

Insert 2

1 (top)   Courtesy of JJ Gonson

1 (bottom)   Courtesy of Michael Lavine

2 (top left)   From the author's collection

2 (middle right)   Courtesy of Steve Gullick

2 (bottom left)   Courtesy of Jens Jurgensen

3 (top)   Courtesy of Chris Cuffaro

3 (bottom)   Courtesy of Lee Ranaldo

4 (top)   Courtesy of Raymond Foye

4 (middle right)   From the author's collection

4 (bottom left)   Courtesy of Ebet Roberts

5 (top)   From the author's collection

5 (bottom)   Courtesy of Hayley McFadden

6 (top left)   Courtesy of Michael Lavine

6 (middle right)   Courtesy of Jim Jocoy

6 (bottom)   Courtesy of Andrew Kesin

7 (top)   Courtesy of Eva Moore

7 (bottom)   Courtesy of Dana Distortion Yevin

8 (top)   Courtesy of Ian MacKaye

8 (bottom)   Courtesy of Sean Ono Lennon